Book
Collaborative
Edited by Theune
from Wesly

FORMS OF EXPANSION

Maine's Narrow Gauge Railroad

"poet should @ some point embrace form, experiment w/

Lynn Keller

FORMS OF EXPANSION

RECENT LONG POEMS BY WOMEN

THE UNIVERSITY OF CHICAGO PRESS

CHICAGO AND LONDON

Lynn Keller is professor of English at the University of Wisconsin-Madison. She is the author of *Re-Making It New: Contemporary American Poetry and the Modernist Tradition* and co-editor of *Feminist Measures: Soundings in Poetry and Theory.*

The University of Chicago Press, Chicago 60637
The University of Chicago Press, Ltd., London
© 1997 by The University of Chicago
All rights reserved. Published 1997
Printed in the United States of America
06 05 04 03 02 01 00 99 98 97   1 2 3 4 5

ISBN 0–226–42970–9 (cloth)
        0–226–42971–7 (paper)

Library of Congress Cataloging-in-Publication Data

Keller, Lynn, 1952–
    Forms of expansion : recent long poems by women / Lynn Keller.
        p.   cm.
    Includes bibliographical references and index.
    ISBN 0–226–42970–9 (cloth : acid-free paper)—ISBN
0–226–42971–7 (paper : acid-free paper)
    1. American poetry—Women authors—History and criticism.
2. Women and literature—United States—History—20th century.
3. American poetry—20th century—History and criticism.   4. Epic
poetry, American—History and criticism.   I. Title.
PS151.K45   1997
811'.54099287—dc21   96-52786
                                                                CIP

for Duncan

CONTENTS

ACKNOWLEDGMENTS

My first thanks go to the poets who are my subject here, not only for their marvelous poems and the heartening example of their persistence through extended literary projects, but also for their generous support of this book. All of the writers I contacted—Beverly Dahlen, Rachel Blau DuPlessis, Judy Grahn, Marilyn Hacker, Susan Howe—responded helpfully. Susan Howe, Beverly Dahlen, and Rachel DuPlessis even read draft material and proffered information to strengthen my analyses. Rachel's wonderfully encouraging cards still brighten my desk. I thank all three for allowing me to quote from their correspondence with me.

Four dear friends who seem always to be there when I need anything—Alan Golding, Betsy Hirsh, Cris Miller, and Ron Wallace—provided valuable suggestions for improving chapters-in-progress. I thank them for that labor and for so much more. The members of the Draft Group of the University of Wisconsin–Madison English Department, a changing roster over several years' time, provided thought-provoking commentary in response to several chapters. In particular, I am indebted to Heather Dubrow, Cyrena Pondrom, Eric Rothstein, Larry Scanlon, and most especially—for her unfailing support and inspiring example as well as her thoughtful criticism—Susan Stanford Friedman. Graduate students in my 1989 seminar on long poems by women helped launch this project, and several former or current students—Susan Koenig, Linda Krumholz, Kathleen McSharry, Marie Paretti—shared their expertise to enhance parts of this study. Robin Becker read a draft of the chapter on Hacker's sequence; Gordon Hutner applied his editing skills to a version of the chapter on Doubiago's epic; Jenny Goodman responded helpfully to a later draft of the same chapter. Many other friends have in large and small ways encouraged and assisted in the completion of this project. I am grateful to the two readers for the University of Chicago Press for their discerning suggestions; however limited my success in addressing their comments, the book is stronger for the care they took. And I am endlessly indebted to Alan Thomas, Senior Editor at the University of Chicago Press, for his wholehearted backing and for allowing me to have a say in so many aspects of the book's production.

Without the financial support of several institutions, this book probably would not have been published before the twenty-first century: my sincere thanks to the University of Wisconsin Graduate School and to the William F. Vilas Trust for repeated summer salary support. A year's American Fellowship from the American Association of University Women in 1994–95 played a crucial role in enabling me to complete this manuscript.

Some of this text has appeared before in another form. An earlier version of chapter 1, " 'to remember / our dis-membered parts': Sharon Doubiago and the Complementary Woman's Epic" appeared in *American Literary History* 4, no. 2 (1992): pp. 305–28 and is included here by permission of Oxford University Press. Likewise, an earlier version of chapter 4 appeared as "Measured Feet 'in Gender-Bender Shoes': The Politics of Form in Marilyn Hacker's *Love, Death, and the Changing of the Seasons*," in *Feminist Measures: Soundings in Poetry and Theory*, a volume edited by myself and Cristanne Miller (Ann Arbor: University of Michigan Press, 1994), pp. 260–86. Two of Marilyn Hacker's sonnets, "And Tuesday III" and "Bloomingdales I" from *Love, Death, and the Changing of the Seasons* (W. W. Norton and Company, 1986), appear on pages 168 and 169 of my text and have been reprinted by permission of Frances Collin Literary Agent (Copyright © 1986 by Marilyn Hacker). I am grateful to these publishers.

Finally, heartfelt thanks to my family: to my mother, Kathleen Clear Keller, who has voluntarily taken upon herself so many time-consuming domestic tasks to lighten my load; to my husband, Duncan Carlsmith, who has patiently encouraged my professional development for the past seventeen years; to my children, Caroline and Joseph, who have had to compete with this project for my time and attention ever since they were born and who have grown into wonderful people despite it all.

Pushing the Limits of Genre and Gender: Women's Long Poems as Forms of Expansion

The importance to literary modernism of the collage long poem—of Ezra Pound's *Cantos*, T. S. Eliot's "The Waste Land" and *Four Quartets*, Hart Crane's *The Bridge*, William Carlos Williams's *Paterson*, H.D.'s *Helen in Egypt* and *Trilogy*—has insured recognition of the long poem as a central genre for early twentieth-century American literature.[1] Extended poetic forms have enjoyed tremendous popularity among writers across the spectrum of contemporary poetries in the last thirty years.[2] Yet the scale and significance of this recent phenomenon have been obscured because critics have not adequately acknowledged the diversity of practices and practitioners in the contemporary long poem. Critical models from earlier decades tend to recognize as long poems only works which fit a single pattern based on a particular generic precedent, usually epic or lyric. Recently, factionalized debates about current poetic schools—concerning the relative merits of "open" and "closed" forms, of free verse and formalism, of lyric, narrative, or language-centered experiment—have resulted in similar privileging of one or another type of long poem as the authentic item. These critical practices have impeded recognition of a pervasive drive among contemporary poets of both sexes and multiple poetic camps toward sustained, ambitious poetic forms.

This study emphasizes the long poem's formal and structural range; it resists imposing a single generic model or dominant tradition, or favoring any particular type of poem. Focusing on poems by contemporary women, it redresses imbalances in previous criticism, which not only favors modernist over more recent poems but also attends almost exclusively to works by white men. The flowering of women's long poems since the 1960s is a significant development in literary history, particularly given the scarcity—or invisibility—of long poems by women in earlier eras. Yet no prior book-length study of the genre has been devoted solely or even substantially to poems written by women. Nor has any acknowledged, let alone discussed, long poems by writers of color.[3] As this book demonstrates, recent gender-conscious play with received traditions of the long poem and the interweaving of non-Anglo-European cultural traditions with Anglo-European forms have significantly expanded the available models and their social implications.

The long poem is, by most accounts, a generic hybrid; one can well argue, as does Smaro Kamboureli, that generic interplay or dialogue is the long poem's most distinguishing characteristic. Yet a good deal of the critical literature has tried to impose on this flexible form a paradigm based on a single genre, thereby limiting recognition to those texts best exemplifying traits associated with that genre. I do not share Kamboureli's objection to what she calls the "generic fallacy that a literary text, no matter how complex, tends to privilege one genre among the many it might borrow from" (1991, p. xiii), for I believe that in individual poems with multiple generic valences, the conventions of one genre or another may well be particularly evident, and awareness of those primary conventions can assist interpretation. What I resist is the imposition of a single model on the whole of a diverse field.

Beyond being open to the multiple genres interacting within and shaping modern and contemporary long poems in varied ways, readers need to be responsive also to the multiplicity of equally legitimate traditions or models of practice upon which writers of long poems may draw. Among poets working from an epic base, for instance, some may look to the example of Homer, others to Dante, to Whitman, to Wordsworth, to Pound, to H.D., or to Charles Olson. While "family resemblance" (a term from Wittgenstein often invoked by critics attempting to allow for differences under the umbrella of a genre label) may link all of these epics, the differences among them are also pronounced. Reading with one or another poem, or with a line or trajectory of poems, particularly in mind, rather than the entire family tree, may best clarify the project of a specific text. Consequently, this study considers individual poems in the intertextual context of particular traditions (single branches from family trees) and specified precursor texts.

Narrative poems, verse novels, sonnet sequences, irregular lyric medleys or cycles, collage long poems, meditative sequences, extended dramatic monologues, prose long poems, serial poems, heroic epics—this is a partial list of the formal varieties that I believe may legitimately be identified as long poems. But what is to be gained from such inclusiveness? First, it allows us to appreciate the pervasiveness of the impulse to expand poetry beyond the limits of the late Romantic lyric. This, in turn, permits more accurate assessment of what is happening in contemporary poetry. It has been fourteen years since Charles Altieri, in the fall 1982 issue of *Contemporary Literature* devoted to American Poetry of the Seventies, identified the highly crafted "scenic lyric" as the dominant mode of American poetry in the 1970s and outlined the profound problems accompanying that mode ("Sensibility, Rhetoric, and Will").[4] Another landmark essay appearing in the same journal issue, Marjorie Perloff's "From Image to Action: The Return of Story in Postmodern Poetry," pointed to some of the same tired conventions in contemporary ("late modernist") lyric—"the solitary 'I' in the timeless moment, the emotive response to the landscape, the reliance on the consort of images to create meaning, the ecstatic present-tense mode, the structured free verse stanzas" (1982, p. 425)—but hopefully identified revitalizing new trends accompanying an increasing recognition that poetry is not synonymous with lyric. Perloff hailed the reappearance of story in "postmodern" poetry and predicted the ascendancy of a kind of narrative that is not primarily autobiographical, that is "fragmented, dislocated, and often quite literally non-sensical" (1982, p. 425; reprinted in *Dance of the Intellect*). Thanks in part to astute critiques like Altieri's and to Perloff's energetic championing of alternative poetic practices, contemporary American poetry in overview looks different now than it did fifteen years ago. Not only have postmodern poetries such as those of the Language poets—many of whom work in extended forms—gained far more recognition, but many practitioners of lyric have been pushing the boundaries and intellectual/cultural limitations of the genre in its "scenic" mode. The very institutionalization of the expressive lyric that has obscured the increasing importance of the long poem, then, has in fact fostered the long poem's development by heightening poets' consciousness of the need to seek alternatives

[margin annotation: included as "long poems"]

if poetry is to regain cultural importance. In that quest, many have attempted to cross genres, challenge dominant conventions of authorial voice, and expand the scale and scope of their work. A great variety of poets are attempting to make poetry more responsive to current understandings of the relation of self to language and to contemporary cultural and social realities, though without necessarily moving in Perloff's favored direction of dislocation and fracture. And many are doing so by exploring the resources of the long poem.

A second advantage of an inclusive definition of the long poem is that it encourages reassessment and expansion of the contemporary canon. Playing on the assumption of "big" within the term "long," Susan Stanford Friedman has called attention to the hierarchy, the "exclusionary politics," implicit in the term *long poem:*

> As poems on the greatest historical-metaphysical-religious-aesthetic questions, big-long-important poems have assumed the authority of the dominant cultural discourses—even when they speak from a position of alienation, like Ezra Pound in *The Cantos* or William Carlos Williams in *Paterson.* The generic grid within which these and other big long poems are read has been established preeminently by the epic, which has a very big-long history of importance in western culture.
>
> (1990b, pp. 10–11)

Friedman's concern, which I share, is that this association of the long poem with the privileged status traditionally accorded epic has contributed to the exclusion of women from the canon; the epic has been "the quintessential male territory whose boundaries enforce women's status as outsiders on the landscape of poetry" (1990b, p. 11). For those troubled by the infrequency with which works by women figure in discussions not only of the long poem but of contemporary poetry more generally (except when the discussions are explicitly feminist and gynocentric), a broad application of the term long poem has strategic advantages: then the respect and status accorded to effective long poems is not reserved solely for a single type, such as the epic or the lyric sequence.

I will return to the issue of gender later in this introduction. At this point, I wish to stress that excluding any kind of long poem from that category is a way of denying that work and its creator—whether or not that person is female—the prestige, the scale of achievement associated with the genre. For instance, claims that only fragmented collage texts are genuine long poems deny to less paratactic sequences—even those that treat subjects of historical and cultural significance—the importance that label confers. I am not defending the notion that to be a major writer, one must work in the "major" form. (Surely Elizabeth Bishop is one of the great poets of our era, yet she never produced a poem longer than a few pages.) But given that such assumptions are widespread, a narrow definition of the long poem may irresponsibly restrict the pool of poets deemed worthy of serious attention.[5] An inclusive definition, moreover, prevents this generic category from becoming merely a pawn, hostage of one camp or another, in current battles over what constitutes poetry appropriate to our era.

To give some sense of the current diversity of the long poem, I have chosen to examine six quite different kinds of poems. The six chapters of this study do not represent a taxonomy, for the variety of long poems being written today—evident, for instance, in the 1993 issue of *Parnassus* on that topic—cannot be represented by only six types. The chapters are, however, arranged in pairs according to some broad heuristic groupings: the poems discussed in the first two chapters draw heavily on epic models; the next two chapters treat lyric sequences; and the final two examine radically experimental, less representationally based texts. The epic-based poems are comprehensive in scope; they focus on an individual's quest, enacted often through educative confrontations with a series of obstacles, which has broad cultural implications. Where contemporary epics offer a sweeping worldview and cultural critique, lyric sequences treat narrower portions of a culture, more confined history, or more inward perspectives. The usually brief units from which sequences are composed may be held together only loosely by subjectivity or theme but, as Joseph Conte has noted, generally appear in a hypotactic structure (Conte 1991, p. 22); elements in one lyric section will enhance an understanding of lyrics that follow. Narrative structure need not be pronounced (one thinks of John Berryman's *Dream Songs*, Diane DiPrima's *Loba*, or Robert Lowell's *Notebook 1967–68*), but the sequences treated here do, with varying degrees of directness and continuity, tell stories. Although most poets composing long poems are engaged in some experimentation, I follow convention in reserving the adjective "experimental" for poems like those in my third category.[6] These are poems that delib-

ideas of experimental poetry— awesome

erately disrupt conventions of ordinary and poetic language—of grammar, syntax, punctuation, of representation and narrative, of lineation, persona, imagery, of intelligibility itself. Such works attempt to reinvent language structures, even to reinvent the silences within which speech sounds.

Lest readers imagine a monolithic practice for any of these three suggested types, the two chapters forming each pair deal with quite different kinds of poems, which may represent different generic mixtures, follow different traditions or models, embody different views of women's relation to received literary traditions, and address different audiences. One epic-based poem I examine—Sharon Doubiago's *Hard Country*—develops from the tradition of sprawling didactic cultural collage exemplified by Olson's *Maximus Poems*, while the other—Judy Grahn's "The Queen of Swords"—reaches back to pre-Homeric as well as modernist epic models and takes the form of ritualistic verse drama. One kind of lyric sequence (and there are many), represented here by Marilyn Hacker's *Love, Death, and the Changing of the Seasons*, revises the tradition of the Petrarchan love sonnet sequence. Another, represented by Rita Dove's *Thomas and Beulah* and Brenda Marie Osbey's *Desperate Circumstance, Dangerous Woman*, is formally less regular and draws upon African American cultural traditions in presenting culturally and temporally specific historical material. Of the two kinds of experimental long poems represented here, one, Susan Howe's "The Liberties," explores innovative ways of using and considering historical documents in the non-narrative collage long poem, while the other, represented by Beverly Dahlen's *A Reading* and Rachel Blau DuPlessis's *Drafts*, adapts for feminist ends precedent traditions of serial form. (A serial poem is constructed from separate but related parts in an exploratory manner that refuses progressive or narrative structure. Where a sequence usually follows a hypotactic arrangement, a serial poem is paratactic; it is, in DuPlessis's phrase, "an argument of leaps." The series discussed here are open-ended, highlighting the resistance to teleological structure and to closure, the emphasis on ongoing process characteristic of even the more contained serial long poems.) An overview of critical approaches to the long poem will further clarify my reasons for structuring this study to emphasize multiple generic types, for selecting such eclectic focal texts by women, and for examining the poems in terms of various specific antecedent traditions or texts.[7]

Early critical studies of the modern American long poem emphasize its roots in epic. Roy Harvey Pearce's chapter "The Long View: An American Epic" in *The Continuity of American Poetry* (1961) offered the first overview of the subject and was the first of several studies to propose a model of modified epic practice in which Whitman's example is central. Influentially, Pearce presents that "strange, amorphous, anomalous, self-contradictory thing, the American epic" as freed from "the fetters and forms of tradition" by forces of American history and the antinomian American character (1961, pp. 61, 59). The strategy of the American epic is "to make a poem which will create rather than celebrate a hero and which will make rather than recall the history that surrounds him" (1961, p. 61); the breadth and scope of traditional epic are retained, but conventional heroes and linear plots are abandoned.[8] Whitman's *Song of Myself* is Pearce's key text initiating this new heroic poem "of ordering, not of order; of creation, not confirmation; of revealing, not memorializing" (1961, p. 83). The three twentieth-century poems Pearce discusses are among those that, at least until recently, have dominated discussion of the long poem: *The Cantos, The Bridge, Paterson.*

James E. Miller, Jr.'s study, *The American Quest for a Supreme Fiction: Whitman's Legacy in the Personal Lyric* (1979) develops a number of the ideas Pearce introduced concerning Whitman's crucial transformation of the epic. Miller sees Whitman as initiating the "personal epic" in which loose or open structure replaces the traditional narrative; a familiar colloquial style replaces an elevated one; the poet's self as embodiment of his time and place substitutes for the "truly heroic hero" (1979, p. 34); interior actions replace exterior ones on a larger than life scale; and new myths—Supreme Fictions—are sought rather than national myths reenacted. Miller's focal texts include the modernist ones Pearce treated, along with Wallace Stevens's "Notes Toward a Supreme Fiction" (regarded as offering a theory for the personal epic) and "The Waste Land." In addition, Miller treats two more recent works by poets of a later generation: John Berryman's *Dream Songs* and Allen Ginsberg's *The Fall of America: Poems of These States, 1965–1971.*

Like Pearce and Miller, Michael André Bernstein sees the nature of epic as a problem explored by modern American poets whose poems enact a quest for the necessary structure of a new epic. Rather than looking back to Whitman, however, he identifies a tradition of modern verse epic "whose first and most significant document remains *The Cantos*" (1980, p. 10), a tradition evolving specifically in an era when the novel had replaced verse as the proper medium for narrating " 'the tale of the tribe' " (1980, p. 15). In *The Tale of the Tribe: Ezra Pound and the Modern Verse Epic*, Bernstein does not claim to characterize the long poem generally. He generates a category appropriate to three major texts—*The Cantos, Paterson, The Maximus Poems*—in order to clarify the contract between reader and poet that these versions of epic invoke. Bernstein emphasizes the communal project of epic—its narration of the audience's cultural, historic, or mythic heritage; its attempt to address an audience of citizens using the voice of the community (rather than the voice of a single sensibility); and its didactic aims. His model provides terms for understanding the modern verse epic's incorporation of prose narrative and historical documentation and for understanding the difficulties the poets encountered as they tried from their own necessarily limited and partial perspectives to "give voice to historical forces transcending any single consciousness or moment" (1980, p. 272).

The epic emphasis, as developed in these studies, offers much that remains useful to projects like mine. Particularly valuable is the stress on genre as something always in process; among today's long poems that might be considered epic, epic is being remade as the poems enact a search for structural and metaphysical principles and for histories and historiographies that can replace those of the traditional heroic narrative. Also relevant here is the recognition that most often these replacement histories have not been previously validated as foundational or central; instead, their communal significance must be discovered within and generated by the process of the poem. Critical emphasis on the epic roots of American long poems has appropriately highlighted the public and didactic impulses behind many long poems, and—in a revisionary, perhaps peculiarly American twist—the poet's position as critic of the dominant values of his or her culture. However, as the recurrence of the same key texts in these studies indicates, the number of long poems that can appropriately be discussed in terms of epic is quite limited. Even when significantly revised in accordance with modern sensibilities, epic's comprehensive heroic narrative and declamatory modes do not accommodate the interests of all poets, so that many long poems do not fit even modified epic models.[9]

At the opposite end of the critical spectrum are treatments of the long poem that do not consider issues of quest, hero, community, nation, history, and the like, and instead regard the form as essentially lyric. Seen through this lens, the long poem explores largely private (though possibly representative) sensibility and emotion, usually through focused moments of autobiography. While several critics have positioned the twentieth-century long poem as an outgrowth of lyric modes, none have championed the lyric model so extensively as M. L. Rosenthal and Sally M. Gall in *The Modern Poetic Sequence: The Genius of Modern Poetry.*[10] The best known of the books on long poems, Rosenthal's and Gall's survey has been hailed for the skillful readings it contains. As a genre study, however, (rather than as a collection of readings) *The Modern Poetic Sequence* demonstrates the drawbacks of imposing a single model on the diverse practice of the long poem, as well as the dangerous ease with which generic description can become prescription and categorization become evaluation.

Positioning Whitman's "Song of Myself" as the "first great unmistakable exemplar of the form" (1983, p. 4), Rosenthal and Gall identify the modern sequence as "*the* modern poetic form within which all the tendencies of more than a century of experiment define themselves and find their aesthetic purpose" (1983, p. vii).[11] Looking back over the past several centuries of poetry in English, they see "an increasing emphasis . . . on a complex music of feeling involving a number of radiant centers, progressively liberated from a narrative or thematic framework" (1983, p. 11). The culmination of this development, the poetic sequence, they define as "a grouping of mainly lyric poems and passages, rarely uniform in pattern, which tend to interact as an organic whole. It usually includes narrative and dramatic elements, and ratiocinative ones as well, but its structure is finally lyrical" (1983, p. 9). This lyrical structure derives from successive intensities of emotionally and sensuously charged awareness.

For Rosenthal and Gall, characterizing the form is inseparable from praising it.[12] Thus, they differentiate the poetic sequence from the Elizabethan sonnet-sequence, "which was too redundant and theme-ridden to provide a genuine dynamics" or from *In Memoriam*, which is "weighed down by its endless succession of uniform stanzas . . . and dominantly meditative tone. . . . It is less a sequence than it might have been, too, because of the steadily developing argument and continuous account of spiritual struggle" (1983, pp. 22–23). Their devaluing of the discursive, the narrative, the meditative, the intellectually speculative leads to troubling omissions from the privileged category they identify as modern poetry's "decisive form." For instance, the "speculative, ratiocinative" character of Stevens's meditative sequences, because it threatens to "smother" the works' lyrical structure, calls into question whether those poems qualify as sequences (1983, p. 361); similarly, most of Auden's extended poems are too "disproportionately discursive" and "continuous" to count as poetic sequences. Rosenthal's and Gall's belief that the discursive and the didactic sap energy from the lyric intensity of the sequence yields an unsympathetic reading of Olson's *Maximus Poems*. Their appreciation of *Four Quartets* is similarly limited:

> *Four Quartets* is *thoughtful*, in stretches, as Eliot's earlier sequences, especially *The Waste Land*, are not. And this mode of thoughtful communication damps down the more strictly aesthetic controlling impulses to a degree that may be considered unfortunate.
>
> (1983, p. 175)

Omitted from the book entirely are the long poems of Robert Duncan, Langston Hughes, James Merrill, John Ashbery, Melvin Tolson, A. R. Ammons, Robert Pinsky, Gwendolyn Brooks—to name just a few well-known figures—as well as all of the women who will figure in this book.

Of course, any critic surveying a genre has to make selections, but the process becomes particularly insidious when the genre slips from a descriptive to a prescriptive category, as it so clearly does here, and when a particular subtype is portrayed as occupying the space where multiple subtypes in fact exist.[13] In effect, *The Modern Poetic Sequence* casts as failed attempts at sequences any long poems that do not fit the authors' conception of the sequence. Naturally, appreciation of any literary work will be reduced if it is held up to inappropriate generic standards. When the didactic character of epic is delegitimized, long poems rooted strongly in epic, such as *The Maximus Poems* or *The Changing Light at Sandover*, will be seen as seriously flawed, if their existence is acknowledged at all.

Some critics, such as Charles Altieri, have discussed the modernist long poem in terms that effectively combine epic with lyric: "The most distinctive feature of the modernist long poem is the desire to achieve epic breadth by relying on structural principles inherent in lyric rather than narrative modes" (1978, p. 653). The long poem "tests a lyric sensibility by elaborating the existential and cognitive consequences of momentary insights" (1978, p. 658). Working from this assumption, Altieri can fruitfully examine long poems in terms not of fixed generic traits but of a tension between what he terms the impulse to lucidity and the impulse to lyricism. Despite efforts like Altieri's, recent studies by younger critics have moved away almost entirely from considering long poems in terms primarily of epic and/or lyric.

Thus when Thomas Gardner points to Whitman as a model, in the first book devoted exclusively to long poems by generations subsequent to the modernists, he is not concerned with Whitman's impact on the genres of epic or lyric.[14] Instead, he argues in *Discovering Ourselves in Whitman: The Contemporary American Long Poem* that Whitman exerts a generalized influence as a "figure wrestling with and empowered by the problems of self-rendering." Whitman models for poets a way of "framing and finding generative the tensions implicit in singing oneself" through the "embrace" of the world external to him (1989, pp. 1, 2).

Interaction with the external world receives even more stress in *Obdurate Brilliance: Exteriority and the Modern Long Poem* as Peter Baker advocates a reorientation of "the analysis of modern long poems away from the idea of the individual self as the center of interest and organization" (1991, p. ix). Poets writing long poems in this century are, in Baker's view, rebelling against the tyranny of the lyric *I*. Countering the widespread "model of *interiority*," he argues that in the form of their poems, his focal poets—Saint-John Perse, Ezra Pound, Charles Olson, Gertrude Stein, Louis Zukofsky, John Ashbery, Clark Coolidge, Michael Palmer, and Bernadette Mayer—are "working out an intersubjectivity or openness to the world and experience of others, while inviting the reader to participate in the creation of meaning" (1991, p. 9). The poems Baker considers and the generalizations he offers represent only one tradition of the long poem, so that another exclusive canon emerges, though in this case it is an experimentalist one.

The recent critic of the long poem who has engaged most thoughtfully with the question of genre is Smaro Kamboureli. The announced intention of her study *On the Edge of Genre: The Contem-*

porary Canadian Long Poem is "to understand the generic restlessness of the long poem, why and how it engages itself with disparate elements only to subvert their functions and ideologies" (1991, p. xiv). As she sees it, "coherence occurs, is marked, only when the contradictory genre systems of epic, lyric, non-epic narrative poetry and non-literary discourse operating within the long poem posit their various interrelationships" (1991, p. 45). I find congenial Kamboureli's emphasis on generic multiplicity, interrelation, and contradiction; her extended critique of the critical literature on the long poem for having privileged "one of its encoded genres at the expense of the others" (1991, p. 50) reinforces my perception, evident in the brief survey above, that poems have been forced to fit narrow molds or been left out of the picture entirely in accordance with exclusive epic or lyric models.[15]

[handwritten left margin: Keller does tell that smtms 1) genre is in the foreground]

Kamboureli and I diverge, nonetheless, in our emphases and interests. As already indicated, while I wish to sustain a sense of multiple genres interacting in the long poem, I do not wish to deny the possibility that particular genres may come to the fore in particular poems. Thus, I do not share her view that quest in the long poem "functions as a metonymy of desire" quite distinct from epic quest (Kamboureli 1991, p. 57). Kamboureli's assertion that this Lacanian desire "manifests itself [in the long poem] as the converging point of self and language" illuminates Beverly Dahlen's work, considered in my final chapter, but does not accurately characterize the quest in either of the epic-based poems I discuss, by Sharon Doubiago and Judy Grahn. Nor do I agree that when the "monological form" of the pure short lyric appears in a long poem, it necessarily appears as a "deliberate undoing" of conventional generic codes, as "an anti-lyric," though that may often be the case (1991, pp. 73–74).

Like a number of the other critics discussed, Kamboureli is defining "long poem" so as to accommodate a more restricted range of texts than those I include under that rubric.[16] This is why she can speak of "*the* ideological intent behind *the* writing practice of *the* long poem" (1991, p. 79; emphasis mine). She identifies differentiation as the "primary trope" of the long poem and dislocation as its consistent theme (1991, pp. 70, 71); such generalizations seem to me not to do justice to the diversity of the genre's current manifestations. In contemporary long poems I see multiple ideologies being encoded through diverse writing practices that employ widely varying structures, tropes, and themes. I regard no single approach as consonant with this era or nation; even uses of forms that lack the fragmentation or the dazzling hybridity associated with both modernist and postmodern art are not necessarily anachronistic.[17]

As already noted, Kamboureli is quite definite that "a generic reading of the long poem should not valorize one of its novelized genres at the expense of another":

> The long poem not only works against any attempt to retrieve the matrix of the specific genres that engender it, but also parodies the nostalgia for the retrieval of generic origins while incorporating this search within its own textual body. The implicit denial of an overriding structure of generic authority posits the long poem as an instance of *mise en abyme*—a genre without a genre, one might even say. It is . . . not a fixed object but a mobile event, the act of *knowing* its limits, its demarcated margins, its integrated literary kinds. The long poem ceases to be a kind of a kind by becoming the kind of its other.
>
> (1991, p. 101)

She perceives always the transgression of genre; the long poem absorbs other elements of other structures so as to create "a textual process of 'betweenness.' This betweenness is not a matter of simple deviation from previously established generic conventions; rather, it is a matter of multiple encodings and decodings, of shifting value systems, of infraction" (1991, p. 77). As theory, I find such formulations compelling, particularly since the women whose poems I discuss here often aspire to de-code and differently re-code the "value systems" of received categories of both gender and genre. Also valuable for my work is Kamboureli's implication that contemporary long poems, innovative in so many ways, should not be read solely in terms of linear models of literary history or simply as revisions of prior works. Today's more process-oriented poets, in particular, may pursue modes of invention unrelated to literary precedent. Yet, in practice, I find that reading with "deviation from previously established generic conventions" in mind, particularly as those conventions animate specific prior texts, illuminates a great range of long poems, including those in which generic hybridity is especially pronounced. Perhaps this is because the long poem—this genre-that-is-not-one—has been evolving long enough for some clear models to have emerged. In consequence, an individual long poem cannot enact simply a self-reflexive "knowing" of its own limits;

rather it knows also the limits of precedent long poems (*The Cantos*, say, or *Helen in Egypt*, or Robert Duncan's "Passages") that in some ways reduce, even as they may define, the contemporary poem's "otherness." Hence, while wanting not to discount innovations in the long poem that arise independent of revisionary gestures, I have chosen to consider individual poems largely in terms of anterior texts and generic traditions.

Questions involving genre and antecedent traditions assume additional complexity when the long poems under discussion are authored by women. In the last twenty-five years, production of long poems has dramatically increased among both men and women writing in the United States. But the burst of production by women is particularly striking in view of the relative dearth of long poems by women from prior periods. Women's historical reluctance to attempt epic poems has been explained by Friedman in terms of an anxiety, not of authorship (Harold Bloom's concept) but of genre, and her insights can be extended to poems that are not specifically epic but are comparable in scope and ambition. Friedman points to "a covert set of expectations about poetic genres that reflects the larger gender system of western culture": "Epic norms—public, objective, universal, heroic—coincide with western norms for the masculine. Lyric norms—private, subjective, personal, emotional— overlap with the concept of the feminine" (1986, pp. 203, 205). Earlier women poets did not possess the cultural authority that would legitimate their attempts at epic, that would allow them to narrate the sweeping "tale of the tribe" or to produce extended philosophical meditation. In consequence, female poets by and large composed lyrics.[18]

Recent poetic production suggests, however, that the "second wave" of feminist activism has proved empowering enough to women writers in the United States that they no longer feel intimidated by the associations of grand poetic scale with the heroic, public realm, with intellectual depth and scope, or with great artistic ambition. That women should take up this ambitious genre at this time follows from struggles by the women's movement in recent decades for expanded attention to women's experiences, to female subjectivity, and to the construction of gender in and through language; for the retrieval of women's history; and for greater exploration and recognition of women's artistic (among other) powers. On a purely practical level, the long poem's openness to sociological, anthropological, and historical material renders it particularly useful for poets eager to explore women's roles in history and in the formation of culture. Victor Li's argument (developed in relation to *The Cantos* and *Paterson*) that the modern long poem's length is a response to the modern poet's questioning of the self's unity and autonomy may suggest another reason why women would feel at this moment drawn to experiment with the long poem: the insights of some feminist theorists have fostered perceptions of female subjectivity as multiplicitous, polymorphous, or fractured. The elusive subject-in-process (to adopt Julia Kristeva's term) may be best rendered in forms other than lyric—that is, in capacious forms which stretch to accommodate multiple voices and discourses, forms which may even defer closure indefinitely.

The iconoclasm that has from the start characterized the American long poem is no doubt another factor which, at the present historical juncture, makes the genre particularly congenial for some women. DuPlessis notes commonalities between the iconoclasm of "female aesthetic" and that of modernism, evident particularly in what is arguably its key genre, the encyclopedic collage long poem.[19] In writing that reflects "female aesthetic," she observes an "antiauthoritarian ethics" occurring on the level of structure, which "coincides with the thrilling ambition to write a great, encyclopedic, holistic work, the ambition to get everything in, inclusively, reflexively, monumentally" (1990, p. 9). DuPlessis argues that to the extent that women's writing is "(ambiguously) nonhegemonic" (the degree of hegemony being affected by such factors as race, social class, sexual preference, and ideological orientation), it shares with modernism a tendency to engage in subversive critiques of culture. This project of cultural transformation easily leads to both didacticism and an encyclopedic impulse, "in which the writer invents a new and total culture, symbolized by and announced in a long work, like the modern long poem" (DuPlessis 1990, p. 17). Though I would emphasize that not all women composing long poems have taken as their model the modernist collage epic with its invention of a "total culture," certainly a great variety of women writers have capitalized on its *formal* innovations. Many have found in the nonlinear structures and radical parataxis of modernist long poems methods for unsettling the traditional forms of narrative in which gender and gender relations have been defined or for conveying a multifaceted female subjectivity. Yet some aspects of male high

ot have found thru th

modernist practice have proved decidedly uncongenial for recent women writers. As DuPlessis has noted, Pound, Williams, and Co. ultimately reinscribed traditional ideologies of gender and of race, of the authority of the white male; these ideologies are among those that long poems by contemporary women generally attempt to reform.[20] Among the poets in this study, Doubiago, Howe, and DuPlessis in particular wrestle with the mixed legacy of the largely male-authored modernist collage long poem, finding different strategies for capitalizing on its liberating dimensions while evading its misogynist ones.

Unable to position themselves fully or comfortably within predominantly male traditions, women poets have often sought alternative female traditions with which they might identify. Because most of the long poems composed by women in earlier decades had slipped from sight or been thoroughly devalued, recent feminist scholarship, by recovering previously slighted poets and poems, has eased such quests. The number of long poems written by women before the 1960s is small compared with the number by men, but several of them—such as Elizabeth Barrett Browning's novel in verse, *Aurora Leigh*, or, more influentially, such modernist experiments as Mina Loy's *Anglo-Mongrels and the Rose*, Gertrude Stein's *Tender Buttons*, "Lifting Belly," "Patriarchal Poetry," and "Stanzas in Meditation," H.D.'s *Helen in Egypt* and *Trilogy*, and Muriel Rukeyser's extended sequences—have recently come to be more widely known, more readily available, and better appreciated.[21] That many of the genres contributing to the hybridity of any single long poem, such as the novel, the journal, the epistle, the lyric, individually have strong female traditions may have lent the long poem a feminine cast that enhanced its appeal for recent women writers.

Nonetheless—partly because the recovery of earlier long poems by women is so recent a development—women attempting to write long poems have been conscious of entering a territory previously mapped by male poets and traditions. Consequently, these women have tended not so much to "think back through [their] mothers" (Virginia Woolf's phrase) as to work with, struggle against, and revise the approaches of their fathers.[22] This is the central reason for my choosing to consider particular long poems by women in the context of male precursors and traditions. A benefit of this procedure is that the genre of the long poem, precisely because it has been so dominated by men, offers—as genres like the novel or lyric,

[handwritten annotation at top: looking @ ot's wk in the Long Poem offers unob-structed views @ ot wking in male-dominated tradition]

say, cannot—unusually unobstructed perspectives for viewing women's interactions with male-dominated traditions.

My discussion of women's poems in terms of men's precedent texts and male-dominated traditions serves another agenda as well. I have already noted that works by women rarely figure in discussions of the long poem. (A recent example of the token representation of women's work: the four-essay section of a 1992 issue of *Sagetrieb* devoted to that subject offers extended discussion of work by six men—Louis Zukofsky, John Ashbery, Ed Dorn, Ron Silliman, Robin Blaser, Robert Kelley, and only one woman, Leslie Scalapino.) In selecting as focal texts only works by women I attempt some compensation here, while hoping also to increase the likelihood of women's poems being fully integrated into future scholarship in the field, discussed alongside men's and with equal frequency. By situating women's long poems in relation to more widely recognized traditions and texts, I indicate the lack of intellectual grounding for the exclusion of women's work from critical considerations of the long poem.[23]

[handwritten annotation in right margin: Keller Hopes to integrate an equal focus on wmn's writing - alongside that of ot]

In their long poems, women enact various models of relationship with the dominant traditions, in accordance with varying assessments of the problems or opportunities traditional structures and procedures pose for women or for other nonhegemonic groups with which they may identify (lesbians, African Americans, etc.). The six chapters of this book suggest quite different patterns of interaction with tradition, and in each case I have tried to allow the texts under discussion to determine how precedent tradition will be defined and represented. Because Howe's "The Liberties" explores how women have been written into and out of history, broadly conceived, that chapter takes a rather generalized view of hegemonic literary tradition; at the same time, it situates Howe herself within the particular iconoclastic historiographic tradition of Pound-Williams-Olson-H.D. et al. What I term the "testifying" long poems of Dove and Osbey invite interpretation within the context of broadly defined African American cultural traditions, not in relation to any particular precedent writer or text. Hacker's sonnet sequence, in contrast, is written particularly with Shakespeare's sonnets in mind, so that his practices within the tradition of the Petrarchan sonnet sequence provide the central intertext for my consideration of *Love, Death, and the Changing of the Seasons*; similarly, Doubiago seems to have Olson's *Maximus Poems* specifically in mind while she conducts her own impassioned epic investigation of American mythology, history, and geography. Both Dahlen and DuPlessis had some biographical connection with Robert Duncan, whose open-ended serial poem "Passages" I use to contextualize theirs in chapter 6, but neither woman's poem rests heavily on direct allusion to "Passages." Rather, Duncan figures as a model in more general ways and as representative of the relatively young tradition of what Conte terms "infinite serial form."

Several of my focal texts (such as Doubiago's or DuPlessis's) would lend themselves to discussion in terms of the example offered by H.D.'s long poems. But, having shaped my inquiry around male-dominated traditions and male-authored texts, for the most part I have left such exploration of female models for others. In the case of Judy Grahn, however, I abandoned the approach I initially intended—a consideration of her lesbian writing in relation to a homosexual long poem tradition represented by W. H. Auden—because it proved less illuminating than the gynocritical context of the "Sapphic" literary heritage Grahn herself constructs in *The Highest Apple*. Of course, Grahn, too, interacts with male dominated traditions—that is unavoidable. But in "The Queen of Swords" she does so indirectly, through the mediation of works by two modernist women, H.D. and Stein. Their strikingly different examples merge with surprising ease in Grahn's work, through dynamics I liken to the interactions of a butch/femme couple. This model of relation to earlier writers further diversifies this study's perspectives on how women poets may find authority and empowerment through their multifaceted literary inheritance.

I have deliberately included in this study texts that address or appeal to different audiences and that pursue alternative, sometimes conflicting, ideals of aesthetic value. Readers who admire the process-based poetics of such feminist experimentalists as DuPlessis and Dahlen (or of Bernadette Mayer, Kathleen Fraser, Joan Retallack, Rae Armantrout, Lyn Hejinian, Carla Harryman, etc.) tend not to appreciate the reliance on representational conventions of lyric and narrative, the imagistic neatness and closural tendencies of "mainstream" works like Dove's *Thomas and Beulah*. For the process-based experimentalists themselves deliberately write *against* the conventions of expressive lyric that writers like Dove respect. At the same time, readers who admire Dove's skill with imagery and rich linguistic texture often fail to appreciate either works like

Keller chose diverse & opposing pieces particularly to attempt to instill an apprec. of varied texts + the rewards of applying diff. reading stratgies

Grahn's or Osbey's, which rest more on oral traditions and employ more mundane and working-class language, or radically disjunctive even hieroglyphic texts like Dahlen's or DuPlessis's. Those who champion formalist control like Hacker's often have little interest in the relatively undisciplined character of omnivorous free verse like Doubiago's. In bringing such works together in the context of a single study, I hope to encourage less sectarian and schismatic responses. I hope to communicate (albeit indirectly) my sense of the rich rewards that follow from a readiness to apply different reading strategies in order to appreciate varied texts. I do not wish to obscure the aesthetic differences manifest here; like the differences in identity politics and feminist positionings among this book's focal writers, the differences in their poetics are profound. Yet a fair account of this diversity makes clear that no single aesthetic can respond to the full range of women's cultural needs. In addition, precisely because these focal poems reflect alternative understandings of how art may contribute to social change, collectively they demonstrate that intervention in or subversion of Anglo-European and/ or patriarchal norms is not limited to any single mode.

Different formal and linguistic strategies reflect different understandings of how art may foster social or cultural transformation, and one approach may be more effective than another vis-à-vis a particular audience. I share Rita Felski's skepticism of "prevailing conceptions of literature which make it possible to identify the literary text as a site of resistance to ideology by virtue of its formal specificity" (that is, its formal character, such as whether it is realist or experimentalist):

> In the context of the women's movement, the necessity and importance of a feminist avant-garde must be balanced against an equal need on the part of oppositional movements for texts which address the particularity of their social experience more explicitly and unambiguously.

(Felski 1989, p. 162)

Accessible revisionary myth-making like Grahn's, which explicitly advances a gynocentric and lesbian-centered understanding of the significance of Helen and the Trojan War, speaks powerfully to a popular audience (Grahn's "common woman") while it challenges established scholarly perceptions of classical epic. Dahlen's highly abstracted and telegraphically obscure analyses of Freudian concepts and their adequacy to the female psyche will seem to some readers more radically transformative than Grahn's poetry and to others more politically retrograde because purportedly more elitist. Both women's poems, it seems to me, represent significant feminist expansions of existing literary traditions. Given the difficulty of correlating literary production and social change, I would not attempt to identify one or the other as more certain to serve feminist goals of social and cultural transformation.

All of the poems I have chosen to examine closely were published in the 1980s and 1990s. Listed in order of the poems' appearance in this book, their publication dates are: *Hard Country*, 1982; "The Queen of Swords," 1987; *Thomas and Beulah*, 1986; *Desperate Circumstance, Dangerous Woman*, 1991; *Love, Death, and the Changing of the Seasons*, 1986; "The Liberties," 1980; *A Reading*, in its first book-length installment, 1985; *Drafts*, the first several collected in a book, 1987. This means that these long poems were written during a period of social upheaval for American women, in the peak years of the second wave of feminism. They were written also in a time when poetry, increasingly institutionalized in the academy and MFA programs since the 1950s, has been going through its own upheavals. I have selected as my focal texts poems that are essentially book-length (in a couple of cases, near book-length or multiple book-length) for reasons related to both phenomena.

First, I want to highlight the boldness of women's entrance onto the field of the long poem. In demonstrating this achievement, I could have chosen to discuss some of the midlength poems, often thematically linked lyric sequences, which women have been producing in great numbers—Adrienne Rich's "Sources," "Twenty-One Love Poems," or "An Atlas of the Difficult World"; Irena Klepfisz's "*Bashert*"; Carolyn Kizer's "Pro Femina"; Mitsuye Yamada's "Camp Notes"; Alice Fulton's "Point of Purchase" or "Give"; Jorie Graham's "The Phase After History," to name but a few that come quickly to mind. Several critics, such as Susan Stanford Friedman and Herbert Leibowitz, editor of *Parnassus*, have considered these or comparable works as long poems, yet here I am reluctant to do so. I don't wish to quibble about how long is long, a particularly fruitless activity given that the scale of a poem as literary/cultural practice cannot necessarily be correlated simply to its scale as an object. After all, "The Waste Land," a central modernist long poem, has only 434 lines, and works like Gwendolyn Brooks's "Anniad," or John Ashbery's "A Wave" or "Self-Portrait in a Convex Mirror," while far from being book-length, certainly have the heft of long poems. In some contexts, the complexity of a poem's intent and conception, as well as its length relative to other works in a poet's *oeuvre*, might better determine whether it should be considered as a long poem than the number of pages it occupies; one could in some circumstances approach midlength poems like Marianne Moore's "Marriage" or Lorine Niedecker's "Wintergreen Ridge" as long poems. Nonetheless, very extended length poses distinctive challenges for the poet, and attending in this book to works which meet these challenges seems to me an effective way to command appreciation of the striking scale of women's recent poetic achievements.

A poem that approximates book length requires a great deal more time both in the writing and the reading (and often treats a greater sweep of historical time as well) than does a relatively short sequence.[24] Consequently, sustaining interest—balancing the need for variety against the need for some structure, coherence, or repetition—requires more resourcefulness. The relation of parts to whole becomes more problematic: how discrete are the parts? how do the gaps between them function? how may their relationship be sustained and/or disrupted? Strategies that work for midlength poems may not serve over a longer haul. Issues of managing voice or polyphonic voices, of incorporating multitudinous facts and perspectives, of the surface textures of language, of the use of page space, of closure, of linkages among parts via theme, image, form, and phrase all become potentially more unwieldy as a poetic structure grows. Ezra Pound, who didn't mind starting out with a rag-bag but ended up crying out for coherence, stands as a cautionary figure here. I have selected works I hope will convey the daring, the confidence, the seriousness of purpose, and the effectiveness with which women have variously met these considerable challenges.

The second reason for my wishing to focus on book-length poems relates to developments in contemporary poetry more generally, wherein the structure of the volume of short lyrics has increasingly provided a space for expressive effects or cognitive reach not obtainable within the format of isolated short poems. Often in recent volumes, image clusters flow and accumulate from poem to poem, multiple poems explore the same concept from different angles and using different voices, and poems are artfully arranged to follow developments in subject matter or emotional tonalities. Composing a long poem, even in the form of a lyric sequence, is an enterprise quite distinct from arranging a shapely volume, yet the two often serve some of the same ends in contemporary poetic production. Significantly, both may reflect dissatisfaction with the lyric as it is codified in contemporary practice—with its representing a single epiphanic moment, its reliance on a unified speaker, its imagistic coherence and tendency toward closure, its restricted intellectual or cultural range—and both may deliberately push the limits of that form. Consequently, the boundary between the contemporary long poem and the contemporary poetry volume is not always clear or fixed.[25] This means that much may be lost in reading (or teaching) short contemporary poems in isolation from the collection in which they appear. The extent to which contemporary poetry composed in brief units may manage to subvert or defy conventions of the "scenic" or "late modernist" lyric will not be fully apparent in the context of single short pieces or of anthology selections. Although I am not here examining any collections of lyrics apart from explicitly linked sequences, I hope that my treating primarily poems that are themselves books might encourage greater use of a book-based approach to contemporary poetry generally.

The trend toward poetry collections that appropriate powers and possibilities of the long poem demonstrates the magnetism extended poetic forms are exerting on contemporary poets. It is one more reinforcement of my contention that the long poem is as important to literary production in the late years of the twentieth century as it was in the decades of the modernist revolution. American poets are increasingly drawn toward inclusive, multivocal, expansive forms. In women's writing, where growth and diversification in literary/generic authority, social critique, and senses of gendered identity have fueled formal poetic expansions, this development has been particularly striking. The following chapters look closely at some notably diverse examples of women's recent achievements in very long poetic forms, beginning with the contributions of two working-class writers to that traditionally most noble and most masculine of poetic genres: the epic.

[handwritten margin note: probs posed by teaching one poem — not the vol. that houses it or part of a long poem.]

"To Remember / Our Dis-membered Parts": Sharon Doubiago and the Complementary Woman's Epic

While Susan Stanford Friedman persuasively argues that women of earlier eras experienced an "anxiety of poetic genre" in relation to the paradigmatically masculine norms of poetic epic, no traces of such anxiety remain in the recent long poems by Sharon Doubiago and Judy Grahn to be discussed in the next two chapters (1986, p. 203).[1] Without temerity, these poets seize the didactic, even prophetic, stance of the epic poet and confidently present their views of a sweeping history in which gender is the fulcrum for power relations. While Doubiago and Grahn foreground different sexual preferences and sexual mythologies, and while they speak for distinct feminisms, the two are nonetheless alike in being comfortable with the substantial universalizing that epic traditionally endorses: the stories they tell and the individual protagonists they depict are also broadly representative or archetypal figures. Doubiago and Grahn share, too, a rejection of the modernist epic's densely allusive texture that—while enhancing the poet's prestige among the intellectual elite—intimidated, indeed precluded, a mass readership.[2] Like their modernist predecessors, each regards her epic's message as ultimately a basis for vital social change. But the styles of these contemporary feminists, unlike the modernists', reflect a desire to communicate that message clearly and directly.

Doubiago's *Hard Country* draws extensively on the tradition of modern verse epic Michael André Bernstein identifies in *The Tale of the Tribe* and particularly on the example of Charles Olson's *The*

Maximus Poems. According to Bernstein, epic verse characteristically presents a narrative of the audience's cultural, historical, or mythic heritage; the dominant narrative voice functions as the voice of the community's heritage, representing values significant for communal stability and social well-being; the proper audience is not the individual but the citizen, the member of a "tribe"; and the didactic element is deliberately foregrounded (Bernstein 1980, p. 14). The modern variant exemplified by Bernstein's focal texts, *The Cantos*, *Paterson*, and *The Maximus Poems*, arose from Ezra Pound's belief that while prose might, like poetry, give memorable formulation to crucial elements of the tribe's heritage and urgent problems the tribe faces, only verse was also "genuinely capable of articulating a vision of beauty, of crystallizing the possibility for a better existence, and therewith of providing an impetus for the attainment of that good" (Bernstein 1980, p. 23). Consequently, Pound's understanding of verse epic, which has shaped subsequent practice in the form, required a precarious balance between two codes:

> the historically analytic and explanatory elements (the "prose tradition" of the great novels recaptured for verse) and the mythological, intuitive insights, the religious revelations of universal truths (traditionally the rightful domain of verse).
>
> (Bernstein 1980, p. 24)

In modern "tales of a tribe," the narrator usually bears strong autobiographical links with the author (think of the incarcerated speaker of the Pisan Cantos, or of the overlap between Maximus's experience and Olson's life in Gloucester) but also represents a sometimes mythologized collective as he confronts the circumstances that threaten his society's continued existence. No longer bound to ancient epic conventions of meter or structure, authors of such works have turned to disjunctive, easily inclusive forms constructed from relatively short units grouped into larger clusters. These short units sometimes attain the focused intensity and completeness associated with lyric, but they need not do so; often, their power derives from their contribution to (what Pound might call their rhyming with) intellectual and imagistic structures developing in the work as a whole. The relationship Doubiago forges between her ambitious epic *Hard Country* (1982) and this male tradition is that of a new form of complementarity, exemplified in the intertextual dynamics between her poem and Olson's *Maximus Poems.*

Hard Country is divided into four major sections composed of individually titled poems, comparable in length to Maximus's letters, which in turn are often subdivided. These lyrics place the female speaker's family heritage within the nation's cultural heritage and her thwarted personal quest for a balanced and reciprocal male-female love relationship within the field of patriarchal power relations.

Part I of the first section, "Headstone," explores the foundations of the speaker's identity by juxtaposing moments from her early childhood and identifications of her earliest ancestors. This part is addressed largely to the paternal grandmother for whom she is named. Part II of "Headstone" explores the early history of Asians on the American continent and then focuses on the contemporary (1970s) presence of the Vietnamese encountered by the speaker in a refugee camp and its family planning clinic. The second section, "Headland," is also divided into two numbered parts. The shorter of them, "Ramon/Ramona," picks up chronologically essentially where Part I of "Headstone" left off, presenting events from the speaker's adolescent years in the southern California town of Ramona and her passionate bond with a Mojave boy, Ramon. "Headland, II" is titled "Bicentennial." In the year commemorating a political revolution, the speaker meets the man with whom she will journey across the country in the epic's third part and with whom she hopes to accomplish a revolution in male-female relations. The beginning of their love is entwined in the painful end of her marriage. Part III, "Heartland," occupying 140 of the book's 260 pages, depicts the couple's journey by car from northern California to Tennessee and back. The history and lore associated with the American geography through which they travel is as much the poem's focus as the speaker's immediate experience or her changing relations to her unnamed companion, as this sample, from the poem "Wyoming," demonstrates:

> *Few of us will forget the wail of mingled grief, rage and horror which came from the camp 500 yards below us when the Indians returned to it and recognized their slaughtered warriors, women and children.*

Now the car bears east
against the century's westering tide.
We climb dark broken masses
to a small dry sky, high
between summits

Behind us, hardly a century,
openings are being found

and Custer's wife, Elizabeth,
starts out that morning from the fort
to join him, he from whom
she is rarely separated

and grandmothers come into the country
sitting on bundles of pieced quilts and blankets
of their own spinning

and soldiers splash across streams
firing and clubbing
as they emerge from their tipis

babies crushed by boots and rifle butts, Joseph
racing by with Sarah in his arms

and the boy Crazy Horse sees with great lightning spears
that are brighter than the sun, as thunders shake the earth,
these dead ones with their faces open to the storm
are his people

(*HC*, p. 141)[3]

In Tennessee—where the man grew up, where his mother drowned herself, and where the speaker's paternal grandparents had lived—recent family history comes to the fore, particularly in relation to the speaker's increasingly conscious quest for the elusive mothers.[4] In the brief final section, "Heartsea," the speaker, having parted from her companion, is briefly reunited with her husband before their final separation. At the poem's close, she attempts to move beyond her grief for the failure of their relationship—essentially, a failure to transform received gender roles—and for the tragic history of the American continent.

This summary suggests a reading experience far more linear and rational than the challengingly elliptical work in fact offers, as multiple voices or documents and pieces of historical narratives play off of and into the protagonist's story. Similarly, the quotations in this chapter, while conveying the often nonliterary language of *Hard Country*, may misleadingly suggest a thoroughly discursive, propositional text. Admittedly, Doubiago's commitment to the integrity of a poetic language true to her working-class roots markedly narrows her range of diction; and frequent employment of straightforward documentary syntax, which reflects a politically motivated wariness of embellishment as potentially falsifying or even dangerous ("the love of beauty above the human / is fascism"), can also flatten the work's individual sections. But relying heavily on fragmentation and parataxis, and on elaborate interweaving of motifs, the work as a whole achieves an overwhelming scale and great emotional power. *Hard Country's* aesthetic force derives from the intricately echoing cumulative conversation among its parts and from the resulting sense of the protagonist's psychic complexity and development. Catharine R. Stimpson's characterization of Doubiago's more recent long poem *South America Mi Hija* as a poem "in which structure is far sounder than diction"—referring both to the metrical structures of the free verse and to the "beautifully connected networks of reference and allusion"—applies as well to this one (Stimpson 1993, pp. 261, 263).

Hard Country embraces the major conventions of modern epic in its massive scale and public sweep, elliptical and paratactic construction, didactic societal critique, quest-based exploration of both past history and the nation's current state, and speaker at once individual and collective. In what follows, I argue that Doubiago creates a female complement to Olson's mode of epic: she transforms his poetics and thematics by incorporating the feminine voice, perspective, and values such works omit. This incorporation is not merely an addition in which the woman artist remains in a subsidiary relation to the established genre; rather, in generating a woman's epic, she recasts central elements of the male tradition, including its conceptions of masculine and feminine.

Underlying the complementary stance is a belief in an ideal of textual and personal androgyny (a balancing of feminine and masculine qualities within the individual or the text which s/he creates) and a belief in the value of heterosexuality (the coming together of male and female individuals in a sexual, and emotional, unit).[5] In this context, Doubiago's understanding of female sexuality as presented in her autobiographical story "Chappaquiddick" is instructive: In the sixties, Doubiago resisted the assertion, widespread among feminists, that vaginal orgasm was only a myth. She herself experienced vaginal as well as clitoral orgasms and preferred the former (1988, p. 331; cited hereafter as *SE*): her vagina "had always been the center of *all* [her] sensate experience." She could "understand the need to liberate the female from male sexual dependency" but to deny the pleasure she obtained from the penis inside her would be to participate in a "dangerous lie" (*SE*, p. 57).[6] Identifying the "center" not with the phallus but with the vagina, she resists radical separation of male and female, taking satisfaction in conjoining male and female parts. Similarly, the complementary woman writer, rather than rejecting the male tradition, claims its powers and pleasures as her own and expands them through transformative grounding in a female center—manifest in voice, perspective, rhythm, values, themes, forms—that has been lacking.

Obviously, this is a controversial stance for a contemporary feminist—and controversial terminology for a contemporary critic. Like Adrienne Rich, many feminists today class androgyny among the "words [they] cannot choose again" (1978, p. 66)—as an essentially androcentric concept that represses female difference. Many view heterosexuality as a patriarchal construction that subjugates women and sustains patriarchal power.[7] Moreover, the notion of the woman artist complementing male creations raises the specter of the ancient oppressive pattern in which woman has no specific being or desire and merely completes man's. There are indeed moments in Doubiago's epic when the speaker seems troublingly male-identified. Yet what she pursues is not a specious complementarity that masks male dominance—what I will sometimes refer to as phallocentric complementarity—but a different feminist complementary process where male and female, or masculine and feminine qualities, together create not Man but Woman:

> our only chance,
> *man, husband, father, brother, son, country,*
> *female*, is to become
> in this late century
> on this nuclear brink
> Woman

(HC, p. 257)

The new complementarity, then, cannot be achieved simply in a harmonious union of matching parts; it necessarily involves contest against the sexism of patriarchal traditions. If we are to become Doubiago's androgynous Woman or to inscribe her text, the misogyny of our culture embedded in heterosexual social structures and in hegemonic literary traditions must be excised or transformed. Yet, in order to write herself, Doubiago has to inscribe her own heterosexually manifest eroticism. The challenge she faces is that of reconciling keen insight into the oppressions of women and other marginalized groups in heterosexually sustained patriarchy with the passionate desire to couple with, incorporate, and love the male. Her solution is an unapologetic yet unblindered demonstration of the "both/and vision, the contradictory movement between the logically irreconcilable" that Rachel Blau DuPlessis celebrates as part of female aesthetic's countering of dualism and hierarchy (1990, p. 8).

Doubiago's poems and apparently autobiographical stories suggest that in her personal relationships with a succession of male partners, she developed from a youthful acceptance of the traditional phallocentric model of complementarity to a conscious quest for the new gynocentric one.[8] In the section of her story "Joyce" that is modeled on Molly Bloom's soliloquy in its structure and its stream of consciousness prose, Sharon concurs with a psychic's interpretation of her goals as she considers in particular her many years' relationship with a man named Max:

> I ground myself through my lovers rather than grounding my own
> body directly into the earth my body she said is made stable
> through sex so that then I can bring cosmic energy down . . . my
> work in this lifetime she said is to learn to draw up the earths cur-
> rent through my own feet and legs to take responsibility for
> grounding my own body rather than being dependent on a lover
> yes because it is an accurate description of Max and me Maximil-
> ian my Boylan my giant boy of the land my rainbow my Leopold
> Bloom my Wandering Jew my Daedelus my artificer of labyrinths
> we were such great pals cosmic pals I always said he gave me the
> earth this world and nature
>
> (SE, p. 230; ellipsis added)

A parallel narrative underlies Doubiago's relation to the tradition of epic associated with Whitman, Pound, Crane, Eliot, Williams, and, in prose, Joyce. Doubiago first seeks grounding in this tradition, discovering in the process particularly strong affinities for the version of epic poetics championed by the recent "artificer of labyrinths" Charles Olson. But Olson's epic, so exemplary in its exploratory eccentricity, proves problematic for being phallocentric and misogynistic. Consequently, her artistic "work in this lifetime," like that of many contemporary women, becomes a quest to move beyond a dependency on phallocentric tradition and to find, in part through her female body, her own grounding for her work. She attempts this progress, however, in a manner that will allow continued acknowledgment of the depth of her love for and debt to Olson and his Max/imus.

Olson and his epic spokesman, then, occupy a position in Doubiago's artistic development parallel to that of her longtime lover Max in her fictionalized personal development. (At one point, she even calls Max Maximus.[9]) Both Max and Olson are energetic iconoclasts, questing thinkers, and, for Doubiago, tremendously important liberators. But their liberation does not extend to their understanding of gender or their attitudes toward women. Through several of her stories in *The Book of Seeing With One's Own Eyes*, Doubiago portrays stages in the painful realization that Max, the new man who has taught her so much that is valuable, is in crucial ways no different from his fathers:

> He may have refused to go to war, chosen prison to maintain his convictions, he may have grown long hair worn in spite of the violent reactions of his own gender, beads and pretty clothes too, he may see through much that is false and cruel about this culture—but he will not love a woman.
>
> (*SE*, p. 203)

Olson, too, the latest avatar of a tradition of innovative works that point to "much that is false and cruel about this culture," typifies his society in being deeply misogynistic, and this misogyny inevitably informs his poetics. Just as Sharon has to confront her male lovers' inadequacies in order to grow beyond her "sexual emotional" dependency, Doubiago must confront the ideological limitations of Olson's poetics and re-form them to create her own female epic. (Later chapters present other poets—Susan Howe and Rachel Blau DuPlessis—conducting their own negotiations with Olson as one who is swaggering and condescending in his attitudes toward women yet also excitingly open and generative in his approach to poetic form.)

Doubiago's interaction with Olson becomes paradigmatic of her procedures in *Hard Country* in that her relation as writer to Olson parallels the relation of Doubiago's epic heroine to her male sexual partners. At times, Olson functions as an essentially emblematic figure: either positively as, say, Rebellious Poet or Critic of Dominant Culture or Poet of the Body, or negatively, as Tough Guy and Sexist. Yet he and his works also retain an individual force as someone/something that entered her life, as a particular lover would, at a given time and place and that continues to provide a personally meaningful context for her writing.

As poet, Doubiago lovingly adopts some of the liberating roles embodied by Olson's Maximus and typically reserved for men: the explorer/quester unencumbered by domestic responsibilities, the tough- and straight-talking worldly individual responsible for him- (and now her-) self, the prophet and teacher. At the same time, attempting to balance masculine and feminine, she reforms Olson's poetics and thematics, as she cannot in life reform her lovers' attitudes. By shifting emphasis to marginalized history and values, she redefines the values central to his epic tradition. Through revisionary emphases in her use of traditional myths, by reconceiving gender traits, and by combining genders within entities traditionally regarded as exclusively male or female, she creates a complementary dynamics between herself and Olson as female and male authors participating in the same literary tradition. By the close of her epic, Doubiago can incorporate the words of Olson's Maximus as essential elements within the most urgent formulation of *Hard Country*'s antipatriarchal message.

In her epic's plot and theme, Doubiago rejects the old form of complementary relations between male and female and dramatizes a progression toward a new one. When Sharon's husband brings home a man he has chosen to be her lover in a partner swap with another couple, she initially submits to her husband's wishes in a self-destructive gesture of traditional female love, figured as drowning herself for him. (That drowning recalls her earlier depiction of herself as a child fishing alongside her father, "a drowned creature" in "the great heartsea" beneath her father's ribs [*HC*, pp. 62–63].) But then she finds herself attracted to this new partner as part of her own constructive quest. Drawn by his mother in him, Sharon—

whose tubercular mother was removed to a sanitarium and conse-
quently absent during part of Sharon's childhood—journeys across
country with this unnamed man to the man-made (T.V.A.) lake in
which his mother, Geneva, literally drowned herself. There, as "A
Drowning Person [who] Sees Her Whole Life Pass Before Her,"
Sharon offers some straightforward summary:

> I am in love with you
> because of your mother.
> I left my husband for your mother.
> I've come all this way to find her.
> She lies at the bottom of you,
> the deep dark water that covers you.
>
> . . . .
> I saw someone in your eyes.
> She was watching from the water.
>
> . . . .
> I heard her crying *you can save me*
> *it's not too late.*
>
> (HC, pp. 189–90)

The speaker's quest, then, which until now she has only half under-
stood, is to rescue the woman who has been drowning in both her-
self and her male partner. Canoeing on the lake's surface, the narra-
tor participates imaginatively in Geneva's suicide:

> But she hardly hesitates on the shore beside him,
> then steps in, slipping down through the last miraculous air
> in her Sunday clothes, entering veiled, in prayer, the hushed
> sanctuary, the green cold, her earthly dress now
> dragging her the long terrible path down
> through holiness and voices, through faces
> lit in darkness, the terrible wrath gone over her
> as her navel, at last, *O Jesus to thy bosom*, oozes her out
> into the beautiful waters her sons swim in,
> floating her mother's farm in golden light, in songs of the planets,
> the jubilant weeds of the glory land enfolding her, a fish now
> going down under the world
>
> (HC, p. 189)

Leaving her partner behind in the canoe, Sharon literally enters that body of water, recognizing as she does so that she has approached love with comparable self-negation, allowing it to engulf her completely—"Take me up and cast me into the sea. / I am in love with you" (*HC*, p. 189). Now, however, she successfully resists patriarchy's seductive glamorization of the woman perfected in death; her submersion becomes not a drowning but a second baptism from which she arises at dawn reborn—"*Now who is it comes / up from wilderness?*" (*HC*, p. 194)—released from at least some of patterns of the old complementarity.

The new complementarity, though sometimes approached or momentarily experienced with her companion, is not something Sharon achieves in any lasting fashion in her relationships in *Hard Country*, for only the mythicized Crazy Horse exemplifies the man capable of true feminist complementarity, a genuine lover of women. But by the epic's conclusion she does end her unsatisfactory relationships, in the process confronting her husband, whom she still loves, with his failure to do his part to change male-female relationships: he failed to learn from her how "to be a woman" although she succeeded, perhaps too well, in learning from him how "to be a man" (*HC*, p. 252). At the work's close, she shifts from pursuing a complementary heterosexual relationship toward a reformation and salvation she can undertake alone in making her own androgynous being into one of feminist complementarity. Her closing concentration on the potential of her own androgynous vision suggests that, though itself unsuccessful, the process of striving for a heterosexual complementarity has yielded an empowered complementary subject.

Doubiago's quest for a new complementarity in relation to Olson, though nowhere so blatant as her narrator's quest for a feminist complementarity with her partner, emerges—as I have already indicated—in the context of the tradition of modern verse epic that Bernstein calls "the tale of the tribe." Olson was a theorist as well as a practitioner of modern verse epic; his propositions concerning "composition by field" were directed ultimately toward the development of expansive verse forms, specifically epic and drama. Near the end of "Projective Verse," he "hazard[s] the guess that":

> if projective verse is practiced long enough, is driven ahead hard
> enough along the course I think it dictates, verse again can carry

much larger material than it has carried in our language since the
Elizabethans. . . . We are only at its beginnings, and if I think that
the *Cantos* make more "dramatic" sense than do the plays of Mr.
Eliot, it is . . . because the methodology of the verse in them
points a way by which, one day, the problem of larger content and
of larger forms may be solved.

(Olson 1966, p. 26)

Both Olson, a self-proclaimed "[son] of Pound and Williams"
(1966, p. 23), and his theories were at odds with the poetic establish-
ment, still dominated by the precepts of Eliot and the New Critics;
in the 1950s and 1960s, the Projectivist writers were an artistic
counterculture. Here again we may think of Olson as analogous
to Maximilian the hippy and ex-con in that both occupy partially
marginalized positions despite their gender. It was to Olson the ex-
perimentalist and unconventional theorist of "larger content and
larger forms" that Doubiago responded enthusiastically when intro-
duced to his work in the late 1960s. Although nearing completion
of her Master's Degree in English, she regarded Olson as "the first
modern poet I ever understood[,] the poet who first awakened the
poet in me" (*SE*, p. 249). His " 'New American' concept of poetry
as, first and foremost, energy" caught her imagination (*SE*, p. 222;
she refers to Donald M. Allen's groundbreaking 1960 anthology,
The New American Poetry); his rebellious poetics "[gave her] hope"
(*SE*, p. 74).

Despite that hope, for some years following the completion of
her degree, Doubiago fought her own desire to be a poet because,
as one trained in formalism and living in the era of the Mai Lai
massacre, she saw "the terrible but very real connection between
the law and order of the army and the law and order of poetry"
(*SE*, p. 222). In *Hard Country* she lists that connection among the
explanations for the vow she imposed on herself and then elabo-
rates:

> I took a vow never to be a poet
> because art I was taught
> is too delicate to sing of genocide.
> But what else could I sing
> while people were being murdered
> in my name?

I hear the dead in Earth.
Their songs and stories cry to me
beyond all notions of Art and Form,
the poem as museum piece
where words are molded like human skin to shade the light
like special collections
of goldfilled teeth.

(*HC*, p. 144)

Although not writing poetry, she continued to study Olson and to expand her knowledge of epic. Taking her master's exam in 1969, she "chose to write on the epic characteristics of T. S. Eliot's *The Wasteland*" (*SE*, p. 51) and subsequently spent five years unraveling the structure of Molly Bloom's soliloquy, producing a 500-page manuscript on the subject and coming to know Homer's epic in the process. In *The Book of Seeing With One's Own Eyes* she refers knowledgeably to the *Cantos*, *The Bridge*, *Paterson*, and to the works of the most widely recognized female modernist who attempted epic poetry, H.D. She reports periods when her journals were "dominated by Olson" (*SE*, p. 76).

The depth of Doubiago's engagement with Olson's ideas in the early 1970s—comparable to involvement with a lover—is conveyed by her story "The Art of Seeing With One's Own Eyes." It depicts an extraordinary night in 1973 when Sharon and Maximilian drop acid and attend a showing of Stan Brakhage's gruesome film on autopsy entitled "The Act of Seeing with One's Own Eyes." (The etymological roots of autopsy mean "seeing with one's own eyes.") Dawn finds them examining "a different kind of autopsy report": they are literally surrounded by the original copperplate photogravures of American Indians taken by Edward Curtis, a display not of dead bodies but of live souls. Olson's ideas provide a grid through which the narrator perceives, while the night's events both test and are tested against his theories. Brakhage's very presence in town is exciting to her because of his "affinity with Charles Olson, the first poet to inspire me" (*SE*, p. 76). In his lecture before the film, Brakhage asserts that vision is part of our separateness, his films being simply his vision, and he urges his audience to "Remember Olson. 'There are no hierarchies, no infinite, no such many as mass. There are only eyes in all heads to be looked out of' " (*SE*, p. 82; he quotes *The Maximus Poems*, p. 33). Later, other statements from Olson pro-

vide structures that help Sharon process Brakhage's disturbing art-
work. Olson's essay "Equal, That Is, to the Real Itself," comes to
her mind:

> The corpses in the movie seemed perfect illustrations of [Olson's]
> thesis, of "what really matters, THE THING ITSELF, that any-
> thing impinges on us its self-existence, without reference to any
> other thing," the corpse itself, not the spirit or soul or history of
> the person as it leaves the corpse. "Matter," he writes of the
> whale, "offers perils wider than humanity if it doesn't do what still
> today seems the hardest for it to do, outside art and science; to be-
> lieve that things, and present ones, are the absolute conditions."
>
> (*SE*, p. 86)

Sharon's wish to be laid naked in the earth without a coffin when
she dies (not to be autopsied, embalmed, or cremated) bespeaks an
Olson-like desire to accept fully one's material conditions. At one
point, she angrily lashes out at this country for its "antimaterial-
is[m]," its hatred of matter.

Yet the night's events lead her to question some of Olson's con-
cepts, including the notion of congruence invoked in the same essay.
As one might expect from the complementary writer, she proposes
the term "synthesis" instead (*SE*, p. 88). Moreover, the Indians'
photographs call into question the "fanatical drive to *see* everything"
(*HC*, p. 88) enacted by the Olson-affiliated movie, as well as the
desire to discover one's separate vision, the Poundian *virtu* that dis-
tinguishes you from others. For, as one character remarks, "Curtis
saw the Buddha in everyone" (*HC*, p. 91). Curtis's photographic
images and the participatory response they prompt present a power-
ful challenge to the Olson-linked view of the soul as something that
separates individuals rather than binds them to each other. These
challenges to Olson suggest that Doubiago was locating a sense of
her own position, partly as a synthesizing of the two perspectives.
As she puts it in *Hard Country*, "my own story / is understanding
our singleness [Olson] / that I am destined to move my body and
time / into the body-time / the story / of Others [Curtis]" (*HC*,
p. 9). Even so, "The Art of Seeing With One's Own Eyes" makes
strikingly clear how fully Doubiago integrated Olson's precepts into
her own thought processes during this period when she was, how-
ever unwittingly, preparing to be a writer.

Doubiago's return to writing poetry is chronicled in the climactic

"Wyoming" section of *Hard Country*, where she recalls coming to
see that poetry could be a powerful political record of even the
greatest horrors of one's time, that craft "is spiritual," that writing
poetry ("a physical act, erotic and dangerous") was necessary for
her own survival. She still identified the canonized poetry she had
been taught as "lies"

> about war between the fascist polarities
> of vision and technique, of good and evil,
> of woman and man, of now and then, of mine and yours,
> of nature and man, of life and death,
> of the physical and spiritual,
> of race against race
>
> fictions made up
> to lead the mind
> into murder
> in the name of
> what God, what happened, what thing

(HC, p. 146)

But now she saw alternative possibilities for poetry suited to her
own sense of truth-telling.

Not surprisingly, once she released herself from her vow, she
turned to a contemporary poetics based on individually determined
form and on process rather than product, one devoted to countering
at least some of those "fascist polarities": she turned to the example
of Olson's poetics. Olson insists that in composition by field, each
poem individualistically "declares, for itself" its own form, thereby
resisting the imposition of "law and order." Although his use of
polarized terminology indicates that Olson does not really escape
polarized thinking, his discomfort with at least some of the hierar-
chies that accompany such binaries is apparent in his emphasizing
how pairs of supposedly separable, opposing categories function
(complementarily) as one. He presents himself as an opponent of
logical thought precisely because logic's categories falsely partition
a continuous reality. His famous dictum in "Projective Verse"—
alluded to several times in *The Book of Seeing With One's Own Eyes*—
that "FORM IS NEVER MORE THAN AN EXTENSION OF
CONTENT" proclaims the union of "vision and technique" that
Doubiago seeks. His theories of poetry arising from the collabora-

tion of two essential elements—the syllable which comes by way of the ear from the head, and the line which comes by way of the breath from the heart—resist neat mind/body dichotomies. He recalls that "the breath has a double meaning," invoking the Latin *anima*, which also means soul (Olson 1966, p. 22). As much as his respect for individualism, Olson's sense of connectedness, his desire to bring together elements and forces that Western thought has traditionally set in opposition, rendered his poetic program appealing for Doubiago.

In Olson's insistence on writing as a physical act deriving from the poet's physiological being, Doubiago may have found encouragement to write from her own body and express her physical desires. Olson laments that modern society, having lost the understanding that the flesh is common and to be held in common, "causes a man for all the years of his life the deepest sort of questioning of the rights of himself to the wild reachings of his own organism" (1966, p. 57). Always conscious of his body's tremendous size, Olson creates a persona whose name can be translated "the largest" and through him, and his own speech rhythms, seeks to express the value of the "Bigmans" type in a country where space, too, comes large. Being in the same way true to her very different physical makeup, Doubiago speaks as the blonde former beauty queen, whose supposedly mindless body is the American male's fantasy of perfectly satisfying, unthreatening womanhood. Frequently linking herself to Marilyn Monroe, she dares to express the "wild reachings" of her own sexual organism while also exposing her intellectual powers. One cannot claim that Olson taught Doubiago to write like a woman—indeed, in a story she honors a woman poet ("Lorrain") for doing that (*SE*, p. 181)—but in instructing the poet to listen to "his" own speech and to chart the kinetics of "his" own body, Olson pointed Doubiago in that direction.

Olson regarded projective verse as arising from a particular stance toward reality that Doubiago also appears to have valued. This stance, which he labeled "objectism," eliminates the "lyrical interference of the individual as ego, of the 'subject' and his soul," thereby allowing "man" to perceive himself as a creature of nature among other creatures, an object among other natural objects (1966, p. 24). Paradoxically, this humble stance is, according to Olson, what gives one access to larger dimensions and generates works of "projective size" (1966, p. 25). Doubiago, who bears a more urgent ecological awareness of the danger humans pose to themselves through failing to understand their place as part of the natural world, is more successful than he in locating her narrative perspective within nature and creating an epic speaker who seems part of America's immense land. Yet in this, too, his work was a model for hers.

Doubiago's profound interest in geography as a shaping force in American history and character antedates her reading of Olson, but here again, he provided a liberating example of how her interest could find poetic expression. However, in her epic she extends this interest in more mystical and marginal directions than Olson; the Mojave Indians, celebrated as a center of value in *Hard Country*, are "geographer[s] of the far borders of the land, geographer[s] of the far borders of consciousness" (*SE*, p. 17).

Retrieving the history of the marginal in her "poem containing history" is one of the major strategies by which Doubiago revises the male "tale of the tribe." Pound, Williams, and Olson flaunt unconventional historical methods and eccentric views of history, and each incorporates into his writing lore or learning of some non-Western people. Yet the history their long poems explore remains predominantly that of European or Euro-American males. Although admiring elements of non-European cultures, they do not integrate them thoroughly into the perspective of their epic spokesmen. Thus Olson writes passionately but patronizingly about the virtues of Mayan culture and appreciates contemporary Mayans from a distanced perspective as "the descendants of a culture and a civilization which was a contrary of that which we have known and of which we are the natural children" (1966, p. 56). He registers the presence of Algonquins and Micmacs in the Gloucester area and retells in *The Maximus Poems* several Algonquin legends (though partly because intrigued by their parallels with or survivals from Old Norse tales). Yet his exploration of Gloucester's history in *The Maximus Poems* does little to revise the inherited hegemonic perspective on the North American Indians as merely threats or obstacles to white settlements. When he speaks of the "the first men" in Gloucester (Olson 1983, p. 139), he means the first Europeans.

Doubiago's historical methodology in *Hard Country* is every bit as willfully idiosyncratic as her male predecessors', but her enactment of Olson's prized " 'istorin" (finding out for oneself) carries her in different directions, particularly in examining the destruction and virtual genocide of Native American peoples in what is now the United States.[10] "[A]gainst the fathers' amnesia" (*HC*, p. 16), Doubiago's narrator devotes considerable energy to identifying the "people back of [her]," linking her white ancestry not to the Puritan settlers but to inhabitants of this continent antedating them. She traces her roots to the " 'children of the Welsh rovers' / led by Prince Madoc in the 1100s / [who] crossed the Atlantic to the Gulf / ascended the Mississippi to the Tennessee / and settled the Highland"; specifically, she asserts a genealogical connection to one E. Edens whose Tennessee headstone dates from 1558, "30 years before / Sir Walter Raleigh's / Lost Colony / on the Caroline shore // 50 years / before Jamestown" (*HC*, p. 7). The family name is appropriate since legend has these white people living among the Indians, suggesting an Edenic situation of interracial harmony. The narrator's paternal grandmother who married an Edens descended from a Corn, and via that name the narrator ties herself to an earlier existence as part of the American earth, "my body / as maize" in an era when women worked the corn "in the fields / owned only by women" (*HC*, p. 9–10). Through the maternal line, the narrator claims Native American ancestry via predecessors identified on marriage certificates simply as "Squaw" (*HC*, p. 16). On both sides of her inheritance, then, she claims to be, in Olson's terms, a "natural child" of those whose history has been largely invisible to the white colonizers who developed our nation, to most historians—and to our epic poets.

Native American history is central to Doubiago's epic in that values identified with Native American cultures represent the best hope for salvation. (Demonstrating a contrasting version of idealizing nostalgia, Olson looks largely to values exemplified in such early white settlers as William Stevens, in members of the "polis" who demonstrate an "old measure of care," craftsmanship, resourcefulness, and connection to primary production rather than capitalistic development.) According to Doubiago, "We [whites] don't love our land / because we're the ones / who always left our land // for some notion of it" (*HC*, p. 42). In contrast, Native Americans never leave, even when dead; this country is crowded with their ghosts who walk the earth, as Seattle prophesied, "For we [Native Americans] still love this land and even / Death will not take this from us" (*HC*, p. 105; see also the title poem, pp. 163–64). Those who fail to establish such a connection to the land are bound for destruction.

Within *Hard Country*, Native American cultures and history are sometimes simplified and sometimes not, generating occasional inconsistencies in representation. This demonstrates a difficulty inherent in the already noted attempt to combine in epic tales of the tribe "historically analytic and explanatory elements" with "the mythological" (Bernstein 1980, p. 24). Where historical research is likely to reveal a mixture of admirable and deplorable behaviors in any social group, myth depends on simplification, often either demonization or idealization. (For an example of how far mythic treatment diverges from historical analysis, one has only to think of Pocohantas and Maquokeeta in Hart Crane's *The Bridge*.) Some mythic idealization accompanies Doubiago's positing a homology between women and Native Americans in their oppression at the hands of white men. Her tendency to mythologize and to reinforce certain stereotypes is tempered, however, by her incorporation of details of Native American history, including occasional acknowledgment of sexism within some Native American cultures. For instance, she quotes Chief Oury of the Utes saying "*The oath of a woman is almost worthless / among the Indians*" (*HC*, p. 140). More often Sharon identifies ideologically with the Indians, and consequently she retraces their travels; "She follows the path of the Nez Perce / across Washington, Idaho, Montana / because she has retreated herself / from the war and the country / ten years to heal the heart" (*HC*, p. 128). The loving male with whom she seeks union is often depicted as an Indian: as Crazy Horse, Sitting Bull, or the modern Mojave, Ramon, who was her first lover.

Having her protagonist identify sometimes with colonizing whites and sometimes with colonized Indians, Doubiago exercises a both/and vision that internalizes the perspectives of both center and margin. This strategy reflects a desire to acknowledge what Rachel Blau DuPlessis would term her "(ambiguously) nonhegemonic" status as a white female (1990, p. 15). For despite her suggestions that she inherited some Indian blood, Sharon situates herself in contemporary society as a white woman, even as Goldilocks, the "little white person / without roots" (*HC*, p. 21). This strategy also extends the androgynous premise upon which women's complementary art rests. If each person contains both male and female—categories which within patriarchy parallel the binaries of center and margin, oppressor and oppressed—no one can project blame exclusively outward or draw credit exclusively inward.

As a perspective for analyzing patriarchal history, the double identification points toward shared responsibility, shared blame, and shared hope. If dwelt on without attention to specific historical realities, such a perspective might irresponsibly equate all experiences of oppression—and at times *Hard Country* verges on doing so. For the most part, however, Doubiago manages to keep specific histories in view while she highlights the mixed positionality of the oppressed in order to prevent a reversal of the existing hierarchy that would only repeat the dynamics of patriarchal oppression. The balancing act a doubly-identified poet must perform to avoid blaming the victim while maintaining a plausible sympathy with the oppressor can be observed in "Headstone, II, American Alchemy." Here, Doubiago considers America's War in Vietnam, but—setting the poems in a family planning clinic within a Vietnamese Refugee Camp she visits in southern California—she does so primarily in terms of conflicts between the sexes.

In *Hard Country*, the Vietnamese, like the Indians, are accorded a pre-Columbian claim to this continent. Doubiago associates the Vietnamese with the band of Chinese Buddhist monks led by Hwui Shan who arrived in what is now California in 499 A.D. and followed the Hopi trail south into Central and South America, the route of their travels still traceable through legends and artworks recording the mysterious arrival of "bearded white men on canes / clad in long robes" ("*Quetzacoatl in Cholua, / Votan in Chiapas, / Zamna and Kukulcan in Yukatan,*" etc.) and through places named either for *Hwui*, his mendicant title, *pi-kui*, or for Buddha, called *Saka:*

> from Port *Hue*neme to *Saca*ton, Arizona
> down through Mexico to Guatemala and north again
> the cities of
>
> *Wicam, Huetama, Huichol, Huizontla, Huepac, Huila,
> Sacaton, Zacatlan, Zacatecas, Zacatepec, Sacabchen, Zacapa,*
> and
> *Picacho, Pichucalco, Picaho, Picchu,*
>
> and finally
> *Guatema-la*
> the place of Prince Guatama,
> the Buddha.

(HC, p. 32)

Thus, although relegated to refugee camps in the poem's present time, the Asians are in fact importantly connected to the American earth, from which white culture is dangerously alienated.

Again like the Indians, the Vietnamese now occupy the position of the feminine in American culture. The conquest and exploitation they have suffered involve dynamics of "domination / and submission" that in patriarchy are strongly gendered (*HC*, p. 40). The Vietnam War replicates on an international scale patterns of male sexual violence common in our culture: *"Vietnam opened itself to seduction and a brief, unhappy affair, but America came for rape"* (*HC*, p. 43). Similarly, the wars against Indians sanctioned violence as much against women as against the Native Americans: frontier soldiers "scalped / the genitals of Indian women // and stretched them over saddle-bows / and stretched them over cavalry hats / while riding in the ranks" (*HC*, p. 40). For Doubiago, war, fought over land, reflects hatred of the land, of the body—and of woman, who traditionally is associated with both. The speaker, who arrives at the anguished perception that every man she has ever loved has wanted to kill her, has known a version of such warfare in her most intimate relationships. Indeed, her identification with both oppressed ethnic groups is made possible largely by her gender, and her recuperation of marginal history may be understood as a recuperation of the feminine.

Doubiago nonetheless avoids conflating all nonhegemonic positions. She calls attention to her speaker's privileged position as a temporary visitor to the camp who exemplifies the Euro-American ideal of blonde beauty. At the same time, she highlights an analogy between her situation—as a woman whose body in sex is invaded by the male, who in patriarchy loses control over her own reproductive functions and over the fate of her offspring—and the situation of their invaded nation. The speaker has suffered through an abortion (*HC*, p. 50), an act of reluctant complicity with patriarchal oppression because carried out not for reasons of her own but explicitly for the father of that fetus (*HC*, p. 253), and both aborted fetus and the woman on whom the abortion is performed are analogous to refugees:

> Refugees. Struggle like a fish out of water. Refugees.
> Aborted. Fighting the dark waters against a midnight riptide,
> in your mouth his tongue, in your body forever.

Cervix scarred open. You have jewelry
you have gold. What he'll do
to get it.

(*HC*, p. 54)

The recurring italicized choric voice in this section presents the
self-destructive desire common to the woman assimilated into patri-
archy, to the invaded nation, and to the conquered people: "*Devour
me, destroy me / Make me as one with your race,*" "*Deform me in the
manner of your likeness*" (*HC*, pp. 48, 49). What these categories
share is at least partial compliance with their own imprisonment in
the role of the traditional, self-erasing complement.

Depending on their positionalities, individual women may or may
not be oppressed on the basis of ethnicity, class, religion, national-
ity, and so forth, but all women are, in Doubiago's view, inevitably
oppressed by virtue of their gender. Consequently, all women have
something to gain in the reformation of patriarchy. Linking war
to the patriarchal structures common to Vietnamese and American
cultures, Doubiago urges women to resist war by identifying as
women rather than as citizens: "*You are a woman. / No nation / recog-
nizes you*" (*HC*, p. 54), "*You see / beyond all / borders*" (*HC*, p. 55).
Because men want mothers' sons only for soldiers and their daugh-
ters for spoils of war, she urges women to claim their offspring and
to run "*for their* [the children's] *lives*" and "*against the man's war*":
"*Leave. Take your children away / from war. Teach them to run / from
all government. Scatter them / among men and women as you go*" (*HC*,
p. 55). Doubiago's narrator blames the patriarchs for certain repug-
nant characteristics she observes in the Vietnamese women—their
focus on material wealth, their complacent disregard of brutal polit-
ical realities. But she insists that women need to take responsibility
for changing themselves. Marcelene, the Swiss woman whose male
psychiatrist tells her that coming to this country "has made [her] too
independent for [her] marriage to work," replies with a summary of
this lesson:

> . . . *I told him the men*
> *in the old world*
>
> *keep their wives innocent and ignorant. I told him*
> *women bring the people into the world.*

They must learn to take responsibility for it
rather than continue to be
the lighthearted slightly stupid wife
happy in bed.

(*HC*, p. 38)

Taking responsibility means effecting fundamental changes in the dynamics of heterosexuality.

This is reinforced by the horrific emphasis throughout this section ("HARD NOW AGAINST THE MAN: FEMALE PROBLEMS," an extended section within "Headstone II, American Alchemy") on the equation between a woman's "fucking" and her taking death into her vagina, between heterosexual intercourse and a woman's abdication of will and moral responsibility: alluding to a song of Billie Holiday's, "She took you in, took you deep within, / the man who could make her do anything." The section condemns women's cross-cultural failure to reach beyond masochistic submission to the male. Sleeping with men within the patterns of phallocentric complementarity is a version of "sleeping with the enemy" (*HC*, p. 39).

Yet, rather than turning to a lesbian alternative, Doubiago remains hopeful about the possibilities for different relations between the sexes; when urging woman to seize her progeny and run from war, Doubiago still looks to an integration of genders (as well as races and nations); the re-educated children are to be scattered, like the body parts of Osiris, "among men and women." One of the epigraphs for this section, "Headstone, II, American Alchemy," reads, "I thought of Jung who said his clients dreamed most often of the movie 'Hiroshima, Mon Amour' and that in the dream the couple had to connect in order that the bomb not be dropped" (*HC*, p. 29). Acknowledging that this dream, however problematic, is hers also, Doubiago attempts to envision and realize in her epic a different quality of male/female connection than that portrayed by the heterosexual male poets who preceded her.

Olson, whose sexism typifies his epic tradition, presents the connection between men and women as, at best, that of the inequitable phallocentric complement. Maximus's Gloucester is a man's world, in which the female appears largely as an abstraction embodied in inanimate emblems that support or embellish the male enterprise. The fishermen's ships and their bowsprits are female, while Our

Lady of Good Voyage doubles as muse and protecting goddess. The city, the earth, polis itself are sometimes identified with feminine pronouns, but real women would seem to have played little role in Gloucester's history. When abstract and nonsexual, the female is treated with reverence, but when female sexuality comes into play, as it frequently does when women appear in the mythology Olson invokes, his misogyny can be blatant. For instance, in *Maximus IV, V, VI* he several times introduces the beautiful woman from Algonquin legend who killed five husbands by transferring to them in sexual intercourse the poison she received from secret sexual encounters with a huge serpentlike beast "in a deep wild place / in the woods." Her sixth husband wisely refuses to have sex with her, so that she dies of the poison and he survives. Relying on a familiar double-standard, the story presents female sexuality in a demeaning light, its expression considered transgressive promiscuity, its effect deadly to men (Olson 1983, p. 191). Olson several times juxtaposes this tale of "the adulteress," who by implication got what she deserved since "she had fucked with the king of the pool" (*HC*, p. 312), with another Indian story of a woman whom "[t]hey said . . . went off fucking every Sunday" (*HC*, p. 192) and who claimed to have been "fucked / by the Mountain" (*HC*, p. 313). In one telling, Olson presents this sexually active woman more positively, as "the happiest / of the tribe," but his locution deprives the woman of most of her agency and insists on the male's dominant role (he fucks, she is fucked). In "Human Universe," Olson savors a narrative of violent male dominance over a wayward and undependable female, seeing there evidence that the Mayans were "hot for this world" and "hot to get it down the way it was." The myth concerns Sun and Moon; Olson narrates its conclusion as follows:

> So he does, he puts out her eye, and lets human beings have what they want. But when he does more, when, occasionally, he eclipses her entirely, some say it is only a sign that the two of them continue to fight, presumably because sun cannot forget moon's promiscuity, though others say that moon is forever erratic, is very much of a liar, is always telling sun about the way people of the earth are as much misbehavers as she, get drunk, do the things she does, in fact, the old ones say, moon is as difficult to understand as any bitch is.
>
> (1966, p. 66)

Doubiago acknowledges the prevalence of myths glorifying violent male subjugation of women, for instance, in her use of Helen of Troy as the archetypal example of woman-as-spoils-of-war. But she critiques such models and highlights her determination not to replicate them. She does not pretend complete escape from the deeply ingrained patriarchal patterns they encode; at one point her fictional self, Sharon, sits in the car "mute, sentenced, as he rides me north / a grinning thief with his loot" (*HC*, p. 110). But she will not rest there; by the time they have crossed the continental divide, Sharon is the one at the wheel (*HC*, p. 148).

Moreover, adapting what T. S. Eliot termed the "mythical method" of modernist epic that manipulates parallels between contemporaneity and antiquity, Doubiago reworks myths that permit changed visions of female-male relations.[11] *Hard Country*'s governing myth is that of Isis and Osiris; as the endnotes announce, the speaker is "an American Isis," the grieving woman who travels the land in search of her lover, reassembling (re-membering) the parts of her husband/brother that are scattered across and buried within it (*HC*, p. 259).[12] That her husband is her brother suggests this male-female relationship is one of equality and particular closeness. In the portion of the myth that most interests Doubiago—that following the dismemberment of Osiris—the woman, an artist as well as a devoted lover, is the active figure in the pair. Gathering the parts of Osiris's body, she recovers all but the genitals; these she must sculpt herself. Besides debunking male pretensions to priority by giving a woman credit for making the organs of masculinity, for creating man's generative power, Doubiago's invocation of the myth positions woman as controlling the difference between man and woman and what that difference represents. Thus, while the protagonist's quest is for "the man / man enough / to love" (*HC*, p. 90), the framing myth suggests her desire actively to shape such a man. Isis/Sharon/Doubiago does more than mourn and re-member, however important those may be; she also creates so as to remake masculinity and thereby gain her own sexual and emotional fulfillment.

One of the aims of Doubiago's complementary epic is to discover alternative ways of envisioning the two genders, in order to render plausible a healthy complementarity. Having exposed early on the worst aspects of both genders in patriarchy—man's inability to love and to understand, woman's inability to act and to resist the self-destructive—she proceeds to tease out what is of special value in each. She also exposes the inextricability of feminine and masculine in the human psyche, largely by yoking the two in functions or entities conventionally assigned to one gender alone. The recurrent figure of boundaries and borders in the poem relates to this twofold project. Women, as those who "see / beyond all / borders," are in a position to transcend the false dichotomies acculturated into our understanding of gender—dichotomies such as: "*Women understand everything / and therefore can do nothing. / Men understand nothing / and therefore can do anything*" (*HC*, p. 85). Such transcendence may be what Doubiago has in mind in quoting the admittedly ambiguous lines from Bob Dylan, "I kissed goodbye the howling beast / On the borderline which separated you from me" (*HC*, pp. 138, 229). Yet she repeatedly refers to the Indian custom of marking the boundary lines of their distinct nations with the graves of infants and in that connection asserts: "There are real borders." Her project then, is to distinguish the various levels of "real" (biologically or psychically essential) gender differences from the artificial, patriarchally imposed ones, to respect the former and eradicate the latter.[13]

The first poem in "Headland" (the section following the scenes in the refugee camp), identifies in the "boy" a masculinity that is not corrupt or misogynistic, but caring and responsible. "I Was Born Coming to the Sea" presents heterosexuality as the speaker's destiny from birth, but the boy who draws her and warns of a world endangered by war is the male before socialization into patriarchy: "I was coming / to the sea when I was born, / the buoy I heard through water and storm / was a boy calling me" (*HC*, p. 61). The narrator's traveling companion also embodies in some ways a more life-affirming version of masculinity. He has not severed himself from the female or from a fluid nonlinearity widely associated with the feminine, so that the story of his drowned mother is his story and he is genuinely open to his sexual partner:

> Your open mouth like the ocean
> where you allow me, swimming.
> Beneath all things, the Bible says
> are the waters
> but men don't usually open this way.
> They are always ships headed for some horizon

(*HC*, p. 95)

This "Love Song For A Man Whose Mother Killed Herself" concludes: "You are the first man who has ever opened to me. / Somehow you have made yourself // the man she would not live without." The potential for intimacy established by the man's opening offers meaning to the speaker's life.

While suggesting a new, loving masculinity, the narrator also redefines and revalues femininity in a quest to free herself from its conventional self-destructive aspects. As part of this project, she revises some of the most degraded female stereotypes. In the poem "Charon," a pun on the name of the author/narrator, she links the woman artist to the waitress—an important figure as early as the epic's opening poem, and one emphasizing Doubiago's working-class identification.[14] (Even the cover photo depicts a blonde teenager in a waitress's uniform—white shirtwaist, gingham apron—presumably Sharon Doubiago, sitting with a boy who fits Ramon's description.) Sharon recalls from family car trips across the desert during the cool of the night, "the neon-lit truck stops"

> where the diesels hummed
> and the laughter carried
> miles out into the waste, and *her* voice
> tough, sexy, bringing food
>
> so that for the rest of my life
> I would think my occupation
> must naturally be
> waitress
>
> helping night travelers
> to get across
> before the light comes up

> (*HC*, p. 64)

This discovery of "*her* voice" constitutes Doubiago's recognition of poetic vocation. The role might seem strikingly nonfeminist: woman as servant and supporter to the male adventurer (most truckers being men), as bearer of nourishment, as provider of sexual diversion. Yet, by making this the image of the female *artist*, Doubiago not only provides a context in which these traits may be revalued but also creates an empowering revision of the stereotype of the woman poet. The female poet, after all, has traditionally been thought of as one who proffers decorative desserts, if you will, rather than substantial meals, and has been expected to sound demure, virtuous, reverent, perhaps mournful, but not "tough" (nor particularly "sexy"). Such powers *as poetic powers* or powers of voice have been regarded as almost exclusively male. Doubiago claims them for the female artist when she takes as her model for the female speaking subject a female embodiment of the tough voice, the waitress. Additionally, as I shall now argue, she attempts to eliminate the misogyny of that model's male counterpart.

Philip Kuberski identifies Olson's "mannered style" as that of "the movie tough guy" and sees in this telegraphic style, also associated with Pound, a "struggle to maintain the thing as a functioning fetish" (Kuberski 1985, p. 191). Applying Freud's analysis of the fetish as a penis substitute, Olson's fascination with "the thing" (a word that in slang usage may mean penis) reflects a fear of castration and a horror of the (castrated) female genitals; "The pointer, indicator, phallus, the thing repudiates the generalizing, corrupting, promiscuous vagina that can accept all interpretations, measures, and meanings" (Kuberski 1985, p. 190). Whether or not one accepts the Freudian reading, certainly Olson's linguistic and syntactic tics suggest a need to distance himself from any effeminacy associated with being a poet.

Doubiago adopts some of the crude bluster of the American tough guy—for instance in her insistence on the word "fuck"—and thereby claims traditionally male freedom of speech and action (formerly women were free neither to mention fucking, nor to go out and find someone with whom to enjoy it). But, employing a style less telegraphic and more grammatically straightforward than Olson's, she sidesteps the tough guy's fear of the female and of the emotionality associated with the feminine in our culture.

The section of *Hard Country* portraying Jack Kerouac and Marilyn Monroe camping together on the beach presents the stereotypically masculine inability to express emotion—what underlies "Gary Cooper's stammering" (Kuberski 1985, p. 191)—as itself leading to a sense of impotence, which generates compensatory violence and cruelty. Monroe keeps trying to get her taciturn companion to talk, especially about sexuality, and to express emotion, but the closest he comes to expressing feeling is saying he is afraid of rain. Even in their repeated sexual intercourse, he evades intimacy and projects murderous threat rather than love. Echoes of Keats's "La Belle Dame" in a tough-guy style suggest his desire to blame their unhappy situation on her, the beautiful woman ("The saddest face she had ever seen / smiled. He said, My name is Jack. / Your name is Marilyn. / And that is why we sojourn here / alone in Kalaloch." [*HC*, p. 116]). But the real danger clearly lies in the emotionally stifled, fetishistic male: "When he can't cry, he will see his own face / above the waves, he will shoot / fictitious elk, he will be without his / gun. He will be ruthless" (*HC*, p. 116).

Doubiago's echo of the opening lines of *The Maximus Poems* in the closing of her own epic demonstrates her complementary modification of the tough-talking male epic spokesman. Here is Olson, beginning "I, Maximus of Gloucester, to You":

> Off-shore, by islands hidden in the blood
> jewels & miracles, I, Maximus
> a metal hot from boiling water, tell you
> what is a lance, who obeys the figures of
> the present dance

(1983, p. 5)

Characteristically, Olson's syntax is chopped up by modifying phrases and appositives and broken by midphrase line breaks. This is part of what gives his writing the no-nonsense forcefulness that typifies the movie tough guy's speech (though, of course, Olson's language is far richer and more surprising). The speaker's stance is cocky, his manner directive—"I, Maximus . . . tell you"—so much so that Olson himself must mock it in the next poem. Maximus, as grandly authoritative as his name suggests, proclaims with a swagger typical of the American hero his confidence that experience has tempered him, maximized his strength. What he will teach is unabashedly phallocentric—"I . . . tell you / what is a lance." A man who possesses answers, he is determined to instruct his reader in the nature of the weapon that empowers one to impale the enemy (for him, "pejorocracy" in its many forms).

In a poem set at the opposite end of the continent, "Los Angeles," in the closing lines of *Hard Country*, Doubiago alludes to that passage:

> until, *alcatraz*, off-shore by islands hidden in the blood,
> jewels and miracles, I am the Pelican:
> the consumed heart between the White House and the Sun
> the human between the male and the female

buoyed for the moment on my barren coffin, my soft-shelled eggs,
with only love for hope
look back onto the whole country, its lethal tide
its love of death
its hatred of love
and warn you

(*HC*, p. 258)

Giving the allusion such prominent place (along side an allusion, via Queequeg's coffin, to Olson's beloved Melville), Doubiago asserts a continuity between Olson's epic and hers. At the same time, by shifting the context and the poetic construction, she remakes Olson into *her* complement, one who speaks for *her* project. She breaks his lines between rather than within phrases and uses conventional spelling rather than the Poundian ampersand, achieving a less clipped and less obfuscating manner. Her multiplication of parallel or apposite phrases clarifies ideas by restating them variously, so that Doubiago's speaker seems more interested in communication and less in bravado than Olson's was.

Although possessing the same sweeping off-shore perspective as Olson's Maximus, Doubiago's speaker, who incorporates a changed Maximus, does not claim for herself a position of strength. As the Pelican (*alcatraz* in Spanish), whose survival is threatened by shell-weakening pesticides, she speaks for the most vulnerable, including by association the isolated prisoner. Her speaking for the disempowered differs significantly from Olson's celebration in the *Maximus Poems* of, say, Gloucester's underappreciated Portuguese fishermen. These he enlarges into traditional heroes, men of effective action, whereas Doubiago's "human between the male and the female" retains a precarious status, as the syntactic parallel with the preceding line suggests how easily the human might be "consumed" between the other excessively polarized terms. Doubiago does not offer a lance or any weapon with her warning—a warning that here appears to be hers-and-Olson's—since that would only perpetuate patriarchy's "love of death." What her re-formed poetic complement offers is an alternative attitude: with love as her only hope, she declares "a love for hope" that elsewhere in her work is identified simply as "innocence" (*SE*, p. 188). Innocence is at the opposite extreme from cynicism, the pose of the male tough-guy.

When Doubiago's narrator talks tough in her frankness about

sexuality and violence, rather than covering sentiment, she boldly expresses what has been silenced. Indeed, as blonde beauty, stereo-typical sex-object, she speaks from an especially muted female subject-position. She strives for a self-respecting toughness in her relations with men, but not one that distances or oppresses them. As the speaker embarks in "Headland, II" on her eastward journey with her male companion, she has just been confronted with her husband's misogyny (he declares of the lover he brought home for himself, *"When I got inside her / she was disappointing. / It was no different / than being inside you"* [HC, p. 85]). She sees the pathology of their relationship of traditional complementarity wherein the wo-man provides all the understanding and the man all the action, where she loves too much and he too little. She determines, "From now on / he must understand. // He must love me / as much as I love him" (HC, p. 85), a mutuality she hopes to create with her new partner.

The "first man who has ever opened to [her]" differs in some crucial ways from her "pornographer" husband, and over the course of several early sexual encounters the new couple manages to shed much of the baggage from their past experiences within patriarchy's deforming gender system. Initially—when she, kneeling to him, en-gages in oral sex—the speaker knows that the man cannot trust her because of "the kind of passion that threw [his] mother into the lake" and that she cannot trust him because of "the violence / and silence I have known of fathers and husbands / the kind of passion that kills Redwoods" (HC, p. 93). Nonetheless, they subsequently achieve a restorative sexual union; when he "come[s] into [her]," "it is the circle of new shoots / from the burnt heart of redwood," "a bird fluttering light / down into the drifts of the mines / where my grandfather worked all his life." In a figure that reverses the drowning motif,

> it is a fish slivering up through
> shafts of light in the dark water's depth
> and finding her, brings her back
> to her lost child

(HC, p. 94)

Although conventional locution would have it that the boy lost his mother at her death (or that the girl, Sharon, virtually lost her mother when she entered the sanitarium), it is the child who has been lost. Reunited with the mother in this sexual union, the boy, the best of maleness, is recovered. But such moments are rare in *Hard Country*.

By journeying toward the drowned woman whom they both need to recover, the two approach what might enable them to attain a more lasting version of feminist complementarity. Yet the narrator benefits more fully from that encounter than the man; on the lake he merges with the patriarchs who enforce female silence and drowning, while she manages to turn away from death and toward a profound connection with the mother and with the earth's generative body. How far he has been left behind is suggested by his resistance to taking responsibility for the past; when she asserts "*It was our grandparents*" who slaughtered the Native Americans, he repeatedly insists, "*Not mine*" (*HC*, p. 142). Doubiago implies that this white man's denial of participation in history's patterns of privilege and oppression leaves him likely to reenact history's violence in a return of the repressed.

Seeing through the woman's eyes, however, we experience significant modifications of traditional modes of thinking, generating the hope that readers, male or female, might be changed as the narrator has been. This suggests that the analogue between the narratives of the speaker's quest for a complementary relationship with a man and the poet's quest within literary history for complementarity in relation to Olson and male epic tradition has a third implied level in the reader's narrative of complementary reading. The reader's perceptions may be altered, for instance, by the poet's revising traditional gender divisions, something she achieves by joining masculine and feminine within entities commonly associated with a single gender.

For example, modifying Olson's approach to the poetry of American geography, Doubiago revises the traditional conception of the female land, adding a male component. While America's male writers, as Annette Kolodny has documented, have conceived of the land as female—initially as the wholly gratifying maternal "garden," then as an object for domination and exploitation (Kolodny 1975, pp. 5–9)—in Doubiago's work the land becomes androgynous. Her use of the Osiris myth gives the land masculine attributes, since the parts of the male lover's body are not merely scattered on and buried in, but identified with the earth ("You taught me this land. You are the land" [*HC*, p. 255]). Yet the related American legend of Ramona

and her lover expands this pattern to identify the land as both male
and female (and to suggest that the ideal union integrates racial as
well as sexual differences). Ramona, a white woman (or perhaps, as
in Helen Hunt Jackson's novel, a woman of mixed blood positioned
within her society as white), married an Indian and fled with him
from the pursuing whites. Her husband's fate was like Osiris's,
though this man's body was scattered by his lover, not just by his
enemy:

> When his murderer blew off his face
> after he was already dead, Ramona
> scattered his pieces to the four warm corners:
> desert, mountain, basin, sea, naming
> with flesh and story, this last edge
> of country.

Thereafter Ramona herself became part of the landscape:

> Then she lay on her back along the southern rim.
> Her silver hair fell as granite
> all the way to Mexico,
> where the mountains, standing in thought,
> turned blue to honor her.
>
> (HC, p. 33)

Legend prophesies her rebirth: "someday soon she will rise from
her sleep. / When this happens, her husband, the land / will once
again be [the Indians']" (HC, p. 33). The woman is the land, but
so is her male counterpart. Sharon, similarly, searches for her lost
Indian lover, Ramon, whose body (in one of several versions of his
death) is "strewn in pieces on Jacinto" (HC, p. 257). (The related
names Ramon and Ramona provide a further gender crossing in
this pattern.) Sometimes her current lover is the land she travels and
whose unheard stories she tells; sometimes her body is the "body of
America [he] enter[s], / her dark unwritten stories" (HC, p. 89).
Their ability to nurture and inspire each other, then, is at least po-
tentially reciprocal.

When presenting the land as female, Doubiago makes this associ-
ation empowering to women. In the "Wyoming" section, set on
the continental divide, while her male companion sleeps Sharon ex-
periences her moment of farthest vision, one expanding from a fem-

inized landscape of breastlike and vaginal forms and from her own body:

> And then I see, north and west across the black sea
> of mountain ranges, floating in the lap of one,
> a single, gold-chartreuse valley.
> . . . .
>
> I'm looking from night across so much space
> I'm seeing before time
> to the day already passed.
>
> The midnight sun shines between my thighs
> My urine sprays across the top of the world
>
> (*HC*, pp. 142–43)

Thereafter she perceives a "woman arched above the sun," a personification of the zodiac who, laying her hands upon the speaker, defines the difference between the narrator's female art and that of the male poet, Orpheus, who also went in search of his dead lover:

> But you must recall
> Orpheus loved the dead too much
>
> looked back and learned
>
> the Dead can't be brought
> onto the living Earth
>
> To bring the song out of the blood that soaks the ground
> you must remember there will be light even at midnight
>
> You must make it living
> for the Dead who do not forget the living
>
> but livable
>
> for the four infants found alive at Wounded Knee
> wrapped in the shawls of their frozen mothers
>
> (*HC*, pp. 146–47)

The life-giving, life-sustaining powers that are biologically and, in patriarchy, sociologically woman's are revealed as powers contemporary art urgently needs. This would be particularly true for epic tales of the tribe, since such works tend to display the blood-soaked ground of western history.

Doubiago develops therefore a model of poetic creation that centers on the female sexual organs, not Irigaray's onanistic and/or lesbian labia touching and generating inexhaustible pleasure, but the vagina both as a "deep eye" that increases the artist's perception, sympathy, and memory, and as a capacious, implicitly heterosexual "slot" that enlarges her life-giving artistic powers (*HC*, pp. 194, 81). Other people's stories, like the "life-sustaining images / of other poets" "enter / the [artist's] body like sperm to the egg." Positioning herself as a heterosexual lover, the complementary writer actively draws them to her and is fertilized by them so that her vaginal passage becomes "an infinite slot, a great unbroken tongue / telling a story" (*HC*, p. 81). Even here, Doubiago's gender-yoking strategy is at work, for she presents the vagina as not only a receptive but also a phallic organ, just as in union with Crazy Horse, his lover's vagina becomes "hard" like the erect penis (*HC*, p. 151).[15] The stories she tells with her vagina/tongue she identifies as female in origin, the gift of her own mother, yet that gift itself takes the masculinized form also of a horse carved by the mother's father, which in turn becomes "a gun in [her] hands" (*HC*, p. 202).

Doubiago's protagonist, having failed to realize an interpersonal relationship of feminist complementarity, focuses near the epic's close on the necessity for precedent change in herself alone. She responds to the crying Earth that is asking from her what she had unsuccessfully demanded from her male partners: *"you must love me / as much as I love you"* (*HC*, p. 255). Recognizing that in relation to the earth she has occupied the masculine position of refusing love, she urges herself to confront the darkest aspects of her own androgyny: her own guilt as "betrayer of the Body, the Earth, Marriage and Love." Her quest now is to regain the knowledge she seems to have lost sight of during her attempt to establish an exceptional relationship with one she hoped would prove an exceptional man: the knowledge that

> to love
> is not to transcend the horrors I have known
> or the earth
> I have never loved
>
> but to know and contain them
> within my body

to remember
our dis-membered parts
and then
to survive
this memory

though my eyes are gouged out
to *see*

though my tongue is cut out
to *sing*

(*HC*, p. 256)

Before embarking on her journey, Doubiago presented a societal "we" that included both men and women, Sharon and her lover, facing this same challenge.[16] By this late point, however, she has had to retreat to challenging herself alone. Having shifted to the future her hopes for a gynocentric complementary relationship with a man, the protagonist as complementary being identifies with both masculine and feminine via the mythical figures of blinded Oedipus and tongueless Philomela; she is at once the dismembered male Osiris (Ramon, castrated Uranus, etc.) and the re-membering female Isis (Ramona, Aphrodite).

This balanced union of genders takes place only within the created speaker—not between her and a man—if indeed it is realized at all on the level of narrative in the epic's present. Yet *Hard Country* itself, as a work that assimilates male achievements and masculine characteristics of the modern verse epic while self-consciously and successfully excising much of their phallocentrism and misogyny, suggests that contemporary female artists attempting to inscribe female experience may, like Isis, successfully re-form their male predecessors, sculpting from those forebears' literary remains figures who may serve as their feminist complements.

CHAPTER TWO

"Helen, Your Strength / Is in Your Memory": Judy Grahn's Lesbian Warriors and Gynocentric Tales of the Tribe

In 1982, self-proclaimed Lesbian poet and "Gay cultural theorist" Judy Grahn published the first volume of a projected quartet of long poems called *A Chronicle of Queens* (Grahn 1990, p. xiii).[1] Each volume is to be named for a queen of one tarot suit: the first, *The Queen of Wands*, was followed in 1987 by *The Queen of Swords*. *The Queen of Wands* presents, through three sections of titled short poems and a fourth of documentary prose notes, the "worldwide myth of a female god of beauty, fire, love, light, thought and weaving" (Grahn 1982, p. xii). Central to the volume is a story, often repeated in mid-Eastern cuneiform tablets dating from around 2500 B.C., of that queen/god having been "stolen from her temple and carried away by ship" (1982, p. xii). Grahn interprets this prototypical theft narrative, which recurs in various forms in *The Queen of Wands*, as marking the appropriation of female creative power and the destruction of goddess worship that accompanied the historical transfer of power from gynarchy to patriarchy and from polytheistic matrifocal religions to monotheistic worship of a male god. In Western tradition, the most "persistently retold" version of this stolen queen's story is that recounted in Homer's *Iliad:* the tale of Helen, Queen of Sparta, who is transported to Troy (1982, p. xii). The continuation in modern society of attempts to destroy, repress, or take possession of female power is emphasized by the book's dedication to Marilyn Monroe as well as by numerous lyrics portraying manifestations of Helen/El-Ana in the modern industrial world. The ultimate project of the book, and of Grahn's *Chronicle* as a whole, is female empowerment; *The Queen of Wands* reminds women of their own powers, those which continue as well as those which have been suppressed. Thus, the widespread association of weaving with this queen/god (variously identified as El-Ana, Helen, Spider Webster, Spider Grandmother, Frigga, Chin-nu, etc.) enables Grahn to (re-)claim for women an ancient power of word-weaving, to assert that in the past the weaving of language was a female art and that it was women who were in "possession of the word" (1982, p. xiii).

The second volume of Grahn's *Chronicle*, *The Queen of Swords*, continues "the saga of the goddess Helen" (1987, p. 1). Its foundational text is the section of the "great cycle of epic myths" about the Sumerian goddess Inanna, dating back to at least 3000 B.C., that tells of her descent into the underworld (1987, p. 2; Grahn includes a translation of the Sumerian text in "Appendix 1"). The Queen of Swords is Ereshkigal, queen of the underworld, associated also with "air, storms, intelligence, science, piercing violence, and strength," whom Helen/Inanna confronts (1987, p. 3). While *The Queen of Wands* frequently portrays Helen in relation to a male consort (Grahn describes its poems as "more related to my mother's life and the tradition of the heterosexual European folk-goddess Helen, than to my own personal life as a Lesbian" [Grahn 1985, p. 78]), *Swords* deals with lesbian relationships. Writing in *Another Mother Tongue: Gay Words, Gay Worlds* of the myth *The Queen of Swords* represents, Grahn describes its "archetypal dance of beauty, judgment, birth and death between the two powerful female forces" as "a drama of elemental butch/fem interaction" (1990, p. 288). And rather than being constructed like *The Queen of Wands* from series of related but not sequentially connected lyrics, the title poem that occupies most of this volume, and on which this chapter focuses, is a narrative presented in a verse drama, what Grahn labels "A Play with Poetic Myth."[2]

Where Doubiago's epic countered "the fathers' amnesia" and sought to re-member the scattered remains of the genuinely loving male in order to enable the ideal heterosexual union, Grahn's verse epic drama challenges a failure of female memory to recall women's powers, whose defeat was clinched with the fall of Troy, and focuses on the reintegration of the woman/queen/goddess. Grahn's protagonist, Helen, asks "How can I re-form from simple dust / to remember myself, how can I ever understand / the nature of my beauty?"

and "how can I ever gather myself together again?" (1987, pp. 69 and 71). Crucial among those forces that Helen must recover in order to recollect and understand herself are her warrior aspect, without which she is a slave of sorts, and her connection to female community, both historical and immediate. These emphases on the martial and the communal, as well as the lesbian, distinguish the quest of Grahn's epic from Doubiago's.

Grahn's play, whose characters' modern names evoke their ancient Sumerian counterparts,[3] begins in the "aboveworld" home of Thomas and Helen Bull, where Thomas (Dumuzi, the Sumerian bull god) holds Venus captive in the lens of his telescope while Helen (Inanna), herself a version of Venus, ponders her alienation from her own forces and her own mind. Living in prosperity in "a glass house / with glass bells / and glass horses" (1987, p. 14), Helen is troubled by the fragility of what supports her:

> Venus shines expectant
> then sets too fast,
> clouds erase her memory
> and shroud her past.
> A queen am I.
> Queen Helen is my office.
> Yet *trivial* is how I feel.
> Venus of what universe am I?

> (1987, p. 16)

Encouraged by her friend Nin (Ninshubar, Inanna's minister, queen of the East), Helen determines to take a journey of self-recovery. She "falls," landing at the Crow Bar, a "belowworld" lesbian bar whose proprietor is Ereshkigal. Helen becomes a servant there, and through interactions with Ereshkigal and her customers—reenacting distant history, recollecting more recent autobiographical events, and exploring lesbian connections—passes through the ordeals of seven belowworld gates. In the Sumerian text, at each of the gates to Ereshkigal's domain Inanna is stripped of one of her powers of office—for instance, her lapis lazuli necklace of rulership or her man-enticing breastplate. In Grahn's version, she is disabused of illusions; for instance, at Gate Two Helen's exchanges with Enki, god of the wisdom of nature, force her to relinquish the notion that nature loves her, and at Gate Four contact with the revived corpse of Pen (Amazon Queen, Penthesilea), by causing

Helen to recall the Amazons' role in the Trojan War, shatters her belief that women are weak and incapable of self-defense. In this process of unlearning, an inverted *bildung* labeled "deterioration," her patriarchally determined identity and assumptions are stripped away. At the sixth gate, she is judged and condemned to death. For three days and nights Helen, having fallen "through a hole / in the eye of death" (1987, p. 110), is reduced to nothing while Ereshkigal suffers the labor pains of Helen's rebirth. Meanwhile Nin has obtained the help of Enki in her attempt to rescue Helen from the underworld. Granting the request of two Fairies created by Enki, Ereshkigal releases the integrated and powerful Helen/Inanna, who is reborn at Gate Seven, requiring only that another "innocent" be sent belowworld in her place. Helen sends Thomas and his new girlfriend (in the Sumerian text, his sister) to Ereshkigal, while Helen and Nin establish themselves in the Bulls' former home.

In deriving its plot and characters from ancient epic, in following the common epic pattern of quest involving a descent into the underworld, and in emphasizing public—especially martial—history, this installment of the *Chronicle* is closer than the first to the genre of epic, and to what Grahn regards as the roots of all poetry in ancient ceremonial forms connected with religious observance. In its gynocentric relation to several versions of epic, Grahn's "The Queen of Swords" establishes possibilities alternative to Doubiago's for the female poet who wishes to speak for her nation or community and shape its identity through myth-based tales of the tribe.

We have seen that Doubiago, in attempting to create a balanced complementarity with men and male literary traditions in *Hard Country*, struggles to come to terms with the legacy primarily of male poets. She confronts epic tradition, I have argued, as mediated most immediately through the *Maximus Poems* of Charles Olson. Though H.D.'s long poems are also a significant example for Doubiago's writing, Doubiago focuses less on that empowering female precedent than on seeking a satisfying relation with the male poets "behind her." Ironically, Doubiago's process seems significantly similar to that of H.D.'s autobiographically based Helen: for both, the quest may ultimately become a search for the mother (in Helen's case, Achilles's mother, the goddess Thetis); yet each in coming to understand her own history must devote much more space to untangling her relation to various men in her life, her literal and literary lovers and fathers. (H.D.'s Achilles, however, manages to discover the mother within himself and achieves the kind of transformation that Doubiago's speaker desires for her lovers, but which they cannot sustain.)

Judy Grahn, in marked contrast to Doubiago, goes to great lengths to identify her writing exclusively with female literary traditions and ancestors. Grahn's prose study *The Highest Apple: Sappho and The Lesbian Poetic Tradition* (1985) situates her own poetry in the context of the writing of Sappho, of four recent "foremothers"—Emily Dickinson, Amy Lowell, H.D., Gertrude Stein—and of four lesbian contemporaries—Adrienne Rich, Audre Lorde, Olga Broumas, Paula Gunn Allen. The three essays on Stein that introduce Grahn's selections from Stein's work in *Really Reading Gertrude Stein* (1989) further testify to Stein's importance as a mentor to Grahn. Grahn does not link her work with male writers either directly or by allusion; the few men whose poetry she mentions or quotes from tend either to be Gay (for example, Robert Duncan)—hence to her mind occupying cultural functions overlapping with those of Lesbians—or to draw heavily, she believes, on gynocentric traditions (for example, Homer). Indeed, in an essay composed some years ago—though this might not represent her position now—she asserted her belief that women never "learned a thing" from the writing of the male masters (Grahn 1981, p. 542).

Grahn's separatist presentation of her position in literary history, including her usually tacit denial of interaction with patriarchal traditions, is partly strategic: it supports the political agenda for which she very consciously shapes her poetry. One of the founders of the gay women's liberation movement on the West Coast, Grahn long ago dedicated herself to "forging a new definition of Gay people in my writing" (1990, p. 42). She regards a separatist stage as having been crucial to gay women's liberation, as to so many recent liberation movements.[4] Effective "shar[ing of] resources between men and women"—resources which presumably include literary traditions—depends on a prior female separatism which can "give groups of women a power base from which to overlap with men" (Grahn 1990, p. 281). This is why Grahn, who in her youth read widely in canonical literature in English, focuses her—and her readers'—attention on the Lesbian Sapphic tradition. For in Sappho's world, "women were central to themselves" (Grahn 1985, p. 7). In the present androcentric social and cultural environment, focusing on male-dominated traditions would hinder women's recovery of that empowering perspective.

Not surprisingly, Grahn resists seeing female-centered literary traditions as reactions to male-centered ones, just as she denies that Gay culture takes its shape as a response to dominant heterosexual culture, or that the basis of Gay faggot behavior is imitation of women. Rather than generating something new or expanding something marginal, Lesbian writers undertake the venerable project of reclaiming something very old and central. Sappho, according to Grahn, "spoke from a whole way of being, not an alienated, fragmented one; she spoke not as an outcast, but as someone at the very heart and center of her culture and of her times. . . . She wrote from such an integrated female place as we modern women have only begun to imagine" (1985, p. 52).

Of course, as Susan Gubar has pointed out, it is "[p]recisely because so many of [Sappho's] original Greek texts were destroyed, [that] the modern woman poet could write 'for' or 'as' Sappho and thereby invent a classical inheritance of her own" (1984, pp. 46–47). The accuracy, perhaps even the plausibility, of any reconstruction of Sappho cannot be determined, though the recent emergence in poetry of what Grahn calls "the public Lesbian voice" is beyond question. I believe—and in this I resist Grahn's direction—that the Sapphic "inheritance" on which Grahn focuses, and which allows her to downplay negotiation with male-authored precedent texts, in its modern manifestations everywhere reflects the impact of male-dominated traditions. Without denying the significance of the separatist aesthetic that distinguishes Grahn from the other poets in this study, I want to show that Grahn writes, as the others do, in the context of male as well as female traditions.

Her negotiations with male-dominated traditions, however, take place for the most part indirectly, through her interactions with women's texts. Moreover, they take place in a less oppositional form, since her primary context is genuinely, as well as strategically, female. (That is, her Sapphic tradition is not just a construction intended to help women writers find their own voices; it provides the consciousness from which Grahn herself already writes.) Sue-Ellen Case's historical analysis of the second wave of feminism helps explain how Grahn could acquire such a gynocentric sense of her literary context. Case claims that the voice of heterosexual feminism, dominant in the 1970s, arose as a counterdiscourse defined "in distinction to the patriarchal masculine voice." In contrast, " 'breaking silence' for the lesbian feminist voice has been situated primarily within the context of feminism and only secondarily within that of the dominant culture" (Case 1988, p. 48). According to Case, this may explain why Grahn's "Swords" has little to do with deconstructive discourse, which proved valuable for those critiquing "the dominant patriarchal discourse": "this historical location [of lesbian feminism] within feminism has aided in forming a kind of limited separatism. Further, this separatism has constructed a lesbian voice that resonates primarily within a gynocentric tradition it has created for itself" (1988, p. 49).

Despite her occasional acknowledgement of a "secondary" engagement with androcentric hegemonic discourse, Case hails Grahn's "Queen of Swords" as depending on "a completely alternative tradition" (1988, p. 47), as "abandon[ing] the dominant tradition altogether" (1988, p. 58). Such claims are overstated, for, with the possible exception of the Sumerian urtext, the female-authored works/traditions on which Grahn draws inevitably reflect some interaction with hegemonic, predominantly male traditions. Case is right, however, to insist on the non-(or perhaps post-)deconstructive stance of "Swords" as Grahn focuses on the utopian "neo-mythologizing" project of "taking back the [originally gynofocal] myths" from their violent, misogynistic, gynophobic, and homophobic appropriations in patriarchy (1988, p. 51).

Grahn's constructive focus on a gynocentric context allows her to expand feminist options for the epic-based long poem. These new options can be understood as emerging partly from Grahn's creation of a kind of formal and thematic marriage between aspects of two texts by very different Sapphic foremothers—H.D.'s revisionary epic *Helen in Egypt* and Gertrude Stein's play, originally intended as a libretto, "Doctor Faustus Lights the Lights." While constructing and using a women's tradition, Grahn is also generating a model of compound, nonlinear literary inheritance.[5]

Grahn's primary concern in her *Chronicle* bespeaks her profound affiliation with H.D., for according to Grahn, H.D. in her writing "concerned herself with little else than describing the power of female godhead" (Grahn 1985, p. 101); her work "centered on defining the essential female mythos for our time," a goal Grahn has made her own (Grahn 1985, p. 28). In significant ways, Grahn follows H.D.'s example of "us[ing] classical mythology and Hermetic philosophy as a code of her own in which to lay down a philosophical exploration of female power in a masculine world" (Grahn 1985, p. 28). In "The Queen of Swords," Grahn pursues H.D.'s fascination with alternate versions of the story of Helen of Troy and centers Helen's quest for reintegration on issues of recollection and forgetting, as H.D. does in *Helen in Egypt*. But Grahn's work is neither so obliquely coded, so privately "her own," nor so concerned with "a masculine world" as H.D.'s, and these differences along with others can be analyzed in terms of Grahn's different approach to epic, sometimes reflecting her different relation to male antecedents and sometimes the alternative model offered by the writing of Gertrude Stein. Because Stein's libretto and H.D.'s long poem, in addition to their considerable gynocentric achievements, engage very directly (often oppositionally) with male precedent texts—with the epic tradition of Homer, Virgil, Dante, and Pound and with Goethe's (and others' versions of) *Faust*—they also permit consideration of Grahn's relation to male literary traditions.

In *The Highest Apple*, Grahn discusses the generic character of H.D.'s epics as follows:

> She turned [from Imagist lyricism] to an astonishing, breathtaking epic poetry, where she explored epic themes in tight, precise, lyric couplets. The pairing together of the two forms was essential for her task of writing modern mythic-occult-prophetic-historic-epics from *within* a female point of view. With her form she, like Sappho, is able to portray both the inside world and the outside world: both the narrative of what happened and the inner dialogue of what the experience felt, looked, tasted, smelled like. In her form, she married the female/lyric/Sapphic and the male/epic/ narrative/Homeric. She reversed their effects: the usually "objective" narration of events is focused on an internal/occult landscape. . . . The usually cold external narrative is told in a warm, lyric, personal voice; yet the story being told is epic, is history. . . . Perhaps only a woman who loved both women and men in her life could have accomplished, would have attempted, such a wedding of forms, forms that have been considered oppositional.
>
> (1985, pp. 60–62; Although Grahn refers to the couplets
> of *Trilogy*, the supporting quotations she presents where
> my ellipses appear are tercets from *Helen in Egypt*.)

Emphasizing the reconciliation of received opposites and the collapse of objective and subjective (a collapse Grahn discerns also in both Stein's and Sappho's techniques), Grahn describes her own project as well as H.D's. I quote the passage here, however, because of its striking linkage of sexual attachments and literary forms. While I don't subscribe to the essentialism suggested by Grahn's equation of generic choices with sexual preferences, her remarks set the stage for a metaphor with which I will describe Grahn's own "wedding of forms": I propose that in her bringing together of precedent strategies of Stein and H.D., Grahn approaches these forebears as a butch/femme couple.[6]

The usefulness of this metaphor lies in its suggestion of an expanded female identity/textuality deriving from the interplay and union of different, but not polarized, versions of the female or of female writing practice. For while femme and butch can be misread (and in the past were theorized) as re-creating the oppositional genders of heterosexual society, in fact (or according to more current theories), as Grahn observes, "the participants in butch and femme are often interchangeable, or actually much more similar than their Saturday-night garb indicates" (1990, p. 155). Theirs are differences within sameness—differences, moreover, not fixed by biology or society but available as roles on a fluid continuum, to be consciously adopted and often playfully flaunted in a mockery of heterosexual norms. Not to be mistaken for *homme* and *femme*, butch and fem/femme are nondichotomous[7]; Grahn's Ereshkigal describes their union (with a telling line break) as one of "self to other / self" (1987, p. 53). As Case wittily observes in "Toward a Butch-Femme Aesthetic," an essay proposing the butch-femme couple as the model for a female subject position capable of ideological change, "[t]he two roles never appear as . . . discrete" [ellipsis hers]:

> They are coupled [subjects] that do not impale themselves on the poles of sexual difference or metaphysical values, but constantly seduce the sign system, through flirtation and inconstancy into the light fondle of artifice, replacing the Lacanian slash with a lesbian bar.
>
> (Case 1989, p. 283)[8]

This model of literary relation implies Grahn's incorporation of traits, either of form or content, associated with the masculine but, unlike the feminist form of complementarity I posit for Doubiago's writing, does so within a nonbinary framework. In lesbian culture, butch and femme are inclusive categories embracing a range of sexual practices and personal styles. Similarly, the figure of Grahn's approaching her primary female forebears as a butch-femme partnership suggests a variety of options in content and style or form; it proposes the availability of multiple distinct, yet harmonizable, female textual practices that press beyond the boundaries of the traditionally feminine genre, lyric.

As nondichotomous women's texts, *Helen in Egypt* and "Doctor Faustus Lights the Lights" in common assert Helen's link to prepatriarchal goddesses and identify horrific war as one tragic consequence of society's turn away from goddess worship. Despite the prominence in both works of male characters and their narratives—perhaps a compensatory masquerade of womanly deference serving to "disguise the fact that [the authors] have taken their father's penis in their intellectual stride" (Case 1989, p. 291)—both subvert the androcentric tradition of the stories they retell. Grahn extends such commonalities, while she brings together the resources of Stein's and H.D.'s contrasting models of womanly writing. The bold directness of Stein's writing, which, as we shall see, Grahn associates with her own working-class orientation, as well as Stein's avoidance of lyrical images in favor of play with simple words and ordinary syntax may be seen as butch literary traits. (Of course, the transformations Stein performs with that vocabulary and syntax yield patterns neither simple nor ordinary.) The incantatory sounds and visionary mysticism of H.D.'s myth-based writing, which also shape Grahn's often ritualized verse; H.D.'s emphasis on the image; the deferral of meaning achieved in her proliferating questions and in the palimpsestic layers of her story; as well as the conventional femininity of her heroine, may be conceptualized as fem practices.

The formal, linguistic, and thematic interplay between the precedent long poems of H.D. and Stein embodied by "Queen of Swords" parallels Helen/Inanna's butch-fem interactions with Ereshkigal and the Crow dikes staged within the play. As a corollary to claiming that Grahn's assimilation of the different examples of Stein and H.D. constitutes a butch-femme literary ancestry for her creation, I shall argue that the process undergone by Grahn's Helen is, in part, a movement from the archetypal femininity of H.D.'s Helen to a fem identity freed from the hobbles of patriarchally determined femininity. It is as if, having discovered in the butch-femme precedents of Stein and H.D. a noncompetitive, noncontestatory model authorizing woman's epic, Grahn reinforces that authorization in her epic's drama of evolving butch-femme partnership.

The Helen of "Swords" (as distinct from the Helen of *Wands*) revises the heterosexual and male-focused, largely passive and broodingly introspective Helen that H.D. presents by radically extending developments that H.D.'s Helen begins to undergo. For just as H.D.'s Achilles discovers a new version of masculinity not defined by martial prowess, H.D.'s Helen in discovering/recollecting her own goddess aspect uncovers dimensions of her own power that she had not previously recognized. Yet one cannot say of *Helen in Egypt*, as Grahn says of her own play, that it undertakes "definition and re-cognition of the warrior, the quintessential Dyke" (Grahn 1985, p. 123). Nor can one say, despite the two works' shared emphasis on the importance of remembering and recovering the past, that the central task of H.D.'s Helen is reconnection with her own history as a lesbian warrior; such is the case, however, for Helen in "The Queen of Swords."

Despite Grahn's following the common practice of identifying "epic" with "male" when she describes H.D.'s integration of lyric and epic (quoted above), she herself revises received understandings of literary history by approaching epic as a genre whose traditions are not primarily, and certainly not originally, male. Where H.D. counters Homer's primacy and authority by turning to an alternate tale of Helen recorded by the male Sicilian poet Stesichorus (ca. 640–555 B.C.), Grahn turns to a much earlier source, one she regards as quite probably female. She follows closely an anonymously authored story of Inanna that is, as already noted, part of a pre-Homeric and purportedly prepatriarchal epic; its poets may well have been priestesses serving the goddess (see Grahn 1990, pp. 287–88). Homer himself Grahn regards as "drawing from, and writing out of, a vast, rich ancient and woman-developed tradition which [he and Sappho] shared in common" (1985, p. 5); consequently, she is less concerned than H.D. with revising Homeric norms.

Both H.D. and Grahn regard the Trojan War, Homer's subject in the *Iliad*, as a crucial event in the demise of matriarchy. H.D. would concur with Grahn that the war (which took place in the early thirteenth century B.C., several centuries before Homer) "marked the beginning of the end of the matriarchal era for Western civilization and had already become the wellspring of literature for Sappho's generation" (Grahn 1985, pp. 7–8). But only Grahn sees the martial focus of the *Iliad*, which extended to much of the subsequent male epic tradition, as something appropriate also for a woman's epic and for a female epic hero. H.D.'s epic is strongly antimilitarist, as well as antifascist, in part because of her experiences in living through two world wars. (Doubiago's epic follows suit, linking war to destructive aspects of the masculine that must be overcome.) Grahn, who was discharged from the armed services because of her lesbianism, rejects not martial behavior but its association exclusively with patriarchal violence.[9] Consequently, Grahn recuperates for female protagonists the Homeric epic's engagement with martial history and pride in martial prowess.

Resisting the Homeric tradition, H.D. for the most part shifts *her* epic's focus away from the war. It is important that Helen remember her presence there, but her investment in the war is solely personal: "I did not care who won, who lost, / Achilles was dead" (*Helen in Egypt*, 1974, p. 241; cited hereafter as *HE*). The recalled events of the war pale next to her meeting with Achilles on the beach in Egypt. Even her fullest remembrance of her wartime experience breaks off with recollections of that encounter; in the midst of vivid recollection of the final battles—"Another shout from the wharves; / I fight my way through the crowd, / but the gates are barred;"— and of the cruel curses hurled by a sentry who prevented her from leaping from Troy's walls, she abruptly falters, "was it seven years, was it a day? / I can not remember . . . // I only remember the shells, / whiter than bone, / on the ledge of a desolate beach" (*HE*, pp. 234–35; H.D.'s ellipsis). H.D., who in her epic reworks the personal relationships of her own life partly in terms of Freudian psychoanalytic theory, focuses much less on public history than on its private psychodynamics.[10] Of course, this need not be construed as reflecting disinterest in the social dimensions of war; rather, H.D. may be pointing to women's social disenfranchisement, subversively enacting a denial—rather like that of Doubiago's protagonist—that women have an interest in how any patriarchal state fares. Helen's love for Achilles, H.D.'s gloss tells us, is accompanied by "*defiance . . . of the whole powerful war-faction*" (*HE*, p. 18; ellipsis added). H.D.'s dismissal of nationalistic history may itself function as implicit cultural critique.

Grahn, however, wearing her politics more on her sleeve, attends to the war in order explicitly to emphasize its cultural meaning: the war's primary significance lies not in the defeat of the Trojans, but in the defeat of the last Amazonian warrior and all she stood for. Achilles's victory over and rape of this woman warrior, Penthesilea, mark the historical transition to a patriarchal militarism ("When he took our Amazon strength / to be his own he became a soldier" [1987, p. 65]) as well as a devastating loss of individual and collective female power. Thus, Grahn's drama extends the Homeric tradition of recounting battles, but does so in order to analyze the nature of pre- and postpatriarchal warfare. H.D., for the most part, distances the martial realm as a masculine world whose appeal is incomprehensible to women[11]; Grahn regards battle and martial heroism as having their place in gynarchy, notwithstanding that these powers have been stolen and perverted in patriarchy.

The key moment which *Helen in Egypt* keeps circling is the encounter between Helen and Achilles on the beach in which he starts to strangle her—"his fingers' remorseless steel" enacting his anger against her as the purported cause of the war in which he lost so much (*HE*, p. 17)—and then, responding to her invocation of Thetis, changes his murderous gesture to a loving embrace. In microcosm, this moment enacts Achilles' transformation from murderous warlord to lover of the goddess (Helen and Thetis) that takes place over the course of the book. The ultimately rehabilitated Achilles takes the role of keeper of lighthouses (*HE*, p. 63). "*He waits*," the gloss explains, "*not as Lord of Legions, 'King of Myrmidons,' but as one dedicated to a new Command, that of the 'royal sacred High Priest of love-rites'* " (*HE*, p. 210).

Such distancing of Helen's partner from martial heroics is essential to H.D.'s project, since she positions military action as antithetical to the values of the goddess. Thetis hid her son at Scyros, "entreating the king to instruct him . . . in the laws and the arts of peace," but Achilles "followed the lure of war" nonetheless and, in so doing, "he forgot his mother" (*HE*, pp. 286, 287, 292). When his glance meets Helen's, his allegiance to the "iron-ring" of the military Command falters and he forfeits "the rule of the world and Greece" (*HE*, p. 60), beginning the shift away from the warrior cult and back toward the goddess and love. H.D. presents Helen's pacifism (a pacifism Grahn locates also in Sappho's writing) in terms that, while they acknowledge women's limited means of gaining or asserting power in patriarchal society, also underscore the inherent superiority of a nonmartial stance:

> does it even the Balance
> if a wife repeats a husband's folly?
>
> never; the law is different;
> if a woman fights,
> she must fight by stealth,
>
> with invisible gear;
> no sword, no dagger, no spear
> in a woman's hands
>
> can make wrong, right[.]
>
> (*HE*, p. 97)

Grahn, in contrast, regards warriors' powers—literal as well as figurative—as wrongfully stolen from women and forcefully urges their reclamation. Ereshkigal admonishes Helen, "You don't have to learn to be a warrior, / You have to remember having been one" (Grahn 1987, p. 81).

Yet the two poets' positions have more common than such contrasts might suggest. Overall, it is true, the questioning meditations of H.D.'s Helen, her inconclusive attempts to read events or temple inscriptions are far removed from the assertiveness, the vigorous self-defense of the warrior. But H.D. also presents Helen as "fight[ing]" for her own identity (*HE*, p. 37). At one point "*an heroic voice, the voice of Helen of Sparta*" emerges from within her, exulting in "the thunder of battle . . . the beauty of arrows" so that she even wonders, "do I love War? is this Helena?" (*HE*, pp. 176–77). And a passage near the epic's close presents Helen as a figurative warrior in courageously withstanding the onslaught of Achilles's fury during their first encounter (*HE*, p. 278). As part of her reintegration, H.D.'s Helen has to claim some responsibility for the Trojan conflict, recognizing that the Love for or as which she is worshipped is "begot of the Ships and of War" (*HE*, p. 96).

Thus, when Grahn touches on the subject of warrior powers in the Introduction to *Queen of Swords*, she mentions H.D. as if to suggest that she herself pursues something H.D. had recognized. Referring to a passage from *Helen in Egypt* (*HE*, p. 85), Grahn notes,

H.D. said that Helen gathered the white rose while her more vio-
lent sister Clytemnestra gathered the red. . . . The image of red
and white roses in my poem ["Descent to the Roses of the Fam-
ily"] is shorthand for the loss and retention of a number of forces,
especially "female blood powers." Fundamentally I think the In-
anna myth is about menstruation, birth and death, that is, female
blood powers and related male warrior powers which in the his-
tory of white patriarchal culture have been violently suppressed
and denied for many centuries.

(1987, pp. 5–6)[12]

Grahn suggests here that in H.D.'s epic the pallor of Helen's rose
signals her having lost connection with that strengthening blood. A
similar alienation from "blood powers" characterizes Grahn's Helen
in the opening sections of "The Queen of Swords"; significantly, her
initial association of militarism and violence exclusively with men re-
calls H.D.'s protagonist's linkage of the masculine with war.[13]

In Grahn's play, however, Helen's denial of violence in both
women and nature ("Men are so violent. / Woman is more like
Nature." [1987, p. 38]) is exposed as a naive delusion she needs to
discard. It is mocked by the Crows, whose extended catalog in the
poem "Women Are Not Violent" suggests the pervasiveness in this
world, the naturalness, if you will, of violence. Part of this poem,
in which sound similarity permits shifts between "violent" and the
traditionally gay color "violet," implies that homosexuality is no less
"natural" than violence:

Crow
  women are not violent
Crow
  and I am not violent
Crow
  and the Queen of Swords is not violent
Crow
  and violence is violet
Crow
  and Americans are not violet
Crow
  and the wind is never violent
Crow
  and the sea, the sea is not violent

Crow
  and nonviolence is not violent
Crow
  nonviolence is inviolate
Crow
  and the earth is not violent
Crow
  and a shooting star is not violent
Crow
  and a volcano is not violent
Crow
  and war is not violent
Crow
  and violet is not violent

(1987, pp. 38–39)

During the course of the play, as Grahn's Helen learns who she is—in large part through violently charged interactions with women—she moves considerably farther than does H.D.'s Helen away from a blanket identification of violence with men (and toward the "violet" as well). It is as if Grahn were picking up where H.D. left off, following through on a process H.D. had begun. By the fifth of the seven belowworld gates, Helen/Inanna, relinquishing conventionally feminine self-definition, recognizes that she needs to become a warrior, though she does not yet recognize that this will be achieved by her "remember[ing] having been one" (1987, p. 81). One stage in her anamnesis involves Ereshkigal's reenactment of the history of Boudica, a Celtic warrior queen who led a rebellion defending "the ancient female and tribal powers" against the Romans in 61 A.D. (Grahn 1990, p. 144). (Grahn locates in her name the origin of "bulldyke.") Boudica and her forces nearly won, and the patriarchs have been working to squelch them ever since:

He fears me still,
  for my shameless guise
  and lesbian ways;
  for undefeated eyes,
  a warrior's spine
  and all my memories
  of women's time.

(1987, pp. 84–85)

Eluding the patriarchal foe, Boudica teaches Helen, depends on remembering "who we are; / we who are never not at war" (1987, p. 84).

If Boudica instructs Helen in the necessity of vigilant, forceful, and unrelenting battle against oppression, the corpse of the Amazon Queen Penthesilea (also portrayed by Ereshkigal) conveys more tragic lessons as she recalls a lost gynarchic context for war in which military prowess and display held a different meaning. An electrifying glance between Pen, as she is now called, and Helen takes the place of the pivotal binding glance exchanged between Achilles and Helen in H.D.'s epic, and Pen repeatedly proclaims that she was thereafter Helen's weapon, part of Helen herself: "I was your last battle ax / and you threw it" (1987, p. 59); "I was your tooth / and they pulled it / I was your dagger / and they tore it / from your hand" (p. 61); "I was your arrow / against the foe / I was your backbone / bent low / oh lady of sorrow / I was your bow" (p. 62). Despite her ferocity in battle, the Amazon was defeated, and she insists that the gruesome violence visited on her was visited on Helen as well. The moment Pen was beaten, raped ("her very soul stolen as she lay dying" [1990, p. 183]), and "dragged around like a dishrag" (1987, p. 61) was the decisive moment of "the fall of women's power" (p. 65) and men's appropriation of Amazon strength.

Helen/Inanna distances herself from the "manlike Amazons" for a bit longer, resisting belief either that she herself had a part in the war or that she should not rely on the protection of men's strength. Positioning herself as H.D.'s epic positioned Helen, she claims, "I was hardly there at all. / I hid out in Egypt, / keeping the occult sciences that once / belonged to me."[14] Her own phrasing reveals how self-defeatingly evasive this stance can become, as she continues: "I have no part of war. / I live in a glass house, with glass horses; / I hardly ever come face to face with my own forces" (1987, p. 66). But with Pen's repeated insistence that Helen plays a key participatory role in the violence ("everywhere there's a war / there you are, beautiful, desired / and right in the middle of it" [1987, p. 69]) and that reliance on her own strength is necessary if she is to avoid slave status, Helen reclaims her memory of "the whole war" and of the powers she had before the war at Troy "scattered" them (1987, p. 70). The scene closes with the crucial gesture of Helen reaching out to touch Pen's bloody finger with her own. This symbolizes her reconnection with female blood powers, in a sense the merging of Helen with her violent double Clytemnestra. (Ereshkigal, who acts Pen's part, at one point identifies herself with Clytemnestra [1987, p. 25] and at another claims to be Helen's "wild cherry sister, red and / black sheep sister of the unkempt realm" [1987, p. 51].) As Case has noted, Helen's discovery of her relation to the Amazon is also a discovery of the Amazon in herself (Case 1988, p. 62). She is developing into a woman more femme than conventionally feminine, defining herself increasingly in terms of women's powers and bonds rather than men's expectations.

The kind of warfare Grahn's Helen now embraces is prepatriarchal, what Grahn in her prose identifies as "tribal."[15] Such battle, whose values Grahn attempts to retrieve, defends tribal honor and demonstrates personal heroism (see Grahn 1990, p. 219). Sometimes serving a ceremonial function, it depends on individual courage and the graceful display of strength and skill; it eschews the tyranny, the gratuitous cruelty, and the linkage of mastery with sexual victimizing represented by Achilles's rape. The willingness to fight, moreover, need not take aggressive forms, as Helen's recollection of herself surrounded by threatening men on motorcycles demonstrates; in that scene she stood her own ground and successfully defended herself against attack by chanting with apparent fearlessness a "woman-naming roar" (Grahn 1987, p. 89).

We have seen, then, that as Grahn extends H.D.'s example of revising the story of Helen, she recuperates for women's epic the martial dimensions of Homeric plot and heroic character as H.D. did not. Similarly, because she does not position Homer as the dominant male antagonist/oppressor, Grahn comfortably adopts the traditional pattern of descent into the underworld. This pattern, too, has perhaps a partial analogue in H.D.'s epic, since Helen in Egypt occupies another realm, a time out of time; the Achilles she meets has been killed at Troy, and her own status as living/dead/phantom/reality remains elusive. But in *Helen in Egypt* the traditional descent pattern is obscured, thoroughly psychologized as a descent into the repressed, a dream-journey into the subconscious, whereas Grahn, by adhering to the Sumerian template, again more closely follows the long-established epic conventions. "The Queen of Swords" is a drama of dangerous literal descent into a world of death and transformation. Moreover, Helen's encounters with mythic/historical figures like Penthesilea, Ildreth, and Boudica function analogously to epic heroes' encounters with the dead in the *Odyssey* and the *Aeneid*. They construct a tribal memory, a national history, in this case of the "queer nation," not the private if archetypally patterned history that H.D.'s Helen re-members.

Epic heroes such as Homer's Odysseus and Virgil's Aeneas choose to journey into the underworld in order to learn their destinies or obtain other crucial knowledge. The Helen of "The Queen of Swords" also actively chooses to descend (unlike H.D.'s fated protagonist who finds herself "mysteriously transported") so that she may "stand face to face / with [her] own forces" (1987, p. 14), learn her own mind, and remember who she is. This important stage in the traditional hero's quest allows the poet to expand the epic's temporal range, as the protagonist surveys or interacts with figures from the past and the future. Such chronological expansion enables Grahn to dramatize the historically shifting status of female-centered power as well as its ultimate durability.

Interrupting the linear heroic narrative, classical epic descents into the underworld enable a flexible movement in history. Grahn, by making what occupies a single episode of classical epic the entire body of her epic, enlarges the possibilities for avoiding a merely linear plot construction, which she associates with a patriarchal order. (Her butch-femme models provide additional examples for achieving this end—H.D. through palimpsestic overlays of different times, Stein by establishing a continuous present in which past and future merge [see Grahn 1989, p. 16].)

Of course, Grahn freely modifies mainstream epic patterns to suit her working-class lesbian feminist agenda. For instance, she deliberately violates the classical epic convention in which matrimonial union is reestablished as victorious Menelaus reclaims Helen or Odysseus Penelope. She follows instead the Sumerian story in which Inanna sends her consort Dumuzi to take her place in the underworld. Moreover, the journey of self-discovery taken by the Helen of "Swords" involves moving from heterosexual marriage and self-identification as "Mrs. Thomas Bull" (1987, p. 22), through erotic and spiritual engagement with the "Butch of Darkness" (1987, p. 51)—a subject to which I shall return—, to a lesbian partnership (also a self-integration) with her longtime "friend and Higher Mind," Nin (1987, p. 9), sustained by a sense of women's community.

By representing her underworld in/as a "seedy" lesbian bar,

Grahn teaches Helen lessons about class-based privilege and op-
pression (as well as gender-based oppression) not contained in the
Sumerian or the classical Greek epics, nor in *Helen in Egypt*.[16] Nin
accurately foretells events when she warns Helen,

> You could begin this day with
> a solid position in your class,
> a marriage built on tradition,
> an education, a vocation and an aim,
> and having no further explanation than that
> you fell through a sky of glass
> on a particular crystalline day like this—
> have none.
>
> (Grahn 1987, p. 18)

In descending to a punningly "underground" cultural setting,
Helen encounters and then becomes part of an underside of modern
urban culture that many heterosexual middle-class women never
see. The first "venial virtue" of which Helen must be cured is think-
ing that she's something; and because her class affiliations, which
are established partly through marriage ("Mrs. Famous Thomas"),
sustain that delusion, they must be stripped away.

None of the characters who contribute to her transformation and
ultimate rebirth in the underworld are conventionally heterosexual
or comfortably middle-class. The majority are lesbian: the bar
owner Ereshkigal, the seven "spicy" crow dikes who are her regular
customers, and the "androgynous" "vegetarian fairy" Kur. Two are
male: Enki, a gardener cum janitor who sometimes crossdresses in
women's clothes, and the other androgynous vegetarian fairy, the
young faggot with the woman's name, Gal. Nothing, by profession
a "bartender, dealer, and bouncer," has "no distinguishable gender"
(Grahn 1987, pp. 9, 21). Pampered Helen's spiritual and psychic
transformation is facilitated by liquor, drugs, and depression that
shatter the superficial bases for her former self-esteem. Her trans-
formation also requires her undertaking menial tasks that are deval-
ued in patriarchy and consequently relegated to women, servants,
or slaves; taking a fall in social class, she becomes "an underground
Maid" who has to (punningly) "work for Nothing" (1987, p. 30).
Knowing her as queen of heaven and earth, Ereshkigal challenges
Helen:

How can you expect to
rule heaven
if you can't make a bed?
How can you affect stubborn earth
if you can't even bake it into bread?
How can you keep the order of nature
if you can't keep a simple house?
How ride the great breast of the wild wind
if you can't even dust?

(Grahn 1987, p. 29)

I can think of no epic poem with a comparable base in characters who are not only working-class but also socially marginal, both in their sexual identities and in their vocations, or any epic poem in which the descent is so markedly a movement down the social ladder. "The Queen of Swords" departs particularly dramatically from the upper-class Hellenism of H.D.'s deities and heroes.

It should be apparent by now that I see Grahn's sense of epic as owing little to the relatively recent interventions in the form offered by, say, Whitman, Wordsworth, or by the collage texts of Pound, Eliot, Olson, etc. In this, her position is very different from that of H.D., whose biographical entanglements among the modernists made intense consciousness especially of Pound's *Cantos* unavoidable; conceiving of her epic as a rejoinder to Pound's, H.D. spoke of *Helen in Egypt* as "my *Cantos.*" As much because of her generational position as anything else, Grahn escaped the need to produce a female version of or response to the *Cantos.*

This is particularly significant since Pound's influence on *Helen in Egypt* at least arguably contributes to the work's obscurity. That H.D.'s reacting to Pound contributed significantly to the difficulty of *Helen in Egypt* is implied by Elizabeth Hirsh's discussion of *Helen* as a multifaceted reworking of H.D.'s relation to imagism and modernism, particularly as formulated by Pound:

> "H.D.," the living doll, the spitting Image of Imagism, responds with a "hieroglyphic" text that, on the one hand, reinterprets the Image in light of psychoanalysis, as a mode of hermeneutic veiling that restores the centrality of reading, and on the other, suggests a purely decorative or "silent" picture writing that prefers the pleasurable illusion of a feminine presence over the desire for knowledge.
>
> (Hirsh 1990, p. 448)

H.D.'s critique of Pound's aesthetic, carried out through a re-
working of the Image, involves a complexly deconstructive play:
"just as *Helen*'s undecidable veil/*eidolon* reinscribes the Poundian
Image, its/her Egyptian 'hieroglyphics' transmute the 'ideo-
grammic method' into a mode of writing that oscillates perpetually
between symbol and image, decoration and genesis, spectacle and
sense" (Hirsh 1990, p. 446). The undecidable and the veiled, the
obscurely hieroglyphic, however crucial to an anti-Poundian mod-
ernism, have little place in the kind of cultural critique Grahn prac-
tices. In examining Grahn's reworking of H.D. in earlier poetry,
Jan Montefiore has rightly observed that Grahn simplifies H.D.;
but her complaints that Grahn reads H.D. "too simply," reducing
mystery and ambiguity, meditation and enigma, that, lacking so-
phistication, Grahn offers "a relaxation rather than tautening and
intensification of meaning in her poems," fail to credit the deliber-
ateness of Grahn's demystification (Montefiore 1987–88, p. 187).
Decoration and elusiveness, Helen's indeterminate multiplicity,
which—following Hirsh's argument—for H.D. constituted a
countering of Pound as well as a feminine self-inscription through
a veil that both disguises and reveals, are unnecessary baggage for
Grahn. To the extent that H.D.'s obscurities derive from her mysti-
cism and constitute revelations of the numenous within the ordi-
nary, Grahn might imitate them. But, thanks in part to what H.D.'s
rereading of Poundian modernism accomplished, Grahn has no
need to reenact H.D.'s critique of male modernism. If any aspect
of high modernism is challenged in "Swords," it is the elitist pre-
sumption of a classical education that H.D. shared with Pound.[17]
Grahn's understanding of useful art demands its accessibility to a
mass audience.

  Gertrude Stein, whose works many find obscure, is for Grahn
a model of an admirable if thoroughly unconventional directness,
ultimately of a nonmystifying accessibility. "She is an extremely sin-
cere writer," Grahn remarks. "She is so completely literal and exact-
ing in what she is saying that sometimes we don't get it because we
just don't believe that anyone could be that deliberate" (Grahn
1989, p. 132). Although Stein is by no means a working-class writer,
many of what Grahn takes to be Stein's fundamental aesthetic prin-
ciples reveal Stein's intellect to be a profoundly democratizing, anti-
elitist one. Stein's remark, "The important thing is that you must
have deep down as the deepest thing in you a sense of equality"

(Grahn 1989, p. 9) reflects a central value of Grahn's, who has for years celebrated the common woman and women's "commonality." Grahn appreciates that Stein's postulation of "a field in which everything is equal" renders her work "subversive at the level of fundamental social relationships" (1989, p. 22).[18] And she sees this democratizing sensibility pervading all aspects of Stein's writing.[19] Employing a "totally simple and accessible vocabulary," Grahn observes, Stein "used the entire text as a field in which every element mattered as much as any other, every part of speech, every word and, good poet that she was, every space and punctuation mark" (1989, pp. 6, 8). Similarly, Stein's sense of equality led to her presenting "characters and subjects situated in daily life, the most mundane and ordinary everyday events becoming for her the stuff of philosophy and meaningful being" (1989, p. 10). These practices have proved model ones for Grahn. "Doctor Faustus Lights the Lights"—like other works by Stein—provides examples unavailable in H.D.'s work of strategies for bringing epic down to earth and back to real speech, for humorous treatment of serious matters, and for discussing philosophical, social, and metaphysical issues via concrete and ordinary examples rather than runic puzzles or recondite allusions.

Stein's distinctive mode of including the mundane and the common offers Grahn a very different model from H.D. for the realistic dimensions of the contemporary lesbian project Grahn dubs "mythic realism." Artists in this mode "use female subjects portrayed realistically on one level, yet with deep connections to a communally held myth at the same time"; taking into account both "the local (the community and the individual) and the sublime (the unknown and the unknowable)," mythic realism yields "art based on our collective consciousness and collective unconsciousness" (Grahn 1985, p. 87). While not all of Stein's work has a mythic dimension, "Doctor Faustus" does, and it is crucial to Grahn's investment in the play. One of her footnotes in *Really Reading Gertrude Stein* refers readers of "Doctor Faustus" interested in its "matriarchal background" to an essay by Shirley Neuman; there Neuman observes that

> part of the theological argument of *Doctor Faustus Lights the Lights* involves an extended allusion to matriarchal religion. That the Greek (sun) gods had displaced a prior matriarchal (moon-identi-

fied) pantheon, and that vestiges of the goddesses remained in the Virgin Mary, was current theory in the anthropology and classicism of Stein's generation, beginning with Sir James Frazer, and continuing with writers such as Jane Harrison in her influential *Prolegomena to Greek Religion* (1903) and *Themis* (1912) and Richard Briffault in this three-volume *The Mothers* (1927). The visual iconography of Stein's libretto invokes these matriarchal goddesses: they were often represented as associated with snakes . . .

(Neuman 1988, p. 183)

By (re-)assigning to her goddess four ancient names—Marguerite, Ida, Helena, Annabel—each with its own history, Stein in Grahn's view recombines traditions that have been split over the centuries, thereby "integrating the goddess' broken personality and scattered powers" (Grahn 1989, p. 260). The mythic preoccupations of Stein, as Grahn constructs her, emerge as strikingly close to those of H.D.—again, the nondichotomous coupling.[20] H.D.'s more runic, elaborately and lyrically costumed work takes an approach to the goddess myth that we can designate "femme" while Stein's is a more direct, more pared down "butch" approach.

In their mythic projects, both Stein's "Doctor Faustus Lights the Lights" and H.D.'s *Helen in Egypt* draw upon and revise Goethe's portrayal of Helen in his *Faust*.[21] Since this portion of Goethe's play is often excised from performed versions and may therefore be unfamiliar, a précis is in order: Goethe's Faust initially summons the phantoms of Helen and Paris at the request of the Emperor in the second part of Act I; Mephistopheles cannot summon them because as heathens they do not concern him ("they occupy a hell that's all their own" [Goethe 1950, p. 80]). It is Faust who must descend to "the Mothers," "Goddesses, to men unknown, / Whom we are loath to name or own. / Deep must you dig to reach their dwelling ever;" (Goethe 1950, p. 80). With a key Mephistopheles provides, Faust steals the Mothers' tripod from which he can summon the spirits. When he views Helen's ideal beauty, he is enthralled and determines to possess her, though his attempts to seize the phantom fail. In Act II, Mephistopheles takes Faust to Greece where Faust searches for Helen until a female seer agrees to take him to Persephone's throne to obtain permission to bring Helen's shade to earth. Ultimately the spirit-Helen is transported from Menelaus's palace to Faust's castle, where she bears him a son, Euphorion. With Euphorion's death, however, Helen returns to the spirit world.

It is relevant to H.D.'s epic that when the spirit of Goethe's Helen is still at Sparta, Mephistopheles taunts her by alluding to Stesichorus's version of her history in order to increase her confusion about her identity and her reality. Hirsh notes that

> To the extent that Goethe [in his portrayal of this interaction] recognizes a kind of pathos in the situation of the woman/phantom his conception begins to approach that of *Helen of Egypt*, for . . . it too is an allegory of art, an allegory of the woman as artwork, but one told, as it were, from the point of view of the work. As such it becomes also an allegory of feminine identity or self-knowledge.
>
> (Hirsh 1990, p. 442)

For Stein, the aspects of the Faust story that concern her have to do with gendered issues of worldly and spiritual knowledge and power, rather than with woman as artwork/fiction or with feminine self-knowledge. Masculine identity appears considerably *more* uncertain than feminine identity in "Dr. Faustus Lights the Lights," and this is implicitly one of the causes for the historical process the play allegorizes, a compensatory process in which female powers are first threatened and then appropriated by men/patriarchy.

Stein, like Goethe, stages encounters between Faust and Helen—and again, since the work is not well known, a partial synopsis seems appropriate. Marguerite Ida and Helena Annabel (Stein's compound name for her female protagonist) initially offers the possibility of a kind of redemption for Doctor Faustus, who desires to regain the soul he forfeited to the devil precisely so that he will be able to go to hell. She comes to him when she is dying from a viper's bite, hoping he will agree to use his powers to cure her. At the close of the first act he does so, and in the second act she appears in her glory, seated with her back to the sun and with an artificial viper beside her, apparently invulnerable and widely worshipped: "She has everything / and her soul" (Grahn 1989, p. 315).[22] The halo of natural candlelight that glows around her contrasts with the unsatisfying electric light which Doctor Faustus, with his different kind of knowledge and power, has invented. But then appears "the man from over the seas," who addresses her with the stifling formulas of romantic love in patriarchy: "Pretty pretty dear/ She is all my love and always here / And I am hers and she is mine / And I love her all the time / Pretty pretty pretty dear." . . . "I am the only he and you are the only she and we are the only we. . . . I am not any one I am the only one, you have to have me because I am that one" (1989, pp. 316, 317). He claims to have been bitten by her but also announces "I have won I have won her," signalling victory over her more than suasion of her emotions. She and the man from across the seas (behind whom stands Mephisto) then sit side by side, indicating a dilution of the goddess's power; the worshippers subsequently address "Mr. Viper." In Act III, taking his cue from Mephisto, Doctor Faustus chooses to use his power not to heal but to murder. He kills his companions the boy and the dog, in hopes that he may indeed go to hell. Mephisto convinces Doctor Faustus to assume the appearance of a younger man so that he might convince Marguerite Ida and Helena Annabel to go to hell with him (echoing a scene with Marguerite in Goethe's *Faust*). She refuses, but as she does so she faints into the arms of the man from over the seas who with ominous protectiveness insists on his dominance and their heterosexual bond: "Pretty pretty pretty dear I am he and she is she and we are we, pretty pretty dear I am here yes I am here pretty pretty pretty dear" (Grahn 1989, p. 329).

The sociopolitical implications of this narrative are grim—not surprisingly so if one notes, as Neuman does, that Stein wrote the play during Hitler's annexation of Austria, "completing it as the last Jews to escape that country fled to France and England, and in daily expectation of the outbreak of war" (Neuman 1988, p. 189). The play suggests that attempts to resist patriarchal power, however valiant, are easily squelched: Helena lifts her viper and asserts "Lights are all right but my viper is my might" (Grahn 1989, p. 318), only to be pooh-poohed by the devil. Grahn, like H.D., tends to be more optimistic about social transformation and the revitalization of female power. Nonetheless, it is easy to see why Stein's legitimation of the goddess and her presentation of a history that includes matriarchal power as well as the corruption and appropriation of female knowledge render this work a particularly likely match for H.D.'s epic. Grahn, whose play is linked to Goethe's only indirectly via antecedents in her Sapphic tradition, combines in "The Queen of Swords" H.D.'s allegory of female self-knowledge acquired through remembrance and reinterpretation of the past (though not, for Grahn, within H.D.'s Freudian frame) with Stein's Faustian tale of

women's knowledge and power stolen as Helen is pressed into patri-
archal heterosexual partnership.

As noted above, the realist aspects of Stein's "mythic realism"
have proved particularly important for Grahn. H.D.'s epic is realis-
tic primarily in its autobiographical dimensions. She makes myth
of "the tragic events and sordid realities of [her] life," particularly
her painfilled relationships with men (H.D., as quoted by Gelpi
1985, p. 75). The mythicizing of this material takes place through
the mediating narratives of psychoanalysis and hermetic knowledge,
as well as through elaborate interweaving with tales of classical
myth. Alicia Ostriker's observation that "To a degree paralleled by
very few poems in our literature . . .[*Helen In Egypt*] is pure psycho-
drama, nonmimetic of the world outside the psyche" (Ostriker
1986, p. 227), though it divides internal from external more neatly
than does Grahn's reading of H.D., is in broad outline correct.[23]
Stein's less internalized refiguring of Helen in "Doctor Faustus
Lights the Lights" combines the ordinary and familiar with the
mythic without relying on correspondences between fictional char-
acters and "real" autobiographical figures and without reference to
psychoanalytic constructs. Stein's play portraying a Doctor Faustus
who sold his soul to the devil in order to make electric lights has
in fact been read autobiographically as representing Stein's reac-
tions to seeing her own name in electric lights on Broadway after the
publication of *The Autobiography of Alice B. Toklas*.[24] But the work's
realism lies much more in its reliance on the verbal patterns of ordi-
nary modern speech than in its autobiographical resonances.

Stein's dramatis personae, unlike H.D.'s, sound a good deal like
real people speaking, despite the apparent quirkiness of Stein's ways
with phrasal repetition. Idiomatic patterns and rhythms are unmis-
takable throughout "Doctor Faustus Lights the Lights."[25] Here, for
instance, is Doctor Faustus in an angry huff:

> Well then I can go to hell, if she can turn night into day then I
> can go to hell, come on then come on we will go and see her and
> I will show her that I can go to hell, if she can turn night into day
> as they say then I am not the only one very well I am not the only
> one so Marguerite Ida or Helen Annabel listen well you cannot
> but I I can go to hell. Come on every one never again will I be
> alone come on come on every one.
>
> (Gertrude Stein, in Grahn 1989, pp. 323–24)

Or, here is a song of the countrywoman, capturing well the gossip's shifting tones as she addresses different characters:

> Well well this is the Doctor Faustus and he has not gone to hell he has pretty lights and they light so very well and there is a dog and he says thank you and there is a little boy oh yes little boy there you are you just are there yes little boy you are and there is Marguerite Ida and Helena Annabel and a viper did bite her, oh cure her Doctor Faustus cure her what is the use of your having been to hell if Marguerite Ida and Helen Annabel is not to be all well.
>
> (Stein, in Grahn 1989, p. 308)

Sometimes speeches—still employing a simple vocabulary and creating a colloquial effect—are heavily rhymed and read like verse, as when Doctor Faustus murmurs, "I cannot go to hell I have sold my soul to make a light and the light is bright but not interesting in my sight and I would oh yes I would I would rather go to hell be I with all my might and then go to hell oh yes alright" (Stein, in Grahn 1989, p. 325).

Though frequently more linear than Stein's, the dialogue in Grahn's "play with poetic myth" is similarly effective as colloquial speech, and it, too, often rhymes. Here, for instance, is the voice of the priggish Helen who first arrives at the Crow Bar:

> I may be everything a woman
> ever wants to be, and more,
> but at least I'm not a bar owner,
> or a madame, or a boy or a whore
> or whatever it is you do here.
>
> (Grahn 1987, p. 25)

Here is the resentful tirade Helen directs at her husband when she returns from the underworld:

> You—who are you?
> you're the one who didn't notice I was missing,
> never saw me
> going down, never thought I might have crashed,
> never wondered, never asked,
> never missed me, never mourned.
> You're the one who assumed my absence

meant you were in charge of the whole bash;
yours is the head
swelling up underneath my crown.
Yours is the big dead end
sweating upon my throne.
You never tried to find me,
you found a silly replacement.
You're the one who's disgraceful.
I'll tell you what's what, now that we know you
for who you are, . . .

(Grahn 1987, pp. 119–20)

Perhaps this imitation of colloquial speech, in addition to ensuring the work's accessibility, is one method by which Grahn approximates the oral character of ancient epic. More certainly, since Grahn regards gay culture and history as having been preserved not through written record but by word of mouth (1990, p. 3), maintaining a spoken flavor in her writing suits her political project.

That the spoken character of Grahn's text is indebted to Stein's techniques is particularly evident from the Crows. They are the characters who draw most directly on Stein's way with words, for besides being idiomatic, their speech constantly challenges single interpretations, opens up alternative meanings, and by repetition and variation transforms understandings.[26] Through their dialogue, these characters serve several functions: because their playing with words generates "patterns" rather than recounts or forwards action (as is at least sometimes the case with the other characters), they create a movement other than the progression of linear narrative which Grahn identifies as a patriarchal structure; the proliferation of meanings in their verbal play "reveal[s] the multiplicity" of situations and perspectives, fostering release from the rigidity of existing (often binary) systems and identities; their banter and their puns lighten an otherwise somber, at times brutal, series of experiences. H.D., one should note, also opens up multiple meanings, for instance through the juxtaposition of prose gloss with more suggestive lyric in *Helen in Egypt*; and, especially in *Trilogy*, H.D. explores associative word play.[27] Her work, however, is not humorous as is Stein's; being what Grahn dubs a "profound clown," Stein seems the primary model for Grahn's often comic verbal patterning.

Consider, for instance, part of the Crows' response to Helen, who echoes the saccharin hymn "Jesus Loves Me" when she asserts, "Nature loves me, this I know, / as she loves the flowers that grow. / Nature loves to give and give / and Nature loves— / what other cause have I to live?" (Grahn 1987, pp. 40–41):

Crow
   What other caws to live?
Crow
   I caws to live.
Crow
   I live to caws.
Crow
   I love a just caws.
Crow
   I love a righteous and good and just caws.
Crow
   I loathe any kind of caws.
Crow
   I prefer first caws.
Crows
   CAW CAW CAW
Crows
   We prefer last caws
Crow
   I prefer long drawn-out caws
Crows
   CAAAAW CAAAAAAWW CAAAAAAAWWW
Crow
   I like edible caws.
Crow
   The caws of peas.
Crows
   CAW CAW CAW
Crow
   The caws of corn.
Crows
   CAW CAW CAW
Crow
   The caws of war.

Crows
   CAW CAW CAW
Crow
   The caws of contemplation.
Crow
   Contemplation has no caws.
Crow
   The BEE caws—
Crows
   CAW CAW CAW
Crow
   The BEE caws—
Crow
   bee caws of you
Crow
   there's a song in my heart—

(Grahn 1987, pp. 41–42)

Through the verbal clowning of such punning passages, Grahn attempts to maintain "the spirit of the paganism that sustained this story for so long" (Grahn 1987, p. 5).

In addition, exchanges like these further the stripping process Helen is undergoing, undermining her certainties. Of course, the constantly shifting ground in this passage deliberately unsettles the audience as well as Helen. Syntactic reversals, crude puns, vibrating realms of reference from lofty principles to scavengers' raucous calls, from vegetable grounding to spiritual aspiration to popular song lyrics dizzy the reader and preclude any fixed, single interpretation. Grahn describes the effect well when she discusses "the continual play of Stein's language":

> [it] shakes our everyday belief that reality is hard-edged and fixed, and at the same time so fragile that we feel our version of reality must be taken seriously lest it crumble and our relationship to it and to our own personalities also crumble into madness. Allowing new dimensions of thought through, however, does not result in madness, but in an endless spiral of creative, motion-filled worlds—worlds of overlapping events.
>
> Reality in Stein's work is never fixed, it is by definition and usage always in motion, taking its meanings from evershifting rela-

tionships which the humor aids by sparking our courage—through
the shifts of ever moving text.

(Grahn 1989, pp. 19–20)

Often the Crows tease Helen with word play involving Nothing,
the character who is Helen's "guide in undertown" (Grahn 1987,
p. 24). Nothing is particularly effective material for fostering "new
dimensions of thought," since he/she/it, being at once nothing and
something, no one and someone, eludes categorization. Here is a
sample of how the dialogue plays on such indeterminacies: *Helen:*
"I've been left here with nothing." / *Crow (to Nothing):* "Is she
complaining?" / *Crow:* "We do have Nothing to offer her." / *Noth-
ing:* "You'd think she would be used to me by now." / *Crow:* "She
can't help it. / Nothing bothers her" (Grahn 1987, p. 33).

A passage in "Doctor Faustus Lights the Lights" introduces simi-
lar play at the moment when Marguerite Ida and Helena Annabel's
voice is heard as she approaches Doctor Faustus's door:

> and together they all say
> Where is there nobody says nobody is there. Somebody is there
> and nobody says that somebody is not there. Somebody somebody
> is there somebody somebody somebody somebody says there is
> where where is it where is it where is it where, here is here here is
> there somebody somebody says where is where.

(Stein, in Grahn 1989, p. 306)

Referring to a character as "nobody" or, more radically, "nothing"
has an epic precedent in Book IX of Homer's *Odyssey*, where Odys-
seus tells the Cyclops that he is Nobody (343; this yields such self-
contradictory lines as Polyphemus's "it is Nobody that is slaying
me" [345]). It is also a powerful example of what Grahn calls Stein's
practice of "unnaming." According to Grahn, Stein "calls" or un-
names things rather than reciting their assigned names so that they
may be distinct, equal, freed from conventional definitions and
ideological baggage.[28] What particularly interests Grahn about
"Dr. Faustus Lights the Lights" is that "Stein collected some of the
archetypes and deep stories of folk tradition and antiquity, especially
in the female tradition, and unnamed them" (1989, p. 259). This
unnaming is itself a kind of making-real, for it refuses socially con-
structed accumulations; it enacts a denaturalization that requires

fresh thinking in the present. In the passage quoted above, discussion of nobody's presence or absence in terms of somebody's or nobody's assertion mockingly strips away common assumptions about identity based on social status (being somebody); at the same time, the passage emphasizes the generative linguistic processes in fact crucial to establishing personal identity.

Grahn's Nothing is at once the agent, the epitome, and the goal of the stripping-away, the "deterioration" so crucial to the transformation the "unnamed" former Mrs. Bull must undergo to rediscover who she is or has been. (Soon after her arrival at the Crow Bar, she discovers that "Someone has stolen [her] name," along with her position, fame, money, credit cards, etc. [Grahn 1987, p. 28].) The paradoxical link between becoming nothing and gaining an identity—or gaining a fruitful understanding of subjectivity as constructed, ultimately from nothing—is suggested early on when Helen objects that her guide's naming itself Nothing "isn't healthy, it's putting yourself down." Nothing's response clearly applies to Helen's quest for self-knowledge (as "I"): "But Nothing *is* down, / Nothing is all the way to the bottom, / that's certainly the right direction— / it's where I can be found!" (1987, p. 24).

As the inverted realm of those once labeled "inverts"—where, for instance, Crows playing with words are told to "[d]arken up" (1987, p. 93), where Helen must rid herself of seven "venial virtues"—Underland is the place "where Nothing matters" (1987, p. 30). Nothing's importance lies partly in the fact that, both as character and as "unnamed" concept, Nothing demands a re-valuing of all sorts of things that have been devalued in the aboveground heterosexual world: boundarilessness, chaos, death, various lacks—including especially lack of self-esteem—and, of course, nothing itself. Hence Helen's transformation as she passes through the various belowworld gates, registered partly in her increasingly unkempt and "disheveled" appearance (Grahn 1987, p. 80), is what Ereshkigal half-mockingly calls "accepting everything Nothing has had to offer" (1987, p. 101). The final stage of Helen's descent— what is in fact figured by all epic descents to the underworld—is an experience of death leading to rebirth, and that experience of death is Helen's most direct encounter with nothing.

In terms of the Steinian precedents for this text, it is significant that this journey into the linguistically slippery state of nothing is a journey to the heart of paradox. For paradox is a rhetorical figure central to Stein's writing and, according to Gregory Woods, central to homosexual writing generally. Woods regards paradox as a linguistic strategy often adopted by modern gay (male) poets to negotiate a kind of double consciousness; paradoxical ways of speaking serve as "weapon and shield,"

> both to reflect the way we are seen and to stamp our own more accurate logic on the world. We strive to make sense of the conflict between the negative versions of our lives and our own more positive versions: to forge some kind of unity out of our contrary needs to be different and to fit in.
>
> (Woods 1990, p. 176)

Noting the false and hierarchical binary organization of homosexual versus heterosexual imposed on "the world's spectrum of sexual variety," Woods sees language itself forced into a divided state under contrary banners—the battleground of paradox (1990, p. 177). And paradox, whose etymological roots *para doxa* mean "contrary to public opinion," is by definition "deviant speech"; "Paradox is syntactical logic working 'against nature'" (Woods 1990, p. 178). Paradoxical language works—often with a kind of violence (Woods 1990, p. 189)—to disturb, to redefine, to subvert the status quo, including its binary system of discrete genders.[29] *Double entendre* and irony are attendant two-tongued strategies serving similar ends. Woods's argument that paradox operates to unsettle binary systems would seem to be supported by both "The Queen of Swords" and "Dr. Faustus Lights the Lights." The emphasis in both women's texts (something Woods's essay does not stress, though it may apply also to gay male writing) is on paradox as a means of opening into multiplicity, particularly multiplicity within wholeness.

In Stein's play, for instance, the nihilistic figure of Doctor Faustus initially wrestles despairingly with paradoxes posed by his relation to the devil; for example, "how do you know I have a soul, who says so nobody says so but you the devil and everybody knows the devil is all lies, so how do you know how do I know that I have a soul to sell" (Stein, in Grahn 1989, p. 300). But he musters confidence that his mental processes which can embrace the contradictions of paradox are less limited than the devil's unidirectional thinking: "I know how I do what I do when I see the way through and always any day I will see another day and you old devil you know very well you never see any other way than just the way to hell, you only know one way. You only know one thing, you are never ready for anything" (Stein, in Grahn 1989, p. 301). A link between empowerment and the embrace of paradox is also suggested by the name of the play's female protagonist; by combining many into one, her name generates and sustains syntactic paradoxes of plural nouns agreeing with singular verbs: "Marguerite Ida and Helena Annabel comes in" (1989, pp. 306–7), or "Of course her names is Marguerite Ida too and Helena Annabel as well" (1989, p. 312). In the final scene, however, when her power is waning and she is reduced to the "pretty one" of the man from over the seas, she no longer maintains the paradoxical fullness of doubled, or doubly doubled, identity; she is "Marguerite Ida or Helena Annabel" (1989, p. 324).

Grahn's play follows a more optimistic trajectory, as her character moves from an extremely restricted sense of her identity as the wife of Thomas Bull to embracing as parts of herself multiple and sometimes contradictory forces, eras, roles, and bonds (a development that has parallels in *Helen in Egypt*). Pointing toward this transformation is the early scene in which Helen tries on Enki's glasses which "see absolutely everything, from every point of view" (Grahn 1987, p. 45). For Enki, they offer "clarity of vision." But Helen says she can't bear to see "from so many / points of view, / one is enough, or at most two" (1987, p. 45). By the end of her quest, however, she has developed a more complex and combinatory vision;[30] in the closing scene she likens her own perspectival powers to those of the telescope:

> I too know how to use mirrors,
> how to weave with lights and sound.
> How to see from at least two points of view,
> a parallax of measurement.
> And I know how to recognize my own being
> in the dark side of the wind . . .
>
> (Grahn 1987, p. 125)

Helen's mention of wind refers back to what she learned from Nothing, that guide with the "howling / hollow center" (1987, p. 53). In the "Gate One: Belowworld" section titled "Where Nothing Lives," Ereshkigal's poem called "How Nothing sees it" conveys that "The wind is Nothing's true lover; / where the wind lives / is Nothing's true home":

Where the wind lives is order,
what the wind leaves is chaos,
what the wind does is blow.
What Nothing does is hold the place
completely still, for Zero.

It isn't pleasant being no one,
the eye in the eye of the storm;
but someone has to make the spaces—
or the sky would never turn around.

(Grahn 1987, pp. 27–28)

Helen echoes and sometimes reverses these lines at Gate Seven in her poem "The light in the eye of death," where she rises from death, a "reconstituted" Inanna born of Ereshkigal's labor. She reports having fallen through a hole in the eye of death and having gone "to where the wind lives":

Where the wind lives is chaos;
what the wind does is blow.

The center of the wind is paradox,
completely orderly and patterned,
a mathematical, coherent person
with a mind, even a soul.

(Grahn 1987, p. 110)

As she describes in sensory and kinesthetic terms that realm of paradox, Helen relies on the gerund form (-ing) so important to the insistent presentness of Stein's writing:

Deep in the eye of death
the light is never standing,
it's dancing, it's unfolding,
light is holding dark,
shy is holding bold,
everything is blowing hot
with cold;

(Grahn 1987, p. 111)

Ultimately, as this passage suggests, paradox is not a matter of irreconcilable contradictions but of contraries that may be located on a continuum or contained within each other.

This fits also Grahn's explication of a "principle of polarity" central to Stein's writing: "This principle expresses the idea that heat and cold, love and hate, poverty and wealth are not categorically different but rather are opposite poles of the same vibratory element. All paradoxes may be reconciled" (Grahn 1989, p. 260). The reconciliation of paradox resounds at the close of Helen's poem in lines resonating between everything and nothing at all:

> I went all the way to Zero,
> leaned in Zero's door;
> and you know what lives in there?
> Absolutely everything—everything at all.
>
> (Grahn 1987, p. 111)

While Steinian paradox serves as the primary model for such constructions, H.D.'s perspectives are similar: Ostriker has rightly observed that "in its theology and its structuring of images, as well as in its quest plot, the driving intellectual impulse in *Helen in Egypt* is the synthesizing of opposites" (Ostriker 1986, p. 227).

Grahn seems to concur with Woods that paradox is a resource particularly for those who write as homosexuals; Gay culture, she claims, works to reveal the other side, and to this end "We [Gay people] act out irony, essential humor, and paradox" (1990, p. 282). It is hardly surprising, then, that one of the ways in which the paradox-loving Stein is a model for Grahn is in her representing lesbianism itself. Here, too, her (butch) role is to be distinguished from H.D.'s. For just as the literal butch through her appearance more directly announces her lesbianism than does her femme partner, who might pass as straight, Stein writes more directly (and more playfully) of lesbian experience than H.D. In *The Highest Apple*, Grahn describes Stein's work as "centered almost entirely on women, and—basic to this—on solving the problems of expressing and naming a Lesbian life in a world that forbade doing so" (1985, p. 26). To demonstrate the presence of such forbidden expression, Grahn in several prose works describes her own slow recognition of the striking "literal honesty" of Stein's story, "Miss Furr and Miss Skeene," "the literal, step-by-step telling of a complete first-love story between two women" (1989, p. 137). Grahn's literal honesty in depicting lesbian love, while no doubt facilitated by the liberation movements of her era, draws on Stein's empowering example.

Helen's necessary descent is in significant part a movement into

socially unsanctioned lesbian sexual practice. And "savage" Ereshki-
gal's invitation "Oh lower yourself to love / in the underground,
the union / of a woman to one other / woman" (Grahn 1987, p. 53)
as it becomes more graphic does not shy away from even the violent
dimensions of that experience:

> Oh descend to me
> mound on mound of Venus meeting
> maddened Earth to be unbound on.
> Fix your gaze upon me
> while I find and flay you
> with my fingers and my tongue.
>
> My tongue is nicknamed
> "Say Everything."
> She's appealing enough
> at first until she nails you fast
> to solid dirt of the fat earth
> and ends your fantasy.
>
> You will moan, Inanna
> you will cry.
> Everyone you ever were
> will die,
> while you go down
> and go down
> and go down
> on me.
>
> (1987, p. 55)

Lesbianism has a central place among the multiple identities Helen
embraces when she emerges as "a warrior Maid" at the play's end
(1987, p. 123); nor does she appear restricted to either the butch
or the femme role. For while Ereshkigal is explicitly butch ("Butch
of the Realm," she calls herself [p. 56]) and clearly takes the erotic
lead with Helen, no obvious erotic roles appear in Helen's loving
partnership with Nin. What seems most important is the fact of
partnership itself or, in expanded version, the development of a
women's community. As Case notes, what really "deteriorates" in
this play is Helen's isolation (1988, p. 65). While staging Helen's
entry into an erotic relationship with Ereshkigal, "The Queen of
Swords" also depicts her entry into the rich support and vital chal-

lenge of an uncloseted lesbian community. This communal emphasis is distinctly Grahn's own, reflecting and celebrating the social context of the lesbian feminist movement neither Stein nor H.D. lived to see.

————————

"But when we had come down to the ship and to the sea, first of all
we drew the ship down to the bright sea"
                    —opening of Book 11, Homer's *The Odyssey*,
                                trans. A. T. Murray (1995, p. 401)

"And then went down to the ship"
                    —opening line of Ezra Pound's "Canto I,"
                a translation of Divus' Latin version of the opening of
                                        Book 11, *The Odyssey*

"ho and ho poor death
our lovers teeth are white geese flying above us
our lovers muscles are rope ladders under our hands
even though no women yet go down to the sea in ships
except in their dreams"
                    —Judy Grahn, "A Woman is Talking to Death"
                    (*The Work of A Common Woman*, 1978, p. 130)

In the early 1970s, when she wrote "A Woman Is Talking to Death," Grahn seems to have felt that ordinary women's heroic aspirations (at least in conventionally male realms of heroism) and women poets' epic ambitions had not yet been translated from dream into reality. By 1987, however, when she published "The Queen of Swords," she could number herself among the female poets now recounting women's epic adventures. The two very different epic-based long poems by Doubiago and Grahn examined in the preceding chapters demonstrate some of the uses for which contemporary women are claiming the resources of poetic epic.

Women whose long poems self-consciously reconstruct epic tales and conventions are appealing to and ambitiously revising their audience's sense of public history. Both Doubiago and Grahn do so in part through revisionary presentation of their mythic heritage, insisting that ancient myths continue to be enacted today and that the roles of women in such epic tales need to be reconsidered, both in the sense of being rethought and altered and/or of being understood in a different way. Their works offer the cultural instruction characteristic of all "tales of the tribe" but from the perspective of a female hero and with particular emphasis on gender roles and gender's place in social power systems. Their public teaching emerges both from reexamining how women have been situated in the androcentric versions of epic tales and from envisioning alternate positions women might occupy (and, in Grahn's view, have occupied).

Differences between *Hard Country* and "The Queen of Swords" that are particularly significant for the long poem have to do with the roles of autobiography and of community. Although exploring a public history going back many generations and including multiple ethnic groups, and although invoking mythic patterns from a variety of cultures, Doubiago's *Hard Country* has a very private base in family history and personal experience; her protagonist serves as an example of rewarding individual quest that is instructive for others, but she cannot serve as a model for cultural transformation. Her final solitude is emblematic. Grahn, in contrast, approaches the retelling of mythic stories not only as revealing things about the structures of our society and the patterns of individual behavior within society, but also as serving a crucial communal, ceremonial function:

> Poetry repeats and recreates the ceremonial myths which give human lives their meaning. . . . Given a ceremonial story, we connect to a group; we connect to a time; we connect to a universe that has a place for us. . . . In the absence of such stories, we not only fall out of public life, we fall out of history. . . . We also fall out of mythic time, out of recognized, central social value.
>
> (Grahn 1985, p. 11; ellipses added)

Grahn's ideal of connection to a group is a key factor determining her reliance on mnemonic devices such as rhyme and word repetition; key components of her epic are rendered as memorable chants. Created with a less participatory aesthetic in mind, *Hard Country* has no analogue to lyrics like the Gate Three celebration, "Lesbians love to dance / inside the thunder" or the Amazon chorus "As for what we do with horses," poems which could be put to music and sung at political rallies or other contemporary ceremonial occasions. Here, as a shorter example, is Helen's poem defending Nin:

> You can't take her
> she loves me.

When I bowed down so low,
she bowed down too.

Even when she couldn't find me
she stood beside me.

Even when she couldn't understand me
she stood by me.

Even when she couldn't stand me
she stood for me.

You can't take her,
I love her as a friend.

Because of her I know more
about being human;

more than "stand up for myself,"
I know "stand up for another woman."

(Grahn 1987, p. 115)

Doubiago shares only part of Grahn's sense of the poet's role as that of "defining the culture around her, giving it name, substance and rhythm so it can grow into a full life" (Grahn 1985, p. 71). As an epic poet, Doubiago indeed attempts to define the culture around her, but like many earlier American authors of long poems (including her mentor Olson), she positions herself as a critical, resisting outsider who warns of societal disaster as she seeks her own way into a full life. (In *Hard Country*, this way is literally as well as figuratively countercultural.) Grahn, by putting her own marginalized culture—lesbian culture—at the center of her epic world, can present her hero's experience as representative, typical, even as she suggests that every individual must go through her own quest and her own confrontation with the forces of "Our lady of the Underground." ("Everyone's / shadows are custom-made / by their own needs" [1987, p. 122].) With characters who are on some level gods and vast natural forces, the emphasis in Grahn's epic is very much on the archetype; Doubiago's work, though also figuring a communal necessity and an at least partially mythicized protagonist, presents a more particularized and idiosyncratic history, geography, personality, and resolution.

Doubiago and Grahn, then, occupy alternative positions in relation to a paradox Michael André Bernstein points out is central to modern verse epic:

> In the narration of history, responsibility is always both collective and diachronic, the truths of the past and the exigencies of the present uniting to shape a particular tale whose spokesman is a single author, but whose true subject matter is articulated in the labor of an entire people. This is the essential paradox of a modern verse epic, a text that can be only the response of a particular individual writing from his own, partial and limited, perspective, but which must nonetheless give voice to historical forces transcending any single consciousness or moment. It is a problem Olson called "methodological," and its implications are as much moral as technical, and as much political (in the broadest sense) as aesthetic.
>
> (Bernstein 1980, pp. 271–72)

In Doubiago's work the limited perspective of the singular individual comes more to the fore, while in Grahn's the foreground features a collective understanding. (We might note that Enki, Grahn's god of the wisdom of nature, proposes that individuals' thoughts do not come from inside their own minds; rather, people when thinking are "Tuned in to radio bands / of collective understandings, / flashes of insight / going inside from outside" [Grahn 1987, p. 73].)

Doubiago grounds her epic in the personally revelatory or confessional lyric that has become a staple of women's poetry in recent decades, thereby expanding the cultural uses of such autobiographical material. The readership she gathers forms a previously nonexistent community that can consider the public issues her story raises and the solutions it attempts. Grahn, positioning herself as spokesperson for a neglected but vital woman-centered tradition, can presume she addresses not a scattering of previously unconnected individuals in an indifferent or hostile nation, but an eager politically conscious community already in existence though insufficiently voiced. As bard-priestess, she recuperates sacred narrative without encountering a distance from the audience she hopes to instruct. It is precisely such a distance, Bernstein persuasively argues, that led poets like Olson to shift in the course of their epic poems from "a public and historical discourse to a private exploration of cherished themes" (1980, p. 266).

Undeniably, the most typical gesture of the modern verse epic is a stubborn attempt to tell the tale of the tribe until the pressures of an indifferent and ethically "incoherent" tribe compel a withdrawal back into the private accents of a lyric or verse meditation.

(1980, p. 268)

Perhaps because prominent American feminists such as Adrienne Rich have so effectively conveyed to women the message that the personal is the political, contemporary female epic poets tend more to question the received distinction between public and private realms and to attempt their merger from the beginning; nonetheless, such gestures appear to varying degrees in their epics as well. Grahn, by virtue of her outspoken lesbianism, is socially a more marginal figure than Doubiago; yet she has found within lesbian feminism a "tribe" that enables her to speak with a collective impersonal authority approaching that of the classical epics.

The two lyric sequences to be examined in the following chapter, which are not based on epic models, approach the relation of public history and private experience from another angle. These works by Rita Dove and Brenda Marie Osbey portray individual lives positioned within precisely defined historical circumstances and deliberately removed from the generalizing realm of myth. The poets' turn to individual histories, however, seems not to reflect a sense of "an indifferent and ethically 'incoherent' tribe." Rather, it reflects a desire to expand historical understanding of ethnically and geographically specific communities.

CHAPTER THREE

Sequences Testifying for
"Nobodies": Rita Dove's
Thomas and Beulah and
Brenda Marie Osbey's
*Desperate Circumstance,
Dangerous Woman*

Rita Dove defines "testifying"—an important term in African American spiritual traditions—as "tell[ing] the truth through story" (Dove 1985, p. 114).[1] The two long poems by African American women to be discussed in this chapter have such testifying as their aim. Both Dove's *Thomas and Beulah* (first published in 1986) and Brenda Marie Osbey's *Desperate Circumstance, Dangerous Woman* (1991) tell, through sequences of shorter poems, stories of historically and geographically specific African American characters and communities. Their projects can be clearly distinguished from the epic-based projects of Doubiago and Grahn, which rest on a mythologizing impulse. Not only do those epic-affiliated long poems pattern their protagonists' stories on revisions of received myths (of Isis, of Helen); they didactically mythologize the modern protagonist so that she can speak for something much larger than herself, even for Woman. While such epic poems give the protagonist an identity at once individual and collective, rendering her archetypal in significant ways, testifying poems like Dove's and Osbey's present the very particularized stories of distinct individuals. A character's situation may be in important ways representative of a group's experience, but it is so precisely because of its embeddedness in a set of specific public historical events and forces. To apply Dove's description of Derek Walcott's earlier procedures, these long poems "[insist] that only through the particular fate can a universal one be posited" (Dove 1987, p. 62). Testifying about ordinary lives, a gesture that deliberately bypasses the epic's comprehensiveness, need not signal a lack of ultimate ambition or an anxiety about cultural authority.

That writers of color might often be among those drawn to the more historically and geographically bounded project of "testifying" than that of transhistorical or cross-cultural mythmaking makes particular sense in view of the near erasure of their immediate, local histories by a racist society (and by its supposedly universal tales).[2] As Dove says, when responding to a question about her relation to Africa, "There's a hole somewhere, you know; I feel like I came from someplace—that a part of my ancestry sprung from a place that is irretrievably lost; but as I said, I don't want to romanticize that. I mean, I can't go back and find it" (Taleb-Khyar 1991, p. 356). Her quest and Osbey's are not for revised representations of long buried matriarchies or matrifocal religions (as in "The Queen of Swords"), nor for revisions of vast eras of history so as to better reveal the costs and processes of white male imperialism (as in *Hard Country*)—nor even for re-creation of an African homeland. In the long poems under discussion, these African American women speak for people of particular American localities living relatively close to their own time; their stories, to the extent that they have been preserved, have been transmitted primarily through oral forms whose survival is at risk in a society where scribal, rather than oral, culture dominates. Some of this orality is captured in the poems' narrative techniques that imitate and "signify on" forms of oral narration found in African American vernacular traditions. The poets aim to rescue more than to revise, though rescue adds to a revisionary process. They salvage stories of their own grandparents and great-grandparents, whether that ancestry is literal or figurative, endowing those characters with the individualized, unstereotyped subjectivity denied them in white-dominated traditions.

Works by people of color have rarely figured in critical considerations of the long poem.[3] Among the explanations for this oversight may be genre critics' reluctance to become embroiled in debates extending back at least to the 1920s about the relation of ethnic writing to hegemonic Anglo-European traditions, conventions, and standards.[4] Both Dove and Osbey, as we shall see, have been caught in contemporary extensions of these arguments. Dove has been criticized by some black critics for not performing more obviously and exclusively as a race poet; Osbey's poetry, on the other hand, has been evaluated by at least one white critic in terms that give too little recognition to the distinctly black traditions shaping it. By including Dove's and Osbey's sequences in this study, I hope to demonstrate the value of integrating works by writers of color into genre-oriented considerations of the long poem.

Such integration fosters fuller appreciation of the writers' achievements as well as better understanding of the interactions among formal and generic traditions of different social groups. After all, when a white female poet is compared only with Dickinson, but never with Whitman, Pound, or Eliot, this may, whether intentionally or not, serve to keep her in her place at the literary margins; similarly, critics identifying a novel as the best work by a black writer since *Invisible Man* might imply that the work does not bear comparison with the creations of Faulkner, Woolf, or Pyncheon. What one might call "mainstreaming" works by writers identified with minority groups is one way of gaining more widespread attention and respect for those works. It also counters erroneously absolute separations of racial (or of gendered) traditions. Given the white-dominated educational system in which contemporary American writers of color have been trained, separation of racial traditions risks not only implicit hierarchizing but false simplification as well.

At the same time, acknowledging the presence of non-Anglo-European traditions in works by writers of color is crucial if we are to avoid further denial of the often suppressed history those traditions embody. This chapter presents Dove's and Osbey's shared choice to produce narrative long poems elliptically composed of brief disjunct parts as a choice shaped significantly, though not exclusively, by specifically black traditions (of slave narrative, coded storytelling, blues, etc.). I attempt to integrate formal/generic with cultural/historical perspectives so as to stress the importance of recognizing particular ethnic or racial traditions and contexts, both as they operate within specific works and as they enrich the conventions available to all writers within a previously Anglo-European genre.

Launching her career in the 1970s and publishing her first volume in 1980, Rita Dove resented and resisted the sense, persisting from the Black Arts Movement of the 1960s, that a black poet should write about prescribed black subjects, usually involving ghetto life, in the language of the street. Brought up in a middle-class household and trained first at Miami University in Ohio and then at the Iowa Writers' Workshop, Dove chose to publish her early work in white mainstream, rather than black, periodicals. Her poetry has been warmly embraced by the white establishment[5]; this is evident, for instance, from her being the sole black woman and one of only four poets of color in *The Harvard Book of Contemporary American Poetry* (1985), edited by Helen Vendler; from her having been selected by Robert Penn Warren for the 1986 Lavan Prize of the Academy of American Poets; from her having won Fulbright, Guggenheim, and NEA fellowships; from her being in 1987 only the second black poet awarded a Pulitzer; and from her 1993–95 appointment as the nation's poet laureate. As these institutional endorsements suggest, Dove's lyrics in many ways epitomize the mainstream aesthetic that dominates academic writing programs (an aesthetic countered by experimentalists such as Howe, Dahlen, and DuPlessis, whose work will be discussed in later chapters).

The reception of Dove's poetry among black intellectuals has been more cautious. Appreciative notices in major African American journals by such prestigious black critics as Arnold Rampersad (writing in 1986) and Houston Baker (in 1990) have had to push to expand the audience's concept of black writing beyond the still influential terms of the black aesthetic in order to argue for Dove's inclusion in the black canon. Yet even these critics do not sound entirely comfortable with Dove's stance.

In his thoughtful piece, Rampersad presents as positively as he can Dove's deliberate rejection of the dominant black aesthetics of verse in the 1960s and 1970s:

> In many ways, her poems are exactly the opposite of those that have come to be considered quintessentially black verse in recent years. Instead of looseness of structure, one finds in her poems remarkably tight control; instead of a reliance on reckless inspiration, one recognizes discipline and practice, and long, taxing hours in competitive university poetry workshops and in her study; instead of a range of reference limited to personal confession, one finds personal reference disciplined by a measuring of distance and a prizing of objectivity; instead of an obsession with the theme of race, one finds an eagerness, perhaps even an anxiety, to transcend—if not actually to repudiate—black cultural nationalism in the name of a more inclusive sensibility.
>
> (Rampersad 1986, p. 53)

He sympathetically positions Dove as a poetic reformer determined "to break new ground and set fresh standards in relation to the black writers of the half-generation before her" and provides strong rationales for her practices, including her discreet handling of specifically racial indignation (1986, p. 53). Nonetheless, he suggests that she has not entirely escaped the pitfalls of writing in a spirit of reaction. While reminding his readers that Dove's poems demonstrate that she is "well aware of black history" (her first volume, for instance, contains a section of poems on antebellum black experience), Rampersad notes with ambivalence that she "writes few poems about racism today" (1986, pp. 54, 55). Echoing Black Arts goals, he briefly acknowledges his own disturbance at the "meagerness of racial feeling" or "racial identification" in her work (1986, p. 55).

Baker opens his review of Dove's 1989 collection *Grace Notes* dramatically: "Rita Dove is not a 'Race Poet.'" He goes on to urge interrogation of the overall wisdom of United States "culture" that insists on essentialist categorizations of the "Afro-American" or "Black" poet:

> For surely, there is no Afro-American critic in his or her proper senses who would want to exclude Dove from our canonical lists. On the other hand, there are few, I suspect, who would be able quickly to say what relationship she shares with Phillis Wheatley, Frances Ellen Watkins Harper, or June Jordan—to select a random and arbitrary group of Afro-American artists.
>
> (Baker 1990, p. 574)

Nonetheless asserting Dove's links to a specifically black and female tradition, he singles out

> Dove's autobiographical lyricism and her astute precision in naming as the distinctive poetical traits that connect her work with Afro-American womanist traditions. Such traits bring her poems into a kind of harmony with, for example, the complex narrative voice of Zora Neale Hurston's *Their Eyes Were Watching God*.
>
> (1990, p. 574)

Like Rampersad, Baker presents Dove as pointing black writing in new, positive directions: race is in Dove's work "transformed into an uncommon commonality" (1990, p. 575). By this he seems to mean that Dove presents the racialized subject as a figure with whom all readers identify and through whom our diversity becomes what we have in common; "If *Black* is the combined richness of all color, then Rita Dove is the singing blackness of blackness" (1990, p. 577). The closing assertion of Baker's review functions as a call to black readers for precisely the critical flexibility and inclusiveness he has been struggling to enact: "The addition of *Grace Notes* to the score of Afro-American poetry certainly fills the space of past omissions and offers a beautiful flexibility for our emerging definitions of Afro-American women's canons of song" (1990, p. 577).

Dove has reported that her awareness of prescriptions for authentically "Black" writing and a resulting sense that she wasn't writing what she was "supposed to be writing" left her "a closet poet for years" (Waniek and Dove 1991, p. 262). It is telling that among the small number of critical essays Dove has published are pieces championing two black poets heavily involved in Western traditions, Melvin Tolson and Derek Walcott; these essays allow Dove implicitly to defend her own poetics in the process of explaining theirs. Her 1985 essay "Telling It Like it I-S, *IS*: Narrative Techniques in Melvin Tolson's *Harlem Gallery*" begins by providing a historical context for the mixed reception of Tolson's epic (and in doing so provides the historical context for understanding debates about her work): in 1965 "Black writers rejected white literary standards, proclaiming their own Black Aesthetic which extolled literature written for the common people, a literature that was distinctly oral, using the language patterns and vocabulary of the street to arouse feelings of solidarity and pride among Afro-Americans" (Dove 1985, p. 109). Tolson's complex work, containing "allusions to Vedic Gods, Tintoretto, and Pre-Cambrian pottery, as well as snippets in Latin and French" (p. 109)—while enthusiastically received by white critics such as Karl Shapiro—made him appear to many black intellectuals a " 'white man's darkie' " (p. 110). Dove complains that the poem itself—including Tolson's "virtuoso use of folk talk and street jive" and his use of "storytelling 'riffs' which are rooted in the Afro-American oral tradition"—got lost in the critical controversy over racial loyalties (pp. 110, 111). Many of his narrative techniques, through which he conveys something analogous to "tribal history," she claims are "based on devices exclusively rooted in the Afro-American tradition" (pp. 114, 113).[6]

Dove presents Tolson as someone who, through his range of reference and heterogeneous diction, "is deliberately complicating our pre-conceived notions of cultural . . . order" (Dove 1985, p. 115). This essay, like the one on Walcott, demonstrates her allegiance to those who resist narrow, programmatic understandings of what it means to be a black artist. Like the Tolson she describes, Dove herself draws extensively on African American traditions; what makes her work controversial among black intellectuals (in addition to her interest in nonblack subject matter) is her determination to mix those traditions with others so as to generate genuinely *multi-cultural* models of "cultural order." Her approach at once high-lights and furthers the symbiosis of black and white traditions always present in African American texts, calling attention to what Henry Louis Gates, Jr., calls the "double voicedness" of black texts. Gates concurs with Susan Willis that black texts are " 'mulattoes' (or 'mu-latas'), with a two-toned heritage," adding, "these texts speak in standard Romance or Germanic languages and literary structures, but almost always speak with a distinct and resonant accent, an ac-cent that Signifies (upon) the various black vernacular literary tradi-tions" (Gates 1988, p. xxiii).[7] Most African Americanists would probably agree, but many have chosen to stress the specifically black elements, perhaps to compensate for centuries of denial that African American artists could be anything more than mimics of white cre-ators. Dove, however, while genuinely engaged with her African American literary heritage, has not given preferential treatment to specifically black traditions. This apparently contributes to the warmth of the white mainstream response to her work; Helen Ven-dler, for instance, is obviously relieved to find in Dove a black writer who feels no need to make blackness her central subject, who will treat black characters as "ordinary" people, with "ordinary"—by which Vendler means nonracial—"physical and social resentments" (Vendler 1995, pp. 82, 80). It also accounts for the cooler recep-tion Dove's poetry has received in the black intellectual commu-nity.

Walcott enjoys far more stature and renown than Tolson, but he, too, has frustrated some cultural nationalists by doing precisely what Dove admires: "resist[ing] being cubbyholed" and "reject[ing] nei-ther his Caribbean heritage nor his British education" (Dove 1987, p. 49).[8] Dove's review of his *Collected Poems 1948–1984*, titled " 'Ei-ther I'm Nobody, or I'm a Nation,' " is another tribute to one who, in his "contrariness," resisted the Black Arts understanding of how the artist can best assert racial pride. He chose

> to present an introspective exploration of his personal past at the
> very moment so many Afro-American writers were writing "for
> the people." Walcott insists that only through the particular fate
> can a universal one be posited; his response to the call for Black
> Pride is to contribute his version of a life, another life, in all its
> ambiguities.
>
> (Dove 1987, p. 62)

This statement reflects Dove's own interest in using poetry to ex-
plore the experience of individuals rather than to champion social
causes as such, just as her approval of Walcott's realization "that
assimilation means embracing every culture around one" (1987,
p. 54) reflects her desire to embrace multiple cultural traditions.
Whereas assimilation has often been condemned as a relinquishing
of one's identity in order to merge with the dominant culture, Dove
presents it as a productive response to the "spiritual and cultural
schizophrenia" experienced by the colonized. It involves not ex-
changing one ethnic identity for another—not abandoning one's
blackness—but absorbing multiple cultures into one's identity and
voice.

Thus, in her statements about other African American writers—
as through the example of her poetry—Dove encourages recogni-
tion that varied traditions from various cultures may nourish and
enrich each other in a single artist's work without depriving the
artist or her work of distinctive racial character. Like Gates, Dove
believes that more than one tradition and linguistic register inevita-
bly operate in works by writers from minority groups; speaking of
"the awareness a writer needs to see many sides of a story" she
observes:

> Of course, as a minority we have acquired that binocular vision
> necessarily. As Du Bois said, to live as a Black person in America,
> you must learn to fit into the main culture even while you are not
> of it. Even if you come from an upwardly mobile middle-class
> background, you grow up with an awareness of Difference and a
> set of cultural values rooted in the Black tradition, so in a certain
> way you are already bilingual.
>
> (Taleb-Khyar 1991, p. 351)

Appreciative use of Anglo-European traditions need not entail
avoiding or devaluing traditions of other cultures. In the case of

Dove's *Thomas and Beulah*, it does not preclude her employing narrative strategies and poetic techniques that, in Gates's sense, signify on African American traditions.

Critics need to recognize, however, that the distinctions between the traditions operating in a single work are not always clear-cut, particularly since racial traditions may be subtly registered through racially inflected uses of widely available techniques (free indirect discourse is a case in point). The specifically black traditions of slave narrative, historical narrative poetry, or blues that influence Dove's and Osbey's choice to produce narrative sequences elliptically composed of disjunct parts provide only some of the traditions at work. (After all, white modernist traditions also model an interest in discontinuous narration.) Moreover, these African American forms themselves evolved partly within the context of Anglo-European cultural traditions, so that what comes from where is not easy to determine. Dove's and Osbey's approaches to the formal possbilities of the long poem demonstrate a complex multiculturalism that highlights the problematics of distinguishing among ethnic traditions interwoven in single works. At the same time, their poems—which I believe are enriched by readings that highlight racially specific genres and historical contexts—demonstrate the importance of our recognizing the several traditions in operation.[9]

Narrative poetic traditions exist in cultures worldwide, so choosing to use the lyric sequence to construct a narrative does not in itself signal a particular cultural allegiance. Yet, as Jay Clayton has noted in discussing the increasing turn to narrative as both technique and theme in American fiction since the mid-seventies, "[s]ome of the most direct treatments of the theme of storytelling in recent years . . . have taken place in the African-American novel" (Clayton 1993, p. 93). Clayton ties the general interest in narrative to current emphases on local political struggles throughout our society but claims that the theme is particularly visible in fiction by writers of color both because of the non-Euro-American heritages on which they draw and because of the "frequently collective nature of a minority group's struggle against dominant culture" (1993, p. 94). "[N]arrative is often viewed by novelists today as an oppositional technique because of its association with unauthorized forms of knowledge, what Foucault has called 'subjugated' and Morrison 'discredited' knowledge" (1993, p. 95). This association

can be and often is emphasized by drawing on oral forms—folk-
tales, myths, legends, oral histories; by exploring less privileged
written genres—diaries, letters, criminal confessions, slave narra-
tives; by identifying the contemporary text with archaic symbolic
modes—rituals, dreams, magic; and by writing about traditional
activities—vernacular arts, recipes, folklore, quilting and other
crafts, native music and dance.

(Clayton 1993, p. 95)

In part because telling stories creates as well as sustains community,
narrative lends itself to being used as a source of empowerment for
oppressed or marginal peoples.

That this applies to poetic as well as prose fictional forms has
already been recognized by Susan Stanford Friedman in "Craving
Stories: Narrative and Lyric in Contemporary Theory and Wom-
en's Long Poems."[10] She builds upon Clayton's argument to claim

[a] historically produced cultural imperative exists that creates a
need for narrative to resist or subvert the stories told by the domi-
nant culture. . . . [T]o counter the narratives of alterity produced
by the dominant society, [members of marginalized groups] must
tell other stories that chart their exclusions, affirm their agency
(however complicit and circumscribed), and continually (re)con-
struct their identities.

(Friedman 1994, p. 17)

In long poems composed by women, Friedman finds a dialectical
play between narrative and lyric that reflects a "need for narrative
based in traditional Western exclusions of women from subjectivity
and from the discourses of both myth and history" (1994, p. 17).
This chapter supports her claim that "women writers whose cul-
tures rely on a living oral tradition have transformed literate narrative
by weaving strands of oral and written narrative conventions" (1994,
p. 21).[11] The poems under discussion here would fit Friedman's cate-
gory of poems "[p]aralleling feminist social history," which

set out to re-create the stories of "ordinary" women's lives, that
is, the texture and feel of everyday life for the kind of women "his-
tory proper" ignores. Like social history, these poems often nar-
rate individual stories and family histories with an implicit assump-
tion of their representability and reflection of the larger social
patterns.

(1994, p. 27)

Perhaps because of its reliance on lyric units, commonly a vehicle for private voice and individual epiphany, these aspects of Dove's long poem in particular have not, I think, gained sufficient critical recognition.

While Dove does not particularly emphasize the non-Western and oral traditions behind her poetry, she nonetheless concurs with the widely held view that African American poets have their own traditions. The essay she co-authored with Marilyn Nelson Waniek, "A Black Rainbow: Modern Afro-American Poetry" (1991) states as an initial premise:

> Confined to a literary ghetto for many of the same reasons Blacks have been confined to physical ghettos, Black poets have created their own tradition, rooted in a song fundamentally different from its white counterpart. Modern Black poetry is nourished by the work of earlier Black poets, and draws much of its sustenance from the folk sources which have nurtured the race since slavery. These sources include Black music, Black speech, the Black church, and the guerrilla techniques of survival—irony, concealment, double-entendre, and fable.
>
> (Waniek and Dove 1991, p. 217)

Dove identifies African American traditions among the forces that made her a writer: "I come from a long line of storytellers—not that storytelling was cultivated in my family, but more in line with black American oral tradition, where anyone who could tell a good story was a favored guest" (Walsh 1994, p. 146). *Thomas and Beulah* in fact originates from an oral narrative: a story Dove heard from her grandmother when she was ten or twelve, about her grandfather "coming north on a riverboat; it seems he had dared his best friend to swim the river, and the friend drowned" (Schneider 1989, p. 115). Dove tells this story in the opening poem, "The Event," beginning the sequence in the manner of a raconteur:

> Ever since they'd left the Tennessee ridge
> with nothing to boast of
> but good looks and a mandolin,
>
> the two Negroes leaning
> on the rail of a riverboat
> were inseparable: Lem plucked

to Thomas' silver falsetto.
But the night was hot and they were drunk.

>   (from *Selected Poems*, p. 141; cited as *SP* hereafter)

The imagery of that poem and the psychological consequences of the event it goes on to depict pervade Thomas's half of the sequence, entitled "Mandolin."

Dove's recorded discussions of her decision to compose a narrative sequence, however, focus not on issues of racial traditions but on her interest in the possibilities of generic combination:

> I thought there must be a way to get back into poetry the grandness that narrative can give, plus the sweep of time. Lyric poetry does not have that sweep of time. Lyrics are discrete moments. On the other hand, a lot of narrative poems can tend to bog down in the prosier transitional moments. . . . So one of the things I was trying to do was string moments as beads on a necklace. In other words, I have lyric poems which, when placed one after the other, reconstruct the sweep of time.
>
>   (Schneider 1989, p. 117)

Her wariness of "the prosier transitional moments" of conventional narrative poetry seems determined by a desire to maintain the kind of intensity M. L. Rosenthal and Sally Gall seek in the poetic sequence.

Even so, her avoidance of a continuous narrative in her historical chronicle, *Thomas and Beulah*, extends several aspects of African American literary tradition. Episodic—indeed, chronological episodic—structure is one of the hallmarks of slave narrative, and Dove's sequential lyrics effectively recreate such a movement. In addition, the disjunctive lyric structure of Dove's sequence puts into play those traditional African American "guerrilla techniques of survival" she has mentioned. Her approach to narrative fits the long-standing African American cultural traditions that depend on innuendo, metaphor, circumlocution, and abbreviated suggestion rather than fully explicit elaboration. These devices in themselves are not race-specific, of course, but their use here is racially inflected. Thus, Lawrence Levine's description of black song in his landmark study *Black Culture and Black Consciousness: Afro-American Folk Thought From Slavery to Freedom* suggests analogues in Dove's long poem:

they generally are not vehicles for the telling of explicit, chrono-
logical, developed stories. They more often embody personal com-
ment and reaction and put their message across through innu-
endo, repetition, hints, and allusion. . . . [T]he structural units in
Negro folksongs are typically the metaphor and line rather than
the plot; Negro songs don't tend to weave narrative elements to-
gether to create a story but instead accumulate images to create a
feeling. These characteristics have made black song an especially
effective medium for complaint, protest, and the venting of frustra-
tions. These same qualities, of course, also make it difficult to in-
terpret the meaning of many black songs.

(Levine 1977, p. 240)

Frustration and complaint are recurrent undertones in the poems
of *Thomas and Beulah*—frustration generated in significant part by
the restrictions of a racist society. The poems themselves, resisting
single or simple interpretations, retain an aura of mystery, for
Dove's writing tends toward the cryptic; she prefers the compres-
sion and understatement achieved through juxtaposition and evoc-
ative sensory detail to propositional explanation. Traditions of
deliberately coding information, thereby rendering it opaque to
outsiders, shape Osbey's *Desperate Circumstance, Dangerous Woman*
as well. Neither of these narrative sequences by contemporary Afri-
can Americans tells its story fully or straightforwardly; both rely
heavily on suggestion in recounting and recreating part of the Afri-
can American past.

Both poems' stories, moreover, while involving distinct individu-
als in very particular circumstances, are nonetheless in some ways
historically representative. Both sequences touch upon or connect
with more inclusive narratives of great racial significance. To put
it another way, both poets demonstrate a commitment to what Dove
calls "the underside of history" (Taleb-Khyar 1991, p. 356), not
only in the sense that they approach history through the daily
thoughts and experience of ordinary individuals who are "nobodies
in the course of history" and on the social scale (Rubin and Ingersoll
1986, p. 236), but also in the sense that these individual histories
connect to historical phenomena which—because of racial bias—
have not received the attention they deserve (Rubin and Ingersoll
1986, p. 232).[12] In Osbey's poem, as I will explain later, this phe-
nomenon is the existence within the continental United States of

escaped slave communities or maroons. In Dove's sequence, it is the immense black migration from the rural South to the urban North in the early years of the twentieth century, an upheaval in which her maternal grandparents (the models for Thomas and Beulah) participated.[13] Dove observes:

> Only very recently have historians begun to explore that entire era in any depth and what impact the great migration, as they call it now, had on not only southern communities and northern communities but a host of other things. So much has been done or talked about the uprooting of the black family through slavery, but this was a second uprooting and displacement. It's the first time that blacks in this country had any chance, however stifled, of pursuing "the American dream." Obviously not with the same advantages as whites, not even as the otherwise ostracized European immigrants, and so it is a very poignant era. . . . It's a major population movement in our country that just went largely unrecorded.
>
> (Schneider 1989, pp. 116–17)

Although each of the forty-five poems in *Thomas and Beulah* represents a discrete moment of individual experience (as is usual in mainstream lyric), Dove specifies that "these poems tell two sides of a story and are meant to be read in sequence" (*SP*, p. 137). That story is of two participants in the Great Migration who pursue the American dream, with limited success, throughout forty years of marriage, four decades of American history. A concluding "Chronology" enables precise dating of the poems' events. The first twenty-three poems convey Thomas's "side," depicting his 1919 migration from Tennessee to Akron, Ohio; his responses to the jobs he finds in the north (in Goodyear's zeppelin factory, as a riveter during WWII, as a part-time janitor) and to periods of unemployment; his perspective on his courtship of Beulah and his disappointment on producing four daughters but no sons; his love of music; and his lifelong preoccupation with the drowning of his friend Lem. Thomas's section concludes with his dying moments in 1963 at age sixty-three. Most of Beulah's poems, which follow, present her perceptions after her life in Akron becomes entwined with Thomas's: her responses to courtship, pregnancy, motherhood, the Depression, to her employment after the war in a dress shop and as a milliner, to widowhood, to the Civil Rights Movement. The sequence ends with her death in 1969.

Helen Vendler is perhaps alone among critics of *Thomas and Beulah* in calling attention to the centrality of the migration to this long poem: "[t]his great social movement—one of the most important for American history in the twentieth century—finds here its first extended poem" (Vendler 1986, p. 50). Writing a review rather than a full-length essay, Vendler immediately moves on to discuss the sequence as "also the history of a marriage."[14] More extended focus on the racially specific sociological drama that unfolds here and on the racially significant manner of its presentation, beginning with attention to the links between this migration narrative and some patterns of slave narrative, can open new perspectives for understanding *Thomas and Beulah*.

The sequence begins with the northward movement that is the backbone of African American slave narrative (itself the generic backbone of the African American written tradition) (*SP*, p. 137). The "two Negroes" traveling up-river (probably the Mississippi or perhaps the Ohio) in the opening poem, set in 1919, are in no danger of being sold down-river, but they are as much fugitives from racist oppression as were their escaped-slave predecessors. Economic forces were at the root of the black exodus from the south[15], but sharp increases in lynching and interracial strife were central causes as well.[16] Dove testifies to this historical reality in the poem "Nothing Down," as Thomas in 1928 recollects in disconnected fragments the events prompting his flight from Tennessee. He recalls what appears to be a manhunt/lynching:

Every male on the Ridge
old enough to whistle
was either in the woods
or under a porch.
He could hear the dogs
rippling up the hill.

(*SP*, p. 152)

(The reference to whistling may point to catalyzing events similar to those that later led to the notorious death of Emmett Till; the usual justification for lynching was the protection of white women from supposed sex crimes by black men.) Thomas was among those who took to the woods—initially *"a child's forest . . . gone wild with hope"*—where he found *"silent forgiveness"* (for his own supposed crime? for white brutality?) in a flower, a *"blue trumpet of Heaven"* dangling overhead. By the end of the ordeal, however, his hope was shattered:

> *The air was being torn*
> *into hopeless pieces.*
> *Only this flower hovering*
> *above his head*
> *couldn't hear the screaming.*
> *That is why the petals had grown*
> *so final.*

(SP, p. 153)

Racist violence and the desire to escape it apparently prompted Thomas's agreement with his friend Lem that they should "run away" together.

The northward movement of the slave narrative is a movement from slavery to freedom, but that freedom is heavily qualified, not merely because of the Fugitive Slave Act, but because of continued racism the black narrator encounters in the "free" states. (In his narrative, for instance, Frederick Douglass finds himself unable to work as a ship's caulker in Massachusetts as he had in Baltimore, despite his skill and experience.) This movement into a freedom that is at once an amelioration and a sore disappointment structures Thomas's migration story as well. Consequently, his *bildung* does not follow the characteristic pattern of Anglo-European literature in which the youth's journey out of country innocence results in an ultimately fortunate fall, the achievement of worldly maturity and social integration or success in a more sophisticated realm. The epigraph to Thomas's half of the sequence, taken from Tolson's *Harlem Gallery*, suggests the difference of the African American perspective: "Black Boy, O Black Boy, / is the port worth the cruise?" (*SP*, p. 139). This is not a question the reader is invited to ask in most white *Bildungsroman*; indeed, a poem like Wordsworth's *Prelude* demonstrates the determination with which authors in the Anglo-European tradition may struggle to affirm that the port is worth the cruise and the gains worth the losses. The question is particularly appropriate, however, "among a people who had recently uprooted themselves in pursuit of a dream which, in the disillusioning years of post–World War I race riots, lynchings, and discrimination and the poverty of the Great Depression, seemed increasingly hollow" (Levine 1977, p. 188).

From the opening poem of *Thomas and Beulah* on, Thomas's story reinforces the epigraph's suggestion that for the black migrant in the early years of the twentieth century the port may not be worth the cruise. Here, responding to Thomas's challenge, Lem dives into the water heading for what we might call the "port" of an island.

> *You're so fine and mighty; let's see*
> *what you can do*, said Thomas, pointing
>
> to a tree-capped island.
> Lem stripped, spoke easy: *Them's chestnuts,*
> *I believe.* Dove
>
> quick as a gasp. Thomas, dry
> on deck, saw the green crown shake
> as the island slipped
>
> under, dissolved
> in the thickening stream.
> At his feet
>
> a stinking circle of rags,
> the half-shell mandolin.
> Where the wheel turned the water
>
> gently shirred.
>
> ("The Event," *SP*, pp. 141–42)

The paradise suggested by Lem's "green crown[ed]" destination proves entirely illusory and treacherous; merely a tree snared in the river, it pulls the black man to his death.

Lem's thwarted quest-journey models what lies ahead for Thomas, representing one of a number of ways in which the boat trip north proves not to be a journey to freedom and the promised land. Of course, beyond being an emblem, the event is of overwhelming importance in itself, and not just as a source of grief. Thomas suffers lifelong guilt as well—for having caused Lem's death through his drunken dare, for having stood by "dry / on deck" during Lem's drowning, for having survived as if at the cost of Lem's life.[17] ("The Charm" closes with Thomas hearing Lem's whisper, "*I ain't dead. / I just gave you my life*" [*SP*, p. 164].) Nonetheless, "The Event" establishes a generalizable pattern of disappointment. And while Lem's drowning itself would not represent a common occurrence, other aspects of Thomas's disillusionment and loss of innocence would be typical of migrating black American men of Thomas's era. "Straw Hat," for instance, depicts the poor working conditions most black migrants found in the industrial cities of the North. The poem begins "[i]n the city" circa 1921 where Thomas is "lucky / to sleep third shift" on a smelly mattress used sequentially by men who work the other two shifts. Memories of the Tennessee ridge offer a striking contrast:

> Years before
> he was anything, he lay on
> so many kinds of grass, under stars,
> the moon's bald eye opposing.
>
> He used to sleep like a glass of water
> held up in the hand of a very young girl.
>
> (SP, p. 145)

For the grown man (more worldly, though deluded if he imagines himself much of "anything" in society's eyes), a very different evocation of a female figure suggests powerful ambivalence about what northern life has brought him; post-lapsarian/urban existence yields sensual pleasure and stylish flair but also expanded suffering:

> To him, work is a narrow grief
> and the music afterwards
> is like a woman
> reaching into his chest
> to spread it around. When he sings
>
> he closes his eyes.
> He never knows when she'll be coming
> but when she leaves, he always
> tips his hat.
>
> (SP, p. 145)

At least in economic terms, Thomas seems for a while to be making the advances promised by the American dream. Within a year or two after his arrival in Akron, Thomas in "Courtship" (SP, pp. 146–47) can wrap his yellow silk scarf around Beulah's shoulders and think to himself, "(He made / good money; he could buy another.)" But that same financial solvency leads him to trade his freedom for marriage; it enables him to assure his future father-in-law, "*I'll give her a good life*," while wondering "what was he doing / selling all for a song?" Moreover, material progress does not enable escape from racism, as a poem from which I have already quoted, "Nothing Down," makes clear. Daring to hope that he may participate fully in the American dream, Thomas in that poem purchases a used car, imagining as he does so the admiration and excitement he and Beulah will stir when visiting Tennessee in their own car. In actuality, eight miles outside of Murfreesboro their "sky blue Chandler"—chosen because it was the color of Thomas's salvific trumpet flower—breaks down, leaving the black couple exposed to the ridicule of white men who "halloo past them." This experience is linked in Thomas's psyche with the hope-destroying manhunt that prompted his migration in the first place.

In subsequent years, work conditions remain poor, for instance at the zeppelin factory, where if Thomas is not literally drowned like Lem he feels nonetheless trapped as the submerged Jonah (or as the slaves in ships' holds in the Middle Passage):

> The zeppelin factory
> needed workers, all right—
> but, standing in the cage
> of the whale's belly, sparks
> flying off the joints
> and noise thundering,
> Thomas wanted to sit
> right down and cry.

(SP, p. 154)

And because of the Depression, the relative prosperity of the black migrant proves temporary; in 1930 Thomas loses his car, symbol of increased social status as well as source of literal mobility.

The "Mandolin" poems show Thomas struggling throughout his life to feel like a real man—what the protagonist of a traditional *Bildungsroman* becomes—when almost every aspect of his life, including the circumstances of Lem's death, feels emasculating. Some of this emasculation has little or nothing to do with race: for instance, his producing four daughters and no sons or his being categorized as "frail" and consequently relegated to riveting when employed in Goodyear's war relief work. His loss of employment during the Depression was by no means an experience reserved for black workers. But black workers were particularly hard hit and the incidence of unemployment among blacks was far above that of whites (Johnson and Campbell 1981, p. 93). Similarly, the part-time janitorial job Thomas holds for eight years beginning in 1934, recalled in "The Satisfaction Coal Company," points to the especially limited opportunities available to black workers. Tolson's epigraph, in addressing the black male as "Boy," reflects social as well as linguistic realities for black men in white-dominated America.

The poem "Compendium" (*SP*, p. 158) provides a summary of what migration has brought Thomas by the mid-to-late 1930s: he has given up his expensive tastes and his flashy image ("fine cordials and / his hounds-tooth vest"); the mandolin whose music so charmed the women and allowed expression of his feelings is now unused, "a bug on a nail" in the parlor; a canary has taken his place in his wife's affections. All this suggests a contraction, not an expansion, of his horizons or his sense of personal power and self-worth. A metaphor in one of the bleakest poems—"Definition in the Face of Unnamed Fury," in which Thomas takes down his long unplayed mandolin from the parlor wall—powerfully conveys his sense of reduction in terms of a failure to escape dehumanizing racial oppression: "Each note slips / into querulous rebuke, fingerpads / scored with pain, shallow ditches / to rut in like a runaway slave / with a barking heart" (*SP*, p. 159).

Yet Thomas's tale is not a tragedy, or not simply that. Thus "Compendium" ends with an image pointing to the pleasure Thomas finds in what also disappoints him: "the girls fragrant in their beds." He is a survivor—at times, as in "Lightnin' Blues," even a lucky one—and the moments when he approaches despair are relatively few. Even in his dying moments, depicted in "Thomas at the Wheel," he manages an ironic detachment from the darkest aspects of his situation. Although literally at the wheel of his own vehicle, Thomas, who is experiencing a stroke, is again (or still) without control. "What a joke—" he thinks to himself, "he couldn't ungrip the steering wheel." While he feels his chest "filling with water"—Lem's fate come home to him at last—Thomas looks helplessly at the glove compartment containing the medicine that might have saved him and "laughed as he thought *Oh / the writing on the water*" (*SP*, p. 172). The final saving irony is that such humor, with its acknowledgment of how long he has lived beyond Lem, places Thomas's immediate experience in a larger perspective; to the very end, humor helps him cope with his lot.

Such laughter, a version of what Dove refers to as "the healing laughter of the blues" (Peabody 1985, p. 11), has for centuries been a crucial "compensating mechanism which enabled blacks to confront oppression and hardship" (Levine 1977, p. 299). Dove, then, achieves a nontragic perspective by calling on traditions of black expression that have long helped African Americans deal with suffering and injustice. Healing laughter or saving ironic distance is often evident in the folk culture and folk music with which Thomas is allied in many of the poems. Dove's use of African American musical and folk traditions, to which I now turn, particularly her presentation of Thomas's relation to various forms of traditional African American music, tempers—even as it reinforces—the sense of emasculation, pain, and disappointment pervading much of Thomas's experience. It reinforces, too, the ties between Thomas's individual story and twentieth-century black history, and between Dove's lyric sequence and African-American cultural traditions.

Dove reports that during the composition of *Thomas and Beulah* she was listening to a lot of black music, especially older blues recordings—"everything from Lightnin' Hopkins to older ones like Larry Jackson or some of the recordings that Al Lomax made of musicians, all the way up to Billie Holliday, stopping about in the '50s. It seemed to be the music for the book" (Schneider 1989, p. 118). Bits of countryblues and spirituals or gospel songs as well as musical references are woven into a number of poems in "Mandolin." This follows a practice Dove and Waniek claim typifies black poetry: "instead of the literary references of generic poetry, Black poetry tends to allude to spirituals, the blues, and jazz, often going so far as to mention specific jazz musicians or pop singers by name, as if to insure the place of poetry in that richest tradition of Black culture" (Waniek and Dove 1991, p. 219). This practice also renders Thomas typical of the migrants to the North in that he holds on to familiar musical patterns rooted in West-African and slave cultures. Music seems in his life to have served many of the functions it has long served for African Americans: it "allowed them to express themselves communally and individually, to derive great aesthetic pleasure, to perpetuate traditions, to keep values from eroding, and to begin to create new expressive modes" (Levine 1977, p. 297).

In Thomas's psyche, music is linked to Lem and all he represents, for in their riverboat days they had been the inseparable "*tater bug twins*" (tater bug being vernacular for mandolin). The name Thomas means "twin," and his being left with a "half-shell mandolin" in "The Event" signals, through Dove's description of the instrument's shape, his sense of having lost half of himself and of his musical being.[18] The next poem, "Variation on Pain," opens with "Two strings, one pierced cry," again linking the instrument's construction (paired strings) to the dreadful progression from a tight pair of musicians to one anguished survivor. The poem's final line, "So is the past forgiven," suggests that it is through playing the mandolin—once Lem's, now his—that Thomas comes to terms with his loss and his guilt (*SP*, p. 143). By the time he reaches Akron, Thomas, a dashing ladies' man, was "always jiving" and the young ladies respond "saying *He sure plays // that tater bug / like the devil!*" (*SP*, p. 144).

In "Straw Hat," the figure of music as a woman reaching into Thomas's chest and spreading around the narrow grief of his work captures the emotional complexity of black music, which can simultaneously laugh and lament, convey suffering and soothe pain. Similarly, Dove's use of music in "Refrain" (*SP*, p. 148–49)—a poem about Thomas's sexual and emotional experience of his new marriage—taps the expressive range and complexity of secular songs in the tradition of black countryblues. Three of the poem's eight quatrains are italicized songs which implicitly comment on the action, conveyed in highly metaphorical terms in the other stanzas. The opening stanza in which "The man inside the mandolin / plays a new tune / every night, sailing / past the bedroom window" suggests the hopefulness of beginnings—a period of creativity, of new emotions and fresh expression. Similarly, the poem's first bit of song conveys Thomas's lively sense of empowerment, of knowing how to play the game and get what one needs out of life—

> *Take a gourd and string it*
> *Take a banana and peel it*
> *Buy a baby blue Nash*
> *And wheel and deal it*

But the lines immediately following sound more ominous notes; the man inside the mandolin, an image for Thomas that reminds us again of his fraught bond to Lem, is now figured as having tied himself to a raised mast with rags, "drunker / than a robin on the wing." Mention of rags recalls the "stinking circle of rags" in "Event," the clothes Lem stripped off that lie at Thomas's feet when Lem drowns. The suggestion is that Thomas has tied himself to marriage as a kind of penance, restraining himself from a wilder life; his inebriation suggests abandon but also a longing to escape reality, perhaps a desire for the lost freedom of the migratory robin. The passage of song that follows returns to being upbeat and confident, though at the same time acknowledging the singer's position of economic subservience:

> *Count your kisses*
> *Sweet as honey*
> *Count your boss'*
> *Dirty money*

The next three quatrains depict the couple's sexual intercourse, largely in positive terms, but not without ambivalence. The heavy bed's "clumsy" "pitching" motion is unromantic at best. The phrase "a man and a wife," however, gives to the husband a priority and masculinity he presumably values. The couple's having sex— Thomas's rolling over to scatter the ruffles and silk of Beulah's nightgown "stiff with a dog's breath / among lilies [ambiguously, flowers of death as well as resurrection] / and ripening skin"—is presented with further ambiguity as a way to "shut . . . up" the man in the mandolin. But his music sounds again at the poem's close:

> *Love on a raft*
> *By the light o' the moon*
> *And the bandit gaze*
> *Of the old raccoon.*

Although invoking the lazy pleasures of the rural South, in the context of Thomas's history and Lem's drowning in a moonlit river, this passage of song reinforces the sense of haunted constraint on Thomas, almost as if Lem were the watching "coon." Reminders of loss, of limit, of guilt qualify the aura of personal and sexual freedom in this final image. Following long-established traditions of black music, this poem infused with song refuses to sentimentalize or glamorize reality; it achieves a distanced, lightly ironic perspective on a multifaceted situation that could be better—but could certainly be worse as well.

Thomas later shifts from the mandolin to gospel singing as his primary mode of musical expression. This move, which reflects the increasing popularity of gospel music in America from the 1930s on, may in Thomas's case represent further penance, a sacrifice of secular music in order to focus on the spiritual realm. Certainly, the shift from blues to gospel signals a change in focus from this world to the next. According to Mahalia Jackson, "Blues are the songs of despair, but gospel songs are the songs of hope" (quoted in Levine 1977, p. 174); this hope, however, is otherworldly, focusing on the rest, peace, and justice promised in the hereafter. In the poem "Gospel" (*SP*, pp. 165–66)—which is linked to "Refrain" by its quatrain form—the figurative ship is not the mandolin sailing past the bedroom window or the marriage bed, but a community of suffering: "*Swing low so I / can step inside— / a humming ship of voices / big with all // the wrongs done / done them.*" Paradoxically, it is the largeness of suffering that makes the congregation's communal voice too "generous" to fail—suggesting not only that those who pay heavily in this world will be rewarded in the next, but also that reward will come to those who, in their generosity, do not dwell unforgivingly on wrongs done them. Paradox and oxymoron continue to dominate the poem: the animal misery of the congregation is a fortress, the tenor's voice is at once chill and enraptured, the sky toward which his notes rise is "blank with promise." Thomas is the tenor "enraptured // with sacrifice." In contrast with his (and the congregation's) suffering-is-good-for-your-soul orientation is the far simpler "healthy" attitude of "the single contralto" (unmarried as well as a solo voice?) "settling deeper / into her watery furs!" Thomas is momentarily tempted by the pleasures of her earthward orientation, but the spirit of immediate self-denial triumphs for the sake of ultimate reward:

> *Carry me home,*
> she cajoles, bearing
>
> down. Candelabras
> brim. But he slips
> through God's net and swims
> heavenward, warbling.

Historically, the rise of gospel music corresponded with a sharpening division between the sacred and secular in black culture (Levine 1977, pp. 176–79). Dove's poetic sequence suggests Thomas ultimately turned back toward the secular and to the sustenance of the secular elements of his folk heritage. The chronology would place "Gospel" close to Thomas's 1946 decision to quit the gospel choir of the A. M. E. Zion Church. The next poem, "Roast Possum," is set in the mid-1950s and depicts Thomas telling stories to three grandchildren, including his only grandson Malcolm. His narratives draw upon his Tennessee roots to demonstrate the triumphs of *"old-time know-how"* and to portray characters (in this case, a horse named Strolling Jim) who, against all odds, earned the respect due *men*. For his sole male heir especially, Thomas enters wholeheartedly into the tradition of African American storytelling, "invent[ing] / embellishments" to his childhood experiences while passing on the survival strategies and the values of the Southern rural community into which he was born:[19]

> He could have gone on to tell them
> that the Werner [Encyclopedia] admitted Negro children
> to be intelligent, though briskness
> clouded over at puberty, bringing
> indirection and laziness. Instead,
> he added: *You got to be careful*
> *with a possum when he's on the ground;*
> *he'll turn on his back and play dead*
> *till you give up looking. That's*
> *what you'd call sullin'.*
>
> Malcolm interrupted to ask
> who owned Strolling Jim,
> and who paid for the tombstone.
> They stared each other down
> man to man, before Thomas,
> as a grandfather, replied:
>   *Yessir,*
> *we enjoyed that possum. We ate him*
> *real slow, with sweet potatoes.*

(SP, p. 168)

Fable, we should recall, is one of the devices Dove and Waniek list among the "folk sources which have nurtured the race since slavery" (Waniek and Dove 1991, p. 217); here it is an antidote to the racist mythology perpetuated by the encyclopedia. Perhaps more than any other poem in the "Mandolin" section, this one suggests how the port may come to seem worth the cruise for the black male migrant: when Thomas in the North himself reaches the rank of elder—traditionally in black culture a position deserving respect—he can feel himself a man in his role of grandfather/griot. Passing on the values he himself inherited as well as what he learned from his own experience, he can enjoy the prospect of their further transmission through his heirs (ironically, he focuses on his male heir, when it is the granddaughter, Rita Dove, who will insure that his stories are not forgotten). He can savor like a possum dinner the experience of simultaneously recollecting the past and shaping the future. Survival itself, and particularly the generational continuity of the family and its stories, is affirmed. That survival, Thomas's wisdom suggests, is achieved through a combination of resources: through traditional tricksterlike strategies associated with the "sullin'" possum (who on one level figures the black man, or the seemingly lazy [sullen] black child); through sheer toughness and courage (also the possum's traits); through the wariness exemplified by Thomas-as-hunter; through specific skills that more conventionally constitute "know-how"; through the cultivation of memory; and through the ability to take pleasure when the opportunity lies—like sweet potatoes or a good yarn—before you.

Through Thomas, Dove emphasizes the sustaining character of black folk traditions. By evoking patterns characteristic of slave narrative and by tapping the resources of oral forms such as the blues, Dove demonstrates in Thomas's poems how weaving African American traditions into the Anglo-European poetic sequence can give the lyric sequence an emotionally and historically charged range and depth of understated suggestion.

In the character Beulah and her section of poems, "Canary in Bloom," Dove presents a very different personality with a different early history, different roots, and sometimes a very different perspective on the circumstances she and Thomas have in common. Dove's strategy of including "two sides of a story" insists on the uniqueness of the individual (a perspective underlying much contemporary lyric).[20] Dove is always cautious about approaching people in terms of groups, wary that it will obscure individual identity and individual difference; she insures here that her readers will not generalize about the black experience—even about the experience of a particular generation of black migrants to Akron, Ohio—on the basis of merely one man's perspective. This "two sides" approach, though not involving different *racial* perspectives, enacts a version of the "binocular vision" she finds necessary to the writer and inevitably developed by African Americans; it fosters recognition of the multiple sides to any story based in historical experience and of the complex relation between personal and historical "truth." In addition, this strategy enables us to see how gender difference affects "the underside of history" (Taleb-Khyar 1991, p. 356). For Beulah encounters limitations and oppressions that have been faced particularly, though not exclusively, by African American women in this century.

Beulah's family, according to the chronology, migrated to Akron from Georgia in 1906 when she was two years old. Consequently, she does not have the direct ties to Southern folk culture that Thomas does, nor does the migration itself figure in her memories. She rarely experiences herself as one who left her cultural home behind her, and her sense of connection to her black folk heritage— though not to the black church—seems more attenuated than his. Her cultural heritage is presumably more mixed than Thomas's since her father is half-Cherokee, though this mixture does not register formally in the poem.

Not just the migration, but public history generally seems to impinge less on the poems in Beulah's section. Reflecting the legacy of the nineteenth-century middle-class ideology of "separate spheres," this difference between the "two sides" of Dove's story reinforces our awareness of gender difference in the narrative. While Thomas in "Weathering Out" leaves every day seeking work and returns "every evening nearly // in tears," Beulah floats placidly through her pregnancy. Even in "A Hill of Beans" (*SP*, pp. 181–82)—where Beulah feeds increasingly desperate hobos increasingly limited fare until, sensing a suicidal edge to their terror, she "made Thomas / board up the well"—she seems at least partially buffered from anxiety by being neither part of the paid work force nor the designated provider for her family.[21] "Thomas tossed on his pillow / as if at sea." Beulah, however, could remain resourceful within her sphere: when "money failed for peaches" for her cobblers, she pulled rhubarb instead.

If Thomas's section is dominated by backward-looking guilt and regret, Beulah's is dominated by longing (the word "want" appears again and again), often projected toward the future as a desire for travel to distant exotic places. The epigraph, from early twentieth-century black poet Anne Spencer, points to the intensity of Beulah's imaginative life—"Ah, how the senses flood at my repeating, / As once in her fire-lit heart I felt the furies / Beating, beating" (*SP*, p. 173)—while subsequent poems reveal how the circumstances of her life prevent its full expression. Beulah is an artist manqué (not unlike the mother Alice Walker celebrates in "In Search of Our Mothers' Gardens"); Dove herself perhaps embodies what Beulah might have been had she lived in an era according greater opportunities to black women.

The second poem, "Magic," reveals the extent to which imaginative curiosity dominated Beulah's mental life in childhood. She is so intrigued by watching knives sharpening on a grindstone that she bends over the wheel long enough to wear away not only the knife blades but her own flesh. Though her brow becomes "stippled with blood," her concentration is so intense she feels no pain. She believes in magic, which she approaches as an art form, and the poem's closing example shows her using this belief to reduce the terror of the racism that surrounds her; like most superstition, her belief serves to increase an illusion of control over her fate:

> One night she awoke
> and on the lawn blazed
> a scaffolding strung in lights.
> Next morning the Sunday paper
> showed the Eiffel Tower
> soaring through clouds.
> It was a sign
>
> she would make it to Paris one day.

> (*SP*, p. 176)

By the time Thomas is courting her, depicted in "Courtship, Diligence," Beulah's desire to reach that exotic otherland takes the form of social pretensions manifest in a silent scorn for his folksy style. She responds to his mandolin as "Cigar box music! / She'd much prefer a pianola / and scent in a sky-colored flask" (*SP*, p. 177). The poem "Dusting" (*SP*, pp. 179–80) reveals that she continues during the early months (perhaps years) of marriage to long for someone/something "finer." As she dusts, she daydreams about a boy who "years before" had given her a kiss and a "clear bowl with one bright / fish, rippling / wound!" She recalls once warming the fishbowl when it froze, releasing the fish to swim free from its locket of ice (not unlike Thomas swimming heavenward in "Gospel"). The only freedoms Beulah enjoys as she patiently dusts the solarium are those of fantasy and memory, suggested by her final recollection of the boy's French name, Maurice.

Hers are different survival strategies from her husband's. Where he finds sustenance in fishing, singing, even walking under the viaduct, her forms of solace reflect the physical limitation, the domestic enclosure of a woman's life. That enclosure and how Beulah copes with its constriction are the subjects of "Daystar," in which, as the mother of small children, she can find "a little room for thinking" only by hauling a chair behind the garage during the brief period when they are napping:

> And just *what* was mother doing
> out back with the field mice? Why,
>
> building a palace. Later
> that night when Thomas rolled over and
> lurched into her, she would open her eyes
> and think of the place that was hers
> for an hour—where
> she was nothing,
> pure nothing, in the middle of the day.

(SP, p. 188)

The next poem, "Obedience," portrays a nighttime version of such imaginative transcendence of her material circumstance, where she allows her "free" mind to re-create her physical environment so that it obeys her wishes:

> That smokestack, for instance,
> in the vacant lot across the street:
> if she could order it down and watch
> it float in lapse-time over buckled tar and macadam
> it would stop an inch or two perhaps
> before her patent leather shoes.

(SP, p. 189)

The world as she would create it would have an expansive freedom lacking in her reality:

> but she would never create such puny stars.
> The house, shut up like a pocket watch,
> those tight hearts breathing inside—
> she could never invent them.

(SP, p. 189)

As Beulah later moves from a life dominated by the responsibilities of motherhood into the public working world, race figures more explicitly as a restriction, and we see her rejecting her earlier idealizing perspective on Paris and the white culture it represents. In the same year that Thomas quits the gospel choir, Beulah takes work at Charlotte's Dress Shoppe. The title of the poem depicting this phase of her life, "The Great Palaces of Versailles" (*SP*, pp. 190–91), echoes, with irony, the palaces in the air Beulah built behind her garage as well as her childhood vision of the soaring Eiffel Tower. While the white girls are saleswomen, Beulah does alterations in the backroom. The "nast[y]" odor of stale Evening of Paris mixed with perspiration rises from the white woman's dress she is ironing, while the white employees chatter and laugh out front. Confronting corruption beneath the glamour of white society, she recalls what she has read about court ladies in the gardens at Versailles. "[L]ifting shy layers of silk, / they dropped excrement as daintily / as handkerchieves," while the *cavaliere* in their fine clothes amused themselves by urinating along the walls of the *Orangerie*.

Part of what Beulah finds offensive about white culture (in addition to the racism it fosters, even if in the North that racism is often disguised, elaborately costumed) is its positioning of women as helpless. This ideology is self-consciously dramatized by Autumn in the dress shop—a "girl" who dresses to make her face appear delicate and who tosses her blond hair in imitation of Lauren Bacall—"sighing / *I need a man who'll protect me*." In contrast to that image of female weakness stands Beulah. Her name itself suggests that she is a source of stability and strength for those around her; meaning marriage, "Beulah" is also the land of Israel in the biblical book of Isaiah and a country of rest and peace in *Pilgrim's Progress*. She lives up to this name, for instance, in "Weathering Out," where she sometimes finds the unemployed Thomas sleeping with his head on her pregnant belly, mirroring their sleeping child in utero.

A tradition, even a community, of strong black women is suggested in Beulah's poems through the portrayal of her mother and of Willemma, Thomas's sister. The opening poem of Beulah's sequence reveals that, although Beulah "was Papa's girl" (as her later preoccupation with her father testifies), her father is an alcoholic described in terms that stress unreliability—changing skin color, swaying stance, slipping smile, intermittent violence. Mama, on the other hand, "never changed." And when he threatens her daughter (the suggestion is of incestuous desire), she responds with fierce determination: *"Touch that child // and I'll cut you down / just like the cedar of Lebanon"* (*SP*, p. 175). The only other poem in which Beulah's mother figures is "Sunday Greens." The short-lined lyric describing Beulah's preparation of the family's usual Sunday ham dinner is another piece about Beulah's sense of entrapment in sameness and domestic responsibility and about her desire for travel and adventure. Her mother provides an image—contrasting with Beulah—of freedom and abandon *within* domestic routine, a freedom tied to rural tradition:

> she pauses, remembers
> her mother in a slip
> lost in blues,
> and those collards,
> wild-eared,
> singing.
>
> (*SP*, p. 195)

Willemma, similarly, combines African American country traditions with personal strength and freedom. As recollected by Beulah, this old-fashioned Tennessee hick achieves a kind of exoticism within authentic traditions, making her one model for what Beulah herself wants but has failed to achieve. In "Pomade"—which follows directly after "The Great Palaces of Versailles"—the perfume of the hair ointment Willemma makes, like her leaning cabin without running water or electricity, contrasts with the stale odor of "Evening of Paris" and all of the "progress" and pretention it represents:

> *Beebalm*. The fragrance always put her [Beulah]
> in mind of Turkish minarets against
> a sky wrenched blue,

sweet and merciless. Willemma could wear her gray hair twisted
in two knots at the temples and still smell like travel.
But all those years she didn't budge.

(SP, p. 193)

The positioning of this poem (like "Sunday Greens") late in the
sequence, so that the occasion when Willemma taught Beulah how
to make pomade appears as a memory of a time long past, may sug-
gest that only late in life was Beulah ready to see the value of Wil-
lemma's (or her mother's) example and of the folk ways they repre-
sent. She came late to appreciate what could be found close to home.
This is suggested, too, by the later poems showing more acknowl-
edgment of her profound bond to Thomas.

Yet even if Beulah is capable of changes in perspective, nonethe-
less, her curiosity, her desire to see the world and to create imagina-
tively, remain largely thwarted. "Headdress," which describes Beu-
lah creating a hat after taking up millinery in 1950, represents the
closest Beulah comes to fulfillment as an artist. The hat she is mak-
ing is an emblem for her own desire ("The hat . . . is no pet trained /
to sit still. . . . The hat / wants more."), which she seems at last in
a position to satisfy. But it also reflects the customer's desires, which
prevent Beulah from making something truly expressive of herself.
This ornate object made of "[s]pangled / tulle . . . in green /
and gold and sherry," with three "pearl-tipped spears," feathers, and a
double rose is too exotic even for Beulah. She "would have settled /
for less"—as indeed she has throughout her life. Now at last that
settling seems potentially valuable and deliberate.

Yet by the time she has completed her work of art (a process so
terrifying and absorbing that it interrupts her usual habits of prayer)
Beulah fully embraces its amusing excess, its bold disproportion, its
refusal to settle for less:

> Finished it's a mountain
> on a dish, a capitol
> poised on a littered shore.
> The brim believes
> in itself, its
> double rose and feathers
> ashiver. Extravagance
> redeems. O

intimate parasol
that teaches to walk
with grace along beauty's seam.

(SP, p. 194)

Settling is never lastingly Beulah's wish. Poignantly, the final poem of "Canary in Bloom," entitled "The Oriental Ballerina" (*SP*, pp. 201–2), portrays Beulah's death as a relinquishing of her fantasies about the "other side of the world" where life is dramatically different and more beautiful. Her final thought: *"There is no China."*

In that testifying is Dove's project, she might more accurately have defined the term not as telling "the" truth but as telling "a" truth through story; for everything about Dove's sequence insists that truth is relative to one's position and experience, and therefore truths are multiple. Even the "Chronology," with its interweaving of public and private events, reinforces this point; referring to that list of dates while moving though the poems strengthens the reader's awareness that moments of historical record take on very idiosyncratic personal meanings. (Thomas, for instance, experiences the Akron zeppelin disaster in terms of survivor's guilt vis-à-vis Lem.) An individual's response to the historical or political import of public events is highly mediated by other factors. Thus, when Beulah in "Wingfoot Lake" (*SP*, pp. 198–99) recalls viewing the television broadcast of the great 1963 Civil Rights March on Washington, the march is for her an emblem of painful solitude rather than primarily an image of solidarity; Thomas had died only weeks before and "she stood alone for hours / in front of the T.V. set." She also experiences it as a reminder that "[w]here she came from / was the past," while the present belongs to her daughters' generation.

By building over the course of "Canary in Bloom" a portrait of a particular woman within her time and circumstances, Dove makes Beulah's fearful response to the "crow's wing" of the marchers moving "slowly through / the white streets of government" something a reader can neither condemn nor condone. It is simply one person's truth, perhaps a common one in Beulah's generation. Yet at the same time, by depicting the march seen through Beulah's eyes as "[t]hat brave swimming," Dove brings us full circle to "The Event" (while recalling as well several other poems with swimming figures, such as "Gospel" and "Dusting"), so as to suggest that the aborted bold swim of the Negro migrant in the early decades of the century is in some ways taken up again by the generation that insists *"we're Afro-Americans now!"* (*SP*, p. 198).

As noted earlier, in her poetry Rita Dove is not given to proclaiming racial identity in terms as direct as those she assigns to Beulah's daughters conversing in the mid-1960s; her writing does not obviously follow the conventions most frequently associated with black writing in recent decades. She has struggled against critical biases that impede recognition of her multicultural, assimilating approach to tradition as legitimately and proudly African American. Because of narrow prescriptions of what constitutes authentically black writing, black readers in particular have been uncomfortable with what many have perceived as Dove's lack of racial consciousness. White critics as well as black have frequently overlooked the importance of race and racial history to *Thomas and Beulah*. In contrast to Dove's sequence, Brenda Marie Osbey's poetry, which relies heavily on vernacular models of narration, in many ways fits the widely acknowledged conventions of African American writing. Osbey's sequence differs from Dove's in employing a simpler and less compressed, as well as more thoroughly vernacular, style; in relying more obviously on verbal or syntactic repetition as a unifying device; and in emphasizing a community larger than the family. All of these traits are widely considered characteristic of black literary forms. Like Dove's sequence, Osbey's is a highly elliptical episodic narrative, but— more obviously than Dove's—its silences are linked to the silences in black America's historical record, which may register deliberate coding and withholding by blacks, deliberate erasure by whites of information challenging their dominance and supposed superiority, and/or the loss to modern culture of knowledge formerly transmitted through song and storytelling. Osbey's different approach to the lyric sequence as a form for testifying narrative—itself a manifestation of the diversity of African American poetry today—demonstrates that the testifying project within the genre of the long poem may be adapted to divergent senses of poetic form and language, to disparate visions of individual and group identity and of the interaction between the two.

Both Dove's and Osbey's long poems are affiliated with Gates's broad tradition of "the speakerly text"—"a text whose rhetorical strategy is designed to represent an oral literary tradition, designed 'to emulate the phonetic, grammatical, and lexical patterns of actual speech and produce the "'illusion of oral narration'"'" (Gates 1988, p. 181). But they employ distinct narrative techniques and alternative ways of incorporating the vernacular so that their texts may, in differing degrees, speak with "a black difference" (Gates 1988, p. xxii). When Dove's third-person poems achieve an oral character, they usually do so by blurring the line between impersonal narrative commentary and the character's spoken voice, as Zora Neale Hurston's free indirect discourse does; language appropriate to the character merges with the language of the poet/narrator.[22] Beulah's poem "Pomade," for instance, from which I have already quoted, opens with the two voices nearly indistinguishable:

> She sweeps the kitchen floor of the river bed her husband saw fit
> to bring home with his catfish, recalling
> a flower—very straight,
> with a spiked collar arching
> under a crown of bright fluffy worms—
> she had gathered in armfuls
> along a still road in Tennessee. Even then
> he was forever off in the woods somewhere in search
> of a magic creek.
>
> (*SP*, p. 192)

The metaphor of the flower's collar arching under a crown manages to sound as if it were part of Beulah's thoughts (particularly given her interest in courts and royalty) in the context of such folksy phrases as "her husband saw fit to bring home" or "forever off in the woods somewhere."

In contrast to Dove's third-person sequence, Osbey's *Desperate Circumstance, Dangerous Woman*—subtitled "a narrative poem" and divided into titled units Osbey calls "chapters"—relies heavily on the first person. The work's simulation of autobiographical statement through the use of monologue places it in the center of African American written tradition. For as Gates has observed, "the predominance of the first-person form" in black writing attests that

> the impulse to testify, to chart the peculiar contours of the individual protagonist on the road to becoming, clearly undergirds even the fictional tradition of black letters. . . . Constructed upon an ironic foundation of autobiographical narratives written by ex-

slaves, the African-American tradition, more clearly and directly than most, traces its lineage—in the act of declaring the existence of a surviving, enduring ethnic self—to this impulse of autobiography.

(Gates 1991, p. 4)

Osbey's sequence, unlike Dove's, employs lots of direct dialogue and internal monologue with a distinctly spoken (and specifically regional) cast in diction and syntax. Here, for instance, is part of an easygoing exchange in which Percy, the obsessed lover of the main character, Marie, responds to his father's asking " 'how is that skinny woman of yours?' ":

> "marie don't change, old man" i tell him.
> "nòn" he says.
> "nòn.
> i wouldn't think she did.
> wouldn't think she did.
> but then you know what you doing.
> (*a grunt*)
> *only* one knows."

(Osbey 1991, p. 42; cited hereafter as *DC*)

Even unspoken thoughts may be narrated as if addressed to another; here Percy recounts his thoughts and actions by inwardly addressing Marie:

> i walk up on you standing there in the kitchen door.
> you turn around
> could be you're right.
> not as if you ever *did* me any harm
> but then you never had to.
> what you put on me
> you put on me day-one.
> i sit down at the table, push back my sleeves.
> and when you turn around
> there's not a speck of kindness in your face for me.

(*DC*, p. 60)

Osbey's narrator, who is not a dramatized character, sometimes speaks directly to the reader as if to an immediately present listener, although one whose outsider status limits what he or she should hear. At one point, the narrator stops her(or him)self from digressing inappropriately: "but that is another tale / and more than is wise for you to know" (*DC*, p. 33).

Osbey identifies a specifically African American ancestry for her narration of ordinary lives in *Desperate Circumstance, Dangerous Woman*: a tradition of the "narrative and historical poem" treating specific episodes in African American history (Osbey 1993, p. 481). In contrast to Dove, she belongs in the camp of African American writers and critics who want to de-emphasize the "mulatto" character of black writing. Her perspective appears similar to that of Calvin Hernton, for instance, who in 1985 described "most contemporary black women's poetry" as continuing and beginning anew "the oral-narrative-poetic tradition of Maria Stewart, Sojourner Truth, and Frances E. W. Harper in the nineteenth century, and of Georgia Douglas Johnson, Effie Lee Newsome, Helen Johnson, Ann Spenser [Anne Spencer], Gwendolyn Bennett, and a host of others in the early twentieth century" (Hernton 1985, p. 524).[23] The "tradition of narrative chronicling the exigencies of black life in America" began with spirituals, Hernton explains, continued in the prose of autobiographical slave narratives, and kept evolving in the musical forms of twentieth-century blues, ragtime, and jazz (1985, pp. 529–30).[24]

It is partly because Osbey does not share Dove's multicultural view of the traditions informing her work that *Desperate Circumstance, Dangerous Woman* extends and diversifies the model of historical testifying I have traced in *Thomas and Beulah*. Before examining *Desperate Circumstances* as a testifying long poem, however, I wish to describe an exchange between its author and a reviewer, Ben Downing, that suggests what is at stake in placing a poem—especially one by a person of color—within particular traditions or generic types. Downing's response to Osbey's poem is limited both by his apparent ignorance of the historical contexts on which it depends and by his evaluation of the work—without consciousness of his own bias—in terms of white standards and traditions, particularly the perspectives and techniques of high modernism. Osbey's rebuttal, which situates her work exclusively in a black tradition as if to deny any white ancestry for her work, overstates the case, much as Grahn's depiction of a separate lesbian tradition exaggerates its autonomy; in context, however, the political impulses for such gestures are easily comprehensible.

Downing's review, "Big City, Long Poem," evaluates three works—by Vikram Seth, Osbey, and Frank Menchaca—which for Downing raise questions about "how best to convey, through poetry, the palpable sense of a city one loves, and how far poetry itself can stray into other genres [specifically, prose fiction] before erasing its signature powers" (Downing 1993a, p. 220). His touchstone is Eliot's *The Waste Land*, which "proved that, given ample breathing room, a single poem could modulate rapidly enough to catch the modern city's jagged rhythms" (1993a, p. 219). Reading Osbey's poem, Downing misses the "speed, cacophony, and swirling activity that usually mark urban writing" (1993a, p. 224), finding instead a "languid" atmosphere, an unhurried rural tempo, and a dearth of action. Among the weaknesses in this text he ultimately finds monotonous, Downing identifies as "most disappointing" that:

> the poem contributes little to our literary image of New Orleans. Never having visited New Orleans, I am familiar with it largely through novels, and had hoped that *Desperate Circumstance, Dangerous Woman* would bring a poet's particular dazzle to my own mirage of that city. Instead I found myself comparing the poem unfavorably with New Orleans novels. It lacks the exuberant lunacy of [John Kenney Toole's] *A Confederacy of Dunces* and [Walker Percy's] *The Moviegoer*'s brooding air of humid ennui. In form it resembles Michael Ondaatje's *Coming Through Slaughter*, but Osbey's poetry is considerably less rich than Ondaatje's prose.
> Tonally, it reminds me more than anything of *The Awakening*'s restrained gentility. Although born in the city of jazz, the poem is remarkably devoid of its energetic riffs.
> (Downing 1993a, p. 229)[25]

The next issue of *Parnassus*, the journal in which the review appeared, contains both a responding letter from Osbey and Downing's reply. Osbey writes in anger to correct what seem to her glaring misreadings involving, for instance, the poem's temporal setting (which Downing takes to be contemporary, but which Osbey identifies as "early in the 20th century" [Osbey 1993, p. 481]) or the efficacy of the main character's quest (Downing sees failure where Osbey intended to suggest her protagonist's spiritual and physical "transform[ation]" occurring "when she learns of her mother's and therefore her own connection to the maroons of the Louisiana swamps" [Osbey 1993, p. 480]). But Osbey's more fundamental purpose is to correct Downing's attempt "to force *Desperate Circumstance, Dangerous Woman* into a tradition of which it is so apparently not part." That tradition is predominantly white and male (as well as novelistic). "There is," she asserts, "a longstanding tradition of the narrative and historical poem among African American writers dating back at least as far as 1746 and Lucy Terry Prince's 'Bars Fight.' Gayl Jones, Sherley Anne Williams, Colleen McElroy, Jay Wright, and Robert Hayden are but a few who have written about different African and African American communities and different eras in the last forty or so years" (Osbey 1993, p. 481). Moreover, she reminds us, New Orleans is an African/Creole city in which 70 percent of the population is African American. "This is the history, language, and tradition, largely unknown—and certainly not explored in the works of Percy, O'Toole, or Ondaatje—out of which I am writing" (Osbey 1993, p. 481). She deplores both the stereotyping on which the reviewer's expectations of New Orleans writing depend and his ignorance of (or disinterest in) the culture and literary tradition from which she writes.

Downing's essential defense in his reply (I omit the more cutting remarks peppering both sides of this exchange) is that the flaws he points to are flaws independent of knowledge about the work's context or traditions: "no amount of background reading could have made me like the things I disliked in *Desperate Circumstance*, or dislike those I liked" (Downing 1993b, p. 483). Offended by Osbey's insinuations of racism, he asserts that she is "mistaken in thinking that I treated her as a trifling epigone of the Great White Tradition of New Orleans Writers"; he claims that the novels he chose for comparison, rather than representing a tradition, were simply works that, like Osbey's, depict New Orleans and desire "to immerse their audience in a specific atmosphere" (Downing 1993b, p. 483).

The issues their exchange raises—concerning the importance of readers' recognizing ethnic traditions and of their possessing specific bodies of historical and cultural knowledge, as well as the role this information should play in critical evaluation of literature—are complex and politically charged. Consensus about some aspects of this exchange may nonetheless be possible. Certainly, a reader who brings inappropriate expectations to a work is likely to be disappointed. In this case, Downing has a prior sense of what it feels like to live in a city and how a writer should go about representing it; he seeks a poem that captures the "ways in which [a city] impinges upon [the residents] moment by moment, a relentless bombardment kindling consciousness one instant and fracturing it the next." His preference for works heterogeneous in form (as opposed to what he labels Osbey's "confinement" within the monologue) stems partly from his own geographically and historically determined sense of urban experience, both shaped by and shaping his allegiance to Eliotic collage. Even while he admits his own "Manhattocentric-ity" (1993a, p. 233), Downing fails to comprehend fully that Osbey's African/Creole milieu is a fundamentally different kind of city. This blindness may be racially inflected, though one can imagine black residents of Manhattan finding alien, and perhaps implausible, the relaxed pace of Osbey's New Orleans. More damning is Downing's inability to recognize the positive significance of the protagonist's discovery of her link to the maroons—a term thoroughly glossed in the notes; this striking failure illustrates the limits of understanding imposed by ethnocentric historical ignorance.[26]

Downing's assertion that "Any poem worth its salt should be self-sufficient" (to which he adds, "which *Desperate Circumstance* certainly is")—that its meaning and value should emerge independent of the reader's prior knowledge—is naive and at least potentially ethnocentric. Perceptions of "self-sufficiency" are relative (and, surely, few readers could construct an understanding of Downing's exemplary text, *The Waste Land*, without critical guides). Many Americans are relatively ignorant of the histories of oppressed groups in the nation, yet such knowledge is necessary for fullest appreciation of works by many writers of color.

Failing to acknowledge the presence of non-Anglo-European tra-ditions not only distorts Downing's interpretation and evaluation of the text at hand but also repeats the dominant society's erasure of the history those traditions embody. Yet Downing might also have been vulnerable to criticism if he *had* written of Osbey exclu-sively in a racially specific context, for positioning minority writers solely or automatically within minority traditions can risk further ghettoization. As noted earlier, absolute separation of racial tradi-tions, while possibly serving cultural nationalist agendas, distorts literary history.

How profoundly will recognizing the appropriate traditions in-forming a work and understanding the historical contexts of its nar-rative affect evaluation? That is a complicated matter. Without knowledge of a blues tradition, for instance, a critic might inappropriately perceive a Langston Hughes blues-based poem as too simple or tediously repetitive. Yet identifying a poem as a work within the blues mode does not guarantee its quality. Such knowledge will shape the appropriate evaluative questions but should not preclude evaluative criticism. There may, then, be some legitimacy in Downing's complaint in his reply to Osbey, "I fail to see how the dullness of the poem's language could be excused or relieved by knowing when it is set" (Downing 1993b, p. 482). Indeed, I myself find greater richness in the metaphorical and imagistic density of Dove's lyrics—traits valued within the white poetic mainstream since high modernism—than in Osbey's more prosaic idiomatic lines. But "richness" is not the only legitimate evaluative criterion, while the perception of linguistic "dullness" may be culturally inflected. (Returning to the example of a Hughes blues poem, might not its repetitions feel monotonous to one reader and richly suggestive to another who hears them with a differently trained ear?) Understanding the traditions shaping the poem's language promises to open up more appreciative perspectives. In the reading of Osbey's sequence to follow, I attend to the relevant history and note the effect temporal and geographical setting as well as ethnic traditions may have on language, form, and technique so that future readers will have broadly informed bases for their evaluation.

The characters in all of Osbey's poetry collections occupy a very particular historical niche as ordinary residents of New Orleans in the first half of the twentieth century (Osbey 1987, p. 40). She describes her poetry as "a kind of cultural biography, a cultural geography": "Louisiana's folklore has far outstripped its recorded history. I try to re-create something of that, of the *experience* of the culture, the family history, and the folk history, in my work" (1987, pp. 34–35). She accomplishes this re-creation by giving voice to female (usually) characters who are distinctly Louisiana women and who are presented in the context of their communities. Osbey has labeled her kind of writing "*community of narrative/narrative of community.* . . . I see narrative as a kind of community—the talking to and the talking about or through" (1987, p. 43). Her linkage of talk and narrative is significant; the primary linguistic models for Osbey's poetry are oral and vernacular. The monologues constructing the story of *Desperate Circumstance, Dangerous Woman* explore the situation and inner realities of three characters: centrally, the young black woman Marie Crying Eagle, but also Marie's lover Percy who is so obsessed with Marie that he feels himself Hoodoo-ed by her, and her recently deceased mother's former friend, the conjure woman Regina. Some sections employ a third-person narrator to flesh out the sense of their community in the Faubourg Marigny, the largely black creole district where most of the poem is set— "this part of town / [where] there is a tale for everything" (*DC*, p. 34).

The structural/thematic commonalities with slave narratives evident in Dove's poem—the movement of northward migration toward a partially disappointing quasi-freedom—appear but in more shadowy form. As already noted, Osbey relies on the first-person testimony that is fundamental to slave narrative. Her protagonist's journey toward freedom, however, is an internal quest that is also an exploration of memory and generational history. Composed of twelve "chapters" followed by a "Glossary of Louisiana and New Orleans Ethnic Expressions and Place Names," this narrative poem recounts little action. The basic situation is established in the eight-part opening chapter via the shifting, often cryptic memories of the protagonist who sits in the parlor of her home that was previously her mother's. Marie's recollections of her mother and of her mother's death interwoven with memories of Percy's impassioned behavior introduce both lovers' inner crises: Marie's sense of overwhelming hunger and Percy's sense that he is being consumed by his adulterous love for Marie, that she "has her hands on him" so that he cannot exert his own will against his attraction. In the course of the sequence, each character consults the old conjure woman Regina, who performs voodoo rituals and offers some wisdom to assist them, but most of the chapters do not so much advance the plot as enrich our understanding of characters or place; much has to be inferred from the "guerrilla techniques" of hint and innuendo. In Marie's quest for self-knowledge that will enable her to come to terms with her mother's death and, secondarily, with her attachment to Percy, her only action (aside from consulting Regina) is to get a ride from the city to the outlying Manchac Swamp seeking Olender, the man who had been her mother's extramarital passion. She meets instead a postman, Walker St. John, who tells her about the community of the maroons, to which Olender belongs. Changed by what she has learned, Marie returns to the city and to Percy. At the work's close—as in slave narrative—the protagonist has established a personal wholeness signaling a significant liberation. And, as in so much black literature, according to Gates's persuasive argument, in Osbey's long poem, black vernacular traditions—cultural traditions like voodoo as well as vocabularies and ways of speaking characteristic of creole New Orleans (Gates: "a blackness of the tongue")—function as crucial signs of African American difference.

Osbey's figuring of voodoo and of the maroons, like Dove's recourse to blues and other folk traditions, serves partly to underscore her characters' (and, metonymically, their people's) strength. Yet appreciating how far this material removes Osbey's characters from positions of victimization by hegemonic culture requires historical knowledge. For although New Orleans is commonly recognized as having been the center of voodoo practice in North America, the extent to which its voodoo represents both an African cultural survival and a tradition of African American defiance and slave rebellion is less widely known. Similarly, knowledge about the substantial and long-lasting maroon communities on the city's outskirts—something rarely mentioned in written histories—clarifies why Marie Crying Eagle should feel transformed upon learning of her familial connection to the maroons. Voodoo and the maroons, then, do not function in this testifying poem simply as local color. They appear as significant parts of a nearly erased history. The historical information to follow establishes both as central to regional traditions of black resistance to white dominance. Characters' participation in the one or affiliation with the other thus registers their carrying on longstanding communal traditions of racial self-determination against overwhelming odds and puts into a racialized context their issues of interpersonal connection and individual identity.

New Orleans voodoo developed from the African religions of its earliest black inhabitants, so that the later influx of voodoo from Haiti and other Caribbean locations only reinforced earlier developments.[27] According to Gwendolyn Midlo Hall, "Almost all the slaves brought to Louisiana under French rule came directly from Africa and arrived within a twelve-year period following the founding of New Orleans. Very few slaves were brought to French Louisiana after 1731" (1992, p. 66). These early slaves, most of whom came from Senegambia, were the creators of Louisiana creole language (Hall 1992, pp. 68–69). Slaves imported later by the Spanish, who took over in 1766, came into a well-formed creolized black culture that included voodoo religious practices (Ostendorf 1993, p. 393).[28] Thus, Osbey's representing all of her main characters as involved with voodoo rites signals an African American cultural continuity going back to transported Africans of the early eighteenth century. (Even the poem's descriptions of women carrying parcels on their heads as they walk along the slave-bricked streets of the Faubourg suggest African ways.) Particularly since, as Osbey notes in the glossary, the maroons were regarded as especially linked to African spirituality, Marie Crying Eagle's vision of the old maroon Olender dancing in the swamps, holding "a piece of bark in one hand / a small pouch in the other" and singing a song in a language Marie does not know, points toward her African roots (*DC*, p. 55)—though not until the work's close does she recognize the empowerment offered by this heritage.

The folk beliefs about the maroons which Osbey reports in her glossary—that "in Louisiana, maroons and their descendants were often believed to possess special knowledge or power of a spiritual nature or to bear special access to African ancestors and therefore [were] regarded with awe and feared by some" (*DC*, p. 101)—signal the unusual extent of African cultural survivals in the region. It was easier for blacks to sustain elements of African culture in New Orleans than in many other colonial areas. Cultural solidarity and stability were fostered not only by the early slaves' common roots in Senegambia, but also by rights accorded slaves in early New Orleans that were denied slaves in other parts of North America. New Orleans slaves were, for example, encouraged by the Catholic clergy to practice baptism and marriage. In addition, New Orleans

> [s]lave families were stable and strengthened by intermarriage with free people of color and Indian networks which in turn had maroon networks. Because of the relative failure of the early plantation economy before the 1740s and the attendant poverty of planters, slaves were allowed a great deal of freedom to provide their own provisions. Hence they were given plots of land, were allowed to hold markets, where they could sell their surplus, and to hire themselves out as craftsmen and workers.
>
> (Ostendorf 1993, p. 393)

Maroon communities, begun during the first half of the eighteenth century, evolved during Spanish rule into permanent settlements in the swamps surrounding the city. Unlike maroon communities elsewhere, these were the refuge of families, not predominantly of single men, and they were populated not primarily by African-born people but by Louisiana creole slaves (that is, slaves born in Louisiana); they actively engaged in trade with the city, to which they were tied by powerful family networks. In this particular locale, then, life in a swamp community of escaped slaves was a genuine, widespread, potentially permanent alternative to bondage.[29]

The city itself, moreover, was a predominantly African American place.[30] The large population of free blacks as well as the intermingling and intermarrying of free and slave in the Creole municipal districts meant that the typical Southern "linkage of negritude and servility" was never thoroughly established in New Orleans (Logsdon and Bell 1992, p. 204).[31] When Ms. Regina states, "my daddy was a building man. / helped build that house you live in. / built this house for mama and his mama" (DC, p. 49), Osbey suggests the black creole's pride in belonging in the Faubourg for generations. Yet even while blacks in New Orleans enjoyed the benefits of the city's distinctively tolerant and racially permeable social fabric, many strove for greater rights and fuller freedom. This heritage of rebellion, of communal action defiantly asserting black rights, is suggested by Osbey's emphasis on both the maroons and voodoo, for both played key roles in slave rebellion. Indeed, Jessie Gaston Mulira suggests that African religious and magical systems such as those represented in voodoo survived in the New World partly *because* of the organizational role they played in slave revolts (1990, p. 36). Certainly, secret religious meetings and dances were among the principal forms and mechanisms for slave resistance. Maroon communities—places where cultural continuities with African tribes were often strikingly direct and where white prohibitions against voodoo practices could not be enforced—were often centers of voodoo. The Voodoos even created a syncretically Catholic St. Marron, the patron of runaway slaves (Teish 1983, p. 348). The link between voodoo leaders and major slave revolts, which was particularly apparent in places like Haiti and Brazil, existed in North America as well, where most slave insurrections before 1800 were lead by conjurers and "obeah men" (Ott 1991, p. 40). Knowing that the maroons represent not just escape from slavery, but powerful resistance and cultural continuity, enables readers better to appreciate why Marie Crying Eagle's visit to the Manchac swamp (the location of maroon settlements) near the poem's close and her encounter there with Walker, a descendent of the maroons, should prove empowering and healing. Without that knowledge, one cannot fully appreciate the significance of the work's closing with a return to Marie's earlier "vision" of an old man (Olender) stepping and singing in another language "somewhere out manchac way."

Marie's journey into the swamp, the place itself a "dangerous / crossing" (*DC*, p. 68), is significantly a pursuit of her maternal history. Critics of African American women's fiction have noted how frequently development of a black female protagonist's empowered subjectivity depends on her exploring her maternal history.[32] Dove seems to have enacted such a quest in the extensive research she did in order to portray the maternal grandmother who seems in many ways to prefigure herself as artist. In the case of Osbey's fictional protagonist Marie, her sense of connection to her mother has been at once threatened and heightened by her mother's recent death. Thus, in the opening lyric of the first chapter, titled "memory," Marie sits in the front parlor of her mother's house with "the little cloth navy pumps mama had given me / set to one side / out of the wet"—as if uncertain how or whether to follow her mother's footsteps—remembering her mother's words, "*do you know what hunger is?*" (*DC*, p. 9). Recalling what it feels like to be touched, she remembers her mother's hands affecting her more powerfully than the hands of her lovers; even while thinking of Percy's claims that she has her hands on him (in the vernacular sense of using Hoodoo to keep him with her and away from his wife), her hunger for her mother is more clearly figured than hunger for Percy:

> and at the wake
> the shameless way i touched her
> holding
> feeling
> her hands and face
> kissing her eyes and mouth
> as though she were a lover
> or alive.
>
> that night you lay against me
> your face pressed deep
> against the pit of my arm.
> i rubbed your smooth neck with one hand.

you kissed my breast.
i thought of mama,
the yellow cotton dress
blowing
hanging
on the clothesline

(DC, pp. 13–14)

Percy's later lines *"your mother's dead and in the ground / and i'm a man / i got no breast to feed you on"* *(DC,* p. 23) convey his pained recognition that Marie's need is for maternal sustenance he cannot provide. When Marie turns to Ms. Regina and her voodoo purification rites, she is turning to a maternal figure; after the voodoo ritual during which she goes "back and forth / between a hard shaking chill / and the calm of yellow cotton dresses," Marie awakens to all the comforts of a mother's care, including "the smell of thick coffee / and biscuits heavy with butter," and to Regina whose activity—"hanging out the wash"—further associates her with Marie's mother *(DC,* pp. 15–16).

To the extent that voodoo is, in Luisah Teish's words, "a science of the oppressed, a repository of womanknowledge," Regina also offers a model of womanhood that assumes power. (Teish points out that Marie LeVeau, the most celebrated voodoo queen, "stepped outside of societal 'feminine' restrictions and used her power in the political arena" [Teish 1983, pp. 334–35]. The preponderance of female voodoo leaders in New Orleans leads Mulira to label its voodooism "a matriarchy" [1983, p. 49].) Yet Regina, whose name points to the city's celebrated voodoo queens, cannot remove Marie's troubles. The limits of her powers may have to do with voodoo no longer being a group ritual—a historical falling off that Osbey mentions in the glossary and which may be signaled by the poem's emphasis on Regina's emotional isolation. But the poem also suggests that no one ever could remove the necessity of Marie's undertaking her own quest; Regina explains, in a passage that recalls Dove's sense of individualized truth,

"it's what you hold to in your middle makes your
memory.
and only you can know what's in your memory,
baby.

and if you got a danger living in you
then you go to take it by the hand
and walk with it.
live with it.
you got to *live* with your danger, daughter."

(DC, p. 50)

Marie's skinniness—along with the many references to hunger—makes it clear that Marie does have a "danger" living in her. Rather than the sensational power over men that others seem to attribute to her, Marie's "danger" is a need to place at the center of herself and her memory something that will sustain her; its lack—not some evil power—threatens to devour her and the man who loves her. To "take [her danger] by the hand," Marie has to confront the legacy of her mother's hunger, which in earlier days had been directed toward Olender. Marie herself is already bound into this extramarital passion in a very material way, since "every letter olender received from her / was in my hand" (*DC*, p. 19); indeed, Marie's mother dictated those letters sitting just as Marie sits in the front parlor during rain in the poem's opening, and—eerily—Walker is carrying one in his bag when Marie meets him. It is the significance of this link to Olender that she has to discover in the course of the poem.

The mother, who remains nameless, was herself miserably cut off from her own maternal heritage; prominent among the things she laments as lost to her late in life are the memory of her own mother and the middle name her mother gave her—as well as "the little lean-to up manchac way" (*DC*, p. 22), perhaps Olender's, perhaps her family's. All these Marie in some way recovers or holds on to in a sequence which stresses the necessity of memory (what is true is what is remembered) and people's responsibility to what they remember. The chapter in which she encounters Walker is entitled "revelation" because it is there she realizes the extent of the community to which she is bound through her mother—what she calls "my people," following Walker's phrasing; this community includes the proud if sequestered tradition of the maroons.

Even Walker's response to her name, with its indication of Native American ancestry, points Marie toward a more inclusive and more positive sense of identity.[33] When Percy had complained about the inappropriateness of Marie's name, Regina could respond only by suggesting a kind of typicality in its inappropriateness:

"marie crying eagle.
what kind of name is that for a black woman?"
"faubourg" the woman answers.
"people in the faubourg have all kinds of names.
you know it is the truth
and what kind of name is good for a black woman?
you know any good names?"
"no" he laughs
"no i guess i don't."

(*DC*, p. 26)

Walker, however—the work's only figure who is not only wise like Regina but also (unlike Regina) content—sees value in the creolization of cultures her name suggests: "nice name. / nice name for a nice lady" (*DC*, p. 81). This man with matte-black skin and chestnut-colored eyes is a repository of new knowledge for Marie, and in the silent space between the "revelation" section and the next chapter, "the breaking of the season," he tells her about his people, the maroons.[34] That the reader is not privy to the information Marie gains indicates that she and Osbey are continuing an African American tradition of self-protective secrecy important to slaves generally but especially to communities of escaped slaves:

"let walker tell you, miss marie,
the last thing these maroon people do
is tell some stranger,
even a nice stranger from the city like you,
where anybody—
especially this mr. r. t. olender—
has gone to
and when or if he's coming back."

(*DC*, p. 82)

The poem, then, reenacts some of the gaps in the history of Louisiana's people of color at the same time that it pushes readers who lack information to take their own figurative walk in pursuit of historical knowledge.

While we do not know exactly what Marie learns, we can see its effect on her. Marie's insistence on marketing immediately upon her return to the city—her selecting a chicken from the "plumper breasted birds" at the coop (when both she and Percy have been figured as breastless) and her purchase of other tasty ingredients "for percy and me"—suggests at last a satisfaction of hungers, a renewed ability to nourish herself and her partner (*DC*, pp. 88–89). Percy is there "reaching her in from the outside" at the end of her walk (one version of the walk with her danger that Regina advised), and in the closing lines of the poem

> his eyes find hers
> set deep in their sockets
> chestnut brown
> the color ma-ròn
> somewhere between the camelback house here on frenchmen [street]
> and an eternity of hunger
> danger
> nothing but vision
> somewhere out manchac way.
>
> (*DC*, p. 96)

The Creole term "ma-ròn" has appeared only once before, used by Walker as the terminology of the maroons themselves: "you think i'd be out here in the sticks / *these* sticks— / if my old man wasn't *ma-ròn*, as we say?" (*DC*, p. 84). In effect, the narrator's voice—and hence the reader's awareness—merges with the consciousness of the group in the know, the "we" whose people come from maroons. The description of Marie's eye color further reinforces her link to Walker and his people, even raising the possibility that she is Olender's daughter. (Her mother's eyes, we know, were "light.") Other aspects of the poem, including Regina's assertion that "*blood will tell / truth will out*," might support such a hypothesis. But Marie's paternity is not, I think, a key issue and need not be determined. She is her mother's daughter in any case, and she has found a way of using that connection—via her mother's former bond to a man and a shack "out manchac way"—to tie herself to the living, not just the dead. The poem closes with Marie at a point of hopeful, if unresolved, crossing: no longer confined within a house or even an urban district, she has expanded her territory and her vision to include the swamp and its heritage of submission refused, of freedom seized and sustained.

Dove and Osbey, I have argued, demonstrate through the discontinuous storytelling of their long poems a desire to interweave histories

of individual African Americans with aspects of public history inade-
quately recognized by mainstream America and a related desire to
resist the mythologizing that would remove their characters' stories
from local truths. Dove, we saw, underlines the complex, sometimes
ironic, interaction between private and public history by appending
a chronology to *Thomas and Beulah*. Osbey reinforces the communal
dimensions of her characters' experiences by including in *Desperate
Circumstance, Dangerous Woman* a glossary of Louisiana terms
through which the reader perceives words and phrases as well as
the material objects they denote (such as the Hoodoo's "chapel
room" or "anklet") functioning as cultural memory. Both Dove and
Osbey dwell on specificities of place—Akron with its viaducts, rail-
road lines, factory smoke stacks; the old quarter of New Orleans
with its slave-bricked streets, outdoor markets, and distinctive archi-
tecture. (In Osbey's poem, the houses equipped with jalousies and
quarter galleries are themselves live presences, listening and speak-
ing, absorbing memory.) How much the particularities of place
function as valued historical preservations is suggested, for instance,
by Osbey's glossary entry under "Manchac Pass," (an official name,
according to the poem, which "never took" [*DC*, p. 67]). She identi-
fies three distinct stages in its existence, each reflecting different
social structures and patterns of habitation: it was first an unpaved
dirt and shell road (its condition at the time of Marie's ride), then
a paved highway, presumably after drainage of swamp areas begun
in the early twentieth century enabled expanded development, and
is now "a seldom used scenic route" (*DC*, p. 101). Such specificities
typify the testifying poet's project. By developing the lyric sequence
as a multivocalic yet historically specific narrative devoted to the
rarely seen "undersides" of history, Dove and Osbey underscore
the polyphonic, multiple, and relative character of historical truth.

A similar interest in using lyrics to tell in a discontinuous manner
the stories of either real or fictional, often marginalized individuals
within localized history is evident among white female poets as well.
One thinks, for instance, of Ruth Whitman's *Tamsen Donner* or *The
Testing of Hanna Senesh*, Jill Breckenridge's *Civil Blood*, Margaret
Atwood's "The Journals of Susanna Moodie," Chris Lewellyn's
*Fragments from the Fire: The Triangle Shirtwaist Company Fire of
March 25, 1911*, Anne Stevenson's *Correspondences: A Family History
in Letters*, or Stephanie Strickland's *The Red Virgin*. But to the extent
that American poets of color can more readily call upon traditions

from several cultures (whereby formal and linguistic elements en-
hance the resonance of any ethnically specific content), they may
enrich the long poem as genre in distinctive ways.

Chapter 5 further examines women's explorations of marginal
history in long poems, this time considering documentary elements
and more radically experimental historiography. First, however, an-
other chapter on lyric sequences will demonstrate how one white
poet has reinvented long-established Anglo-European forms of the
storytelling poetic sequence without calling on other cultural tradi-
tions. Marilyn Hacker, in *Love, Death, and the Changing of the Sea-
sons*, shows none of the interest in public history evident in both
the epic-based and the determinedly nonepic poems considered so
far. As we shall see, however, the history of the sonnet sequence is
very much in Hacker's mind as she subversively recasts for a nonhe-
gemonic speaker that most conventionalized form of lyric-based
personal narrative.

CHAPTER FOUR

Measured Feet "in
Gender-Bender Shoes":
Marilyn Hacker's *Love,
Death, and the Changing
of the Seasons*

The sonnet sequence, originating with Petrarch in the late fourteenth century and enjoying its biggest vogue among English poets of the later sixteenth century, is a far less ancient extended poetic form than epic and possesses a somewhat more visible history of female practitioners. According to Thomas P. Roche, Jr., one might well consider Anne Locke's *A Meditation of a Penitent Sinner* (1590) to be the first sonnet sequence in English (Roche 1989, p. 155). Better known are such love sonnet sequences as Elizabeth Barrett Browning's *Sonnets from the Portuguese*, Edna St. Vincent Millay's *Fatal Interview*, and Christina Rossetti's "Monna Innominata." Nonetheless, in the last several decades a number of feminist literary critics have pointed to problematic gender biases in the sonnet tradition. Some have questioned whether either the sonnet itself, specifically the love sonnet, or the love sonnet sequence can adequately render female subjectivity. According to Jan Montefiore, for instance, the love sonnet's traditional positioning of the woman as the desired object through whose responses the desiring male speaker defines himself, its feminizing of the beloved (of either sex) as the "passive reflecting Other" or a "blank Platonic mirror" to the masculine lover, problematically constrains women writers (Montefiore 1987, pp. 109, 112). Margaret Homans argues not only that the love sonnet, or the traditional love lyric more generally, constructs speaking subjectivity as masculine, but also that its rhetorical structure embodies a specular and hierarchical plot of masculine heterosexual desire. This plot—embodied in the language and tropes as well as the thematics of the poem—is incompatible with female sexuality, which emphasizes touch rather than sight, and female textuality, which privileges metonomy rather than metaphor (Homans 1985).

Debates about the limitations of the sonnet's suitability for women writers intersect with more general arguments among critics and creators of contemporary poetry about the powers and limitations of regular poetic forms (forms with prescribed patterns of meter and rhyme). The recent revival of poetry in set verse forms identified as New Formalism has renewed disputes, particularly heated in the 1960s, about the politics of poetic form.[1] Advocates of free verse have claimed since the days of the Anthology Wars that regular forms preclude rendering the energies manifest in acts of intense, immediate perception and prevent the sounding of an individual's voice and speech rhythms. (Arguably the most extreme statement of this view was made earlier by W. C. Williams: "To me all sonnets say the same thing of no importance" [1963, p. 5].) Proponents of set forms, on the other hand, claim such structures compensate for the purportedly impoverished prosodic and expressive resources of the free verse that has dominated recent American poetry. Each camp tries to position the other as inherently conservative and elitist.[2]

To counter essentialist understandings of poetic form that often underlie these debates about the ideological implications of free or metrical verse and "open" or "closed" forms and to demonstrate one set of strategies a woman may use to inscribe her subjectivity and sexuality within the love sonnet sequence, this chapter examines the "performative" formalism of lesbian feminist Marilyn Hacker. I adopt the term "performative" from Judith Butler, who uses it to describe acts and gestures which might purport to express the essence of gender identity, but which she sees as signifying on the surface of the body an illusory internal core. These acts of gender reveal not its substance but its fabrication: "That the gendered body is performative suggests that it has no ontological status apart from the various acts which constitute its reality" (Butler 1990a, p. 336). Hacker, I will argue, takes analogous de-essentializing approaches to gender and to poetic form, thereby undermining myths that formalist verse necessarily embodies a particular (patriarchal) ideology or that the sonnet can express only desire based on a masculine model.

The current popularity of formalism appears to some critics as an alarming mirror of the increasing conservativism of American culture.[3] Ira Sadoff argues in a 1990 issue of *American Poetry Review* that "neo-formalists have a social as well as a linguistic agenda. When they link pseudo-populism (the 'general reader') to regular meter, they disguise their nostalgia for moral and linguistic certainty, for a universal . . . and univocal way of conserving culture" (Sadoff 1990, p. 7). While acknowledging that the "masters of received form—Justice, Bishop, Wilbur, Kunitz, and Walcott . . .—articulate form with vision" (1990, p. 7), Sadoff claims that the resurgent neoformalists and their champions tend to separate form from vision. "The dissociation of sound, sense, and intellect . . . reminds us of the danger of . . . appreciating esthetic beauty, formally and thematically, at the cost of the observed, sensory, disturbingly contingent world" (1990, p. 8). Going further, he asserts that the neoformalists' "exaltation of the iamb veils their attempt to privilege prevailing white Anglo-Saxon rhythms and culture"; they are guilty of "cultural imperialism" (1990, p. 8). They sidestep the problem American artists need to confront of "finding a sense of 'relation' between self and other, the inner and outer world, the personal and social worlds" (1990, p. 9).

In presenting the neoformalists as the most egregious exemplars of a pervasive failure among contemporary American poets to connect themselves with the social world, Sadoff overlooks much feminist poetry, as Adrienne Rich points out in a subsequent issue of *APR*. While announcing her agreement with much of Sadoff's essay, Rich observes that it provides a striking demonstration of the invisibility in nonfeminist publications of "the groundswell of feminist and lesbian writing":

> There are, close to home, among feminist, gay and lesbian poets, among poets from the communities of color, a profusion of what Sadoff is seeking: "poems that make engaged, dramatized, and surprising connections between the self and the social world, the moment and history."
>
> (Rich 1990, p. 17)

Yet most feminist poets and critics in the United States, Rich among them, remain wary of received poetic forms. Whether sympathetic with Anglo-American or with French theories of language and representation, feminists have tended to share assumptions like

Sadoff's that equate aesthetic choices with political stances; they tend to see in more "open" or experimental forms greater possibility for subversion of the patriarchal and expression of the feminine. Many doubt the ability of language—here I quote Marianne DeKoven as a representative example—"to represent adequately, through relatively conventional literary forms, the specificity of women's experience" (1989, pp. 75–76). Drawing upon Kristeva and Irigaray, DeKoven argues that writing which fails to obstruct normal reading practices and encourages construction of coherent meaning fails to challenge patriarchal and phallogocentric structures. A proponent of experimentalism like that of Gertrude Stein, DeKoven would find comparable limitations in a narrative sonnet sequence as in, say, Osbey's free verse "narrative-as-community," since neither significantly obstructs normal reading practices. But even those who do not share DeKoven's insistence on *radical* experimentation tend to regard the inscription of women's experience as new to our literature and perceive, as Rich does, the "necessity to break from [traditional structures] in recognition of new experience" (1986a, p. 181).

Rich—a member of a generation who in the 1960s came to see regular metrical verse as emotionally or politically repressive, as incapable of capturing authentic experience or individual speech—long ago rejected the "asbestos gloves" of formalism that once shielded her from the burning political issues she needed to address (Rich 1979, p. 40). She continues in more recent work to deplore the political backwardness of traditional poetic forms. *Time's Power: Poems 1985–1988*, contains a "Love Poem" that dismisses the sonnet as inappropriate to politically engaged feminist writing: the beloved woman addressed is a "bristler" with "a warrior's mind," "testing the world / the word," and consequently "to write for you / a pretty sonnet / would be untrue" (Rich 1989, p. 7). The presence of irregular rhyme throughout her love poem suggests Rich is not insisting on abandoning traditional poetics entirely, yet received forms remain in her eyes "untrue" to the gynocentric world her poems attempt to help bring into being.[4]

Marilyn Hacker (born in 1942, thirteen years later than Rich) is a notable exception to the feminist trends I have sketched. Since the publication of her first volume, *Presentation Piece*, the Lamont Poetry Selection for 1973, she has continued to delight in the technical challenges posed by villanelles, canzoni, crowns of sonnets, sestinas, heroic and tetrameter couplets, and the like. Her poetry of the 1980s chronicles her life within lesbian communities in New York and France and is committed to many of the same political goals as Rich's. Yet Hacker does not equate prescribed forms with hegemonic ideology. A 1978 interview demonstrates that while Hacker shares Rich's interest in unearthing women's contributions to literary history, she is confident that contemporary women can express themselves through the resources of received tradition. Moreover, without making Judy Grahn's move of positing ancient gynocentric precedents from a matriarchal era, Hacker refuses to see the tradition as predominantly masculine:

> Traditional forms . . . aren't in any way inimical to women's po-
> etry, feminist poetry. . . . It is important for women writers to re-
> claim the tradition, to rediscover and redefine our place in it and
> lay claim to our considerable contributions, innovations, and inven-
> tions. Traditional narrative and lyric forms have been used by
> women for centuries—even if our professors of Western literature
> never mentioned Marie de France or Christine de Pisan. The lan-
> guage that we use was as much created and invented by women as
> by men. . . . We've got to reclaim the language, demand acknowl-
> edgement of our part in it, and proceed from there.
>
> (Hammond 1980, p. 22)

Not surprisingly, in a largely admiring review of *Time's Power*, Hacker takes issue with Rich's perspective on the sonnet. She observes that "the echo of the mnemonically compelling iambic pentameter . . . is never really absent from [Rich's] work. This puts that work within, and in relation to or dialogue with, a whole body of narrative and didactic poems in English written in that meter." She therefore questions why Rich had to "bad-mouth a tradition that helped to form her art" in the lines from "Love Poem" quoted above. Objecting to Rich's limiting conception of the sonnet as "pretty," Hacker asks, "Why not a beautiful sonnet, or an ugly, thorny, passionate one?" She expresses doubts whether "Twenty-One Love Poems"—"a cycle that, although in free form, has the heft and feel of a sonnet sequence"—could have been written by a poet without Rich's earlier expertise in fixed forms. And, in the context of this particular issue, she laments Rich's influential position:

"next year some college junior, some fourth-grade teacher, some bookstore clerk is going to decide that sonnets are 'pretty' and 'untrue' because Adrienne Rich said so. And that's too bad" (Hacker 1989, p. 467).

Hacker's desire to place her own work conspicuously "within, and in relation to or dialogue with" the tradition of iambic pentameter verse, especially the sonnet tradition, is apparent in her 1986 sonnet sequence, *Love, Death, and the Changing of the Seasons*. The book's first epigraph, Shakespeare's sonnet 73, "That time of year thou mayst in me behold," not only anticipates Hacker's speaking as an older lover in a May/December same-sex relationship; it also signals the multitude of links between her cycle of love lyrics and the Petrarchan sonnet tradition, in particular with Shakespeare's Sonnets. Not content with merely laying claim to this tradition, however, Hacker is reforming it so that it can represent a contemporary lesbian feminist's experiences in a love relationship and convey her romantic ideals, many of which differ markedly from those of the male lovers/poets who preceded her. Of course, Hacker is hardly the first to reform this evolving tradition in which Shakespeare himself was an innovator; it has been recently reworked by John Berryman, Robert Lowell, James Merrill and others. Hacker's sequence is distinctive, however, in its self-conscious invocation of Shakespeare's sequence as a central intertext. This foregrounded archaism renders *Love, Death, and the Changing of the Seasons* particularly useful for critical intervention in the debate about the politics of current poetic formalism and in the corollary feminist debate about whether the sonnet form in particular can accommodate a feminine speaking subjectivity or whether it is, as Montefiore has argued, "masculine in conception" (Montefiore 1987, p. 105).

Expressing her excitement about her new love relationship as well as the sonnet sequence developing from it, Hacker's speaker announces early in the work that she's getting "some / brand-old ideas," an apt phrase for the combination of innovation and conservatism evident in Hacker's formal sequence. Love, death, and aging have preoccupied lyricists for centuries; in choosing to explore her relation to these experiences in a sonnet sequence, Hacker accepts many of the traditions of the egocentric personal lyric that presumes a recognizable subject—if, for her, one that commands a wide variety of roles—using language representationally to address a discrete—if no longer oppositionally defined—other. She accepts a continuity with the given tradition that is resisted to some degree by Rich's organicist insistence on free verse and more strenuously by Hélène Cixous' striving for a new language in *écriture feminine* or by Monique Wittig's efforts to "pulverize the old forms and formal conventions" (Wittig 1992, p. 69). Yet Hacker's play with and against the Shakespearean/Petrarchan model reveals that working from the basis of an established tradition (especially from its most popularly known text) can also enable a poet to define clear differences from an inherited patriarchal norm, precisely because the poet can diverge from that invoked norm in ways readily discernable to a nonspecialist audience. The differences Hacker establishes denaturalize gender roles and broaden the identities available to both lover and beloved. Her politically significant play within the tradition, which parodies both the limits of the sonnet form and the limits of gender coherence, enables a multifaceted, performative approach to sexuality and gender that calls into question conventional notions of gender and opens up a range of possibilities for the female subject.

At the most basic level, this chapter's reading of Hacker's sequence refutes the idea that contemporary formalist writing is necessarily any more coopted by hegemonic ideology than free verse. Works like hers should help temper current exaggerations of the differences between those writing in received lyric forms and free verse writers, who often trained in the same academic workshops. Arguments about whether didactic, earnest free verse like Rich's is more political than Hacker's playful exploitation of the artificialities of received conventions of womanhood, gender, and poetic form, may be largely disputes about personal taste. The most significant political division may fall not between the formalists and those writing in open forms, but between those writing personal lyrics, whether in free or set verse, and the experimental politicized avant-gardes (for example, the often Marxist-affiliated Language writers and the feminist experimentalists associated, if sometimes loosely, with the Language movement; the materialist feminist experiments of Wittig; or the quite different innovations of *écriture feminine*). *Thoroughly* innovative work—brand-*new* ideas—may well demand a break from the personal lyric mode and from the conventions of logic and representation on which it depends.

Yet Hacker's poetry confutes a simple opposition between formally experimental and more conventional (formal or free verse) lyric as well. Hacker's formalist verse becomes radically innovative as she pursues the implications of nonorganicist assumptions about form and nonessentialist assumptions about gender. Like recent (also anti-organicist) Language poets, Hacker highlights the ways in which genre and language itself constitute, rather than reflect, our realities. Clearly, how one approaches one's formalism—for example, whether one regards the repetitions of metered verse as arbitrary or, alternatively, as reflecting "the recurrent structural principles to be found in nature" (Golding 1991, p. 85)[5]—or, for that matter, how one approaches one's experimentalism, has more potential political significance than the formalism itself.[6]

To the extent that Hacker's epigraph reminds readers of the homoerotic dimension of Shakespeare's sonnets—something the mainstream critical tradition has tended to downplay[7]—it undermines any monolithic understanding of the Petrarchan sonnet tradition and of generic traditions more generally. (We are reminded, for example, that the speaker's beloved need not be a woman, and when the beloved is a woman she need not be fair or chaste.) The more varied a tradition, the more room for diversity within it and the less restrictive it need be for those claiming a place in its development. In context, then, Hacker's first epigraph alone encourages an expansive view of literary traditions, and of the sonnet tradition in particular, as varied and adaptable.

That all of the love relationships—indeed, all of the relationships—Hacker portrays in *Love, Death, and the Changing of the Seasons* are between women (or women and girls) radically distinguishes her sequence from the Shakespearean model. Lacanian critics and theorists might argue otherwise: that the gender of the lovers is irrelevant in the sonnet's dynamics. Montefiore, for instance, claims that what is really at stake for the Petrarchan lover-poet (whose poem she sees as structured on the Imaginary I-Thou dyad of mother and prelinguistic infant) is not the success or failure of his courtship but rather "defining his own self through his desire either for the image of his beloved or for his own image mediated through her response to him" (Montefiore 1987, p. 98). Regardless of gender, the beloved is positioned as a passive reflector and thereby feminized:

> in any poem where the lover's self is being defined in and through
> a relationship with a beloved, that process of definition implies the

masculinity of the lover and the femininity of the other; which is
why . . . the love-poem presents problems to women poets.

(Montefiore 1987, p. 109)

I would agree that a woman sonneteer faces significant challenges
if she is to inscribe a speaking subjectivity that does not repeat the
objectifying dynamics and the hierarchical power structure of the
Petrarchan tradition's romantic couple. But Montefiore's ahistorical
model does not allow for the genuine alteration in power dynamics
that results from different gender configurations in love relation-
ships nor for the difference of female, particularly lesbian, sexuality
that Hacker represents.[8]

What one might see as merely the substitution of two lesbian
women for Petrarch's heterosexual couple or for the homosexual
pair at the center of Shakespeare's sonnets in fact transforms the
power dynamics and social significance of the relationships de-
picted. Hacker's use of entirely female love triangles furthers this
transformation. Eve Sedgwick's analysis of the homosocial ele-
ments in Shakespeare's Sonnets calls to our attention the ways
in which his sequence, as much as Petrarchan heterosexual se-
quences, reinforces through its triangular dynamics the power
structures of heterosexual patriarchy. For all its homoeroticism,
Shakespeare's sequence—in which the male characters are bound
to each other in a love triangle via their competition for the dark
lady's favors—is dominated by "male heterosexual desire, in the
form of a desire to consolidate partnership with authoritative males
in and through the bodies of females" (Sedgwick 1985, p. 38).
In contrast, the world Hacker creates in *Love, Death, and the
Changing of the Seasons* is almost exclusively a (lesbian) woman's
world and, for the most part, seems removed from the forces of
compulsory heterosexuality. Men appear seldom and in only the
most peripheral roles; unlike Rich in "Twenty-One Love Poems,"
Hacker downplays the impact of heterosexual patriarchy on the
lovers, giving it virtually no role in the disintegration of their rela-
tionship. The significance of Hacker's removing her characters
from relation to men is illuminated by Wittig's argument that the
figure of the lesbian is removed from the gender divisions and
social systems of patriarchy. Wittig declares in "One Is Not Born
a Woman":

> Lesbian is the only concept I know of which is beyond the categories of sex (woman and man), because the designated subject (lesbian) is *not* a woman, either economically, or politically, or ideologically. For what makes a woman is a specific social relation to a man, a relation that we have previously called servitude, a relation which implies personal and physical obligation as well as economic obligation . . . , a relation which lesbians escape by refusing to become or to stay heterosexual.
>
> (Wittig 1992, p. 20)

Establishing a lesbian world is fundamental among the many strategies, often evident as revisions of Shakespearean sonnet conventions, by which Hacker challenges received gender categories. It helps her make a place both for an exuberant lesbian eroticism quite distinct from the phallocentric erotic economy and for relationships that are not merely mirrorings by which the lyric speaker establishes her own identity.

In broad outline, Hacker's plot follows the Petrarchan model. Her speaker is initially the more desiring partner for whom sonnets are partly rhetorical devices for seduction; tracing a wide range of intense emotions, the sequence often records the discomforts of being in love and of experiencing unsatisfied desire. As in Shakespeare's first 126 sonnets, the beloved is significantly younger, marking a potential difference in power between them: the speaker (who refers to herself in the poems as Hacker, Hack, and Marilyn, and whom I will call Hack) is 42, her beloved Ray (also Rachel) is 25. Hacker's sequence, like Shakespeare's, is much preoccupied with time's passage and with mortality. Several romantic triangles threaten Hacker's relationship, as they seem to have threatened Shakespeare's, and like his fair young man, her fair young woman ultimately becomes involved with another. Before that event, Hacker's speaker, like her forebears', must frequently deal with absence from the beloved, not only because the lovers' New York apartments are separated by four miles, but also because in the year covered by the sequence Hack travels several times to France without Ray (twice in the company of her prepubescent daughter, Iva). Yet unlike the male Petrarchans, Hacker's primary interest is in overcoming metaphorical distances that exist between lovers in a consummated partnership which is fully integrated into their daily lives, what she terms "our doubled dailiness" (Hacker 1986, p. 71; cited hereafter as *LD*).

What Hack desires, from the very beginning, is not merely the satisfaction of her erotic desire or even reciprocal emotional attachment, but a lasting relationship involving shared domestic existence. At the beginning of the sequence, she asks with as much seriousness as humor, "What are you doing for the next five years?" (*LD*, p. 10) and before long she is saying she'd like their relationship to end "when I die / at ninety-seven" (*LD*, p. 126). While the Petrarchan lover's desire for sexual conquest is often thwarted either by the lady's reluctance or by the moral duty of sexual renunciation, in Hacker's sequence sex is perhaps the most easily attained dimension of what the speaker seeks. As she announces early on, with characteristic colloquialism and sexual explicitness: "Although I'd cream my jeans touching your breast, / sweetheart, it isn't lust; it's all the rest / of what I want with you that scares me shitless" (*LD*, p. 12). When Ray, in the early pages, is still living with another woman, Hack feels free to fantasize about the sexual exploits she and Ray might enjoy, but censors her imagination when she wonders about their "dailiness," feeling she doesn't have a right to that (*LD*, p. 55). Allotting such value to a nonidealizing context for love significantly revises the tradition of the love sonnet and, as we shall see, the distance between speaking subject and silent object on which poems in the male tradition depend.

Hacker's images of romantic fulfillment are domestic, and their apparent triviality provides a parodic reworking of the lofty, moralized Petrarchan norm. Hack longs to have her beloved's "PJ's" hung on her bathroom door (*LD*, p. 13), their laundry thrown in together (*LD*, p. 178), a common home address (*LD*, p. 155). Even her erotic fantasies may include a mundane domestic context: "After the supper dishes, let us start / where we left off . . ." begins one vision of the consummation she is still anticipating (*LD*, p. 50). Figures of homes and houses recur as spaces within which Hack imagines the two as individually fulfilled partners:

> I think the world's our house. I think I built
> and furnished mine with space for you to move
> through it, with me, alone in rooms, in love
> with our work. I moved into one mansion
> the morning when I touched, I saw, I felt
> your face blazing above me like a sun.
>
> (*LD*, p. 69)

In another poem she imagines them sharing a home in Lacoste:

> It's almost as if we're already there,
> in the narrow stone house, me upstairs
> writing at the splintery pine table,
> you in the downstairs study. . . .
> . . . I'm cooking
> a sonnet sequence and a cassoulet
>
> (*LD*, p. 25)

Given Hack's desire for a long-term domestic connection, her use of figures associated with heterosexual marriage is perhaps not surprising. The spirit of her invocations, however—ranging from tongue-in-cheek to broad parody—makes clear that she is not aspiring to imitate that patriarchal institution of heterosexual partnership. The first allusion to marriage, which occurs early on when Ray still lives with Alice, is obviously self-mocking:

> I venture it's a trifle premature
> to sign the china-pattern registry
> before you are, at least, at liberty
> to hang your PJ's on my bathroom door.
> A funny pair of homebodies we are,
> as wicked as we like to paint ourselves:
> I kiss you till my clit's about to burst,
> and catch myself reorganizing shelves.
>
> (*LD*, p. 13)

Hack's not taking the marriage analogy seriously is apparent, too, in her being taken aback by Ray's speaking, "not kidding," of Alice as " 'my wife' " (*LD*, p. 34). Hack subsequently characterizes herself in a butch haircut ("short-back-and-sides") as not "the most orthodox of brides" (*LD*, p. 71) and humorously invokes the marriage-bed in a poem recording her feelings shortly after the consummation of their love: "I broke a glass, got bloodstains on the sheet: / hereafter, must I only write you chaste / connubial poems?" (*LD*, p. 65). Both allusions to marriage may be read as making fun of Ray's locution.[9]

A few pages later, having characterized one of her own poems as an "epithalamion," Hack admits that if she wants to be ironic about "wives" and then appropriate language associated with marriage for serious use, she had better "explain [her]self." Here's what she offers:

> No law books frame terms of this covenant.
> It's choice that's asymptotic to a goal,
> which means that we must choose, and choose, and choose
> momently, daily. This moment my whole
> trajectory's toward you, and it's not los-
> ing momentum. Call it anything we want.
>
> (LD, p. 72)

Hack distinguishes the ongoing voluntary renewal of her and Ray's commitment from the false ideal of marriage's fixed state attained by legal decree and by one occasion's vows. In her closing statement Hack both signals and accommodates herself to the lack of a single term for the process of ongoing active choice in which she and her lover are engaged. Whatever designation they employ is recognized as a shorthand approximation, its value depending on its being jointly chosen—whatever *we* want. At one point Hack, while "suppos[ing] / you [Ray] want what I want," describes the relationship she desires as "Connecting what gets wilder as it grows / with what's safe, known, quotidian, routine / and necessary as pairs of old jeans" (LD, p. 194); the marriage figure, like the sonnet form itself, provides the safe and familiar apparel with which to clothe something wild, unfamiliar, and subversive.[10]

One of the central ways Hacker incorporates this wildness is through the sequence's very explicit eroticism. Borrowing the descriptive categories Jan Zita Grover sets up in her review article "Words to Lust By," we could say that Hacker's portrayal of lesbian sexuality often has more in common with "bad-girl porn" than with the "good-girl erotica" of lesbian-feminist writings. That is to say, she does not restrict herself, as "good-girl" writing does, to earnest, gentle lovers who "enact their passion in rustic cabins, in nature, in beds"; nor does she often describe sex "by allusion to flowers, fruit, waterfalls, pounding waves, illimitable oceans" (Grover 1990, p. 21). Although she also does not go in for sex toys, S/M, and the like, her work frequently fits the "bad-girl" model in that she attends to the mechanics of arousal as much as to the subject's psychological state; she explores role-playing and fantasy; she does not rely on heavily metaphorical descriptions of sexual activity; she does not suppress everything culturally associated with maleness; and she employs an "emphatic, workaday vocabulary" (cunt, clit, fuck, etc.) (Grover 1990, p. 22). In portraying sex graphically with four-letter words, themselves adopted from male discourse, Hacker is claiming the traditionally male prerogative of voicing sexual desire and flaunting sexual experience. But she goes beyond merely claiming for women the position men have enjoyed: as she invokes male terminology, plays with butch/femme dynamics, or presents the two women in stereotypically heterosexual scenes, she is engaged in a conscious masquerade revealing gender roles to be performative rather than natural, inevitable structures. Hack's assertion that what "our bodies do together is unprecedented" suggests not only that the couple's sexual relationship is the richest she has ever enjoyed, but that they (and other lesbians) are in fact moving into new realms of sexual freedom and pleasure. Hacker renders their *jouissance* convincing largely by revealing the range of roles they feel free to explore—"We do it once like ladies, once like tramps" (*LD*, p. 93)—in fantasy or in actual lovemaking.

As a sample of the range of sexual roles represented, here are two poems that appear on facing pages (the first concludes a crown of six sonnets linked by repeating the final line of one as the opening line of the next):

> Toward what was after, all our rendezvous
> turned, fine-tuned as a classic Howard Hawkes:
> the silken lady in the black suit walks
> through the hotel bar, smoking. Point of view
> hers: battered tweed with something on the rocks
> near empty, quipping with the bartender,
> glimpsed between bulky shoulders. Pan, then: send her
> around the tables, till the eye-hook shocks:
> "Hi, babe, have you been waiting for me long?"
> Walking west on Twenty-Second Street,
> in wind, near midnight (earlier Godard)
> you held my coat closed, blocked gusts like a strong
> and silent type; the dénouement inferred
> upstairs: denim and silk pooled at our feet.
>
> (*LD*, p. 82)

> "If I weren't working, I'd sleep next to you
> an hour or two more. Then we'd get the car
> and drive a while, out of Manhattan, to

a quiet Bloomingdale's in Westchester.
If we saw anything we liked, we'd buy it!
We'd try things on, first, in one cubicle.
You'd need to make an effort to be quiet
when I knelt down and got my fingers full
of you, my mouth on you, against the wall.
You'd pull my hair. You'd have to bite your tongue.
I'd hold your ass so that you wouldn't fall.
Later, we'd take a peaceful walk along
the aisles, letting our hands touch every chance
they got, among the bras and underpants."

(*LD*, p. 83)

In the first poem, titled "and Tuesday III," Hacker places her lovers in thoroughly stereotyped heterosexual roles and allows them to enjoy this play, yet by presenting the scene through camera techniques, she calls attention to the manipulation of the gaze upon which such images depend. Consequently, the couple's impersonation of a heterosexual cliché appears a politically conscious and ultimately subversive act. The academic sobriety of Judith Butler's explanations, however incongruous (as is my own discourse) next to Hacker's outrageous play, provides valuable insight: "The notion of an original or primary gender identity is often parodied within the cultural practices of drag, cross-dressing, and the sexual stylization of butch/femme identities" (Butler 1990a, p. 337).[11] Butler goes on to argue that in fact "part of the pleasure, the giddiness of the performance [of drag, cross-dressing, etc.] is in the recognition of a radical contingency in the relation between sex and gender in the face of cultural configurations of causal unities that are regularly assumed to be natural and necessary" (1990a, p. 338). "The proliferation of gender style and identity . . . implicitly contests the always already political binary distinction between genders that is often taken for granted" and promises instead "the possibility of complex and generative subject-positions" (1990a, p. 339).[12]

The second poem also opens possibilities for more complex subject positions, though in a quite different way, for here the speaker is the beloved object traditionally silenced in the sonnet sequence. (This is one of two poems presented entirely as Ray's voice; the title of the other, "What You Might Answer," identifies it as only hypothetically Ray's speech.) In this poem, "Bloomingdale's I," Ray is the very active subject of her own erotic fantasies in which she refuses on several levels the constraints of what is hegemonically proper. She and her lover will not conform to standards of p.c. lesbian feminism by eschewing the stereotypically feminine love of clothes shopping (in another poem Hack demands, "why shouldn't girls *parler chiffons?*"); they will not restrict their lovemaking to the respectable privacy of their bedrooms, nor will they reject fetishistic behaviors.

The figure of trying things on in Bloomingdale's may provide a metaphor for Hacker's poetic situation. However much the epitome of patriarchal capital consumerism, Bloomingdale's is a given in her world, just as the sonnet tradition is a received reality. Yet rather than boycotting either one, she uses them as she wants and for her own kinds of self-definition. Within the establishment, so to speak, she seizes the freedom to "try on" a variety of roles, styles, and behaviors, revealing in the process the performative nature of all subject positions and poetic conventions—even the apparently stable ones whose seeming naturalness bulwarks the status quo.

As if to instruct the reader in the performative nature of sexual and gender identities, the villanelle "Conversation in the Park" (like Petrarch and Sidney, Hacker occasionally interpolates other regular poetic forms among her sonnets) shows Ray moving toward such an understanding in the context of the larger homophobic society (an atypical context, as noted above). Ray opens the poem's dialogue with an attitude not of liberating parody or cocky rebellion as in the poems just quoted, but of painfully alienated self-consciousness. She asks, " 'Do people look at me and know I'm gay?' " and confesses how it gets her " 'down! The stares—that way // my back aches when I wonder what they say / behind it . . . But you wouldn't know. You *chose!* " [Hacker's ellipsis] (*LD*, p. 101). It seems that Ray regards Hack's appearance—presumably her haircut, her style of dress—as a deliberate announcement of her lesbianism.[13] But apparently Hack would not have thought so, since she replies, " 'Do people look at *me* and know I'm gay?' " Here is the rest of the poem (Ray speaks first):

> "Honey, you look like a twelve-year-old boy.
> But you go down on me the way, God knows,
> only a girl goes down!" "The stairs! That way

out of the park, or else I'm going to lay
you right here, right now, on the grass!" "Yes, boss!
Do people look at us and know we're gay?"
"Why *would* two girls go down the stairs this way?"

(LD, pp. 101–2)

Sexual and gender roles—merged in the slang designation of lesbian as "girl"—may be socially coded according to details of physical appearance, but such codes are fluid and depend for their interpretation on context and the interpreter's own social position and experience. The only reliable index to the characters' sexual preferences or even their gender is finally performative: it's not clear that a broadly inclusive "they" would recognize either Ray or Hack as a lesbian or as a woman merely by how either one looks; only the couple's lustful dash down the stairs is a clear sign of their immediate sexual orientation.

Significant parallels exist between Hacker's handling of her lovers' sexuality and her approach to the sonnet form itself, for both enact a kind of liberation via excess. In patriarchy's approved representations of female sexuality, as in approved treatments of the sonnet, the potential for wildness has been largely squelched, rendering both, in the terms of Rich's "Love Poem," merely "pretty." Hacker's aggressive irreverence, her ostentatious indulgence in practices many would regard as improper or tasteless opens up new possibilities in both areas.

The rhyme pattern of the sonnet, whether Italian or English, lends itself to expression of a binary order. Some critics even claim that its two-part structure has served primarily to present first a problem and then its solution or resolution. In Hacker's hands, however, the form does not support a dichotomous intellectual/emotional structure. Her heavy use of enjambment thwarts the rhyme scheme's tendency to divide the octave from the sestet or to divide quatrains from one another; her tendency to employ in the sestet rhyme sounds very close to those in the octave gives a fluid unity to her sonnets (when, according to Paul Fussell, "the poet who understands the sonnet form" is the one who exploits its principle of imbalanced halves and therefore "tries to make the rhyme-words of the final six lines as different as possible from those of the preceding eight" [Fussell 1979, p. 115]). Hacker's fondness for linked series (crowns) adds flexibility to the length of the units constituting her sequence.

Indeed, Hacker sometimes so pushes the limits of the sonnet that her poems parody the form and the rules determining it. The heterogeneity of her diction is outrageous, mixing archaisms with contemporary urban vernacular, demotic French with highly educated English, Shakespearean allusion with topical references. The significance of the polyphony of languages from which Hacker constructs her poems is suggested when Hack calls attention to herself and her friends being "polyglot queer / women" while Iva who is "pre- / pubescent" is also "pre-polyglot": Hacker links fluency in multiple languages with the flexible self-construction and gender-construction her sexually mature lesbian characters are engaged in (*LD*, p. 52). Hacker's delight in the play of language—in puns, homophones, and the like—echoes that of Shakespeare and other Renaissance sonneteers, but her playfulness goes far beyond theirs as she flagrantly twists and extends syntax, calling attention to the way received forms shape both what is said and how it is said.[14] Mid-word line breaks and unlikely rhyme pairs—such as "VIS- / A" to rhyme with "colloquies," "Troj- / an" with "Maleboge," "inadept- / ly" with "re-schlepped"—further highlight the demands of the form and the often arbitrary relation of formal characteristics to semantics.

In both her representation of gender and in the form containing that representation, then, Hacker undermines an ideology of transparent "naturalness." The rules for being a "woman" and generating a proper "sonnet" are ideologically weighted constructions; while not entirely outside either of these, the formalist lesbian poet who is ready to play with both categories and thereby denaturalize them opens the way for different constructions of both gender and generic literary conventions.[15]

That Hacker's lovers, both individually and together, feel free to adopt a variety of conventionally male and female roles, signals their consciousness that gender is not given, but enacted. The sequence demands that the reader, too, grant gender's constructedness, allowing the characters to step in and out of roles even as stereotyped as those exploited by Howard Hawkes. Hacker does not suggest an ideal of androgyny—as does Doubiago, who presents only some gender differences as constructed and acculturated—nor of bisexuality. When an interviewer asked Hacker what she thought about Virginia Woolf's notion of the great artist as mentally bisexual, she replied first by criticizing the idea that certain qualities of mind are essentially female and others essentially male, and then added:

> There is, I believe, an enormous spectrum of human possibilities; and none [is] except culturally, more female or more male. The artist must be a whole human being, and that isn't a question necessarily of being "mentally bisexual." In my case, it isn't a question of being or wanting to be anything "more" than a woman. I am a woman. I would like to enlarge my own and everyone's definition of what a woman is.
>
> (Hammond 1980, p. 27)

This is the context for lines like, "You're an exemplar / piss-elegance is not reserved for boys. / Tonight we'll go out in our gangster suits" (*LD*, p. 66).

When, following the tradition of the Petrarchan sonneteers, Hacker depicts her lovers in terms of traditional mythology, she does not restrict her metaphorical positionings to female ones. She thereby attempts to expand our acculturated sense of what a woman is, while also acknowledging commonalities between lesbian lovers and other heterosexual or male homosexual lovers who have been portrayed in Western literature. Where Rich's speaker in "Twenty-one Love Poems" insists "[n]o one has imagined us [lesbian lovers]" (Rich 1978, p. 25), Hacker, as is consistent with her attitude toward the sonnet itself, sees the tradition in less exclusive terms. Thus Hack, thinking of her daughter's understanding of the term "lovers" as applying only to couples who have had genital sex (when she and Ray have not yet made love), says, "Two thousand years of Western literature: / potions and swords, the quests, the songs, the trysts, / call us what Iva, if she knew [that we'd not had sex], would not" (*LD*, p. 33). Without insisting on lesbians' separation from the perspective of those thousand years, her flexible assignment of multiple gender positions undermines the old myths' portrayal of narrow, fixed gender identities. This is the case in "Mythology," where Ray is identified as "Penelope as a *garçon manqué*" who "weaves sonnets on a barstool among sailors"; Iva as both daughter and son, "Persephone / a.k.a. Télémaque-who-tagged-along"; and Hack as "Ulysse-Maman" (*LD*, p. 48).

Hacker's portrayal elsewhere of Ray as a "hero" likened to Achilles demonstrates how she can simultaneously claim for women a conventionally male role (here again from mythological tradition), mock it, and revise it to generate an expanded sense of womanhood. Hack acknowledges that "hero" is a "big word," but she insists ordinary women like Ray and herself "have a claim to" that enlarging label. Taking a revisionary stance, Hack emphasizes the mundane character of heroism, applying the term to coping with "the harder times" in daily living (*LD*, p. 123). At the same time, she makes fun of the puffery in male heroic images, so that her portrayal of Ray in the hero's role is both sympathetic and teasing: When Ray is a "hero grown morose," Hack observes that "Achilles hung out in his tent and pouted / until they made the *Iliad* about it" (*LD*, p. 123). And when Ray is troubled about indecision, Hack ironically notes that indecision is "epic":

> Until they made the *Iliad* about it,
> nobody would have seen a fit of pique
> as quintessentially *geste héroïque*
> . . . .
> She whose mind's made up fast as she'd eat cake
> has not got that right stuff of which bards make
> heroes.
>
> (*LD*, p. 128)

Despite the joking, Hacker seems seriously to suggest that the poet has power to alter our perception of received myths and to shape gendered cultural concepts like heroism.

Expanding our understanding of what a woman is, and in particular what a woman/lover/poet may be, entails embracing a variety of traditionally female roles as well. In *Love, Death, and the Changing of the Seasons*, the speaker's being a mother is integrated into her identity as a lover. The contrast with the role assigned to parenting in Shakespeare's sonnets is illuminating. When Shakespeare's speaker in the "procreation sonnets" encourages his fair youth to become a father, he is concerned only with a narcissistic reproduction of the young man's beauty in his son. Parenting in Hacker's sequence has nothing to do with leaving oneself "living in posterity" (sonnet 6) or with insuring that "beauty's rose might never die" (sonnet 1). Hacker underlines the contrast by alluding to Shakespeare's sonnet 2 ("When forty winters shall besiege thy brow / And dig deep trenches in thy beauty's field,") in a poem which opens "Forty-two winters had besieged my brow / when you laid siege to my imagination" (*LD*, p. 133); the poem expresses Hack's desire to extend the lovers' relationship—with no mention of anyone's beauty or offspring—another forty-two summers.

Instead of serving as a repetition of her mother, Iva forms the third point in the sequence's most important love triangle. But rather than representing an unstable arrangement of rivalry in which someone will inevitably receive diminished love, this triangle is a potentially stable unit that the speaker attempts to sustain. Hack's hope is that she and Ray can "fill out each other's family"; her love for Ray does not supplant her love for her daughter. "[M]issing you can't obliterate / how I've missed her," Hack frankly tells Ray (*LD*, p. 188). Thus, as she becomes involved with Ray, Hack remains always concerned about how Iva is feeling. The importance of her maternal love is perhaps most clearly registered in the fact that the poem recording the lovers' long-awaited consummation focuses on Iva and how *she* spent that night in her own room. "[N]ot sure / of what she made of what she thought she heard," Hack goes to her early in the morning so that the poem ends recording a declaration of love not to Ray but to Iva, " 'I love you, you know, down to my last, best word' " (*LD*, p. 61). Ray and Iva are "my two girls" and Hack, despite the freedom gained during the intervals of Iva's absence, seems happiest when the three are together, for then she has "a family." The presence of Iva, then, further strengthens the emphasis on a domestic ideal while expanding the kinds of love between women that the sequence celebrates.

Hack's loving friendships are also a major focus in the volume, and this, too, broadens the Petrarchan lover's roles. Not only does Hack emphasize the importance of being her beloved's friend; in addition, a number of the poems are composed as letters to friends, most often to Julie in France. Through these epistles Hacker builds a sense of a richly supportive web of lasting relationships, many of them quite intimate without dependence on an erotic bond. When Julie experiences tough times, separation from her is painful just as separation from the beloved might be. Deaths of Hack's friends on both sides of the Atlantic are central events in the sequence; and these crises help the couple counter the imbalances fostered by the inequities of their age and experience. The younger woman takes the guide's role: "my own love," Hack reports, "walks me through / hangovers, death, and taxes like a scout / leader" (*LD*, p. 114).

Hacker's representation of Ray and the roles she plays—that is, her presentation of "the beloved," a tellingly passive critical term—

is an area where her alterations of Petrarchan norms are particularly clear. Hacker gives herself what we might call a feminist sonneteer's handicap by presenting a beloved who is not only significantly younger—and often addressed with diminutives such as "little one"—but who is literally the speaker's student; Ray and Hack met in a writing class Hack teaches. These inequities in power and experience would tend to set up a dynamic similar to that between traditional Petrarchan lovers. In examining Hacker's response to the challenge this poses, I will focus on three sometimes overlapping areas: giving the beloved voice and agency; depicting the beloved's physical being; negotiating phallocentric narratives of desire. We shall see that Hacker makes a place in the sonnet tradition for a speaking subjectivity that is not locked into a masculinized position and that she does much to lend voice, agency, and dimensionality to her speaker's beloved.

That Hacker's sequence is about an affair between two poets, even if one is teacher and the other student, signals the revisionary character of her representation of the beloved, for (as noted in discussing "Bloomingdale's I") this beloved is not the traditional silent other. In the androcentric Petrarchan tradition, as Marilyn Farwell points out, the poet/lover

> is active and creative; he is the one who speaks. The female, the beloved, is acted upon, her usual response to the ardent declarations of her lover being "no." This answer is not an expression of her own sexual choice, but, rather, it is an expression of woman's symbolic function vis-à-vis men: to help the poet transcend the lower world of change and physicality by reminding him that the real object of his sexual passion is his own creativity.
>
> (Farwell 1988, p. 106)

In *Love, Death, and the Changing of the Seasons*, both partners throughout their relationship are recording their experience in sonnets and exchanging them, through the mail or in person, as a mode of reciprocal communication. None of Ray's poems are included in *Love, Death, and the Changing of the Seasons* (though Hack quotes a line from one), but Hack reports translating and reading a poem by Ray at a reading of her own work in France, and she shows Julie Ray's poems together with her own. One could perhaps argue that in choosing to publish only her half of this co-authored love story, Hacker has in fact left Ray as silent as Petrarch's Laura; Ray's voice where quoted is either invented or appropriated. Yet the device of keeping constantly before the reader Ray's writerly vocation invites the reader to imagine Ray as possessing a voice and subjectivity that Laura, Stella, and the like did not attain. At one point Hack, who frequently uses popular song titles to sketch her situation, characterizes the members of the writing class as "our back-up group" (LD, p. 119); she thereby situates both herself and Ray as the lead singers. Such narrative details help destabilize the tradition of one-sided creativity in which "the active male engenders his poetry upon the body of a passive female muse" (DeShazar, quoted in Farwell 1988, 106).

As for "transcending the lower world of change and physicality," neither Hack nor Ray makes claims about immortalizing her lover through art.[16] Sonnet writing is part of the fabric of their lives, essential to their ongoing conversation and valued primarily as an immediate link between them. Thus, Hack on the transatlantic flight "find[s] a clean page to find you again" (LD, p. 29) and when she misses Ray across the ocean relies on "these few lines connecting me to you" (LD, p. 141). Hack is self-conscious, but unapologetic, about the textualizing drive of "left-brain righteousness that makes me / make of our doubled dailiness an art" (LD, p. 71). Presumably, the mutuality of this activity renders it an enhancement of their relationship.

Ray's being a poet provides another revision of a Shakespearean love triangle: Ray herself in this sequence is in some senses "the rival poet." A "competition" over who can complete her sonnet first is staged in the poem "Sunday Night." The complex dynamics of this contest emerge from its being compared to a battle fought by a young Spartan lover, which he wins and in which he dies, in order to save his (male) darling. At the close of this mock-heroic poem, Ray swaggers through "victorious," yet the analogy suggests that her triumph is as much a tribute to her lover/teacher as a victory over her. In contrast with the situation sketched by Shakespeare's sequence, if the rival wins here, the speaker is not the loser. The two partners do not occupy such polarized positions as the military metaphors (again a Petrarchan convention) might seem to suggest.

One of the best known—and for women most problematic—conventions of the Petrarchan sonnet tradition involves objectifying the usually female beloved through celebration, part-by-part, of her various beautiful features. As Nancy Vickers notes in "Diana Described: Scattered Woman and Scattered Rhyme":

> Petrarch's figuration of Laura informs a decisive stage in the devel-
> opment of a code of beauty, a code that causes us to view the fe-
> tishized body as a norm and encourages us to seek, or to seek to
> be, "ideal types, beautiful monsters composed of every individual
> perfection."
>
> (1981, p. 277)

Distancing her speaker from this dismemberment in the guise of idealization, Hacker takes pains never to have Hack speak of her beloved as beautiful and keeps to a minimum descriptions of her physical attributes. The only characteristic of Ray's appearance re-ferred to with any frequency is her blonde hair; its first mention, in the third sonnet, demonstrates how thoroughly Hacker has ap-propriated the Petrarchan sonnet tradition. Hacker's lines, "She hides her blushes in her leonine / hair, that was more like tinsel than like butter / when I ruffled it—the feminine / of *avuncular*" (*LD*, p. 5), repeat Shakespeare's gesture in sonnet 130—"My mis-tress' eyes are nothing like the sun. . . . If hairs be wires, black wires grow on her head." In mocking the exaggerations of a literary tradi-tion of "false compare," Hacker commits an anti-Petrarchism that is firmly within the tradition. At the same time, she reveals how undaunted she is by what others—such as Rich—would see as the masculine bias of the language she has inherited: "leonine," which dictionaries define as "characteristic of a lion," in uses like the above invokes the characteristics of *male* (maned) lions. Similarly, there is no familiar word denoting "like an aunt," only one meaning "like an uncle." Hacker's appropriation of these terms, like her appropri-ation of other "male" activities, calls into question our established gender categories, denying that the "male" is in fact male (or the "female" female).

Thereafter, descriptions of Ray's appearance are rare. On the only occasion when loveliness is explicitly attributed to the beloved, what is described is genitals in orgasm as Hack imagines making love to Ray: "with my whole hand, I / hold your drenched loveliness contracting" (*LD*, p. 21). Here the contrast is most directly with the misogynist portrayal of female sexuality in Shakespeare's poems addressed to the dark lady whose vagina figures as a "hell" in which his (male) angel lover is turned devil, a site of venereal infection (sonnet 144), and a "large and spacious" harbor promiscuously available to all (sonnet 135).

When Hack does provide brief notations of her beloved's physical appearance, she usually accompanies them with comparable descriptions of herself—"My olive skin, your creamy skin" (*LD*, p. 112), "She's / red-gold, I'm brown" (*LD*, p. 165)—rendering both partners embodied beings the reader might envision, neither one the exclusive object of our gaze. On one occasion, writing from France to her beloved in New York, Hack describes herself in order explicitly to remind Ray—and the reader—of the physical attractions she herself offers:

> Not averse to being seen
> as an amelioration of the view,
> I wore that black nubbed-raw-silk *salopette*,
> —but with a lurex cowlneck under it;
> the neckline-to-the-waist take was for you.

(LD, p. 51)

Isolated by a line break, the phrase "Not averse to being seen" suggests that what needs revising in the tradition is the onesidedness of observation that renders only the beloved an object of visual pleasure.

At the same time, Hacker has her beloved speak out against being used as a "masturbation fantasy." In "What You Might Answer" Hack imagines Ray—still unavailable and somewhat reluctant—expressing the kind of resistance the sonneteers' beloveds must have been feeling for centuries:

> "Nobody needs her Frye boots cast in bronze.
> I don't like crowds, and now I'm feeling crowded.
> I can speak tongues, but not the ones your friends
> gossip with you about me in. The end's
> still moot, jackboots. I have to think about it.
> . . . .
> You want a masturbation fantasy?
> Some girls you know put out a magazine
> full of them—but I'm not the centerfold."

(LD, p. 35)

The poem signals Hack's self-consciousness about the dangers of repeating male appropriations when, "horny as a timber wolf in heat" (*LD*, p. 10), she voices her sexual frustration as traditionally only men might. However much she enjoys that freedom, she is aware that she risks repeating the errors of her male predecessors: rendering her beloved yet another statue on a pedestal, albeit in modernized footwear. Consequently, a later poem finds her choosing not to use Ray as a "masturbation fantasy" when that opportunity arises as Ray, now her bedmate, is rendered passive by sleep. Masturbating while watching her would be easy—the technique is even described, "two fingers along my clit," etc.—"but I don't—take you against your will, / it seems like, and I wouldn't" (*LD*, p. 100).

In the many times Hack depicts sexual fantasies involving Ray, she attends to Ray's pleasure as much as her own; indeed, the two are inseparable. One preconsummation fantasy begins, "First, I want to make you come" and describes fairly explicitly how she would bring her lover to orgasm several times in succession; it closes with instructions for her lover (what to do with hands and tongue) so that the poem ends, "I want you to make me come" (*LD*, p. 21). Similarly, she frequently emphasizes her wish to give Ray time and space "to get to me / your way" (*LD*, p. 80). The poem "Future Conditional" reveals how such regard for reciprocity and mutual pleasure may alter the inherited subject/object positions of the sonnet sequence's lover and beloved. Its language recalls Montefiore's claims about the beloved functioning as a mirroring means of self-definition. Hack, writing from France, begins by urging Ray "let us start / where we left off" but soon moves from the hortatory stance to the future conditional, describing her fantasy of their first genital sex. "Sweetheart," she pleads, "your body is a text I need the art / to be constructed by." Yet having apparently announced explicitly the self-construction that Montefiore finds implicit in the traditional love sonnet, Hack proceeds to make this same self-construction available for her lover. As she imagines herself undressing Ray, her own body becomes a text (book) for Ray's use:

> . . . I'll find the hook,
> release promised abundance to this want,
> while your hands, please, here and here, exigent
> and certain, open this; it is, this book,
> made for your hands to read, your mouth to use.
>
> (*LD*, p. 50)

Opening her legs or the lips of her vagina to expose the clitoris merges with the act of opening the book of sonnets. In the latter act, the reader merges with Ray, suggesting not only an erotic invitation to us but also a textualization that extends even to the reader. No one escapes being textualized, rendered an object by which others may construct their own identities, but by the same token, self-construction becomes an activity common to all. This more abstract version of the "I want to make you come" poem reveals a significant change in dynamics between speaker and beloved, one made possible simply by an insistence on the equality of their sexual needs and capacities, an equality missing from the heterosexual Petrarchan tradition.

This mutuality is underscored by Hacker's frequent recourse to a metonymic rhetoric of contiguity and touch for portraying her lovers' connections rather than a metaphoric rhetoric which, Homans has argued, hierarchically depends on specular distance between speaker and beloved.[17] Not wanting either of her lovers to be rendered merely objects, Hacker explores the pleasures of a sexuality that is not primarily specular. Once again, however, she sees no need to excise what Homans identifies as the "male" plot of desire or the referentiality to which it is bound, any more than she entirely rejects "male" roles or language for her characters. As we have seen in other contexts, her project is an expansive one: she appropriates a quest plot yet also places new emphasis on the pleasure of touch in women's sexuality.

Distance, according to Homans, is the motive for the (male) sonneteer's writing. This remains true in Hacker's work to the extent that otherness—that is, the lovers' inhabiting individual bodies— itself is a form of distance: Hacker rarely exploits the figure of sameness, a potential disguise of separateness often present in lesbian representation (especially, Grover reminds us, in "good girl" writing, where it tends to downplay tensions generated by differences, for instance, in class, race, and ethnicity [Grover 1990, p. 22]). But as noted above, the distances that most concern her are emotional, not physical or hierarchical, and the story she tells is not primarily the phallocentric story of looking. The spatial figure she returns to several times as depicting her lovers' closeness/separateness is that of asymptotes—lines forever drawing together more and more closely, though never in fact touching. For example, in a poem whose opening line ("From you will I be absent as the spring") echoes Shakespeare's sonnet 98, Hack on the eve of departure for France voices her hope that

the clearer focus of a distancing
lens will show both of us separately
comet trails marking your trajectory
and mine, convergent, or continuing
asymptotes, toward a human finity
of works and days.

(LD, p. 137)

While the first sixty pages of *Love, Death, and the Changing of the Seasons* which precede the couple's first lovemaking are dominated by a quest similar to that of the Petrarchan male lover—initially, Ray is "just the kind of boy / I would have eyeballed at the bar" (*LD*, p. 17)—the remaining pages depict a struggle both lovers undertake (at least according to Hack) to reduce psychological and emotional distances: "We've both got work to do / to work our different ways across the distance / between us" (*LD*, p. 140). Since the goal is a touching on all fronts—"I want our lives to touch / the way our minds do. What our bodies do / together is unprecedented. (Minds / dreamed it up; can the dichotomy.)" (*LD*, p. 111)—even words and gazes may be presented in terms of contact: "wished I could touch / you now with words . . . that there'd be eye // contact and talk across a dinner table" (*LD*, p. 187). When the breakup does occur, at Ray's instigation, Hack describes the bond she still feels in terms of physical contact and presence that virtually eliminate distance. Yet "I" and "you" remain distinct: "As my eyes / open [upon waking], I know *I* am; that instant, feel / you with me, on me, in me, and you're not" (*LD*, p. 209).

Hacker's ways of revising the Renaissance Petrarchans' tropes depicting the beloved in astronomical figures also demonstrate her interest in representing nonphallocentric narratives of sexual pleasure. The traditional metaphors, Homans points out, "depend for their effect on the analogy between the distance between poet and lady—the distance of desire—and the distance between the lady and the stars to which she is compared" (*LD*, p. 571–72). Hacker works against this distance. In lines quoted earlier, for instance—"I moved into one mansion / the morning when I touched, I saw, I felt / your face blazing above me like a sun" (*LD*, p. 69)—the specular economy with which the comparison of beloved to sun is traditionally yoked merges into a tactile one in which the mutuality of touching and being touched [feeling] is emphasized. Similarly, shortly after the relationship is sexually consummated, Hack announces "This is the second morning I woke curved / around your dreaming. In one night, I've seen / moonset and sunrise in your lion's mane" (*LD*, p. 65). Rather than staring across space at the star/beloved, she sees the motion of astronomical bodies through and "in" the hair of the lover whose body is curved against her own. What Homans terms the "story of looking" here is not one of looking at the beloved, but looking with and alongside her. Nor is Hack the only partner who gazes; Ray has eyes, too, and "What they see sometimes are scabs and scars / on my thin hide. Not always a forgiving / gaze" (*LD*, p. 166).

It should be apparent by now that Hacker does not aspire to sever her work—or her romantic couple—from the traditions of heterosexual patriarchy; yet her feminist parody and play challenge traditional ideology by undermining patriarchal gender categories. The three poems on "Having Kittens about Having Babies" (*LD*, pp. 104–6) permit a closing recap of this formalist feminist poet's position both inside and outside of hegemonic norms. Ray, wanting her own child, has proposed spending "a few months fucking a high-school friend / or, failing that, cruis[ing] bars and pick[ing] up men / until one takes"; she believes this arrangement need not impinge on her lesbian relationship. In order to make Ray understand why she finds this proposal outrageous, Hack asks her to imagine a comparable situation involving a hypothetical heterosexual couple in which the man is infertile because the child of his first marriage gave him mumps. Hack apparently assumes that the emotional dynamics and interpersonal responsibilities of her and Ray's situation will be clearer if presented in terms of heterosexual relationships, for which there's a more general agreement about what is acceptable. Through her speaker, Hacker suggests that because lesbians have to devote so much energy to forging new patterns, they risk losing sight of some basic obligations that she holds apart from issues of gender and sexual preference: "There are two readings to the text: because / no law defines this love, we are outlaws. / We're not, each to the other, marginal." That Hack and Ray are literally and figuratively outside patriarchal law would not justify behavior violating some more fundamentally human laws of respect for the feelings of those one loves. In the first two of the three poems, then, Hacker seems to caution against exaggerating the difference of lesbian relationships.

Yet after Hack has explicitly presented her situation as "the same" as that of the infertile man in her fictive couple (except that "[i]t's not by mumps that I'm disqualified / as child begetter"), in the third poem she distances herself from the heterosexual narrative by fore-grounding privileges accorded the heterosexual male that no lesbian lover can enjoy. Analogies between heterosexual and lesbian couples are accurate only within certain areas, while the dramatic social differences oppress lesbians materially and psychologically:

> They get to make their loves the focal point
> of Real Life: last names, trust funds, architecture,
> reify them; while we are, they conjecture,
> erotic *frissons*, birds of passage, quaint
> embellishments in margins.

(LD, p. 106)

Presenting "we" through "their" eyes enacts the marginalization— the expulsion from the subject position—that Hack is talking about here, and her tone is as angry as it ever gets in the sequence. But she rejects anger for the consolations of her lover, and, after several long kisses restore her composure, she looks to the ways in which lesbians can turn their marginalization to advantage. Refocusing attention away from reproduction and babies, Hack urges:

> Look what we're mak-
> ing, besides love (that has a name to speak).
> Its very openness keeps it from harm, or
> perhaps it wears our live-nerved skin as armor,
> out in the world arranging mountains, nak-
> ed as some dream of Cousin William Blake.

(LD, p. 106)

The relationship these lesbian feminists are creating is expansive (open), and the work it is doing is substantial. No doubt Hacker holds similar aspirations for the sonnet sequences they are making. Yet she does not hesitate to identify the visionary character of this work with a man rather than a woman; in her view, neither women nor lesbians have exclusive claims on marginality or productive social change. Nor do free verse writers—or notably avant-garde ones—have exclusive claims to political engagement; as Hacker once asserted, "If there is such a thing as a New Formalist, s/he may be a black activist as well" (1989, p. 4).

Among contemporary poets generally and women composing long poems specifically, there nonetheless remain those skeptical that regular, closed forms and unfragmented narratives may be adequate either to the postmodern era or to exploration of female difference. Joan Retallack, for instance, an experimental feminist poet affiliated with Language writing, admires Hacker's "extraordinarily sensual intellect," "her linguistic straddling of high-low culture, and her transvaluation of values from implicitly masculine to explicitly, even randily feminine" (1990, pp. 500, 502). But Retallack remains uneasy about the consequences of Hacker's "unsurpassed facility" with regular forms:

> I wonder whether Hacker is fully aware of the consequences of form in the reader's mind—that there is a kind of eradication of difference (the very thing Hacker must value greatly as a feminist poet) in uniform packaging. I want Hacker to claim Gertrude Stein as a genuine spiritual ancestor [not just as a lesbian one]—to claim some of her lust as non-Euclidean poetic geometer. This is not to abandon discipline but to recognize the specific gravities and honors of formal choices.
>
> (1990, p. 504)

In her view, Hacker's performative revelation of the arbitrariness and conventionality of inherited forms remains a valuable but still constraining project.

The final two chapters examine works by poets who, in attempting to sustain poetic mapping of women's history or subjectivity, feel compelled to pursue more radical formal interventions than Hacker. Where Hacker sees women as having contributed importantly to mainstream traditions (even if their contribution is underacknowledged), these avant-garde feminist writers suspect the dominant conventions (positioned within Irigaray's "masculine imaginary" or Kristeva's "symbolic order") of excluding what is distinctly feminine. Where Hacker perceives set forms as arbitrary constructions inherently no better suited to presenting one person's experience than another's, Susan Howe, Beverly Dahlen, and Rachel Blau DuPlessis regard those regular and closed forms, even if initially arbitrary, as at least historically determined to produce particular kinds of meanings and exclude others. For these experimentalists, revolutionary disruption of formal and linguistic convention appears necessary for any fresh perspectives to emerge, including expression of the feminine.

Susan Howe, whose "The Liberties" I shall examine next, possesses an interest in history analogous to that evident in Dove's and Osbey's sequences. Unlike those poets, however, she has focused on developing non-narrative formal strategies and often asyntactic linguistic structures for incorporating into long poems the silences of women. Highlighting women's absence from the poetic and historical record, Howe registers the difficulties and hesitations of feminine or feminized expression that her historical research has revealed.

CHAPTER FIVE

"The Silences Are Equal to
the Sounds": Documentary
History and Susan Howe's
"The Liberties"

E‍zra Pound defined epic, the genre in which he placed his *Cantos*, as "a poem containing history," and a great many men and women writing long poems since the *Cantos*—not necessarily in obviously epic modes—have carried on Pound's desire to produce work that would include and shed light on history. Experimental poet Susan Howe, for instance, who works exclusively in extended forms, has stated "[i]t would be hard to think of poetry apart from history. This is one reason Olson [a key participant in Pound's tradition of epic] has been so important to me" (Foster 1990, p. 17). Pound himself came to regard the modern attempt at epic as "rash," perhaps doomed, because of the absence of social consensus in the modern era.[1] But if writing poems containing history has been difficult for modern male poets because faiths are eroding, master narratives crumbling, and readerships fracturing, this project has presented further challenges for women poets interested in women's history. Pound and Olson at least had little difficulty finding heroes documented in historical record through whom to project their own values and experiences, as well as their aims for modern culture. In contrast, "if you are a woman," Howe has observed, "archives hold perpetual ironies. Because the gaps and silences are where you find yourself" (Foster 1990, p. 16–17).

Contemporary women poets interested in using long poems to explore women's history—or histories of others inadequately represented in archives—have responded to this ironic situation in a variety ways. This has already been apparent in the very different approaches to history already observed: Doubiago, while mythologizing her own experience, emphasizes parallels with histories of oppressed nations and tribes; Grahn instructs her readers in the prior existence of matrifocal cultures and asserts present continuity with them; Dove and Osbey in their fictionalized portraits of ordinary lives highlight the historical context of ethnic communities underrepresented in mainstream historiography. Another current strategy involves attempting to retrieve and to bring to center stage the lives of specific figures who have been recognized in received histories yet have been relegated to peripheral positions there. This retrieval relies partly on scholarly historical research methodologies that enable incorporation into poetry of documentary evidence. This chapter examines Susan Howe's distinctive approach to such documentary poetic historiography.

A brief comparison with a contrasting and more widespread approach, represented here by Ruth Whitman, will provide an initial means of defining and situating Howe's work. Howe and Whitman share a passionate interest in the particularities of individual past lives, which entails both of them in extensive archival research. At the same time, they believe that, in Monique Wittig's formulation, the writer, even if she speaks from the minority position, "must assume both a particular *and* a universal point of view, at least to be part of literature. That is, one must work to reach the general, even while starting from an individual or from a specific point of view" (Wittig 1992, p. 67). Thus, although their long poems have focused on either female or feminized historical figures, they hold similar convictions that poetry's greatest achievement is in its transcendence—neither feels shy of that lofty term—of the merely individual, the temporally specific, the singly gendered. Despite her belief that gender inflects poets' voices, Howe announces early in *My Emily Dickinson* (a prose study in the tradition of Williams's *In the American Grain* or Olson's *Call Me Ishmael*), "A poet is never just a woman or a man. Every poet is salted with fire" (Howe 1985, p. 7); perhaps consequently, she believes that "poetry leads past possession of self to transfiguration beyond gender" (1985, p. 138). Similarly, Whitman sees the aim of her preferred genre, what she terms the "historical persona poem," as enabling readers "to perceive the persona's experience in its symbolic essence. Not only is the persona's historical instant thus illuminated, but beyond that, human experience in general—the reader's own experience and understanding of universal experience—is intensified" (Whitman 1987, p. 69). For both poets, exploration of gender functions within, and is necessary to, a more encompassing goal.

Yet their approaches to poetic language and historiography differ dramatically. Ruth Whitman—like Dove, Osbey, and most mainstream poets today—relies on conventions of realism; her lyric sequences render historical narratives by imaginatively recreating her subjects' thoughts and feelings. Susan Howe, in contrast, is affiliated with the postmodernist avant-garde Language writers, who deliberately thwart perceptions of language as reproducing rather than producing our reality and reject poetics based on personal voice.[2] Howe shares the Language poets' desire to disrupt conventions of representational realism, though the centrality of her interest in historical subjects and historiography also distinguishes her work significantly from theirs. (Indeed, her practices may implicitly challenge the predominantly male theorists of Language writing to engage more with history and historical discourse in their poetry.)

To put the matter in terms not of present affiliations but of inherited traditions, the striking differences between Whitman's and Howe's poetic treatments of history reflect their alignments with distinct male-dominated traditions demonstrating different relations to collagistic prosodic experiment and different senses of personal psychology's usefulness as a probe of history. Whitman identifies John Berryman's *Homage to Mistress Bradstreet*, usually seen as a transitional work marking his move toward the confessional mode, as in many ways "the model for contemporary poets interested in translating the historical persona." In this model, immersion in data about one's historical subject enables the poet to "meld" with him or her: "Berryman tells that as he read Anne Bradstreet's poems and investigated her social, cultural and historical background, he began to fall in love with her, and in a certain mystical sense, to become her" (Whitman 1987, p. 67). Such union depends on a recognition of profound kinship, fostered by "Freudian and post-Freudian" insights that make it "easier to recognize the links between one's own dark subconscious and another's" (Whitman 1987, p. 67). Thus, Whitman, who first found herself writing in the persona of Tamsen Donner when coming out of ether after surgery, pursued her obsessive sense of identification with that woman through historical archives and across the American landscape until she "knew that [she] must write [Tamsen Donner's] lost journal for her" (1987, p. 72). According to Whitman, in poems in this tradition "the poet aims to *become* the other, not merely to tell a tale to an audience, but to reveal the essence of a well-known historical character" (1987, pp. 65–66). In Whitman's sequences *Tamsen Donner: A Woman's Journey* and *The Testing of Hanna Senesh*, this revelation focuses especially on the psychological mechanics of survival in extraordinarily stressful or life-threatening situations.

It is typical of Whitman's poetics that, in constructing her *Tamsen Donner* as a chronologically ordered journal giving voice to the pioneer woman married to the leader of the doomed "Donner Party," she does not significantly disrupt linearity. She appreciates precisely the long poem's linear expansiveness (Vance 1982, p. 66) and identifies in the narrative coherence of her work a principled resistance to modernist or postmodernist fragmentation:

> Most modern music is so difficult because it reflects the randomness, the chaos of our lives, the fragmentation of our lives. And that fragmentation I believe is part of our decadence. One either wants to reflect it or work against it.
>
> (Vance 1982, p. 69)

Work like Whitman's, "written to elucidate another life" through versions of dramatic monologue—a mode which includes Pamela Alexander's *Commonwealth of Wings* or Frank Bidart's "The War of Vaslav Nijinsky," among many others—draws upon readers' powers of empathetic imagination. It invites recognition of the full subjectivity of specific historical individuals and lends a sense of actuality to their experiences. Poets who extend this mode beyond the voice of a single speaker—for example, Jill Breckenridge in *Civil Blood*, Dolores Kendricks in *Women of Plums*, Mark Kaminsky in *Road from Hiroshima*—can expand beyond one person's psychology to develop fuller portraits of society and of forces behind events.[3] This is a valid poetic enterprise; entering into the consciousness of richly rendered personae like Whitman's can move readers deeply while offering insight into particular histories. When the subjects of these works have appeared largely in the gaps and silences of historical record, however, poems in this mode tend to mute the dynamics of the silencing they counter. The impulse to invent lost voices and events itself acknowledges their erasure, but a skillful poet's invention in this mimetic mode deliberately creates an effect of recovered record, even of immediate presence. The poet's ability convincingly to recreate those lives diverts attention from their earlier erasure and the systems of power behind it, as it focuses attention on prior individuals' subjectivity.

Howe's poetry places very different demands on its readers and offers them alternative rewards, for her approach to documentary histories demonstrates a more mediated sense of identification with and retrieval of her historical subjects and an abiding concern with the processes by which history's silences have been generated. The tradition she invokes is one less interested in psychic states and "essences"—one more interested in the individual's interaction with systems of power, in language's role in these power relations, and in the larger dynamics of intellectual and cultural history.

Howe positions her work in a predominantly male iconoclastic tradition in which fragmentation appears inescapable:

> I hope that I am working in an eccentric twentieth-century American tradition that embraces among others Duncan, Olson, Williams, Stevens, H.D., and Hart Crane. Seven poets move in puzzling ways through the ruins of our violent patriarchal history— what has been handed down to us—echoes of memory and myth. Six men and one woman.
>
> (Becket 1989, p. 18)[4]

> I work in the tradition of other poets who have inspired me; poets in the 20th century most of whom are men. Why are there so few women (until just recently) in this tradition? This tradition that I hope I am part of has involved a breaking of boundaries of all sorts. It involves a fracturing of discourse, a stammering even. Interruption and hesitation used as a force. A recognition that there is an other voice, an attempt to hear and speak it. Its [sic] this brokenness that interests me.
>
> (Howe 1990, p. 192)

In addition to serving to "shatter hierarchies," this brokenness linked to "an other voice" is something she associates with hesitation and, importantly, with the feminine.[5] Thus, Howe describes Emily Dickinson's achievement in terms of fracture and stammering which she opposes to the sounding of confident masculine hegemony:

> [Dickinson] built a new poetic form from her fractured sense of being eternally on intellectual borders, where confident masculine voices buzzed an alluring and inaccessible discourse, backward through history into aboriginal anagogy. Pulling pieces of geometry, geology, alchemy, philosophy, politics, biography, biology, mythology, and philology from alien territory, a "sheltered" woman audaciously invented a new grammar grounded in humility and hesitation. HESITATE from the Latin, meaning to stick. Stammer. To hold back in doubt, have difficulty speaking.
>
> (Howe 1985, p. 21)

Howe finds this feminine element also in Olson's poetry, despite his work's disturbing elision of women:

> If there is Woman in Olson's writing (there aren't women there), she is either "Cunt," "Great Mother," "Cow," or "Whore." But the feminine is very much in his poems in another way. A way similar to Melville—It's voice . . . It has to do with the presence of absence. With articulation of sound forms. The fractured syntax, the gaps, the silences are equal to the sounds in *Maximus*. . . . It's the stutter in American literature that interests me. I hear the stutter as a sounding of uncertainty. What is silenced or not quite silenced. All the broken dreams.
>
> (Foster 1990, p. 37)

Like Doubiago, she critiques Olson's representation of the female. But she reads very differently the holding back of speech that Doubiago rejects as a problematic masculine emotional withholding. Howe's perceiving a feminine dynamic in the fractured, telegraphic character of Olson's prosody redeems its resources for her own use. Consequently, the formal impact of projectivist writing registers far more clearly on Howe's distinctively arranged pages than on Doubiago's.

In contrast to Ruth Whitman, Howe is committed to fragmentation, not as a mirror of modern life, but as a politically necessary disruption of the forms of knowledge that confine us. She criticizes those artists and feminist critics who imagine they can destroy hierarchies and hegemonic systems without shattering form and linear progression (Howe 1985, p. 116). Moreover, she regards fragmentation as part of a rhythmic process fundamental to her writing:

So I start in a place with fragments, lines and marks, stops and gaps, and then I have more ordered sections, and then things break up again. That's how I begin most of my books. . . . these sounds, these pieces of words come into the chaos of life, and then you try to order them and to explain something and the explanation breaks free of itself. I think a lot of my work is about breaking free. Starting free and being captured and breaking free again and being captured again.

(Foster 1990, p. 24)

The historical figures who interest her include authors of captivity narratives such as Mary Rowlandson, the women authors of early American conversion narratives, the colonial minister Hope Atherton (whose feminine name intrigues her), the minor Irish poet Clarence Mangan, as well as better-known writers such as Emily Dickinson or Herman Melville. These individuals are not necessarily connected with events that have garnered attention within mainstream history; accounting for her subjects' near absence from or misrepresentation in historical record is a major concern in Howe's work.

Here, too, gender plays a central role. Thus, in an interview where she discusses Esther Edwards Burr, Jonathan Edwards's daughter and Aaron Burr's mother, whose mid-eighteenth-century journal was published in 1984, Howe remarks:

Until now her life has been a blank in historical consciousness. You will hardly find her mentioned in Biographies of these two men. Women must rectify what Irigaray calls "this aporia of discourse." We have to try to understand how and why historical domination has put mothers, wives, and daughters in a position of inferiority. We go back through the masculine imaginary, Irigaray also says, to discover a beginning and a future for our imaginations. It's a very exciting time to be a woman writing. I don't think Esther just dies and that's that. . . . Esther is in many of us, particularly if we are New Englanders. . . . Esther Edwards Burr and an anonymous Delaware woman are members of that silent faction—the feminine. They *were* and somewhere they still *are*. Traces are here.

(Becket 1989, p. 23)

Rather than attempting imaginatively to give life to someone now dead, Howe seeks the traces of those lost women who live as buried parts of our consciousness. She explores the past within the present and the constitution of the present by the past, without believing there is any direct access to the feminine. To tease out that repressed reality, one must go back through the dominant discourse and see how what is not (or barely) there shapes or makes possible what is.[6] Howe's connection with her historical subjects, while no less obsessive than Whitman's,[7] depends little on identification with their emotions in extreme situations. It depends on recognition of a common intellectual and ideological inheritance and on a sense of existing at least partly as an aporia outside of coherent discourse. The struggles she shares with them reflect not only their common traditions, or the earlier figures' having shaped what Howe inherits as traditional, but also a certain liminality that removes them from those same traditions. Often the issues she explores have to do with gender identity and its transgression, sometimes with the "feminine" aspects of individual men or the "masculine" behavior of particular women.

The singularity of individual voices intrigues Howe and is something she seeks to discover and salvage, at the same time that voice and identity emerge in her writing as highly mediated, elusive constructions. Instead of rendering a realistic mimesis of her subjects' thoughts, Howe weaves a text from heterogeneous traces: fragments of archival material, of literary intertexts and echoes, her own thoughts and lyrical inventions, audible (and visible) silences, puns, parts of words, new combinations of letters and phonemes. The visual presentation of these elements is crucial for Howe, who was a painter before she became a poet. In her historical essays and poems alike, she generates for earlier figures complex collagistic portraits which are frankly the creation of an invested onlooker (*my* Emily Dickinson, for instance). Her work may contain fragments of the other's documented or imagined voice, but Howe foregrounds the artifice and the idiosyncrasy of any attempts at ventriloquy.

The disjunctive fabric of Howe's poetry, then, dramatizes the ineradicable gaps in our historical record and our consciousness, making them essential to the portraits she paints. Unfilled, holes in our knowledge or understanding attain a quite specific shape; absences gain an emphatic presence. At the same time, the allusiveness of Howe's writing insists that language is inescapably steeped in history; any word carries historical layerings that expand its meaning and extend its force into silent spaces. As Rachel Blau DuPlessis observes of Howe's understanding of language, words bear "the fused detritus of all their imbeddings" (1990, p. 127). Howe's work enacts an understanding that one can gain insight into past lives through attention, at once historically disciplined and imaginative, applied equally to preserved words and preserved silences—to sounds and their interruption, to inscriptions and blank spaces.

Besides giving stuttering tongue to some of the nearly lost or unintelligible voices, Howe's writing also dramatizes the processes by which marginal voices are silenced and leaves many of the silences to speak for themselves—a particularly significant difference from work like Whitman's. In order to illuminate the workings of Howe's historically conscious experimental long poems, this chapter focuses on "The Liberties" (1980), in which Howe goes back through the masculine imaginary—especially via Jonathan Swift and William Shakespeare—to explore, among other things, the history of a woman at once famous and virtually unknown. Rather than emphasizing Howe's relation to the particular American modernist tradition within which she situates her long poems, I will attend most to what her poetry suggests about the impact on women writers of the inherited patriarchal cultural environment generally— that imaginary which may be as well represented by Shakespeare as by Pound, by Swift or Samuel Beckett as by Olson.

As in Howe's work generally, in "The Liberties" historical particulars both do and do not serve representative functions. For while Howe's collagistic text is constructed from fragments—participating in what Hugh Kenner, characterizing poetic modernism, termed an "aesthetic of glimpses"—their status as shards from a whole is simultaneously denied and asserted (Kenner 1971, p. 69). One of Howe's more recent terms, "singularity," may be more appropriate than "fragment" for referring to the historical particulars that enter her work, since "singularity" suggests distinction without necessarily denoting a part broken from a whole. Singularities may well figure in systems, but they also may act as elements of dynamism and transgression, not merely as representative samples. Howe's discussion of the term (the title of her 1990 Wesleyan collection), deriving from her reading of work by mathematician Rene Thom, emphasizes this transformative dimension:

> In algebra a singularity is the point where plus becomes minus. On a line if you start at x point, there is $+1$, $+2$, etc. But at the other side of the point is -1, -2, etc. The singularity (I think Thom is saying) is the point where there is a sudden change to something completely else. It's a chaotic point. It's the point where chaos enters cosmos, the instant articulation. Then there is a leap into something else.
>
> (Foster 1990, pp. 30–31)

As historiographer, Howe charts the general laws and systems (including, notably, those of language within patriarchy) that govern or restrain individuals, thereby keeping her readers conscious that orderly systems are coercive and render particularity difficult to discern. But she is especially interested in those points of chaos (events, or more often, particular people) that are at once part of the system and outside of it: points of fracture at which the anomalous, the unique agent of destabilization and change, emerges. "Woman" itself may be understood as a point of singularity interjected into the cosmos of the "universal" male (thus Wittig argues that there is no masculine gender because the masculine is the general and abstract, while only the feminine is concrete, specific). Certainly, the individual women in "The Liberties"—Stella, Cordelia, sometimes Howe herself—are themselves singularities: they operate within controlling systems, but in their particular defiant histories they are also points of disruption and potential transformation. Her desire is to "abstract" these disruptive elements "from 'masculine' linguistic configuration" (Howe, in Frank and Sayre 1988, p. 209).

Many of the operative assumptions in "The Liberties" pertaining to women's place in history and in historical record can be discerned in "Fragments of a Liquidation," Howe's opening prose biography of the woman widely known as Jonathan Swift's Stella. Although Howe's biographical narrative is constructed as a paratactic arrangement of facts with little commentary, relations among the data in this section are relatively clear. The polemical title identifies what has happened to Hester Johnson (Stella) in terms of an economic transaction by which debts are erased; the woman has been disposed of, she and her value have been transformed in order to be eliminated. If Stella has not been entirely eliminated from history, she has been misnamed and rendered unsuccessful in naming, and thereby defining, herself. Howe has remarked in an interview that "it takes a name to make something visible" (Becket 1989, p. 18), yet Stella attained no visibility as Esther, the name she preferred. Her near-erasure from historical record and her thwarted self-definition typify what Howe sees as the situation of women in history. Moreover, Howe's adoption of the name Stella acknowledges that the twentieth-century writer has access only to the woman inscribed in a male text, not to the real historical woman who stands behind that construction.

"Fragments of a Liquidation" clearly suggests a powerful bond between Stella and Swift. It emphasizes their willingness to risk "rumors damaging to them both" in order to live in proximity in Ireland. But contradictions are central to the couple's behavior, as they are to most figures of interest to Howe. Despite certain bold moves, in other ways Swift and Stella risk no semblance of impropriety; in twenty-seven years of companionship they "were never seen together unless a third person was present" (*Defenestration of Prague*, p. 66; parenthetical references to "The Liberties" are to this edition and will be cited hereafter as *DP*). While making choices atypical of their era, they were nonetheless constrained by its conventions.

That Stella because of her gender had more to lose—and indeed lost more—through the couple's unconventional arrangement is also stressed in Howe's opening biography: Stella forfeited friendships with women; she was left behind in Ireland when Swift went to England and pursued his affairs, romantic as well as professional; she sacrificed the possible benefits of marriage; her literary talents are recorded, if at all, in three poems (scholars question whether these poems attributed to Stella are in fact hers) and her letters were not saved. Despite her tremendous emotional and material importance to the celebrated Dean (she managed his household, took care of him during his illnesses, transcribed his poems), in her final illness, according to Howe, he seems to have been more concerned about propriety than about his bonds to her. It is clear that a woman's position of reduced social liberty and power renders her acts of resistance particularly costly.

Extant characterizations of Stella, Howe emphasizes, are minimal and sometimes inconsistent: "No authentic portrait exists" (*DP*, p. 67).[8] In some senses, the multigeneric work that follows this prose section attempts speculatively to generate a possibly more authentic portrait, to correct past errors and oversights by displaying the singularities of Stella's life. More centrally, however, what follows continues to be "fragments of a liquidation"—that is, a collagistic reconstruction of some of the processes by which Stella's "real" identity was erased from history, including those ways in which Stella herself contributed to or complied with that liquidation.

But, as Howe's fascination with "feminine" elements in Melville, Olson, and American literature generally would suggest, she is not interested only in the situation of actual historical women. Stella is not Howe's sole focus, and from the complexly echoing structure of "The Liberties," Stella emerges also as representative of western woman, whose position is partially analogous to that of Ireland and of colonized peoples more generally. As Duplessis has noted, Howe participates in "two feminisms: the one analyzing female difference, the other 'feminine' difference"; the 'feminine' position may be occupied by men as well as women, by "[a]nything marginalized by patriarchal order" (1990, p. 135). Often Howe's palimpsestic overlay of oppressed subjects makes it difficult to distinguish which one(s) she is considering. What justifies Howe's seeming conflation of individual, national, and literary history in "The Liberties" is her understanding of their common entanglement in systems of domination and oppression in which language plays a key role. Thus, as I shall demonstrate, in the more dramatically ruptured parts of "The Liberties," Howe subverts literary devices and linguistic structures essential to traditional interpretive methods not only by foregrounding their artifice but also by highlighting their integration into systems of patriarchal or colonial oppression. Howe's understanding of the culturally constituted and relative "feminine" is crucial to her movement between the particular and the general.

Howe seeks a balanced representation of her characters' powers: to present a "feminine" figure (or entity such as Ireland) as entirely disempowered would be to negate her/his subjectivity and agency, while to empower that figure too much would downplay the repressive operation of the hegemonic/colonizing system, which is both manifest and reinforced through conventional language use.[9] Howe conveys the pervasive power dynamics that render Stella a distinct but often representative figure among diverse versions of the "feminine" through adaptations of Poundian methods of "subject rhyme"[10] and through a nonlinear organization of her history around recurrent rhyming elements similar to Pound's "luminous details."[11] Yet her focal figures do not occupy the positions of clear villainy or heroism occupied by historical characters in the more overtly didactic *Cantos* or *Maximus Poems*. For instance, to the extent that Swift himself was disempowered through his assignment to an Irish church, he occupies a "feminine" position similar to Stella's. No character emerges as unambiguously hegemonic or nonhegemonic, and the details generating rhymes between characters or events often reveal parallels between apparent victim and victimizer.

The at least partial rhyme between Stella, Swift, and Ireland—partial because the "feminine" status of these entities is in constant flux—is set up from the earliest moments of "The Liberties" (with Shakespeare's Cordelia added later as what we might call a further "feminine rhyme"). Ireland enters the text before Stella, through the reproduction of a postage stamp on the dedication page facing the title. The 8-pence stamp, on which the Gaelic *éire* appears in large print, is dominated by a flying angel with immense feathered wings, across whose chest flows a banner with the words "*vox hiberniae.*" As the poem develops, this image of the voice of Ireland takes on an irony comparable to that which historical archives possess for women's history: it is audible as much in its silence and silencing as in its cries. Bird imagery recurs throughout the poem in connection with Ireland, Stella, and the usefully named Swift, ambiguously functioning sometimes to suggest vulnerability, sometimes the liberated empowerment that may be associated with flight.

Like Ireland, Jonathan Swift is introduced before Stella, in an apparently stammering epigraph preceding "Fragments of a Liquidation." The passage—" 'so adieu deelest MD MD MD FW FW Me Me Fais I don't conceal a bitt. as hope sav'd' "—derives with slight alteration from Swift's *Journal to Stella* of April 1712, written while Swift was in England pleading the cause of the Irish clergy and during the period of "his growing entanglement with Esther Vanhomrigh (VANESSA)" (*DP*, p. 67).[12] Only after reading "Fragments of a Liquidation" will the potential ramifications of this passage emerge. For just as Howe's method of construction—including her near-simultaneous introduction of Ireland, Swift, and Stella as partially rhyming focal interests—precludes a single focus, one's reading of Howe's work cannot develop through solely a linear accumulative process or through adherence to single interpretations. Not merely permitting multiple readings, as all "rich" texts do,

Howe's text presses on the reader a sense of partiality in any one interpretation, thwarting adherence to a single reading.

The multiple ways in which the reader, having read well into "Fragments of a Liquidation," can fruitfully interpret the passage from Swift's journal suggest the complex positionality typically allotted to individuals in this text. Swift's lines may be read as a confession of love, implying that in his loving address to Stella Swift reveals his true feelings; as a revelation of his duplicity toward her, in that while reassuring Stella that he conceals nothing, he is in fact concealing from her a significant romantic involvement; as a reminder of the intimate exclusiveness of their communication via the "little language" they share; as an unveiling of facets of Swift's "authentic portrait" (the baby-talking, playfully affectionate side of his character) that the ferocious satirist effectively concealed from the public world. Moreover, presentation of this singular language signals a source of Howe's interest in and identification with Swift, since Howe herself so often engages in conscious play with letters and phonemes. These coexisting readings emerge more easily if the reader has consulted Swift scholarship enough to learn that in the little language Swift often substituted L for R and vice versa so that "deelest" meant "dearest," MD probably meant "my dear" or "my dears," FW "farewell" and/or "foolish wenches." Thus, the work not only engages the reader in a purposefully unsettling process of making constantly changing connections between textual elements—a reading process that is a liquefying, rather than a liquidation, of the text; it also encourages the reader's involvement in history via independent archival investigations.

While the historically informative "Fragments of a Liquidation" seems more straightforwardly accessible than much of what follows, it too is a collage; it includes lines from poems by Swift and Sheridan, the epitaph Swift composed for himself, and Yeats's poetic commentary on the epitaph. Here, as elsewhere, Howe attains an interpretive multidimensionality through the play of her intertextual juxtapositions. Thus, Swift was genuinely, and for the Irish poor especially, a strenuous "defender of liberty"; the indignation that Ireland's subjection to England roused in him makes him indeed the awesome figure Yeats admired. Yet to say, as Yeats did, that "he / Served human liberty" is clearly inadequate in view of what Howe has revealed of his treatment of Stella. He may well have helped liberate her from certain constraints on women—for instance, the notion that women need to marry in order to live fulfilled lives, or the emphasis on external beauty that can exacerbate for women the pain of aging. But particularly in Stella's last years, as Howe portrays them, Swift seems to have taken more liberties with or from Stella than he protected for her.

The revelation through parataxis of both the accuracy and the inadequacy of Swift's famed epigraph exemplifies Howe's position on mainstream history more generally. She does not entirely reject received views, yet they are clearly insufficient to her project. Her negotiation of this dynamic may have roots in her own family history. Indeed, the poem's quest for an alternative poetic historiography of the disempowered seems rooted partly in negotiation of her conflicted inheritance from her historian father. Mark Howe taught constitutional law and legal history at Harvard and was a close associate of such seminal Americanists as Perry Miller and F. O. Matthiessen. In an interview, Howe comments on their work:

> While Matthiessen leaves out women, Miller leaves out Native Americans. How could he have written so many books and essays, one of them called *Errand into the Wilderness*, and have left out the inhabitants? Yet after faulting him for that I come back and back to his work. I am trying to indicate how conflicted the whole thing is in my mind. These democratic ("leftist" if you like) professors of English, Law, and History were politically idealistic at the same time they were elitist and sexist.
>
> (Foster 1990, pp. 19–20)

She goes on to recall her father's extravagant love of his work, his reading "some old Mather or Sewell diary for relaxation" after hours of labor on his biography of Oliver Wendell Holmes.

> And now I have taken this long journey back through Puritan history, although I entered another way. I find myself reading about the Mathers for relaxation, and I [too] love my study to a kind of excess. I would dearly love to sit down and show my father what I know now. We would talk about the Garden and the Wilderness together [she alludes to the title of one of his books], and all would be well. All manner of things would be well. Yet this place I want to come home to was false to women in an intellectual sense. It was false.
>
> (Foster 1990, p. 20)

Moreover, her own "journey" into historical study was one her father prohibited: "There was the sense, I suppose from my father, that because I was feminine, anything would do *except* law or history. Those disciplines were for men" (Falon 1989, p. 29).

Howe's depiction of her personal history suggests a commonality bonding her to the central female figures in "The Liberties," Stella and Cordelia, both of whom experienced a conflict between powerful love and transgressive self-assertion, a high-stakes tension between emotional bonds and bondage. This kind of conflicted love, which we saw was a driving force behind Doubiago's *Hard Country* as well—powerful love felt toward someone or something that is also a source of one's oppression, a force responsible for one's exclusion from power or privilege, a focus of one's anger—is one of the fundamental "rhyming" patterns shaping the poem. In addition to determining Stella's exile and Cordelia's banishment, it generates Swift's embittered advocacy for Ireland and propels Howe's explorations of such powerful, and at times powerfully misogynist, literary fathers as Swift and Shakespeare. The bond/age of such love may prove self-destructive or empowering or both. But acknowledging the love and its terrible restrictions is crucial in moving toward "a future for our imaginations"; as Howe remarks (in the context of explicating Dickinson's "My Life Had Stood a Loaded Gun"), "First I find myself a Slave, next I understand my slavery, finally I re-discover myself at liberty inside the confines of known necessity" (Howe 1985, p. 118).

An additional familial dimension affecting Howe's historicist's project in "The Liberties" is the association of Ireland with her Irish mother; the poem dramatizes her own quest for connection with her maternal line and homeland, a quest that pulls her not toward history but toward myth. Howe's polarized sense of her inheritance from her parents is symbolized in her recollections of the family library. Her parents' individual book collections occupied shelves on different walls; in a division she associates with a stereotypical male/female dichotomy, her father's American books, classics, and dictionaries on one side "represented authority and reality," while her mother's Irish books on the other side "represented freedom and magic" (Falon 1989, p. 40).[13] Her mother had been a rising playwright and actress in Dublin before she came to the United States (where she continued to be involved in the theater while being *"first* the wife of a professor" [Falon 1989, p. 30]), and from her Susan Howe acquired a love of Ireland and of the theater.[14]

When she started writing "The Liberties," she was in Dublin and her mother was hospitalized in the old section of the city, called The Liberties.[15] St. Patrick's, where Swift was Dean and where he and Stella are (at his request) buried together, is in the vicinity; indeed, The Liberties was inhabited by the poor working-class Catholics whose rights Swift championed, and who adored him. Howe began writing as much about the local landscape, with its rich history, as about the figures of Swift, Stella, and Vanessa, whose story she had grown up on as "another Grimm's Fairy Tale. But real." She has acknowledged that she hoped through this exploration of place to gain understanding of her mother (Foster 1990, p. 24).

In "The Liberties," Howe gives poetic form to the conflicted dynamics of her outsider's love for Ireland: "One of the problems I have always had has been the pull between countries. A civil war in the soul. I can't express how much I adored Ireland, especially when I was young. But at the same time at that very moment of loving it I felt an outsider and knew there was no way I could ever really be let in" (Falon 1989, p. 37). These remarks suggest similarities between her relation to Ireland and her relation to the scholarly territory of her father; in the latter case, the place she wants to come home to is false, in the former, the very desire for home is a falsification. Both sides of her inheritance offer tempting—indeed beloved—but ultimately unacceptable illusions with which she must come to terms.

Given these autobiographical contexts, it is easy to see how Swift's ambivalence about Ireland would have drawn Howe to write of him; she even speculates that his having been constantly wrenched between England and Ireland in childhood—an explanatory fact that "makes him more likeable"—helps account for "the fracturing of language in his writing" (Foster 1990, p. 24). It is equally easy to see how her consciousness of patriarchal constraints on her own and her mother's professional development would have drawn Howe to Stella. Through consideration of these historical figures, but without—in Ruth Whitman's terms—"melding" with them, Howe can gain insight into her present situation.

So: Howe identifies both with Stella, the nearly silenced woman writer, and with Swift, the deracinated explorer of fractured writing who is also, partly, Stella's oppressor. Howe experiences Ireland as a personal field of imaginative freedom yet recognizes it as a historical site of colonial subjection verging on enslavement, if also a site of sustained resistance. In her work, such contradiction and ambivalence are generative; they counter tendencies toward falsifying closure and foster her writing's rhythmic contraction and dilation between poles of captivity and freedom, acquiescence and agency, between articulations of order and release of words from explanatory or syntactic constraints.

Contradictions also give impetus to her pursuit of what has been concealed, of the processes of concealment, and of countering processes of exposure. Announcing in "Fragments of a Liquidation" that "Nothing is known of Stella's feelings, or what she suffered from" (a partially ironic statement, given the betrayals Howe has outlined) (*DP*, p. 68), Howe proceeds to expose some of Stella's probable emotions. But she does so always through a markedly elliptical text that foregrounds the limits of our knowledge of the actual Esther Johnson. Here, for instance, is a section of the poem (a full page, and in this text pages tend to stand as units, comparable to the lyrics in a more conventional sequence like Dove's) which would seem to describe Johnson's diary:[16]

> her diary soared above her house
>
> over heads of
>
> those clouds
> are billows below
> spume
> white
> tossed this way
> or that
> wild geese in a stammered place
> athwart and sundered
> for the sea rose and sheets clapped at sky
> and sleep the straggler led the predator away
> (Say, *Stella*, feel you no Content
> Reflecting on a Life well spent?)
> Bedevikke bedl
> bedevilled by a printer's error

the sight of a dead page filled her with terror
garbled version
page in her coffin. . . . .
Do those dots mean that the speaker lapsed
into silence?

Often I hear Romans murmuring
I think of them lying dead in their graves.

(DP, p. 72)

I will discuss this passage at greater length shortly, but for now I
simply wish to note Howe's focus on the forces shaping Stella's writ-
ten expression: on an ambiguous sense of the diary as a mode of
liberating escape and/or forced flight, and on Stella's writing as be-
deviled by the priority given to Swift's, threatened by both silence
and confusion. If Howe attempts imaginatively to *recreate* the con-
tents of Stella's diary, she does so only in the last two lines.

As this example suggests, Howe implicitly criticizes both the fal-
sity of mimetic recreation of an earlier consciousness and the em-
beddedness of conventional linguistic structures in patriarchal op-
pression (ironically extended into her own text via the parenthetic
embedding within the passage of lines from Swift). But this critical
project in no way precludes her attending to historical—or liter-
ary—verbal records as sources of precious information about the
past. Nor does her disruption of conventional methods of represen-
tation prevent Howe from taking intellectual positions regarding
the historical territory her work surveys.

For the world Howe explores via innovative linguistic assem-
blages is not constituted solely by language, as might seem to be
suggested by the writing of some Language poets. As Ming-Qian
Ma notes, Howe views history in two disparate ways: not only as
" 'Documents . . . written by the Masters.' As a predominantly male-
gendered, rationalized fabrication," but also as " 'an actuality,' one
that exists 'outside' that patriarchal process of intellectual fusion or
agreement . . . and with which women identify themselves" (Ma
1994, pp. 718–19). When a member of the audience at her talk
"Encloser" observed that he never encountered a "real event" and
challenged Howe's belief that she could judge, for instance, the ac-
curacy of perceptions widespread in the eighteenth century, Howe
not only refused to accept his separation of past and present ("But

what if then *is* now?" she asked). She also challenged as ludicrously "theoretical" his denial of "real" events:

> Come on. . . . Have you ever been really hungry? Did the dentist ever hit a nerve when he was giving you a filling? Have you ever had someone you love die? Did the Holocaust never *really* happen? Did we never *really* drop an atomic bomb on Hiroshima?
>
> I found that when I tried to explain one poem of Emily Dickinson's it was a work of the imagination I was trying to decipher but embedded in the work were traces of *real* events. There was no end to the traces.
>
> (Howe 1990, p. 194)

She regards archival details as "uncompromising," though subject to new interpretation (Foster 1990, p. 17), and the same may be said of the various verbal singularities of her poems. Despite the provisional and partially idiosyncratic nature of any individual reading, one can nonetheless discern a specific complex of concerns being purposefully addressed through Howe's imaginative expansion of historical or legendary events registered in the masculine imaginary of historical or literary records. As the following detailed examination of the poem will demonstrate, the reader confronts more than the disruption of linguistic or literary convention; "The Liberties" invites sustained interpretive acts that incorporate not only the "how(e)" of the text—the disjunctive forms so central to its meaning—but also the "what"—the multifaceted yet specific "content" generated by its particular combinations of particular words.[17]

The reader constructing a coherence, even a coherence of tensions and disturbances, in such a disjunctive and elliptical text inevitably takes some liberties, yet Howe herself sets one at liberty to do so. For while her selection and painstaking arrangement of material suggest she has her own passionate convictions about it, the openness of the poem's structure precludes her assuming a dictatorial role or imposing a totalizing vision. Didactically, she wishes to convey a set of facts or ideas the omission of which from our consciousness distorts our understanding of the world.[18] Yet the reader/writer dynamic she establishes is noncoercive; rather than forcing upon her reader a principle of historic interpretation (like Pound's use of Douglass's economics, Grahn's assumption of a matriarchal past, or Doubiago's endorsement of idiosyncratic theories of "discovery" of the Americas), she demands that readers be conscious of their participation in constructing the text as they contemplate a particular selection of information and a specific—often achingly lovely—set of aural and visual designs. In the multivalent interpretive process, the quest initiated by Howe the poet-historian becomes a collaborative endeavor.

The extent to which "The Liberties" engages a complex poetics of process for both writer and reader is evident from Howe's deployment of organizational cues in the text following "Fragments of a Liquidation." The text appears to be divided into three numbered sections, yet the confusing visual signals provided by (sub?)headings and shifting typefaces make it difficult to distinguish divisions from subdivisions. The large title "TRAVELS" appears before the Roman numeral for section one, suggesting perhaps that all three sections that follow are subsumed under that heading (see *DP*, p. 71; figure 1). Yet two pages later, a title appears in the same large capitalized type, "THEIR," followed on the next line by "Book of Stella" printed in italics slightly larger than those used in the heading "Fragments of a Liquidation" (see *DP*, p. 73; figure 2). Are we no longer within "TRAVELS?" And would "Book of Stella" be a subheading or merely the completion of the heading "THEIR"? When the Roman numeral II appears, printed in the same style as the "I" after "TRAVELS," it immediately precedes the masque— a distinct unit—titled "God's Spies" (see *DP*, p. 96; figure 4). Yet "God's Spies" would seem to be the second section of a portion of the text labeled "WHITE FOOLSCAP" in slightly slanted (but not italic) capitals the same size as the unslanted letters "TRAVELS" and "THEIR" (see *DP*, p. 86; figure 3). Does the II divide only "WHITE FOOLSCAP," or "The Liberties" as a whole? When Roman numeral III appears, on an otherwise empty page following the masque, it is written in slightly smaller font than I and II. Questions proliferate about relations between parts and of parts to wholes, making it clear that Howe wishes to unsettle ordinary interpretive procedures.

One is reminded of Olson's methods of organizing his composition by field and of his erratic numbering of Maximus's "letters": On the one hand, his indentations, numberings, etc. signal genuine conceptual divisions; yet often his organizing gestures serve primarily to advertise the resistance to closure characteristic of "projective" writing. Like Olson's marginal shifts or open parentheses, Howe's divisions and titles may mark new directions or conceptions,

As for Patrick's bird, he brought him for his tameness, and now he is grown the wildest I ever saw. His wings have been quilled thrice, and are now up again: he will be able to fly after us to Ireland, if he be willing — Yes, Mrs. Stella . . .

TRAVELS

I.

Figure 1. Page 71 of Susan Howe's "The Liberties" from *Defenestration of Prague*. The same material appears, in slightly different format and with less white space in *The Europe of Trusts*, p. 157 (Los Angeles: Sun & Moon Press, 1990), ©1990 by Sun & Moon Press. Reprinted by permission of Sun & Moon.

THEIR

Book of Stella

dilapidation at erected original
irish granite   south was added
effected   attempted   wintering
struck the bay's walls mathemati
cal   indicating   perfect choir
system measuring from breach to
floor to roof the place tendered
ancient   famous   latin
external aisle or isle   eternal
ante pedes   the door opened em
braced   appeased
an ancient cliff or cleft   the
ende   recoiled   attempted

and quarreled in churchyard wall
surmising   that this drift
this treachery Lady East may use
the arms   and highbacked chairs
wattled dwelling on a thingmount
perpendicular structure walk and
purlieus   wall   perilous
rotten wood gives light   in dark
mouth of river   head of tide
poddle inlet pool   blue china sp
arkle of view If there be in the
land   Famine   wisdom is a fox
Liberties   unperceived

Figure 2. Page 73 of Susan Howe's "The Liberties" from *Defenestration of Prague.*
The same material appears, in slightly different format and with less white space
in *The Europe of Trusts*, p. 159 (Los Angeles: Sun & Moon Press, 1990), ©1990 by
Sun & Moon Press. Reprinted by permission of Sun & Moon.

WHITE FOOLSCAP

Book of Cordelia

> heroine in ass-skin
> mouthing O Helpful
> = father revivified waking when
> nickname Hero men take pity spittle speak

> only nonsense
> my bleeding foot
> I am maria wainscotted
> cap o'rushes tatter-coat
> common as sal salt sally
> S (golden) no huge a tiny
> bellowing augury

> NEMESIS singing from cask
> turnspit scullion the apples pick them Transformation
> wax forehead ash
> shoe fits monkey-face oh hmm
> It grows dark The shoe fits She stays a long something
> Lent is where she lives shalbe shalbe
> loving like salt (value of salt)

Figure 3. Page 86 of Susan Howe's "The Liberties" from *Defenestration of Prague*. The same material appears, in slightly different format and with less white space in *The Europe of Trusts*, p. 171 (Los Angeles: Sun & Moon Press, 1990), ©1990 by Sun & Moon Press. Reprinted by permission of Sun & Moon.

II.

God's Spies

CHARACTERS
STELLA
CORDELIA
THE GHOST OF JONATHAN SWIFT

SCENE: *A wilderness.*

> **MONDAY** *evening.*
>
> *When the curtain rises* CORDELIA *and* STELLA, *dressed as boys, are seated on a large rock near the back right. Both are in their early teens.* COR-DELIA *carries a knapsack and staff. The knapsack contains some white blackboard chalk, a white blindfold, stones of various shapes and sizes, and three coats.* STELLA *holds a large book. The book is filled with fold-out maps, alphabets and pictures.*
>
> *A painted waterfall on the backdrop cascades from painted rocks to form a stream at the base. The stream bisects the stage.*

STELLA (*Reading*): Her heart was in her throat —

CORDELIA (*Looking straight ahead*): Her words —

STELLA: — were unintelligible.

CORDELIA: You see —

STELLA (*Turns pages of her book and reads again*): An instance quoted by W. L's remark "Faith resides under the left nipple."

Figure 4. Page 96 of Susan Howe's "The Liberties" from *Defenestration of Prague*. The same material appears, in slightly different format and with less white space in *The Europe of Trusts*, pp. 181–82 (Los Angeles: Sun & Moon Press, 1990), ©1990 by Sun & Moon Press. Reprinted by permission of Sun & Moon.

but these stand in a fluid relation to one another and are likely to reach no conclusion. Apparent orders give way as one direction of inquiry merges into another, while untitled individual pages emerge as distinct units, and titles—partially false clues—call attention to the slippage of conventional ordering structures.

This very slippage is potentially liberating; through rupture of oppressive orders and continuities, and through attention to gaps that are usually glossed over, one may begin to address the challenge which Howe (like her Emily Dickinson) faces: "How do I, choosing messages from the code of others in order to participate in the universal theme of Language, pull SHE [for which we may read the feminine as much as the female] from all the myriad symbols and sightings of HE [the dominant masculine as much as the male]" (Howe 1985, pp. 17–18).

For Howe, this quest demands sustaining multiple foci, or at least a multifaceted focus, as I have already suggested in noting her multiplication of "feminine" figures; such compounding is evident in the pages following "Fragments of a Liquidation." Regarding "Travels" as a provisional section heading, and as a reminder of the text's concern with deracination, we can read the pages between that heading and "White Foolscap" as loosely unified around the travels of Swift, Stella, Howe, and other exiles in Irish history (all of whom perhaps contrast with the traveler Yeats scornfully addresses at the close of "Fragments," "Imitate him if you dare, / World-besotted traveller; he / Served human liberty"). Parallels among these focal figures are suggested by the unattributed italicized quotation that appears just above the word "Travels." This passage comes from Swift's *Journal to Stella*, where he describes a bird purchased in England by his Irish manservant, Patrick, to bring to Stella's companion, Mrs. Dingley. When purchased (against Swift's counsel) the linnet showed no will to fly, seeming "to have neither hope nor fear" (Swift 1948, 1:156). Now *"grown the wildest"* Swift ever saw, the bird promises to become another international traveler/exile and, like Stella, one who will follow Swift to Ireland, as she did despite society's attempts to *"quill"* her figurative wings. Explicitly male, Patrick's bird is nonetheless a figure for Stella (who is punningly the "bird"—modern British slang for girl—of St. Patrick's Dean) and for what might be construed as her liberating flight from conventional expectations of womanly decorum. Patrick's bird is also linked to the "wild geese" referred to on the next page, that is, the Irish Catholic exiles who fled from anti-Catholic penal laws after 1691 (a designation famously used by Yeats in "September 1913"). The multiple, partially rhyming travels invoked in this section all raise issues of freedom restricted by social and/or physical disempowerment—again what we might code as femininity.

At least intermittently, Howe remains particularly concerned with the individual woman whose liquidation so troubles her. The page (quoted earlier) exploring the possibly liberating flight Stella may have achieved in her own diary writing is the first lyric in "TRAVELS / I." Initially, Howe imagines a written expression of Stella's untamed, empowered will, envisioning the diary's contents as figuratively, as well as literally, over others' heads. From the lofty perspective of that liberated bird/woman/*vox* the clouds would appear as sea billows appear to those traversing the Irish Sea. But succeeding lines point to the vulnerability of those undertaking such risky flights and to the sometimes fine distinction between willed travel and forced exile, between bridging nations and being broken between them ("athwart and sundered"). The rest of the lyric emphasizes the fears of the isolated woman writer, particularly of madness and an associated garbling of letters and meaning; here and elsewhere in the text such fears induce a lapsing into silence. In this context, the parenthetically included lines from Swift's poem for Stella's birthday 1727—"Say, Stella, feel you no Content / Reflecting on a Life well spent?"—sound patronizing and stupidly blind to the constraints on the woman's life, particularly on her literary self-expression.

Set against her silence is the murmuring of the Romans. The woman writer hears them even though they are dead and buried, presumably because the Romans have left on the English language the audible imprint of their conquest (though they did not conquer Ireland) and because their significance is proclaimed throughout historical record. Howe's poetic task remains the investigation of the unheard "other voices"—"If history is a record of survivors, Poetry shelters other voices" (Becket 1989, p. 25, and Howe 1990, p. 180)—even if that investigation must take place largely through the language, and the male imaginary, of the Romans/patriarchs/conquerors. "In Western Literary Tradition," Howe has remarked, "all roads seem to lead to Rome. A poet is a foreigner in her own language" (Becket 1989, p. 27). Hence the pronoun at the top of the next page: "THEIR *Book of Stella*." Howe cannot write HER or even MY book (again, her route toward this author *manqué* must be through the male imaginary), but she can write theirs differently through her poetry.

Howe's own travels as tourist in Stella's adopted home, Ireland, contribute to that endeavor. Thus, the telegraphic piece opening "THEIR Book of Stella"—a symmetrical column of text—seems to depict some of the floorplan and history of St. Patrick's as well as noting something of the "purlieus," presumably the working-class region of the Liberties, originally in Dublin's purlieus (see figure 2). This is an appropriate inclusion in a "Book of Stella" because the cathedral is her place of burial—for Howe, a burial site that indicates the contradictions of Stella's relationship to Swift. To have buried her in this "ancient   famous   latin" (DP, p. 73) place was on the one hand a "flagrant gesture. A swipe at respectability. The 'imitate me if you dare' aspect of his character Yeats wrote the epitaph for." On the one hand, Stella's position near the Cathedral door means that one walks over her marker "as if there was a dog buried there. Swift's pet or something" (Foster 1990, p. 24). The lyric closes with the line "Liberties   unperceived" announcing a failure or multiple failures, in Swift's time and in Howe's—failure really to see the place, perhaps, or to understand the kinds of freedom buried there, or to recognize those freedoms due to all individuals, or even to discern ways of releasing the feminine imaginary. Such failures negatively define the speaker's quest: she seeks perception of what has been overlooked.

She proceeds with a kind of wandering ("trackless") self-exploration that is also an exploration of the place, in which she remains alert to the parts of Swift, Stella, and Ireland that are alive in her or echoing in the terrain she traverses. The first-person speaker of the next lyric, a deracinated figure who explores a temporary "homeland till dusk," I take to be Howe seeking her Irish antecedents (both her blood relatives and her literary—or, as is the case with Stella, thwarted literary—forebears) within and around her: "there in me   them in me   I / halted   I heard footsteps" (DP, p. 74).

Archaic language (including bits of Gaelic, kenning-like phrases) and mythology (both Christian and pagan) contribute to the echoing footfalls of the past. Both are evoked in the lyrical passage that follows, where they bring comfort, as "her voice"—that of Stella, of Howe's mother, and of her female ancestors—sounds in a pastoral landscape depicted in imagery of prelapsarian Eden and postlapsarian salvation. The evening sky, in which sounds the "fearsad bell" of evensong, is (Mary's?) "blue of sweet salvation"; there are "as many lives / as there are loaves / and fishes"; and the woman as ordinary homemaker offers something comparable to communion:

> her voice
>   a settled place
> table spread   flesh and milk
>   in mystery
>   in the room
>   in the sunlight

(DP, p. 75)

But this idealization is at best a partial truth. We must not be lulled by its soothing beauties. Hence, set off at the bottom of the page (and in the later edition from Sun & Moon Press moved to stand alone on the following page) is the declaration, "She must be traced through many dark paths / as a boy." That is, one must trace her as one would a boy, with all the expectations of complexity that implies. In addition, the lines suggest that she must be sought in disguised, perhaps diminutive, form—for instance, as Patrick's male bird—that her paths involve concealment and gender-crossing, just as her voice, although sometimes spoken from a woman's approved domestic context, speaks also "in mystery." The poet's quest for Stella and the feminine figures that rhyme with her demands invention and ingenuity.

The next section—opening with a pun on the name of a type of bird, "light *flickers* in the rigging" (my emphasis)—returns to the sea journey motif associated with travelers torn between nations and to the

> small boy-bird of the air
>
>   moving or capable of moving
> with great speed
> rapidly running   flying   following
>   flight of an arrow
> known for the swiftness of her soul

(DP, p. 76)

Howe considers the choices available to a woman like Stella: she may use her powers for escape, for self-liberation, for submission or dutiful attachment. In received history, Stella has come to be known for the last of these, her soul's attachment to Swift. But that view alone appears "false" in the way that Perry Miller's history is falsely incomplete. Historical data must be reexamined and redeployed.

Yet in seeking to understand Stella more fully, as having something more than swiftness in her soul, we have only a few archival bits that serve as "flags   charts   maps // to be read by guesswork through [meaning "via" and/or "seeing past"] obliteration" (*DP*, p. 76). Applying her process-oriented poetics, Howe here plays with a few of these documents in splintered form: the centrally positioned "GUIDE" evokes Stella's tribute to Swift as "My early and my only Guide" (in a poem that Howe subsequently quotes in full), and lines praising her appearance in formulaic terms come from Swift's "On the Death of Mrs. Johnson." Howe's arrangement of and amplification around these selections emphasize the young Stella's vitality, her eager confrontation with life's challenges, her early promise. But the line "A PENDULUM SWUNG BETWEEN TWO COUNTRIES"— describing Howe, Howe's mother, Stella, and/or Swift—ominously reminds us that lives are determined by forces beyond such personal attributes as promptness or the perfect facial features Swift commended.

Lacking much information specifically on Stella but always recognizing gender as one such determining force, Howe turns to the "charts" provided by partially parallel tales of other women. "She" necessarily functions flexibly and inclusively, since access to truths about Stella, or about Howe and her female ancestors, may be available only by incorporating into their hypothesized experience what is known about other women. Thus, the next lyric depicts a "she" who disguised herself in men's attire—a common strategy for women who have sought power or liberty of movement equal to men's. Such cross-dressing brings to mind Swift's tendency to praise Stella for her manly attributes, for her distinction from the typically female; in "To Stella, Visiting Me in my Sickness," for instance, he claims that Prometheus stole for her "The Fire that forms a manly Soul" which he then molded "with Female Clay"; Swift commends her as one who never "affected Fears" or fainting spells (*The Poems of Jonathan Swift* 1958, 2:725–26). In this passage (and on the following page, where spears, shields, and battle standards appear),

Howe perhaps invokes Ireland's legendary warrior queens such as Queen Medb (whose name appears much later in the text) as rhyming figures for Stella, especially in her more assertive aspects.[19] But, unlike Medb's, the journey Stella undertakes is once again partly into written expression, and her success is severely qualified, both by the line division "mad/e," which suggests the threat of madness to maids who dare verbal making, and by the lines, "how far I writ // I / can // not / see // days trifled away" (*DP*, p. 77). Stella's eyesight is known to have been weak (and as he aged, Swift's eyesight failed, though he refused to wear glasses). But the difficulty the would-be woman writer has in seeing her life as productive is not a consequence of poor eyesight.

So that we may see more clearly, Howe relies on visual figures to sharpen our understanding. Throughout the text the predominance of visible space represents the surround of women's history that remains blank—unspoken, unspeakable, or irretrievable. At this point in the text, the scale of the obstacles she faces ("she" being Stella/Howe/the woman who would express herself/any oppressed person who would know liberty) is suggested by the drawing entitled "crossing the ninth wave" that itself crosses over the next two pages; waves are thought to increase in regular series with the ninth wave being the largest.[20] And as if for protection of the traveler in this difficult journey, the lyric after the drawing takes the form of a delicate cross. The words forming its arms seem to depict Stella in her weakness: as a squinting orphan, "a / thin / nine / year / old / child" "starlit / outlasting mother's hood" (*DP*, p. 81). If her history is partly that of a warrior queen, it is also that of a vulnerable girl.

Perhaps the poem's speaker here despairs of finding Stella with such inadequate "charts," for below the cross appears, "*O cinders of Eve, what is my quest?*" Or perhaps she fears she has lost sight of her quest, and that either the search for Stella itself or her methods of conducting it are off the mark. As if to start over, the next page finds her turning back to the landscape and to the androcentric history of Ireland. Here native "traditions still flit" (*DP*, p. 82). Clearly, more information is available about male heroism ("he was born / kingly descent / made great progress / in learning" etc.) and about (men's) martial rebellions against colonizing restraint than about women's struggles for liberty; mention of Howth, the port on the north side of Dublin Bay where nationalists armed in 1914, points to one such male rebellion. And in contrast to women's, men's madness is taken for valor, even invulnerability—"John the Mad or Furious, fought like a true Berserker" (*DP*, p. 82). The boundaries defining what constitutes transgression or crossing, whether of national boundaries and seas or mental states, are radically unstable and gender-inflected. The madly brave soldier may with "a LEAP" become the violent suitor/rapist ("the pursuer / stained mantle") in mad pursuit of his female prey (*DP*, p. 83).

This image of the violent hunt returns the focus to women's—specifically Stella's—history: "SHE DIED OF SHAME / This is certain— / That is mist— / I cannot hold—" (*DP*, p. 83). The last two of these lines may suggest either that the speaker's grasp on women's truth slips, or that she cannot remain focused on men's history ("that," as opposed to the "this" of women's history) despite her easier access to it. Succeeding lines suggest that, whatever the difficulties, Howe remains committed to relaying women's power and agency that historical record and folk "wisdom" have denied. She insists that numerous women, even if equipped only with "broken oar or spar" in fact rowed as supposedly they never did, with amazing strength:

> whomsoever
> even the least
> rowed as never woman rowed
> rowed as never woman rowed
> through the whole history of her story
> through pain
> and peril
> the shores rang
>
> (*DP*, p. 83)

Howe the writer is surely among those propelling themselves through "the whole history" of Stella's story and her own.

Given the inadequate documentation of women's stories ("The real plot was invisible" [*DP*, p. 84]), imaginative records take on added importance, if only for the insight they may offer into the male imaginary. Consequently, the speaker's quest for a more authentic portrait of Stella moves next "in a fictional direction" (*DP*, p. 84), specifically toward exploration of *King Lear*'s story of Cordelia. Cordelia's story provides some illuminating parallels and contrasts with Stella's. One reason for Howe's linking the two is suggested by the passage from Act I scene i that appears as a kind of epigraph for "WHITE FOOLSCAP / Book of Cordelia," in which Cordelia refuses to speak in order to "draw / A third more opulent than [her] sisters" (*DP*, p. 85): Both Stella and Cordelia gain presence through their (speaking) silences that tell much about women's painful disempowerment, especially vis-à-vis language. The virtual "nothing" that remains of Stella (her liquidation, the blank foolscap that contains her unwritten history), like the "nothing" of Cordelia's reply to her father, provides substantial information about women's frightening dependence on the beneficence of the patriarchs. Cordelia's silence is an assertive gesture, however; the extent to which Stella chose silence is less clear. Both figures also point to the bind experienced by women in patriarchy who feel deep love for men; essential to the power of both tales is the depth of love they suggest, and the costs of love they reveal.

Of course, the themes of bastardy, introduced in the prose discussion of both Swift's and Stella's parentage, of poor sight/blindness, of madness, and of exile also link these tales. In addition, the Lear story is linked to Ireland: it can be traced to the Gaelic legend, alluded to also in Pound's "Canto II," of the ocean god Lir whose daughter, Fionnuala, and three sons, Aedh, Fiachra, and Conn, were changed into swans by his jealous second wife, Aoife. (The children's names appear in slightly different form in Howe's text, page 87.) The transformed children were to spend three periods of three hundred years each on different bodies of water.

Tellingly, when Howe turns her ostensible focus to Cordelia, whose story several male authors have written, her work becomes even more telegraphic and disjunctive. Rather than recapping existing coherent narratives Howe tries out increasingly visual arrangements of words, verbal progressions that are more obviously sound-generated or orthographically prompted, and a linguistic texture that seems more densely allusive than what preceded. Through her experimentalist fracturing of the recorded male imaginary, Howe attempts a breakthrough to feminine voices; she finds it necessary to "undo or sever / HALLUCINATION OF THE MIRROR" (*DP*, p. 84), that is, the illusion of realism that more mimetic art like Ruth Whitman's leaves intact.

The opening lines of the "Book of Cordelia" suggest a number of this section's major concerns and can demonstrate Howe's exposing, through the shattering of received texts and visions in her cryptic collage, glimpses of a female/feminine subject:

> heroine in ass-skin
> mouthing O Helpful
> = father revivified waking when
> nickname Hero men take pity spittle speak
>
> only nonsense
> my bleeding foot
> I am maria wainscotted
> cap o' rushes tatter-coat
> common as sal salt sally
> S (golden) no huge a tiny
> bellowing augury

(*DP*, p. 86)

As I read it, the main concern here is woman's agency, the constraints on it, and how these may translate into her heroism. The already developed themes of concealment and disguise as necessary strategies for women are quickly evoked, along with the theme of the difficulty of woman's expression (the heroine only mouthing words). Allusions to Lear as the revived father brought to speech highlight the irony of woman's contrasting situation; rather than being urged to speak, she is discouraged from speaking for herself. Where he is "revivified" in sharply sounding consonants "take pity spittle speak," she is "wainscotted," rendered part of the decorative environment, "only nonsense." Heroic and powerful as a woman's perhaps unarticulated love may be, it is likely to be taken for granted—"common as sal salt sally / S (golden) [Silence, presumably] no huge a tiny / bellowing augury," "loving like salt (value of salt)." If unspoken, like Cordelia's and probably Stella's love, it may be denied entirely and turned against her.

The heroine, moreover, is relegated to the largely passive role ("The shoe fits," evoking Cinderella as well as the proverb); when not passive or silent, she is stereotyped as dangerous ("NEMESIS singing from cask," Eve evoked in "the apples pick them") [see figure 3]. In a phallocentric world, Howe suggests, women are caught in a double bind: self-assertions invite denigration, but self-silencing does the same. Although this is Cordelia's book, her situation is not unique. Thus, the phrase "nickname Hero" may refer to Stella as well as to Cordelia, particularly since Swift in "On the Death of Mrs. Johnson" recalls an incident when Stella at the age of twenty-four, in Howe's words, "shot and killed a prowler after her servants had fled the house in terror" (*DP*, p. 67). Swift declares, "she had the personal courage of a hero" (Swift 1962, p. 229).[21] Yet it would seem that most of Stella's and Cordelia's heroics—like those of so many liquidated women—were enacted more passively in endurance of suffering: "Lent is where she lives" (*DP*, p. 86). Although such strength of character is surely admirable, stoic acceptance of pain and imposed silence may support the status quo. Cordelia's heroism lies in her rejection of the kind of self-silencing involved in the dutiful mouthing of prescribed words.

In Howe's retelling of the stories of Lir's/Lear's agonizing losses of their children in the pages that follow, we see how her experimental prosody "pull[s] SHE from all the myriad symbols and sightings of HE," without denying the legitimacy of the male's suffering. The names of Lir's children provide a sonic base with which Howe can play in order to draw forth the disempowered female: the name "Conn" generates the (off)rhyming "One," which in turn rhymes with "sun," seen as the birds/children "pass overhead . . . threshing the sun" (*DP*, p. 87). Sun leads associatively to "corona"—the outer layer of the sun's atmosphere and the emblem of royalty, (Lear's) crown—the first syllable of which corresponds to "Cordelia." Metamorphosis and resemblance are principles in fruitful tension here. Through echoes, whether orthographic or phonetic or associational, words are transformed into other words possessing other expressive possibilities. Following a series of transformations—via translation from one language to another and association from one element to another—we may move toward clearer perception:

> the hoth(heath
> sline(clear
> crystal
> song
> le
> lac
> pure
> semblance
> aperçu

(DP, p. 87)

Yet, gone awry, metamorphosis (also the subject of Pound's "Canto II" in which the daughter of Lir appears) may entail derangement. Madness—experienced by Lear, feigned by Edgar, both feared and experienced by Swift—is a condition Howe sees as a real danger for women writers who dare to thwart the system alone (and equally a threat to those who don't dare).[22] The theme of mental derangement comes to the fore in the next lyric, where it is set against the possibility of empowering verbal (re)arrangements. The second line, "unbonneted he runs" (*DP*, p. 88), depicts Lear mad on the storm-battered heath. Set counter to this loss of mental control are first (in a neat diagonal) a stuttering movement toward meaningful speech—"hrr / hrru / hurry / hare / haloo / cry Whoop / and cry Spy!"—second (in a horizontal line) the orders imposed by poetry, "pauses measures feet in syllables caesura," and third (in a vertical column) rational explanation—"Copernicus / the sun / is a cloud / of dust." Once "bonneted" within such bounds, rage may gain safe expression via questioning, as in Howe's quotation of Lear's question about Mad Tom, "has his children brought him to this pass?" (*DP*, p. 88).

The role of stammering-toward-expression in managing rage and perhaps evading derangement underlines the significance of Howe's coining a new word—"Whowe"—to occupy the line immediately following the question in which Lear reveals his continued denial of responsibility for events. With this word containing her own name, Howe asserts her claim to language with all of its powers of expression, exploration, control, explanation, and explosion. As a response to Lear's question, "Whowe" challenges the father's blindness to his own fault (who? how?, who? we?). It asserts Howe's feminist participation in an undoing of the patriarch, by positioning her among the undutiful children. The neologism's suggestion of several questions may point to Howe's sense of stuttering uncertainty, but it also indicates a principled stance: that Howe chooses to engage language as a vehicle not for domination but for inquiry. In her linguistic exploration, her individual identity is at once present and submerged, fused into other terms, multiple, fluid (again she seizes the positive "liquid" within the negative "liquidation").

The coinage "Whowe" demonstrates the flexibility Howe demands of her language in order to render the complex dimensionality of her subjects. On the next page, the phallocentric king/father

"in colonial core" appears as a figure at once pitiable, terribly re-
duced, and supremely threatening:

L E A R

leans on his lance   he

has holes instead of eyes

blind (folded)

bare (footed)

nuclear (hooded)

w i n d b r i d l e d

for how or to who

(DP, p. 89)

This dangerous masculine power, which is linked to militarism, is
one Lear both wields and—as the chief protestor against Cordelia's
murderers—suffers. Swift, too, is implicitly a perpetrator contribut-
ing to Stella's decline and a sufferer at her loss. The lines "I will
go to my desk / I will sit quietly / (as if nothing / has happened /
what is eaten is gone. If I wasn't lucky I'd starve)" (DP, p. 90) draw
Howe herself into this picture. For they may depict Swift's behavior
at Stella's death, perhaps his composing a memoir during her fu-
neral; or they may describe Howe struggling to write (in an inter-
view, she describes her own writing process in similar terms: "I sit
quietly at my desk . . . " [Foster 1990, p. 23]) and perhaps evading
personal or social crises. They also echo Lear's suggestion that he
and Cordelia retreat from the world's events to prison where the
two alone could sing like caged birds—"ere they shall make us weak;
we'll see 'em starved first." Of course, Lear and Cordelia die almost
immediately thereafter. The unavailability of stable positions sug-
gested by the allusion—particularly of positions removed from the
games of politics and society (in Lear's words, "who loses and who
wins; who's in, who's out")—is a recurrent emphasis in the text. It
is one point Howe makes via the frequent recurrence in telegraphic
form of key terms, phrases, and concepts from earlier pages in "The
Liberties." For as elements or figures recur in different contexts,
their placement in changed combinations alters the tones and values
associated with them.

What happens to words and phrases in the course of "The Libert-
ies" enacts in microcosm the sedimentation that occurs around indi-
vidual words in our language over time. Each word carries with it

not only the accumulated meanings of its etymological history (suggested, for instance, in the progression of "sal salt sally")—but the history of its usage, traces or memories of the particular, ideologically and intellectually charged contexts in which it has appeared. The large amount of white space in Howe's text allows some of this historical sedimentation to rise to consciousness.

By the time the reader nears the end of what I have been treating as section I of "The Liberties," s/he experiences the radically disjunctive text as a network of partially reflexive echoes; each word is burdened with its past both inside and outside "The Liberties," yet freed into dynamism by the very multiplicity of its usages. For instance, the lyric which opens,

> children of Lir
>   lear
>
>   whistling would in air ha
>   nameless appear—
>   Can you not see
>   arme armes
>   give tongue
> are you silent o my swift
>   all coherence gone?
>
>   (DP, p. 91)

re-presents through heavy repetition of earlier passages issues of power, voice, naming, and the difficulty of seeing truly. Yet the new combination shifts emphasis to a previously underdeveloped concern: the need for memory, for a confrontation with what has been repressed or denied. The lines,

>   have forgotten—
>   must go back—
>   so far—
>   almost there—
>   vagueness of the scene
> where action takes place
>
>   (DP, p. 91)

lead to revelation of a fall and/or shooting and the assertion, "Behold / is *is* / you see / he brought her down." The shooting suggests a revision of the Lir legend (modified to echo the hunt motif that runs throughout "The Liberties," partly via Ibsen's *The*

Wild Duck) in which the king shoots down his own child/bird.[23] The struggle to see and remember this tragedy/abuse yields a momentary clarity about a man's responsibility for a woman's fall—Lear's for Cordelia's, Swift's for Stella's, perhaps Adam's for Eve's.

The anguished quest into memory also risks a deeper plunge into madness, suggested by the narrow line of text on the following page:

> I can re
>
> trac
>
> my steps
>
> Iwho
>
> crawl
>
> between thwarts
>
> Do not come down the ladder
>
> ifor I
>
> haveaten
>
> it a
>
> way
>
> (*DP*, p. 92)

This stuttering voice combines empowerment with mad desperation. She speaks with a strong sense of self, the pronoun "I" a marked recurrence, and she asserts her ability to retrace her own history (seizing the active position in "[s]he must be traced through many dark paths" [*DP*, p. 75]). But the price of this empowerment is isolation, and even destruction of the means of her own escape. As elsewhere in Howe's work, the dynamic between escape and enclosure, or liberation and imprisonment, is a tangled one.

The entire passage reappears a few pages later as the close of part I—now broken ("athwart and sundered"?) between two pages. Before its second appearance, the speaker considers the relation between fictionalized record and historical reality and her relation to each. Fiction, figured in "story migration" and "tall tale," is constructed too much in service of approved social or moral orders: "Rat-roofed caution of a cautionary tale / swallows the rat, a pin, wheat / while singing birds recover lost children." In contrast, "crucial words outside the book / those words are bullets. [they bring her down?] / Lodged in the ebbing actual / women in the flight of time stand framed" (*DP*, p. 93). Yet despite her sense of the inadequacy of "some tall tale" depicting "great Fairly, little Fairly, liar Liar [a name close to Lir/Lear, derived also from letter play with "fairly"] / and lucky Luck," the speaker has to have recourse to the fictions. "I am looking for lucky Luck," she announces. Writing from the inherited fictions of legend and from legend's active form, ritual (where myth and history interpenetrate), she exposes the violence within the inherited patriarchal tales and ceremonies. She focuses particularly on the prevalence of the hunt, directed against the most vulnerable, whether that be a woman fleeing with her child, or a wren:[24]

> Once again
> we'll hunt the wren
> says Richard to Robin
> we'll hunt the wren
> says everyone.
>
> (*DP*, p. 94)

By juxtaposing against this meditation on the violence of patriarchal tradition the recurrence of the strained, near-broken voice of the figure crawling between thwarts, the poet-historian suggests the urgency of finding new discursive and social configurations.

Howe accepts that constructing a "poem containing history" demands constructing the history contained in the poem. Using whatever means serve to disrupt old assumptions and suggest new possibilities, she opens past realities and earlier fictions to new interpretations. Hence, in part II Howe takes her quest for Stella into a theatrical staging, which further distances her from conventional historiography and—as with Judy Grahn's dramatic work "Queen of Swords"—allows more direct exploration of women's relation to the forces that silence them.[25] But where Grahn used drama partly to give historical characters voice so that they could authenticate a particular version of past events, Howe presents without apparent didacticism a more abstracted, ahistorical realm at a further remove from the conventions of realism.

The title of Howe's play, "God's Spies," is yet another allusion to *King Lear*; in the "let's away to prison" speech where Lear envisions himself and Cordelia as singing birds in the cage, he proposes they will take upon themselves "the mystery of things / As if we were Gods' spies: and we'll wear out, / In a wall'd prison, packs and sects of great ones / That ebb and flow by th' moon" (V, iii). The allusion suggests a subversively empowered role for the powerless, one dependent on intimate co-conspiracy. That the work can be staged only in the imagination—where directions like "*The* GHOST *rises, crosses the stage to the pulpit, and walks through* STELLA" (*DP*, p. 104) can operate—draws the reader into the intimate invention/empowerment of being God's spy.

In the fantastic, semi-allegorical world of the play, Stella and Cordelia are alive, while Swift is present only as a ghost. The female characters, in their early teens and dressed as boys, are on the verge of womanhood. Their situation and exchanges often echo Beckett's *Waiting for Godot*. That Godot should provide an intertext here is hardly surprising, not only in view of Beckett's being ambiguously Irish (Dublin-born, he attended Trinity College but emigrated ultimately to Paris) but also in view of his writing's reliance on minimalistically charted absence. Beckett once contrasted his work with that of James Joyce in terms that would align his stance with Howe's: "The more Joyce knew, the more he could. He's tending towards omniscience and omnipotence as an artist. I'm working with impotence, ignorance" (quoted by Reid 1975, p. 66). By working with and from positions of ignorance, Beckett and Howe take the non-coercive stance toward their readers described earlier. Neither author holds a hidden key; rather, each demands that the reader construct meaning for her/himself but prevents the reader from legitimizing a definitive, exclusive interpretation.

One crucial difference between "God's Spies" and *Godot* is the gender of the focal characters, and in light of that difference Stella's reliance on the "large book" from which she reads assumes particular significance. Throughout "The Liberties" Howe is concerned with the role played by language, particularly written language, in identity formation for marginalized or oppressed people. The stage directions showing Stella repeatedly reading from the book literalize women's situation: the resources available to Howe's Stella for understanding or responding to her situation are largely prescripted ones. The play opens with Stella reading a description of Cordelia that revises from a third-person perspective Cordelia's line from *King Lear*, "I cannot heave / My heart into my mouth" (I, i): "Her heart was in her throat—. . .—[her words] were unintelligible." One can hardly miss the point that what traps Cordelia and Stella—for like Estragon and Vladimir, they seem unable to go anywhere—is at least in part woman's inscription in western literature.

Educated in patriarchal literary and historical traditions, the two female characters are well acquainted with the seemingly inescapable violence of patriarchal history: "They murdered each other." "Of course. Always." (*DP*, p. 101). They are equally aware of the brutal victimization of those who have little power; their conversation refers to a falcon throwing to the ground the (Irish) "wild goose / dazzled by light" (*DP*, p. 97). They are unsure whether they themselves survived this, but if they did so, they "[l]eft without regrets . . . flying swiftly—past fleecy stars" (perhaps evoking liberated versions of Swift and Stella, Lir's swan children, and Stella's imagined diary).

Yet inevitably, the two characters have to some extent internalized the patriarchal views of women inscribed in the "great"—one possible synonym for "large"—book(s). Thus, when Howe's Cordelia in the line "Wide of the mark" echoes her Shakespearean words upon Lear's awakening, Stella replies by herself voicing the patriarch's judgment, "Blind to a father's need" (*DP*, p. 98).[26] Similarly, Stella consults her book to set up a pointless game of hopping forward and back in which she places her companion at a disadvantage by blindfolding her and turning her until she is dizzy. Following the patriarchal text—and Stella's leadership—in this game, the women compete instead of collaborating. At the end of the first section, however, they speak "together," determining to explore their history in words that recall the spirituals of African American slaves: "Lets [*sic*] go back." "Lay our burdens down" (*DP*, p. 101).

Of the two, Stella seems especially trapped within patriarchally inscribed expectations. In the scene that follows, set in St. Patrick's at midnight, the hour when both Stella and Swift were buried, Stella still reads from her white book; she remains blind to the Ghost of Jonathan Swift, who enters decked with wild flowers like Ophelia and, like Ophelia and Lear, seems partly mad. As she recites the full text of Hester Johnson's poem "To Dr. Swift on his birth-day, November 30, 1721," his kneeling ghost mouths the words. This mouthing suggests how much Stella's poem, a gracious tribute in which she credits Swift with enabling her to avoid the usual failings and dismal fates of her sex, is mediated through male perspectives and expectations; men seek to authorize, and in many ways effectively control, women's expression.[27] The self-destructiveness of women's dependency on male guidance and authorization is emphasized in Stella's suicidal gesture at the close of her recitation; shooting herself in the heart, she enacts the wish expressed in her poem's close that she not live after Swift's death.[28] Stella's subsequent request, "speak to me" (also scripted within the patriarchal tradition since she reads from her large book, echoing both Hamlet addressing his father's ghost and Lear addressing Cordelia), produces only a "silent sermon" and "superfluous words" from Swift's ghost. The words she herself reads are from Swift's "To Stella, Who Collected and Transcribed his Poems," a complexly teasing poem that, even as it praises Stella, cruelly challenges the accuracy of her transcription by requiring her to record his depiction of her faults. Her oppression by "the book"—and her collaboration in that oppression—could hardly be clearer.

In the sixth day of the play's seven-day action (a mockery of the biblical creation myth) Stella puts down her book, potentially a significant gesture of liberation. Nonetheless, her speech suggests her continued colonization, for now that she is listening instead of reading, she still hears someone else (quite possibly Swift "snarled in the wrack of [his] wit") and his words. Cordelia, whose perceptions were clear enough to dictate principled resistance to societal expectations conveyed through the demands of the man she loved most, is more enlightened. Though still blindfolded, when Cordelia enters after two full minutes of silent blackout, her words summarize women's situation as Howe has dramatized it:

> We
>
>   storied and told
>
>   are adrift
>
>   we turn away
>
>   mute.

(*DP*, p. 107)

In subsequent lines, the motif of the violent patriarchal hunt recurs in allusions to the hunter Actaeon punished for his pursuit and sight of Artemis ("Can you not see? / Her hurt / harte / the gored hounds leaping") and to Apollo's pursuit of Daphne, which ended in her transformation into a laurel ("Leafy I / labyrinth am / lost in the woods (or hiding)" (*DP*, p. 107).[29] These rhyming allusions place Cordelia in a long line of legendary women who have preferred silence to violation; she has nonetheless seen clearly—"blind to / *nothing.*" She goes on to "*[speak] softly as if remembering*"; it remains necessary to look back into personal or cultural history, even if what one sees is only the painful fact of one's own invisibility to the fathers: "swift hours unseen swift years unseen" (*DP*, p. 107).

Sunrise of the final day of the play's action finds the two female characters again reciting evidence of patriarchy's violence, with Stella again speaking in terms suggesting self-destructive complicity: "we shoot them there / there where they swim—we lay nets for them— / from a blind you see, we shoot them down" (*DP*, p. 108). But the women do not remain within this male-identified perspective, just as the V of the wild geese may be reversed to "lead off the A's." A gunshot and the "[t]ransfigured cries" of wild geese "*flying over and away*" force upon Cordelia a recognition of women's disinheritance through literature. She cries out, "Nothing is our own!" and adds, alluding perhaps to Yeats's portrayal of Zeus's rape of Leda:

> I learned in leafy woods hmmm—depths of the sea
> that Noone in first father—so soon a terror
> of feathery wings—soft and tremblingly swift—
> How did we happen—because we were written.
>
> (*DP*, p. 109)

She "*tears off her blindfold. Blinks in the light.*" and again searches her memory, this time seeking reconnection with "true love." The "cradlegrave cords" of love remain strong; romantic memories of loving and beloved times leave Cordelia "*[r]adiant.*" Once again we see the importance to Howe's invisible plot of her major sources being powerful stories of deep and tender love, even as they are tales of misogyny.[30] The flight into exile with a beloved—like Lear and Cordelia's venture into prison, or the romantic aspects of Swift and Stella's relocation to Ireland—is paradoxically "a homeward rush of exile— / flight—Liberty." The exile's "going forth" may even be "lucky." Yet Cordelia's speech ends with a grotesque vision of the bodies of "those who are gone" strewn haphazardly at the bottom of the sea "grinding their teeth" (*DP*, p. 110). Love, for all its power, does not cancel out oppression or brutality.

Howe does not suggest a simple teleology any more than Beckett does; there would seem to be no easy route out of women's entrapment in social conventions and patriarchal constructions, and no quick way free of complicity in those constructions. The masque's final scene finds the female pair again repeating "They murder each other." "Of course." If there is substantial progress, it may lie in Stella's articulating more clearly than before the problem of identity she confronts—"Who can tell me who I am?" (*DP*, p. 110); and her gesture of measuring the river they wade into may suggest a more direct approach to self-knowledge than that offered by her book. Yet the two women, like Estragon and Vladimir, suffer from failing memory. And while Cordelia's last words, "I knew a child," may launch a productive interrogation of childhood memories as a source of self-knowledge, we cannot know whether she was herself the victim of the final gunshot that sounds in the darkness. According to Stella, "Truth is what always remains," and what remains here, the last word, is "*Silence*."

Silence, rendered in pages' white spaces, plays its most visibly active role in part III of "The Liberties." The section's first page parallels the opening page of "THEIR Book of Stella"; it too is a fractured description of objects in the landscape, probably a Dublin scene. Here, however, the focus is not architecture but statuary. The number of figures depicted is unclear, but at least one statue represents a woman—"woman standing curling tendril her left hand rest" (*DP*, p. 113)—perhaps as part of a sundial. Here too, echoes of earlier portions of "The Liberties" and of earlier intertexts abound: "lip" may be that of a fountain or the woman in the statue, or may invoke Cordelia's lips, which Lear would have us look upon in his dying moments. The "tiny horn" may identify a statue of Diana, the huntress; the "leaf frame shadow leaf" recalls Daphne's retreat to security as a mute laurel. While this section may in part mark the speaker's return from her explorations "in a fictional direction" to the material ground of Dublin's historically many-layered Liberties, the emphasis on statuary also reminds us how woman in western artistic tradition has again and again (here, in a dozen kinds of stone—WHITE MARBLE, SUBCRYSTAL-LINE LIMESTONE, PENTELIC MARBLE, etc.) been objectified, rendered beautiful and silent.

To shatter the solidity of such distorting stone renderings—which parallel the distorting images of women perpetrated in patriarchal narratives—much of the rest of Howe's text takes the form of airy grids, scatterings of words in nondiscursive arrays. The constructive nature of the reading process, which the highly disjunctive text has foregrounded all along, is dramatically emphasized—and also resisted—here. For all along, developing interpretations has depended on giving greater importance to one word or phrase or juxtaposition than another, asserting linkages, allowing individual words or phonemes or blank spaces to reverberate, sounds to recall other sounds, figures to recall other figures. The exaggerated disjunction and insistent equalizing of elements in this portion of the text seem deliberately to render such procedures almost unsustainable.

The punning title, *"Formation of a Separatist, I"* playfully indicates the instability and novelty of the terrain. "Formation" operates here in at least two senses: One suggests a search for origins, making this the story/demonstration of how a separatist was/is being formed, just as the entire text has been partly a search for the sources of women's silence/absence from history. The other sense of "formation" emphasizes form or arrangement, suggesting that what follows will be the structure created by a "separatist." The last term, too, is multivalent—suggesting perhaps that the speaker/creator is a dissenter, or that she advocates separatism: separating Ireland from England, women from men, women's history from men's, or the history of the individual from that of the group.[31] Most obviously, of course, the separatist here is a poet who separates words from one another and from the syntactic web in which we usually make sense of them. Even the "I" in the title is ambiguously letter, number, phoneme, and/or pronoun; the act of separating words from each other, this indicates, may open up new ways of forming or representing the subject, particularly the female subject.

The abstractly regulated "formations" that follow, in which words and sounds (and sometimes numbers) are freed from the hierarchic arrangements of grammar or syntax and almost cleansed of semantic context, reassert the importance of discrete particularities. The usual interpretive strategies are so thoroughly thwarted that verbal particulars require our fresh inspection. (I hear in the silence Lear's, "Look there, look there!") The allusive sediment attached to the words does not go away, but attracts attention when some of the surroundings are erased. ("See better, Lear.") Howe's practice suggests we have been blinded by the clumping together of words into systems, into apparently cohesive images whose validity is difficult to challenge. Pondering words wrenched apart from narrative, from syntax, from speakers, we may see more clearly the ways in which words woven into language have formed a fabric perpetuating women's oppression.

In this section, that oppressive fabric is rent to tatters, evoked largely through the briefest allusions. Now the reader is no longer trapped within the received system, as were the characters in "God's Spies"; instead, we are invited to see through it (in the senses of seeing beyond it, of discerning its falsifications, of registering the light that comes through its cracks). The lines preceding the arrays—"Crops / his horse / drew his sword / swung his sword / said he would slash and slay" (*DP*, p. 114)—suggest that, as in "God's Spies," the context and impetus for this linguistic experiment is destructive patriarchal violence, both enacted and spoken.

Whether headed by a number or by a letter (either C or S), the individual arrays on subsequent pages seem reconceived experimental "portraits" of either Cordelia or Stella. Perhaps Howe wishes to demonstrate how a composite image of multiple portraits may approach an "authentic" representation. The first array, Stella's, opens with an air of pastoral delicacy that contrasts sharply with the slashing and slaying preceding:

"only   air   most   lovely   meath"—the last word naming the place where Stella owned property. A number of words in this array can be related to Stella's life in rural Ireland; by contemplating them separately and by considering them as sketching the outlines of a gestalt, perhaps we can take a fresh look at that life. Many of the words here connote pleasant freedom and vitality, but there are darker overtones of restriction in terms such as "weir" and "enclosure." The empty brackets immediately above the centrally isolated "stellar" ominously suggest the erasure and/or restraint of Stella (though perhaps one might argue that "stellar" stands apart as a free singularity). Particularly in the second half, violence or violent victimization is also suggested, in words evoking physical attack, perhaps Christ's passion—"blade / pierce   side"—and in "boyne," the famous battle of 1690 which led to the "flight of the wild geese" into exile.

Struggles to write and to write powerfully are also invoked in this portrait/array. The words "churn" and "foam" could well allude to Pound's Canto II, where "So-Shu churned the sea." According to annotator Carroll Terrell, Pound alludes to Li Po's criticism of the poet So-Shu "for creating foam instead of waves," for "stir[ring] up decayed (enervated) waves" (Terrell 1980, p. 5). The sequence "here   foam   pen   still   yew" may suggest literary paralysis or enervation (the pen motionless). It may suggest also the difficulty a contemporary woman still encounters in feeling the pen to be hers, rather than belonging to another you/yew.

Musical links here are as provocative as semantic ones, with each word a kind of bell tone reverberating into the silence around it. Sonic progressions move not only from word to word— "boyne   churn   surely"—but also across pages; the opening line of array 1. reads "only   air   most   lovely   meath" and that of 2. reads "only   fury   cleave   most   air"—with "cleave" echoing "meath," and "fury" echoing but jarring against "lovely." Words recur from one array to another, or recur with slight variation within one array (as when "easter snow" becomes "estersnowe"), their meaning shifting with the context. Whether established by sound or by semantic/allusive association, however, the tonal clusters refuse to yield a seamless whole, though enticingly they suggest scattered bits of a remote gestalt.

Thus, while several of the arrays have at the top of the page an initial S or C, suggesting a focus on Stella or Cordelia, individual identity or personal history nonetheless serve as only partially organizing forces, and some of the words refuse to "fit." The C sections do contain a number of words that occur memorably in *Lear*— on page 117, for instance, "physic" (as in "take physic, pomp"), "dower" (as in "thy truth then be thy dower"), "tom   sa" (as in "poor Tom's a-cold") or "fum" (as in mad Tom's lines concerning Child Rowland), among others. Just as the first array could be provisionally read as suggesting Stella's pastoral isolation in Ireland, this one might suggest fragility and vulnerability, especially the threat of madness. But such a reading is suspiciously selective. (Where do, for instance, "crisscross," "laminate," and "concept" fit in this imposed coherence?) In the next array, which opens "love   tongue   milk   pasture   words," a number of the same terms recur, but the addition and repetition especially of "cause" (echoing Cordelia's "no cause, no cause") puts another lens on Cordelia's experience; more terms point to the importance of love, tenderness, forgiveness. Again, however, the fact that not every term will fit into any such organization, renders suspect—or at least inadequate, falsely limiting—the act of privileging those that do. Howe's iconoclastic forms insist that understandings of historical figures must remain provisional (a perspective very different from Judy

Grahn's, Rita Dove's, or Ruth Whitman's) and must always be chal-
lenged by meditating on words one by one, and allowing them to
speak to each other in a more random way.

In the final C array (*DP*, p. 118), along the right-hand margin,
six descending repetitions of "words" form a kind of literal barrier,
as if to say, "look there," look at the minimal units of the language
in which we give shape to our experience and through which we
experience personal identity. The four descending "no"s that follow
may indicate the importance of resistance (like Cordelia's) to patri-
archal methods of dividing the kingdom, in this case, the realm of
language.

Having broken down her portraits of Stella and Cordelia to sepa-
rate component words, Howe proceeds to anatomize her own iden-
tity as constituted through her name. "I am composed of nine let-
ters," Howe announces at the top of the next page, giving a
definition to each letter of her name in sequence ("1 is the subject
of a preposition in logic. / 2 is a female sheep, or tree." etc.) (*DP*,
p. 119). Where Charles Olson sought to return to the syllable as
"the minimum and source of speech" (Olson 1966, p. 18), Howe
goes even further toward the atomic unit not of speech but of speech
imprinted in writing—the letter. Hence, "THE KEY" appears
above three lines of letters, the second and third of which are the
alphabet.

It is here, Howe suggests, that women's innovative self-portrai-
ture must start, with a separation of and fresh attention to even the
smallest linguistic units. That women's experience might be suc-
cessfully encoded this way is indicated by the half hidden, suggested,
and overlapping words composing the first line of this "KEY":
"e n i g m a s t i f e m i a t e d c r y p t o a t h" (*DP*, p. 119). This
contains (among others) the words, enigma, ma, cry, and crypt, the
syllables fem and crypto, a coinage femiated which would mean
something close to feminized, and half of the word stifled. The key
to the feminine—particularly its voice (cry)—that has been left
mysterious, concealed, silenced, even murdered, lies in a reexamina-
tion and redeployment of our most fundamental linguistic elements.
The poet-separatist's act of verbal reclamation is also a gesture of
self-definition in her own terms. Thus, the "I" with which Susan
Howe speaks is taken from Ireland, leaving the word without its
first letter to suggest Ireland's contribution to her sense of self.

In response to italicized questions, "*What are eyes for? / What are ears for?"* Howe presents a list of Latinate "feminine" rhymes that aptly describe the forces she has applied in her writing: "Tension / Torsion / Traction / Unction / Vection / Version / Vision" (*DP*, p. 119). She pursues rather than elides contradiction; twists, turns, and stretches conventional ordering structures; capitalizes on the plastic and moldable rather than the fixing attributes of language; and seeks in all this a means of carrying new meanings, of seeing differently and more fairly—again to invoke Kent's terms, to "see better" than the patriarchal past and the male imaginary have done.

Like Olson, Howe would have us approach language with tremendous care; even the tiniest shifts are significant—the lines "Nor is t-here / colorless in colourlessness" (*DP*, p. 120) remind us that a single letter transforms here to there, distinguishes an Irish context for language from an American one. Our situation, as Lear, Swift, Cordelia and Stella all remind us, is critical; like Beckett's characters in *Happy Days*,

> We are
> in a sandheap
>
> We are
> discovered
> not solid
> the floor
> based
> on misunderstanding.
>
> (*DP*, p. 120)

If we are to establish a truer understanding, we will have to abstract language painstakingly from the forms in which we misunderstand (the lies within the conventional are suggested in "the li-on roars. / . . . The book fakes. / The snake hiss-es") and allow both chance and vision to act upon language to generate alternatives.

The final pages of "The Liberties," headed by the title "HEAR" (*DP*, p. 123), challenge us to attend to an even more intense mix of genres and discourses—stage directions and dramatic dialogue, cryptic autobiographical anecdote, biography, lyric, quotation and allusion, abstract array, shifting letters and phonemes, etc. The reflexively textual rubs against—and further erodes—the purportedly mimetic: "(. . . *With a bundle of straw*, BRIDE, BRIDEGROOM, / PARENTS. / *A cry.* / *There are transitions.* / *Draft finished & etc.*)"

[ellipsis mine[32]]. *King Lear* again provides the dominant literary context, but its transformation via radical fragmentation here suggests great possibility: when the BASTARD enters, "solus with a letter" (*DP*, p. 126), that letter is not a document of deceitful prose, but rather a single alphabetical character, the initial letter of both Stella's and Susan Howe's name, as well as the first letter of silence and speech. (In an interview, Howe—probably echoing H.D.—also observes that " 'S' makes word a sword" [Falon 1989, p. 34].) Single letters—themselves compressed names or portraits—and this significant initial in particular, are surely part of what Howe declares "Here set at liberty."

Torquing conventional linguistic and generic formations may indeed open writing to new visions and new forms of portraiture, both of historical figures and of oneself. Howe suggests that a radically deconventionalized approach to language opens the possibility of both a less mediated engagement with the "ebbing actual" and a fuller awareness of imposed forms of mediation: her final lines read, "Tear pages from a calendar // scatter them into sunshine and snow" (*DP*, p. 126).

The work's final inscription is a visual and linguistic pun that can serve as an emblem of the entire poem's historical project. Apparently from an old map, it depicts an island with the word Stagg below, and in large print "IRELANDS EYE" above. (Ireland's Eye is a small quartzite island a few kilometers offshore from Howth in Dublin Bay. Once the site of a monastery, it is now a bird sanctuary—a fact that must have intrigued Howe as much as the rock's suggestive name.) The drawing of the island resembles lips as much or more than an eye; that, combined with the eye/I pun, reminds us of the interrelation of perception or vision, identity, and voice. Clarifying one will reinforce the others. This image from an antique map also provides a final insistence on the historical and geographical specificities affecting identity and expression: just as any language is intertwined with specific topographies and histories, the linguistic resources available to any speaker will depend on the places she or he inhabits as well as on various kinds of colonizing experience she or he has known. With Ireland's eye, Howe urges us to look to innovative form and the perspective of the disempowered in order to illuminate the blind spots of recorded history. "The Liberties," along with her other long poems, models processes of exploring the dominant discourse of the past; its remapping of that territory may help us discern and articulate the female/feminine that has been expropriated within the masculine cultural imaginary.

Few, if any, women writers in American poetry's current avant-garde possess an interest in historical subjects and a commitment to historical research as profound as Susan Howe's. A number of female experimentalists, however, share her concern with interrogating the masculine authority of tradition and rendering what has been present there for the most part as notable absence. Beverly Dahlen and Rachel Blau DuPlessis, whose long poems will occupy my final chapter, are among them. They share with Howe a belief, distinguishing them from traditionally formalist and mainstream free verse writers alike, that the genuinely different writing practice they seek—the nonauthoritarian voicing of the feminine—requires radical and continual disturbance of normative conventions of syntax, grammar, lineation, versification, genre, etc. The distinctive contributions of Dahlen and DuPlessis to feminist experimentalism lie in their adaptations of unbounded serial form pioneered by, among others, Robert Duncan. In their hands, the endlessly inclusive poetic series becomes an unfolding succession of attempts to inscribe—but not to impose fixity on—feminine/female difference.

CHAPTER SIX

Grand Collage "Out of
Bounds": Feminist Serial
Poems by Beverly Dahlen
and Rachel Blau DuPlessis

The title Rachel Blau DuPlessis gives to the collection in which
the first installments of her open-ended series *Drafts* appear is a
telling one: *Tabula Rosa* signals that in language there is no clean
slate. Language, inevitably carrying traces of past usages, is deeply
implicated in constructions of gender, and gender is entangled in
the structures of language; hence the word *rosa* alone connotes
woman as erotic exotic bloom and as baby-pink delicate weakness.
The suggested/erased term *rasa*, woman's apparent blankness and
silence, is precisely what has been inscribed on her by her society.
And in the view of many women poets—including DuPlessis and
Beverly Dahlen, author of another open-ended series, *A Reading*,
which was begun eight years earlier than *Drafts* and helped prompt
its inception—that representation of prescribed femininity requires
overwriting. But—here's the catch—how? "A woman, while always
a real, if muted or compromised, or bold and unheard, or admired
but forgotten (etc.), speaker in her own work is most often a cultural
artifact in any of the traditions of meaning on which she draws"
(DuPlessis 1990 [*Pink Guitar*] p. 141; cited hereafter as *PG*). For
those aspiring to a feminist practice of writing, those wanting to
"rewrite the rose" (*PG*, p. 82), *poetic* traditions may be particularly
problematic. DuPlessis has argued that western lyric (in which, of
course, roses abound) depends on a "foundational cluster of gen-
dered notions" that position woman as the beautiful sexual object,
the icon inspiring the male subject's creative acts (1994, p. 73). The
contemporary woman poet must write "otherhow" (*PG*, p. 151).

Modernist poetry, which polyphonically ruptured the lyric voice, points in some fruitful directions. Looking back on her own selection of the modernist period as her field of academic specialization, DuPlessis has speculated that her choice as a graduate student expressed a desire for critique she was otherwise still repressing (M. Keller 1987, p. 22). Drawn to modernist collage, to its practice of rupture and "constant critique," DuPlessis wrote her doctoral dissertation on two of the great modernist long poems, Williams's *Paterson* and Pound's *Pisan Cantos*. But her relation to the male modernists is charged with ambivalence—an ambivalence that recalls Doubiago's and Howe's responses to Olson. For while they provide a powerfully liberating example of nonhegemonic writing that defies literary conventions in order to reconstruct culture—an example in which DuPlessis is deeply invested and for which she is passionately grateful—nonetheless, "the great male poets of that generation repeat tradition where male-female relations are concerned" (*PG*, p. 39).[1] Indeed, they depend on received gender narratives for intelligibility: "Their radical forms are made relatively accessible—readable—by the familiarity of gender limits, the iconographies they inherit and repropose" (*PG*, p. 42).

> They were all, all revolutionaries except for one idea, one feature, one substance. The writing they perfected, the eloquent emptiness, drawn to the burble, the midden, sheer rhythm, a dance and not a mirror, an electricity
>
> was deflected from the contemporaneous revolution in, and of, gender.
>
> (*PG*, p. 62)

Consequently, the most celebrated modernist long poems position women essentially as traditional lyric does:

> The cultural production and reproduction of "Woman" is central to many of the linked chain of major long poems of modernism, poems intertextual, inter-influenced, mutually read. *The Waste Land, Paterson, The Pisan Cantos*. All want to construct a ritual site in which (hetero)sexuality is returned to its spiritual or primary ("primitive") meanings, and the fertile conjuncture of man and woman is affirmed.
>
> (*PG*, pp. 48–49)

Many women interested in experimental writing, including Howe as well as DuPlessis and Dahlen, have dealt with the problematics of an inheritance that positions man as writer and woman as written partly by seeking out a female tradition of writers who explored language innovations with a consciousness of the relation between gender and language.[2] Duplessis's interest in female experimental traditions is evident in her extensive critical writings on female modernists H.D., Stein, Woolf, Moore, and Loy; in her essays on her female contemporaries, Howe and Dahlen; and in her collaboration with Kathleen Fraser, Dahlen, and others on *HOW(ever)*, the experimentalist journal Fraser founded.[3] Dahlen, though less invested in academic criticism, has pursued similar interests through *HOW(ever)* and in essays examining work by Dickinson, H.D., and Stein.

Scrutiny of H.D.'s career has been important to both Dahlen and DuPlessis, but for DuPlessis in particular "the career of that struggle" in which male modernists are heavily implicated has provided an important forum for confronting the complexity of her own relation to male modernist practice.[4] She remains conscious of her dependence on male traditions and examples that cannot simply be escaped. (Dahlen's similar awareness is evident, for instance, in her preoccupation with Freud, Lacan, and their influential dogmas.) DuPlessis's acknowledgment that the page is never a *tabula rasa* does not, however, diminish the fervor with which she champions "the gesture of turning away from poetry as already written, however quixotic or impossible that task, by the repeated, stubborn, and self-contradictory practice of postulating an elsewhere, an otherhow!" (*PG*, p. 151). This gesture is Dahlen's as well.

Given DuPlessis's acceptance of destabilizing self-contradiction (see above) and of a precarious both/and stance (see especially "For the Etruscans" [*PG*, pp. 1–19]), given her refusal of simple and simplifying binaries (evident throughout her literary criticism), it is not surprising that a male poet, Robert Duncan, should have helped lead her into H.D.'s work and, through the example of his own work as well as H.D.'s, into poetic methodologies that would release some of the binds of the male modernist long poem. Dahlen, who, like Duncan, was living in the Bay area, took an even more extensive and formative interest in Duncan's work; she first heard him read in the mid-1950s and went to hear him read and speak with increasing frequency from the late 1960s throughout the 1970s.[5] Although she characterizes her reading in his poetry as "extremely spotty," at times it has been "very intense" so that she identifies Duncan as a writer whose influence on her is probably "out of all proportion to the amount read" (letter to author, 10 January 1995).[6]

Serial form was a dominant compositional method for Duncan, who, as Michael Davidson explains, found in the serial poem "a form flexible enough to handle both the wide range of his readings and his characteristically paratactic, nonlinear thought" (Davidson 1989, p. 141). The term "serial poem," though it means slightly different things to its various practitioners, denotes a work constructed from separate but related parts in an exploratory manner that, in contrast to most lyric sequences, refuses progressive or narrative structure. Its aspirations are more modest, more investigative, than the grandly didactic cultural projects of modernist epic.[7] Not following any predetermined plan, its flexible structure is generally disjunctive, so that meaning develops as much from the gaps between the constituent parts as from their suture. In DuPlessis's words, "a serial poem is an argument made of leaps" (letter to author, 4 February 1995). No prescribed relation exists between part and whole, though as DuPlessis observes, "The sequence will change the heft and nature of any individual poems or units in the series. The sequencing of serial forms changes the individual units, making them larger in implication but less complete" (letter to author, 4 February 1995).

Duncan's serial practice was a significant example for both DuPlessis and Dahlen and provides a useful context for examining their serial works. I do not wish to suggest, however, that his version of seriality is the only, or even the primary, example for either woman. DuPlessis's interest in this structural method derived initially from her close friend and mentor George Oppen, for whom seriality meant an expansion of imagist practice, aiming "to construct a method of thought from . . . the imagist intensity of vision" (M. Keller 1987, p. 174). Oppen explains the title of his book-length series, *Discrete Series*, as follows:

> That's a phrase in mathematics. A pure mathematical series would be one in which each term is derived from the preceding term by a rule. A discrete series is a series of terms each of which is empirically derived, each one of which is empirically true. And this is the reason for the fragmentary character of those poems. I was at-

tempting to construct a meaning by empirical statements, by imagist statements.

(Dembo 1972, p. 174)

Dahlen recalls her earliest interest in the serial poem arising in response to the work of George Stanley:

> The notion of the serial poem is something I remember discussing with George Stanley after he and I became friends in the late '60s. George had been a member of the Spicer circle (he was also a friend of Duncan's) and I think his idea of the serial poem was based more on Spicer's.
>
> (letter to author, 10 January 1995)[8]

Jack Spicer adopts an analogy from Robin Blaser to describe the poetic series: "it's as if you go into a room, a dark room, the light is turned on for a minute, then it's turned off again, and then you go into a different room where a light is turned on and turned off" (Spicer 1973, p. 233). Oppen would find congenial this emphasis on momentary flashes of intense perception. But where Oppen emphasizes empiricism and an ethics of sincerity, Spicer stresses "dictation." Spicer proposes as a reason for writing a series, that "if you can get focused on the individual part enough you have a better chance of dictation, you have a better chance of being an empty vessel, being filled up by whatever's outside" (1973, p. 233). Dictation is also crucial to Spicer's sense of the larger form of the whole: "you have to go into a serial poem not knowing what the hell you're doing. . . . it should be structured by dictation and not by the poet" (1973, p. 233).

The different emphases of Oppen and Spicer emerge in muted form when one compares DuPlessis's and Dahlen's approaches to serial composition; DuPlessis's structures of thought often develop in response to empirical data perceived in the external world, while Dahlen strives to take dictation from her unconscious. Both poets insist on a processive understanding of the series as something that discovers its own path, but DuPlessis is more open to some degree of regulation in relating one poem to another.[9]

Even if Duncan is not *the* shaping example of serial practice for DuPlessis or Dahlen, both are aware of him as a central figure in the tradition of serial writing they have entered, and his practices illuminate theirs. In addition, Duncan has occupied a crucial mediating position between the practices of male and female innovative writers and between modernist and postmodernist literary generations. Consequently, a brief discussion of his poetic theories and practices—particularly his unbounded series, "Passages"—will provide an important context, setting the stage for this chapter's examination of DuPlessis's and Dahlen's feminist refabrications of the modernist long poem in their own "interminable" *Drafts* and *A Reading.* Thereafter, readings in Dahlen's and DuPlessis's serial works will reveal how each poet, extending the modifications of modernist paratactic techniques evident in Duncan's *"grand collage,"* achieves a "depoeticization" sufficiently radical that she can hope to overwrite inherited inscriptions of woman.

Duncan occupies a curious position in relation to poetic modernism, as Michael André Bernstein notes in "Robert Duncan: Talent and the Individual Tradition":

> It is difficult to think of any major poet except Duncan who has located his writing as so deliberate a continuation of the same enterprise. And yet there is also no poet whose work more seriously challenges the premises and boundaries of that very tradition, whose writing has been more responsive to all the impulses modernism sought either to repress entirely or to relegate to the margins of serious writing.
>
> (Bernstein 1985, p. 177)

Duncan's tradition, according to Bernstein, is in fact his own creation, reflecting his "syncretistic imagination [that] has always drawn strength from a plurality of sources, many of which, moreover, have been conceived hitherto as incompatible" (1985, p. 182).[10] Davidson argues that Duncan transformed the notion of tradition altogether and observes that the "litany of artists whom he is ambitious to 'emulate, imitate, reconstrue, approximate, duplicate' would confuse even the most subtle literary genealogist" (Davidson 1989, pp. 126, 128). Yet precisely such an example of selective identification within an eclectic array of precursors is helpful for poets like DuPlessis and Dahlen, who, largely because of their feminist perspectives, can comfortably share only some of Pound's or Williams's goals and practices. Additionally, Duncan's particular selections and practices—the distinctive ways he fabricated his tradition and his poems—have been important to them.[11]

Crucial has been his emphasis on a method, an approach with formal consequences especially evident in his serial work, aptly described by Bernstein:

> The emphasis in Duncan's poetry is on the *process* of discovery, on the ways in which he himself has been moved to a new understanding by the illumination of an often unexpected source, rather than [as in Pound's *Cantos*] on the hortatory truth-content of that source itself. A kind of gradual, often hesitant and incomplete, working-through of an initial predicament characterizes many of Duncan's major poems, so that the distinction between the psychological and the textual, between a strictly personal quest and the discovery of communal values in different traditions is collapsed.
>
> (1985, p. 187)

In contrast to Pound's ideogram, Duncan's poem-as-*grand-collage* (Duncan's term) is "ready to welcome the play of shadows and halftones," open to contingent secondary impulses that may require new principles of order and interpretation (Bernstein 1985, p. 188).[12] Pound seeks

> to attain a maximum transparency to the already securely guaranteed principles (of government, nature, or culture) so that these laws are "made new" for new readers. But the *grand collage* is a process that represents primarily itself as a quest; more than anything else, it enacts the different paths a search for knowledge may follow. . . . [T]he *grand collage* is centrifugal not centripetal, and it often proceeds by undoing the certainties of its inaugural premises.
>
> (Bernstein 1985, pp. 188–89)

This openness to alternative "paths" has constituted a crucial permission for those experimental female poets whose writing is itself a quest for how to write and for the subject that writes, and who deliberately compromise telos and reject as authoritarian the delivery of a predetermined message. They write in the centrifugal tradition of *grand collage*.

Duncan's calling extended attention to the centrality of women in his poetic development (what Davidson calls his "feminization of tradition" [Davidson 1989, p. 130]), his openly criticizing the male establishment for its erasure of women poets, and his clearly subverting male heterosexual norms in his own poetry have further contributed to the power of his example for feminists like DuPlessis and Dahlen. In 1963, the first selections began to appear of Duncan's *The H.D. Book*, an extended meditation on modernism focusing on H.D.'s poetry; this series of essays comprises a remarkable tribute to a poet who subscribed as neither Pound, Williams, nor Eliot did "to the psychological universe," who pursued an interest in "the unfolding of the poem that corresponds to the unfolding of the psyche" and did so with a sensual intensity and an interest in the occult that mirrored Duncan's own (Duncan 1963, pp. 5, 12). In *The H.D. Book*, Duncan asserts that it is perhaps because he "found [his] life in poetry through the agency of certain women" that he had a "special estimation not only of the masters of that art but of its mistresses" (Duncan 1967a, p. 27).[13]

Dahlen has testified to the importance to her not only of *The H.D. Book* but also of "the example of [Duncan's] devotion to H.D. in the poetry" (letter to author, 10 January 1995). DuPlessis credits him with opening for her, via his knowledge of H.D., the doors to a life-project of "understanding culture with the women in" (DuPlessis 1988, p. 9). In a brief tribute, "For Duncan," she recalls her own shocked recognition, prompted by Duncan's essays on H.D., that he was

> a unique example of a male critic and poet who consistently and throughout his studies not only "included" women writers, but saw them as real cultural forces, functioning richly and authoritatively in modernism. Sitwell. Stein. Butts. Moore. Richardson. Riding. Woolf. H.D. The depth and attention which Duncan devoted to these and other figures as co-equals with the male producers (those more readily "canonized" because of gender)—this was a lesson that has barely yet been assimilated.
>
> (DuPlessis 1988, p. 8–9)

Duncan recognized the idiosyncrasy of his own perspective: the creative genius, he acknowledged, is considered male, and "[m]en live uneasily with or under the threat of genius in women" (Duncan 1979, p. 43). Yet he distanced himself from those whose orthodoxies exclude female revelation; as DuPlessis indicates, H.D. sits in his pantheon as high as Williams or Pound.

Duncan honors in the work of the artists he most admires an intention "to project the wholeness of [their] experience—in this way close to the psychoanalytic process—as the content of a work that will present the scales, the ratios, chords and discords of the soul's own creative order" (Duncan 1979, p. 71) He does not share the "dis-ease" of Pound's generation—or the more acute discomfort of New Critics such as Randall Jarrell—with poetry's emotions as womanish things; his sense of his own difference as a homosexual man contributes to his readiness to embrace "even embarrassing sentiments" (Duncan 1985, p. 220) or what others find "queer" (Duncan 1979, pp. 80–81). Dahlen and DuPlessis—whose knowledge of feminist and psychoanalytic theory (and particularly their reading in Kristeva) fosters an interest in presymbolic linguistic registers—are primed to follow his interest in "the truth of how consciousness moves, where form has been developed to bear testimony to undercurrent and eddy, shifts, breaks and echoes of content" (Duncan 1979, p. 75). This flexible multivalence is part of what DuPlessis acknowledges when she speaks of the impact of Duncan's voice: "ruminative, learned, passionate. A voice—synthesizing, evaluating, filled with its own gift and sense of necessity. It is a voice reading—a voice of mulling and interpreting, turning and returning" (DuPlessis 1988, p. 8).

Duncan's practice in the long poem extends the boundaries set by male modernist practice in a number of ways, some of which have been crucial to Dahlen and DuPlessis. As already suggested, most important is his structural/methodological example in his refusal of a plan, his generation of an ahierarchical, polyphonic, nonlinear, nonteleological writing. In a late interview, Duncan identifies as a problem in the *Cantos* their having, in his view, a "preplan": "the crucial experience in art is coming upon something, which is why the preplanned won't do at all" (Bernstein and Hatlen 1985, pp. 92, 93). For experimental women poets seeking an "otherhow" of writing, the hope of coming upon something bears increased urgency and the preplanned carries even less promise. As "a series having no beginning and no end as its condition of form," a work scattered across three volumes published over more than twenty years in which no section occupied a central or climactic position, "Passages" was logically an exemplary text (Duncan 1974, p. 53).

Related to this sense of boundless and unbounded form is Duncan's abandonment of Pound's focus on the integrity of the line. Duncan's line is "compromised": "there's not even a commitment to syntax, and that means every phrase can be compromised by the coexistence of other phrases" (Bernstein and Hatlen 1985, p. 92).

While *A Reading* seems closer to the portions of Duncan's composition that are more syntactically coherent and *Drafts* to those that are more relentlessly paratactic, both works capitalize on the way phrases can "compromise" each other, multiplying possible meanings and intertexts. Like Duncan, these poets are drawn to the impure, rather than the pure, the disequilibrated struggle rather than the crystalline order.

A second area in which Duncan's example (along with H.D.'s) sets the stage for Dahlen's and DuPlessis's practice is in his embrace of Freudian thinking and his adoption of Freudian analysis, particularly dream-work, as a model for poetic process. "[T]he great invitation of Freud," he says in an interview, "was the sense of multilayeredness" (Bernstein and Hatlen 1985, p. 99); his own polysemous writing practices are designed to pursue shifting perspectives in consciousness with minimal censorship. Dahlen appears to share Duncan's sense that "What we experience in dreaming is not a content of ourselves but the track of an inner composition of ourselves," and that track is also the one writing follows (Duncan 1967b, p. 19). The epigraph from George Steiner's *After Babel* introducing *A Reading* indicates that Dahlen's serial poem, as "[a]n exercise in 'total reading,'" follows the unending "process of free yet potentially linked and significant association in psychoanalysis." Freudian association provides the poem's generative and organizing procedure.

At once Freud's devoted follower and his rebellious rival, Dahlen originally thought of *A Reading* as challenging Freud's "heroic claim" that he alone could perform self-analysis (Dahlen 1984a, p. 9). Epistemologically as well as formally, she both relies on and defies him: "I have arrogantly appropriated [Freud's] ideas for my own uses" she brags and confesses (1984a, p. 9). Her involvement with Freudianism is particularly evident in *A Reading 1–7*, but throughout the series she frequently invokes Freudian concepts, comments on Freud's writings, and (as Duncan often does) presents her own dreams. Dahlen also often ruminates on, quotes from, or alludes to the psychoanalytic revisionary work of Kristeva. In addition, a lack that figures centrally in her thinking is linked to Lacan's psychoanalytic theories concerning the lack or loss of the maternal body suffered with the entry into the symbolic and into the position of speaking subject.

Similarly, DuPlessis's poetry reflects extensive reading in feminist exegeses or revisions of Freud's work by Kristeva, Luce Irigaray, Juliet Mitchell, and others. But her writing is less thoroughly steeped in Freudian ideas. Less burdened than Dahlen by the sense of Freud as "a figure of the father . . . whom I have honored and defended, resisted and feared," DuPlessis appears particularly conscious of Freud as part of an intellectual tradition attentive to the revelations of language, intent on listening to the insides of words (Dahlen 1984a, p. 9). In this she, too, comes close to Duncan, who notes, "[i]n the revelation of psychoanalysis there had been, a trick between the mind and the ear, . . . the syllable that hid the pun within the word. Care, attention, had opened doors for souls in what they were saying, doors of other things they were saying" (Duncan 1969, p. 34). Duncan regards Freud as continuing the Kabbalistic tradition; conversely, he sees the modernist writers of "the new interior monolog" reading "their lives as the Kabbalists read the Torah, exploring the permutations of meaning in each letter and diacritical mark" (Duncan 1979, p. 72). Similarly, DuPlessis suggests a relation between her own play with permutations of words, her exploration of puns and homonyms, and the rabbinical exegetical tradition of Midrash: "Tracking the intricate meanings of one's own accidents—a practice related to H.D.'s writing practice in *Tribute to Freud*—gives rise to a midrash-like quality of continuous linkage of interpretation, where the production and productivity of meanings is continuous" (DuPlessis 1996, p. 147).

A third area of affinity between Duncan and these feminist experimentalists is his acceptance of the artist's alienation from hegemonic society—something crucial to his take on modernism—and his determination to use poetry as social critique. In *The H.D. Book*, Duncan presents the modernist writers, including Freud, as facing social ostracism because of their opposition to the major wars of their time. Writing at the peak of (and in opposition to) U.S. involvement in Vietnam, Duncan proclaimed, "We too, in a hostile environment, taking our faith and home in our exile, live in creative crisis" (Duncan 1968b, p. 134). A number of the later Passages in *Bending the Bow* (1968) confront U.S. involvement in the war and its grim meaning for American society. His social critique extends also to gender roles and their verbal codification, since Duncan is bravely determined to explore the power of Eros where "my Other is not a woman but a man / *the King upon whose bosom let me lie*" (Duncan

1968a, p. 65).[14] He becomes a model not only of courageous outspokenness, but of a fully inclusive poetics: DuPlessis speaks admiringly of his

> desire to make an erotics/a politics/a gnosis of the processes and engagements of meditation. In Duncan, I had found on the page [referring to his "Poem Beginning with a Line by Pindar"] what I found in Oppen in person, people who understood that the debates and issues of modernism were not the pickup sticks of literary history but were the basis of a poetics of cultural critique and passionate commitment.
>
> (DuPlessis 1988, p. 8)

A fourth area in which Dahlen's and DuPlessis's poetic practice may be linked to Duncan's is their shared response to linguistic belatedness, their being frankly and unembarrassedly "derivative" writers.[15] Quotations are embedded everywhere in their texts. They are sometimes incorporated seamlessly, sometimes presented as distinct material prompting the poem's meditation and argument. In part, the quotations constitute, as Bernstein notes, gestures of responsibility and even of tradition-formation, acts acknowledging one's masters (Bernstein 1982, p. 177). But beyond that, the poets share an awareness—also evident in Howe's writing—that words are a used medium, each one carrying with it a history of prior uses that shapes our perceptions. Duncan, rather than approaching his poetry as "an expression of what is really his own," experiences instead an

> extreme persuasion to the reality of the world created by the written and read word, where the meaning in language has its definitions in the community of meanings from which I derive whatever meanings I can, . . . at times a feeling that there is no real me, only the process of derivations in what I have my existence.
>
> (in *Poetry/Audit* IV, 3, 1967: 48–49,
> quoted in Bernstein 1982, pp. 179–80)

As noted in the chapter's opening, this sense of being defined within a community of meanings, in particular of the construction of woman in and by the received language of a patriarchal society, is central to Dahlen's and DuPlessis's poetic procedures.

A final area in which the women's serial poems find a model in Duncan's is in their construction of the reader's role, a role affected by the character of the poetic subject. Duncan has spoken of "Passages" as "a work in which I seek to lose myself in the hearing of the voice of the work itself, a work not of personality or oneself but of structures and passages" (1985, p. 227). Similarly, DuPlessis speaks against "writing the personal" as that is understood in today's expressive lyric ("the notion of having a voice . . . of establishing a consumable personality complete with pix, of engaging in self-revelation") and claims that instead of finding a voice, she is "losing one" (*PG*, p. 172, ellipsis mine). And when describing Dahlen's *A Reading*, DuPlessis observes, "there is no fictional center of things; although sometimes there is *I*, *it* also occurs, and *you*, and *she*. . . . The 'I' who is a woman cannot be a writer, must be a 'reader' of these pronominal facts. She must write a reading" (*PG*, p. 121).[16] The reader enters these works, then, not to reconstruct a personality or situation represented by the poet, but to explore those same structures and passages in which the poet has lost him or herself. The poet is as much reader as writer, and the reader is necessarily involved in the act of writing the poem in the process of reading it. Thus, Duncan asserts that the design of "Passages" "does not begin in a certain place but where the admirer's eye chooses to begin in seeing" (Duncan 1974, p. 53); the reader "if he is intent in reading becomes a new poet of the poem" (Duncan 1968b, 153–54).[17]

Just as Duncan himself selected what he found useful from the examples of Pound, Lawrence, H.D., and others, neither Dahlen nor DuPlessis adopts Duncan's poetics in its entirety. They do not share the preoccupation with the visionary and the occult that drew Duncan to H.D. (though Christian texts frequently enter Dahlen's thinking), and they do not write of romantic love. Nor do they participate in the Romantic sense, so central to his writing, of an intrinsic order of the cosmos in which the poem's order fits. Much that he can take from Romantic tradition, they, largely because of their gender, feel called upon to question. For these women, beauty itself is suspect since ideas of beauty are so caught up in gender narratives (woman as object of "sugared loveliness" [*PG*, p. 54]) and in the literary conventions sustaining those cultural structures. More radically—and riskily—than Duncan, then, they must "Depoeticize: reject normal claims of beauty. Smoothness. Finish. Fitness. Decoration. Moving sentiment. Uplift" (*PG*, p. 144).

Admittedly, most experimental poetry today, including the particularly visible movement of Language writing, might be seen as practicing a "depoeticization" more extreme than Duncan's. But I would argue that the Language movement's experiments do not *necessarily* disrupt gender constructions any more than the male modernists' did. The distinctive character of the depoeticization practiced by Dahlen and DuPlessis is particularly well illuminated if their serial poems are approached as self-consciously gendered, feminist extensions and modifications of the example (especially, though not exclusively) of Duncan's form "without bounds."[18] Their practice is, to quote a phrase of Dahlen's, "out of bounds" because it is composed with the transgressive awareness that while a woman writes within the gender system, her position is also radically and inevitably "outside the law" (1992, p. 120; 1985b, p. 43).

Kristeva's theorizing of the semiotic and its importance to the transgressive character of poetic language helps illuminate how gender informs Dahlen's and DuPlessis's radically experimental poetic practice. DuPlessis observes that "Kristeva's location of two developmentally distinct registers of normal language [the semiotic and the symbolic], whose intensity and relationship are heightened in poetic language, offers a powerful picture through which certain elements of gender cruise" (*PG*, p. 85). Kristeva links the semiotic, which involves a "*heterogeneousness* to meaning and signification" dominant in poetic language, with the "maternally connoted" chora (and the opposing modality, the symbolic, with the law of the father) (Kristeva 1980a, p. 134). She does not equate the semiotic with the feminine; rather, as Toril Moi points out, it is the marginality they have in common which allows the two categories to be theorized in roughly the same way (Moi 1988, p. 166). DuPlessis is among those nonetheless troubled by Kristeva's peculiar failure to address the subject of women writers: "It is odd to read of things 'maternally connoted' or to hear that we may 'call the moment of rupture and negativity which conditions and underlies the novelty of any praxis "feminine"' when this still leaves a little in the air what the specific relations of a woman writer to the semiotic register could be" (*PG*, p. 87). Questions Kristeva largely ignores concerning the woman writer's negotiation with the semiotic and the relation of gender to poetic language lie at the heart of the transgressive quest of DuPlessis' poetry and of Dahlen's as well.

DuPlessis does not assert that there is any particular or inherent affinity between either the feminine or female and the experimental. (Note that her characterization of male modernist practice in terms of "the burble, the midden, sheer rhythm, a dance and not a mirror" underscores its semiotic dimensions.) But, along with Dahlen, other writers associated with *HOW(ever)*, and some of the female Language poets, she re-forms Kristeva by positioning her gender as a crucial factor driving *her own* experimentations in poetic language and structure. In "On Drafts," DuPlessis offers this humorous formulation: "I leave as an open, and perplexing question whether there is a female difference within what has been called a 'feminine' position in relation to language. If there is, I am playing it; if there isn't, I am sometimes playing it anyway" (1992, p. 75). Such a writing practice, then, involves a deliberate political deployment of semiotic elements and, "to tally with [the] heterogeneity" of this signifying economy, replaces the transcendental ego with "a questionable *subject-in-process*" (Kristeva 1980a, p. 135).[19] These depoeticizing poets choose to explore—as DuPlessis says of Dahlen's serial work—"some procedure for writing so excessive and marginal that it may begin to say: woman" (*PG*, p. 114).

The importance of gender to the genre of Beverly Dahlen's *A Reading* is highlighted by Language poet Ron Silliman when he claims in a blurb on the back cover of *A Reading 1–7* (appearing with blurbs by both Duncan and DuPlessis), "Only a feminist could have seen the point at which the form of the journal and the tradition of the American longpoem meet." Silliman's implying a novel hybridization of genres might at first seem to exaggerate Dahlen's originality. Duncan's "Passages," for instance, comes to mind as a long poem which possesses journal-like traits—and not because of Duncan's feminism, but because he sought a form of the long poem that could be, as Davidson says, "poems of a life, a compositional field where anything might enter: a prose quotation, a catalogue, a recipe, a dramatic monologue, a diatribe" (Davidson 1983, p. 177). Thus, in "The Architecture" ("Passages 9") Duncan describes as one might in a diary the interior of his home, himself "reading while the music playd / curld up among the ornamental cushions" (1968a, p. 27). Dahlen, who identifies locations and inclusive dates of composition and revision at the close of each of her Readings (a practice DuPlessis also follows), achieves immediacy and openness in much the same way as Duncan, by incorporating the dailiness of her ordinary living into her poem's meditative process. What distinguishes the journal-like aspects of her poem—what I believe Silliman is responding to as he implies a new achievement in her journal-like work—is the extent to which they serve her deliberate, politicized reflections on and of gender.

Details of the season or of seasonal activities like gardening, of the domestic surroundings in which she writes, of mundane conversations or passing thoughts, occasionally of her everyday awareness of her own body come into her poetry as the texture specifically of a woman's life and as integral to her quest—insistent, desirous, recursive, vagrant—for an understanding of herself, both as a particular woman and as generic woman, in language. "I am haunted by a lack of definition at the center of my experience, this absence which, like a centrifuge, propels me toward the peripheral" Dahlen observes in "Forbidden Knowledge," an essay on *A Reading* (1984a, p. 5). The lack she speaks of is for her not only the universal one Lacan posits as inevitably accompanying movement into the symbolic order with the disruption of the dyadic unity of mother and child at the time of the Oedipal crisis; it is also a specifically female one tied to the pervasive Freudian view of woman's "lack" of the phallus.[20] As Dahlen puts it in the opening lines of "A Reading 6," woman is "*the* negative space, since all that is (real) defines it. // what is real in this fantasy of the real is the phallus. everybody believes it" (1985b, p. 85). The peripheral toward which this fantasized lack or absence propels her includes the sort of "trivia" largely excluded from the traditions of serious literature prior to modernism. Such material, long associated with either the infantile or the feminine, provides the consistent ground for and grounding of *A Reading*'s often highly abstract intellection—a basis for the work's attempt to inscribe woman.

To support and develop the assertions I have been making, I believe the most valuable procedure will be to offer a fairly close reading of an entire Reading. Of course, no explication of a Dahlen Reading can be, or even aspire to be, either exhaustive or definitive. The procedure I propose risks giving an impression of Dahlen's text as more linear and stable, less polysemous and polythematic than it is. These dangers seem to me outweighed, however, by the potential benefits of following at some length the process of the poem's unfolding.[21] Through this process, as one perceives the heterogeneous linguistic registers, levels of consciousness, and referential realms Dahlen simultaneously evokes and successively interweaves, one experiences the feminist deployment of resistance to poetic finish that distinguishes this kind of experimental work by women.

Since all parts of Dahlen's "theoretically open-ended" work are of equal importance to the form of the whole, theoretically one can—as with Duncan's "Passages"—enter *A Reading* at any point. My selection of "A Reading 2" (composed in November and December of 1978) is arbitrary except that its relative brevity renders it suitable for treatment here. Like most parts of *A Reading*, this one is arranged in what look like (and what I will refer to as) paragraphs, and sequences of paragraphs are divided into larger groupings (which I will call sections); consequently, the appearance of the text conveys little disruption. However, as is true throughout *A Reading*, the paragraphs are chopped into short, rhythmically insistent phrases by punctuation marks, most often commas and periods.[22] Aurally, this can generate a graceful effect of cadence, but the abrupt units also convey fragmentation—an impression furthered by the use of small letters to begin sentences, by the frequency of grammatically incomplete linguistic units, by frequent semantic disjuncture and tonal shifts. (Duncan's comments on why he came to articulate his line "into a series of smaller elements" illuminate Dahlen's practice as well: "So the caesuras widen, and there's no longer a punctuation within a syntax. It calls attention to the fact that the mind is in full attention on the minutiae of the poem" [Cohn and O'Donnell 1980, pp. 538–39].) Referents are often ambiguous, and pronouns—sometimes reflexively considered within the writing—shift frequently. The writing, then, occupies a borderland where various forms of conventional order and of their disruption interact in constant tension.

On the more conventional and orderly side of things are two centered initial lines which function essentially as epigraphs, "*I sing of a maiden* / ' . . . German tree cults . . .'" (1985b, p. 31). These alert us to this Reading's thematic concern with the supposed link between woman and nature, a long-accepted link that contributes to woman's silenced existence as the body or object displayed in, rather than the subject speaking in, literature. "*I sing of a maiden*" (echoing, with notable differences, male epic claims, "arms and the man I sing," "I celebrate myself, and sing myself") also points to Dahlen's project of representing woman in her own terms, of challenging and complicating received views, like those of the tree cults.

The orienting function of these lines is further enhanced by contextual information Dahlen provided in correspondence (letter to the author 20 March 1995): the first derives from a medieval English Christmas carol, which opens (in modern rendition), "I sing of a Maiden / Who no equal knows. / The King of all Kings / For her Son she chose." "German tree cults" alludes to a passage in Duncan's *H.D. Book* which comments on the work of Hayyim Vital in *The Tree of Life*. There Duncan explains that the Christmas tree with which the birth of the Christ child is celebrated "came from the tree-cults of the German tribes, ancestral spirits—a burning tree." (In finding a catalyst in Duncan's text, Dahlen follows a procedure Duncan often employs of taking some other text, some piece of cultural information, as the starting point for a poem's exploration.) The commonalities in these two sources highlight themes this Reading will explore. Both evoke the midwinter season of Advent and Christmas, during which the poem is being written. Both call to mind the maternal Mary and the birth of Christ, bonds between generations (maternal, ancestral), and the subject of procreation. With this sense of the Reading's central preoccupations in mind, hereafter the reader must work to discern or generate meaning and to distinguish Dahlen's own "song" of female identity from the inherited songs—of myth and religion, of psychoanalysis, of language itself—that her writing reads.

The opening lines of the first paragraph focus on the centrality to society—and the burden to women—of humans having evolved so that the female of the species can give birth throughout the year: "the celebration of that freeing of the bond, in nature, of conception and increase so that women might bear at any time in the year. a birth in the winter. that was the burden, the necessary burden, the import of the song, the argument of the play" (Dahlen 1985b, p. 31). One may see here the cultural dominance of a masculine perspective, since the "celebration" (used, perhaps, with an ironic edge?) of woman's freedom from the estrous cycle—an advantage for the species—marks something linked to great suffering by women. Yet "celebration" may also suggest a solemnization; one may "celebrate" a great sacrifice, as Christians celebrate the Eucharist. Read that way, what follows is an unironic, mournful tribute to motherhood and to women who have given birth, sometimes in the most extreme circumstances: "she died, and the children also, and none would have lived to tell the tale without her labor." The vision of the labor to which woman is "bound" is grim—she gives birth in the dark, without shelter, when there is ice on the trails.

In most renditions of the story of Christ's "birth in the winter," of his life and death, the figure making the great sacrifice is God the Father or Christ his Son; here, by quoting Christ's rebuke to Mary (John 2:4), Dahlen reminds us of the sacrifice made by the Mother as well: *"what have I to do with thee?*, she who pondered all these things silently" (Dahlen 1985b, p. 31). In the Bible, one of the things Mary ponders silently is how her son must be about his Father's business—she "kept all these sayings in her heart" (Luke 2:51). Read orthodoxly, this means that she takes to heart her son's divine purpose, but one can also imagine the anguished loss Mary must feel knowing that her child (as is the case also in the Freudian developmental narrative) must shift allegiances to the Father. Dutiful mother that she is, however, she does not contest this fate. And perhaps the poem would rebuke her for that.

One explanation of woman's silence, this Reading seems to suggest, is her own repression ("denial") of the suffering that is her lot, or her denial that there might be any injustice in that pain, anything beyond what is inescapably "in nature." Another may be man's "devouring," his predatory desire to deny her an identity beyond that of reproductive body: "our hollow mouths, mourning backwards, the ice on the trails, the blood on the ground, that little patch to which she was bound. no wonder no mouth, all breasts and belly, it is there by the rule of denial, devouring" (Dahlen 1985b, p. 31). Does the very power of the reproductive body prompt a denial by patriarchal culture, so that when the female body looms as an awesome vision of fertility, "all breasts and belly," its womb/mouth is demonized as threatening to engulf and "devour"?

The second paragraph in its entirety reads: "rather the stars / *neaten the stars* / she was screaming and then *it's so unfair* she said. agreed, yes to that no, skin to skin, how that softness persists." [virgules are Dahlen's] (1985b, p. 31). The disjunction between this and what precedes demonstrates how thoroughly Dahlen embraces an openness like Duncan's to "alternative paths," to "undercurrent and eddy, shifts, breaks" in her process-based poetics. Here this embrace serves Dahlen's feminist agenda of complicating received views of woman. With the preceding paragraph in mind, we might understand the woman's screaming as noncelebratory behavior during labor: she cries out against her lot in a world governed by chaotic natural forces (hence the desire for greater neatness in the firmament) or cries out for a more equitable arrangement of gendered destinies (what might seem to be in the stars, but is culturally arranged). This woman is a different kind of mother than the dutifully silent and widely idealized Mary. The second sentence adds other dimensions to Dahlen's portrait of female identity: the speaker's reinforcement of the screamer's resistance to the given order (or disorder) and to the burden of giving birth—"yes to that no"—leads into what I take to be an affirmation of the joys of motherhood, the pleasure of skin to skin contact between mother and infant. No longer silent, but screaming and saying, Dahlen's woman is self-contradicting, multiple, unresolvable.

Perhaps thoughts of infant as *tabula rasa* or of the culturally scripted denial of woman's intellect and voice are what lead associatively to the next paragraph's opening word, "blank." A fairly obvious associational progression follows: "it was a rule of thumb, black thumb, someone's new press, imprint, printer's ink" (Dahlen 1985b, p. 32). The next sentence, however, seems to take an abrupt leap: "how could you call that a clock?" Perhaps the word "rule," taken in a different sense, as measure, has prompted thoughts of time. But does Dahlen refer to a particular object, perhaps even a piece of writing? Or is she thinking of the biological clock and its common application to the aging premenopausal body? In addressing "you" does the I address herself, the reader generally, or a particular other? Possibilities proliferate. The confusions of referents increase with the recurrence of "it" in the lines that follow:

> how could you call that a clock? it was winding, trailing, the shadows filling up the forest on a June evening, I was reading that, reading it with a falling for summer which is always long ago and far away. even in childhood it never came, it was a fairy tale, something to look back on. I cannot tell myself a straightforward story.
>
> (Dahlen 1985b, p. 32)

What is clear is that clock and story have in common a seamless progression—"winding, trailing"—from which the speaker feels at least partially removed. Even common temporal designations like "summer" have mythic dimensions, apparently linked to nostalgic narratives of some prior, more perfect state that she finds at once seductive (she reads with a "falling for") and alien.

The next two paragraphs appear to tell another story of sorts, a possibly autobiographical story of transformations and suggested fears, which perhaps brings to mind the "ancestral spirits" of the passage from Duncan's *H.D. Book:* "the crooked paths, or the woods without trails, she wrote how she followed her grandfather in the pathless woods, hunting, how a log became a crocodile, snakes in the water, how things became animals, enemies, enmity forever, my heel shall crush thee" (Dahlen 1985b, p. 32). Yet the placement of the word "how" thwarts narrative structure (this is, after all, a trailing "without trails"); we are invited to consider processes (Freudian condensation, literary composition) more than a series of events.[23] Dahlen's merging of individual experience with Christian mythology through her allusion to Eve's fate in Genesis suggests how much our experiences—particularly our experiences of gender—are shaped by received cultural narratives. Like the German tree cults, and like psychoanalysis, Christianity reflects a masculine perspective. In a passage Dahlen may well have in mind, Kristeva discusses the biblical phrase Dahlen alludes to, noting not only that "woman disappears altogether into seed: generation" (as she does in the "celebration" with which "A Reading 2" opens), but also that "God formulates the code of eroticism between the two sexes as though it were a code of war" (Kristeva 1977, p. 21).

As if such revelations of phobia or antipathy involving a series of phallic "enemies" generate anxiety about the reader's response, shortly thereafter the writer announces, "you and I know the many reasons why these thoughts come crowding into the mind. they come in a crowd, in a swarm." Such a gesture constructs a sympathetic addressee, one who shares a Freudian understanding of repression and its devices, and perhaps also a recognition of woman's sexuality as polymorphous. In the middle of the next paragraph, the speaker uses traces of anecdote to anticipate and then counter the reader's possible objections to this sort of writing:

but this is not literary, I said to him, and she isn't Proust, she has no memory, her mind is full of holes. she sees, god knows how, and speaks, but still there must be some language, a language I am trying to learn from her. I call it aphasia, what do I know. a word covers a multitude of emptiness, if that is not the void, what kind is this?

(Dahlen 1985b, p. 32)

If woman (as aphasic) has lost—or been denied—the power to use or understand words, there is nonetheless some language to be recovered (the semiotic, perhaps?), a language that represents not what is remembered but what is, for the post-Oedipal speaker, lost. If "a word [any word] covers a multitude of emptiness[es]," then even the apparent fullness of Proustian recall is only a richly embroidered cover for holes, a disguise for absence. In that case, the literary advantage of the adept male writer or speaker rests on an illusion. The "lack" that afflicts us afflicts us all and has to do not with the penis but with language.

This "void" that is the site of language points to some lost presence in the presymbolic: Dahlen writes elsewhere,

> language begins with loss, with the loss of the *chora*, however that
> may be imagined by each of us. The inevitability of that loss is
> one of the boundaries of the "speaking being." It is just there, at
> that boundary, that desire is born, desire as the signified always be-
> yond reach.
>
> (1986b, p. 174)

"A Reading 2," however, is at this point less interested in lost presence than in present absence as a condition of language's relation to the real. Some of the ideas Dahlen seems to be exploring are developed more propositionally in her later, densely philosophical essay "Tautology and the Real"; there she considers how the insistence of repetition in the work of certain writers, such as Gertrude Stein, seems intended to reveal "language . . . at the boundary of the real . . . miming the real, discovering that form which is, as the Buddhists say, empty" [ellipses added]. This emptiness, the void, or silence "is the ground of being and desiring" (Dahlen 1989b, p. 215).

In the poem's depiction of desiring, what is always just beyond reach is identified with the id:

> human language is not a code, it is something else in which we
> speak the third world, a world unconquered. where id was there I
> shall be, shall come to be, going there, as if it were another coun-
> try. I would not be looking for it if I had not already found it. or:
> *I desired to desire thee.* falling in love again. her musky voice.
>
> (Dahlen 1985b, p. 32)

To say that language is not a code (a phrase that recurs also in "Tautology and the Real") is to say there is no simple correspondence between words and world, that the poem is not a "message": "One cannot that simply transcribe the real. There is always something left over" (Dahlen 1989b, p. 216). Here what is left over is the psychic realm most heavily censored in the symbolic. Even as the writer tries to approach it, she is caught in erotic cliché—"falling in love again. her musky voice. // now *smoke gets in your eyes.*" The shift into familiar formulas underscores the circularity of language and the inaccessibility of what Dahlen in "Tautology and the Real" calls the "otherness of the real" (1989b, p. 217).

Thoughts of voices (the seduction of the adult singer's "musky voice" in contrast to "our light voices") lead to a nostalgic childhood memory and a quite different evocation of the grandfather than the earlier one. A member of the audience listening to children sing *Finlandia*, "my grandfather"—and Dahlen's grandfather was a Finnish immigrant—is associated with sentimental myths of home, another version of the fairy tale of a promised land displaced either into past or future. In the very telling, the speaker seems to shift from emotional participation in this fantasy to ironic distance. She ends parodically, while suggesting national investment in such myths, "so long boys, I said, I'm on my way to California."

The internal division suggested by these shifting tones then becomes the poem's explicit subject, reinforcing earlier suggestions of woman's unresolvable multiplicity. The speaker feels herself to have "many faces, not one of them recognizably myself." The only binding of her identities seems to be biological (and with this we return to the concern of the opening passage with birth and generational bonds): "the visible history of flesh, the chains of a family." Uncertainties about personal identity lead back—via questioning of Christian dogma—to uncertainties about language:

> you, whoever it was, wherever there are two or three gathered together in my name. but she did not have a name for it. she said we could call it red if we wanted to, that would be all right, it would be a place to begin, but . . . there was no naming that, no word for it.
>
> [ellipses added] (Dahlen 1985b, p. 33)

"Red"—perhaps a label applied to woman's sexuality? certainly a curious word to place where one might think of "prayer" or "worship"—may function as a pun here; the passage questions the adequacy of reading, making it inseparable from the problematics of naming, perhaps specifically of naming female experience, and of faith as well.[24]

"Red" provides an associative link to the next paragraph, where "the red sand or the green" introduces a memory of building uninhabited towns in the sandbox. These are towns with a notably vaginal character: "the lumps of wet sand becoming a tunnel, a road, a place where the train went, where people walked, but there were no people. the miniature town, the pool, the tiny garden, a secret place." The next paragraph introduces another artwork which also might be seen as "a landscape"—or as "a wall, nothing"—that turns out to be more troublingly feminized and returns the poem to issues involving language, representation, and gender. Because its medium is paint, this artwork

> refers to nothing but color, paint, the size and shape of the canvas, the way the paint is laid on, the thickness or thinness of the paint on the surface, the way it dried, shiny or dull, the quality of the reflection of light in the particular room where it was hung. that was all.
>
> (Dahlen 1985b, p. 33)

But even a nonreferential medium, through the weight of association accumulated over time, cannot remain entirely free from connotation. And words are more inevitably tainted:

> except that it was pink. it was not empty of pink. it was full of pink. one might ask: why pink? this detail of pink. then there is language. hard to avoid the connotations of pink.
>
> (Dahlen 1985b, p. 33)

Even writing like Dahlen's that refuses conventional representation (of story, character, scene, interpersonal relationships, etc.) and emphasizes its own material qualities as linguistic object cannot release words from the implications of their past uses—particularly their roles in constructions of gender. *Tabula rosa.*

As if the speaker were making an effort to avoid precisely those stifling gender-loaded connotations, the shift to the succeeding paragraph is abrupt and the paragraph's associational movement is particularly disjointed. Disjointedness, a depoeticizing disruption of conventional structures, becomes a tool for creating something not "rosa," of what DuPlessis calls writing "otherhow." The paragraph seems to be concerned predominantly with relationships and loss. The mother's comment, "but you were such good friends" indicates surprise at the dissolution of a personal relationship. A few sentences later, the speaker suggests in implicit rebuttal that relationships are only constituted by and in language: "a relation of pronouns. that's all." Then the speaker didactically presents language as the structure constituting relationships and as the vehicle for mourning loss, particularly the loss of a unitary identity which, according to versions of psychic development like Lacan's, precedes a recognition of otherness—that is, the loss that makes relationship necessary:

> a language is about relationship, that's what grammar does. it's a structure of relations. grammar prior to vocabulary. naming, what is the need to name unless there is something out there to name, realizing in that act that I am not this, that is other. me wants it. me wants to name what is lost, to cover the losses, to show (as in a play) by a word that it is gone, out there, no longer part of me. o language, the first and last sign of loss.
>
> (Dahlen 1985b, p. 34)

This explanation, which brings to mind Freud's understanding of the *fort/da* game, is followed by a critique of another biblical assertion: "this word that was in the beginning was never no word and it wasn't the beginning. it was later." Although the tone suggests defiant correction, exactly what Dahlen asserts is elusive and not simply oppositional; the double negative of "never no word," for instance, leaves open the possibilities both that there was never a word in the beginning and that there was never not a word, suggesting that language may be removed from reality and/or may constitute it.

A similarly double sense of language as at once nothing and something leads Dahlen frequently to speak of language as a "substitute" for the real even as its emptiness defines the boundaries of the real: "Sacrificial language, standing in for, taking the place of the body which deepens in silence around it" (Dahlen 1986b, p. 172). This statement reverberates with the opening of "A Reading 2," where sacrifice centered on the female body and silence was linked to the mother Mary. At this later point in the Reading, Dahlen suggests that the whole Christian narrative of father sacrificing son—along with Freud's Oedipal narrative where son takes the place of father—enacts a verbal cover-up that excludes the female. Dahlen focuses on the grammar of the story; in addition to being constructed in grammar, so that its reality is purely linguistic, the biblical narrative of Christ's life, death, and resurrection metonymically presents the substitution that any language enacts:

> we are talking about a father who was already dead. this word was supposed to cover that. it would be a sign unto you. he was not dead forever but born again in the son. who also died. again. that is the grammar. the sign of the dead father is that his word lives. the word lives as if it were his body. that being so, words behave as bodies, beget children, are children, ghostly swarms and crowds.
>
> (Dahlen 1985b, p. 34)

The word covers the death of the father and makes possible a type of procreation (words as children, themselves begetting—that is, siring—children) independent of the female reproductive body. Within the phallocentric frames of Christian theology or of Freudian/Lacanian theory (frames reinforced as well as resisted in Dahlen's Readings), women are alienated from the symbolic order of language: "for women, perhaps, language as a second language?" (Dahlen 1984a, p. 13).

This section of the Reading ends with a one-line paragraph, "the sign of the father. the sign of the lamb." These are signs of patrilineal heritage and of self-perpetuating phallic power from which daughters—and mothers—are excluded. More than woman's biological role in begetting children, these particular signs or cultural narratives and all they have begotten have governed the writer's experience.

The second section of this two-section Reading continues exploring from a variety of directions the difficulties of establishing female subjectivity in the face of both its confusing multiplicity and the surrounding phallogocentric culture. Here, however, Dahlen emphasizes the value of language as a means of recalling what has been lost through forgetting and repression, of "writing as an aid to memory" (she adopts the title of a book by Lyn Hejinian). Language need not be merely the sign of or cover for loss, as stressed in the preceding section; apparently, it may also be the counter to loss. (Dahlen, we note, concludes her essay on "Tautology and the Real" by asserting that "There will always be a reading of 'nothing' in which it is full, rather than empty" [1989b, p. 218].) Thus this section presents words and poetry as potential vehicles for gaining knowledge, for finding out "why"—not for "preserving the mysteries," but for penetrating and shattering them.

Language may be particularly a vehicle for understanding if one has the benefit of Freudian insight. Thus, referring apparently to "eyes in the dark" (in turn referring back to an anxious moment in the first section of this Reading, where "a senseless rock suddenly had eyes"), the writer explains:

> those were the eyes of my double, loose and crazy. I might never have known this except for the accidents of history. truth may be forbidden, might not be level as a desert. the desert landscapes I drew, that place which I had never seen, always mountains in the distance. how anything might mean its opposite.
>
> (Dahlen 1985b, p. 35)

One who happens by accident of history to be part of Anglo-European culture in the twentieth century is likely to know Freud's spatial model of human consciousness and understand that the human psyche is not a level plain on which all truth is easily visible. Truth may be censored ("forbidden") and repressed. "How anything might mean its opposite" Freud explains particularly in his essay on the uncanny, where he investigates why the word *heimlich* may mean the same thing as its opposite *unheimlich* (an essay in which the phenomenon of the double is also elaborated[25]). Freud argues that we perceive as uncanny whatever reminds us of the repetition-compulsion. What is repressed comes from pre-Oedipal infantile complexes; the feeling of the uncanny results from an encounter with "something familiar and old-established in the mind that has been estranged only by the process of repression" (Freud 1950, p. 394). This phenomenon is particularly linked to female genitalia and to the maternal body; Freud asserts that his male patients find something uncanny about the female genitals because they are "the entrance to the former *heim* [home] of all human beings" (1950, pp. 398–99). We are again reminded, as in the opening "celebration" of "A Reading 2," that our phallocentric culture sees woman as womb, as incubator. At the same time, the very instability, noted by Freud, of a term like *unheimlich* may suggest the possibility of alternative perspectives—perspectives that *A Reading* attempts to open.

This section of "A Reading 2" develops more fully the speaker's ambivalence about Freudianism, already suggested in the first section. On the one hand, Freudian ideas lend to language new value: "I would not have written poetry except for that opening." Freud's ordering insights concerning the unconscious, repression, neurosis, and so forth are the basis of powerful, if dark, understanding ("I should not have thought this otherwise, I might never have known. that part of myself which might turn against me, that had seemed something other. fixed on it. fixed.") All Freud's naming charts what had previously appeared as chaos. And yet Dahlen may well refer to the woman who had screamed "*neaten the stars*" when reporting "*and still she cries.*" For Freud's positioning of woman and his view of woman's psychic makeup are terrifyingly, infuriatingly limiting; his charting leaves her unconsoled.

As it draws to a close (without necessarily reaching some final position, however), the section seems to endorse at least the tools and processes of Freudian analysis—especially if self-administered? —as helpful to, and accessible to, women. The analytic process, as a naming "which carries us back" in order to carry us forward, "completes the circle" so that we may no longer have only "the sign of the father and son, but . . . also the mother as a circle, the limit of what we are" [ellipses added] (Dahlen 1985b, p. 36).

One of the last paragraphs opens, "how bound to our chains. the work of a lifetime. one by one unknotting that, taking it apart at night in order not to be trapped, suffering that fate, for ten years waiting" (Dahlen 1985b, pp. 36–37). The word "unknotting" is closely related to other terms that Dahlen elsewhere links to "the etymology of 'analysis' ":

> "a releasing . . . to undo . . . to loosen." Kristeva's concerns have sometimes led her to prefer 'semanalysis' to 'semiotics'—owing to the etymology of 'analysis': to dissolve; dissolving the sign, taking it apart, opens up new areas of signification . . .
>
> [ellipses hers] (Dahlen 1984a, p. 7)

In the passage from the Reading, the analysand (or the Freud-defying, Freud-imitating self-analyst) who unknots the net of psychic repression merges with Penelope, who unravels her weaving to avoid entrapment in unwanted marriage. The word "bound" echoes the opening paragraph about women's labor, where woman is "bound" to the bloody little patch of ground, read as the place where she gives birth. Now Dahlen seems to suggest that analysis can unbind us, and perhaps rather literally "[open] up new areas of signification." Thus, in the concluding paragraphs, the speaker may lose herself not, or not only, in the labor of childbearing, but in other forms of work; the "work of a lifetime" referred to may well be her poetic vocation, even perhaps the "interminable" writing of *A Reading.*

There is no easy optimism here, however. Work, after all, may be "alienated labor," as "nature is God's alienated labor." Moreover, according to the closing lines of this Reading, what we "bear" more inevitably than children is "guilt":

> we are already caught up in it the moment we are born. bearing the guilt. it was not ours but we are born into history. it becomes ours. we cannot do otherwise. we cannot refuse it. Freud's prayer to Eros. there is nothing in the unconscious that corresponds to *no.*
>
> (Dahlen 1985b, p. 37)

Following Freud, Dahlen in the last sentence stresses the difficulty of regulating human beings' unconscious drives. Why she emphasizes guilt and history in this connection—and why she suggests in "Forbidden Knowledge" that "Freud confirm[s] the myth of original sin" (Dahlen 1984a, p. 3)—is clarified by this passage from Freud's "Analysis Terminable and Interminable":

> there is a force at work which is defending itself by all possible means against recovery and is clinging tenaciously to illness and suffering. We have recognized that part of this force is the sense of guilt and the need for punishment . . . ; we have localized it in the ego's relation to the super-ego. But this is only one element in it. . . . If we consider the whole picture made up of the phenomena of the masochism inherent in so many people, of the negative therapeutic reaction and of the neurotic's sense of guilt, we shall have to abandon the belief that mental processes are governed exclusively by a striving after pleasure. These phenomena are unmistakable indications of the existence of a power in mental life which, according to its aim, we call the aggressive or destructive instinct.
>
> (Freud 1963, pp. 260–61)

The situation of struggle into which a woman is born derives partly from nature and from history and culture; it is shaped, for instance, by woman's biological ability "to bear at any time in the year" and by received views of women conveyed in the Bible, or Freudian psychology, or perhaps in ancestral tree cults—powerful, and powerfully limiting, views. Yet, even with the benefit of analysis, the struggle also derives inevitably from within her own psyche, from the opposition between the drives toward destruction and pleasure signaled by guilt. She labors toward self-understanding and its articulation—without ever arriving satisfactorily at either—within a dynamic of ceaseless conflict that she "cannot refuse."

There remains "Freud's prayer," a sentence from the conclusion of *Civilization and Its Discontents* mentioned twice in this Reading and a number of times in later Readings, which appears as one of the epigraphs to "A Reading 17": "And now it may be expected that the other of the two 'heavenly forces,' eternal Eros, will put forth his strength so as to maintain himself alongside of his equally immortal adversary" (Dahlen 1989a, p. 90). This is the poet's hope as well as Freud's; but knowledge of the results of the contest between Eros and Thanatos is endlessly deferred. Quite characteristically, the close of this Reading refuses closure; it both invokes limits and points to the possibilities of an uncertain future. While the entire series opens recursively with the words, "before that and before that," its structure—like that of "Passages"—is centrifugal;[26] its parts tend to break off pointing toward new beginnings—or as Dahlen puts it, "a terminal as a point of embarcation also" (Dahlen 1985b, p. 118).

The foregoing, inevitably partial reading of "A Reading 2" demonstrates how each of Dahlen's Readings, however multilayered and polysemous, nonetheless pursues certain identifiable informing concerns. The poem's process may suggest some shaping intellectual movement (here, for instance, the shift from emphasis on language as a woman-excluding cover for loss to language as a fruitful means of "unknotting"), but it does so without imposing any definite development or closural form. Images, phrases, single words recur suggestively within a single Reading. Yet the fractured, paratactic, and associational character of the writing precludes any fixed identifications of what these things "stand for," just as this 'song of a maiden' thwarts fixed and singular identifications of woman and her relation to language. Within one Reading the meaning of recurring elements is in flux, though the range of that flux, as a function of the writer's language, is bounded by the writer's psychic history, especially her social/physical/intellectual experience of gender. Again, order and its disruption, boundaries and the boundless operate in tension.

The "interminability" Dahlen claims for her text echoes not only with Duncan's insistence on an open-ended poetic form "without bounds," but also with Freud's argument, articulated in "Analysis Terminable and Interminable," that analysis is not terminable; with Kristeva's assertion in "The Novel as Polylogue" that "the collision between *semiotic operations* (those involving instinctual drive, phonic differentials, intonation, and so on) and *symbolic operations* (those concerned with sentences, sequences, and boundaries) . . . produces an infinite fragmentation that can never be terminated" (Kristeva 1980a, p. 174); and with Cixous's statement, quoted by Dahlen in "Forbidden Knowledge," that "A feminine textual body is recognized by the fact that it is always endless, without ending: there's no closure, it doesn't stop" (Dahlen 1984a, p. 12). That there can be no final resolution is stressed by Dahlen's tendency to repeat specific verbal material in more than one Reading—that is, by the ways in which she develops her individual Readings into a long poem. Each Reading is autonomous, yet some of its elements are subsequently reconsidered as its shadows flicker across other periods in Dahlen's life and writing, her life-in-writing.

Duncan's "Passages" provide one model for this approach to serial structure (operative in DuPlessis's *Drafts* as well). In discussing the *Cantos* and Pound's autonomous "uncompromising line," Duncan suggests that Pound's focus on the line is "so extreme that Pound really doesn't remember what's going on in that poem." Pound's need for a preplan reflects precisely that failure; a preplan is "the only alternative if you can't remember what's going on in the poem." For Duncan, however, "now that you've made that line, hasn't it changed everything around it?" (Bernstein and Hatlen 1985, p. 92). Thus, when Duncan writes, he has very much in mind what goes on in the rest of his serial poem to date. In his composition, the emphasis is on elements coexisting not simply within a single section of "Passages" but in the work as an unfolding whole. As Thomas Gardner observes, a "notable characteristic of 'Passages' is its constant testing and revising of itself. Because no embrace of the ensemble is full, each new proposition is itself potentially shatterable, the ground for a movement backward as well as forward" (Gardner 1989, p. 109). Since propositions in Dahlen's work are often qualified by semantic or contextual ambiguities or by some degree of irony, it can be difficult for a reader to determine the exact path of a "rethinking." But, as with "Passages," the whole of *A Reading* as so far constituted remains present in the writer's mind as she writes, and earlier parts may be glimpsed palimpsestically in later sections.[27]

Because repetition conventionally functions in literature as a unifying device, the reader is likely to interpret the recurrence of phrases as a signal of the text's unity. However, as Lyn Hejinian says in "The Rejection of Closure," it can be that

> where certain phrases recur in the work, recontextualized and with new emphasis, repetition disrupts the initial apparent meaning scheme. The initial reading is adjusted; meaning is set in motion, emended and extended, and the rewriting that repetition becomes postpones completion of the thought indefinitely.
>
> (1984, p. 135)

Examining some recurrences of material from "A Reading 2" in later parts of the series will demonstrate how Dahlen combines these two possibilities. Through repetition, Dahlen gives the reader some sense of unity in *A Reading* at the same time that she sets meaning in motion (as she also does within any single Reading) so that her polysemous series evades functioning as a teleological sequence.

Words from the opening of the second Reading—"that freeing of the bond in nature"—recur in "A Reading 7," now followed by the word/sentence "proliferation" (Dahlen 1985b, p. 106). This later Reading, which was composed in the summer (20 May–5 August 1979), often records thoughts and activities linked to gardening. (Gardening, like the poem itself, is one activity the speaker has in mind when she asserts "this interminable work is women's work, it is never done, is there again and again. I live here, an unreconstructed housewife" [1985b, p. 102].) It is in this context that the phrase reappears. Knowing the earlier context—and approaching the repetition in terms of unification—allows us quickly to suppose that the proliferating plants are in a position analogous to the reproductive body of woman. It sensitizes us to the misogynist overtones in the sentence a few paragraphs later, referring most directly to "a vine he called a weed": "it is not beautiful it proliferates" (1985b, p. 106). That this devalued proliferation has relevance particularly to women is confirmed by announcement a bit later. Yet taking a different course from "A Reading 2," that announcing passage in "A Reading 7" quickly swerves from specifically female to more general, not gender-specific, processes:

> they are the same as we are, lady ferns, lady palms, hooded, cobra, pitcher plant, 'a novelty,' augh, our simian cousins. the writhingness of everything, the snaky shoots of the morning glory twisting on the fence. everything spinning, that movement in waves.
>
> (1985b, p. 106)

Certainly, the biological realities of being female, as well as the male perspective on these realities, are here invoked more richly for the echoes of earlier formulations. At the same time, through repetition as rewriting, these formulations are disrupted. The notion of a "freeing" accomplished within natural process, which in the opening of "A Reading 2" was linked heavily to loss, suffering, and sacrifice, here acquires a less negative meaning linked to the inevitability of change and evolution.

A considerably larger section from the opening of "A Reading 2" crosses the text again in "A Reading 8" in the longest "sentence" in the series to date. New introductory material suggests a winter setting, presumably *"winter, 1985–86"* when the poem, originally composed in September and October of 1979, was revised. The season apparently brings to the writer's mind the text of "A Reading 2," which tumbles forth, up to the passage about the sandbox, first in somewhat abbreviated and slightly altered form, then in more abbreviated and garbled form, a third time more briefly still. Thus, this section of 8 opens as follows (I present only a small portion of the page-long sentence):

> not to have to account, to make the report how she rolled her hollow oral sex. the gloss it over, winter the bare reaching I myself, hauling wood, the waves and the cold I think the celebration of that freeing of conception so that women a birth in the winter that is the burden the necessary in this way she made it deliver in the dark even so, children also and none would have our hollow the ice on the trails the blood she was bound no wonder no mouth devouring the mouth of death she who pondered and rather the stars then it is so no
>
> (Dahlen 1992, p. 45)

In the second iteration this much appears as

> this is Monday the sun the day of the not to have to account to
> mad winter the waves and the celebration of that winter birth the
> necessary even so and none would have the devouring mouth of
> even so know
>
> (1992, p. 46)

and in the third as: "this is the sun the day of the not to have to
account the devouring of even so" (1992, p. 46). The section closes
with the following two paragraphs:

> this is the day of not to have to account desire there is part some
> kind our light
>
> of not to have to account
>
> (1992, p. 47)

As I understand this pattern, it conveys a determination to work
toward the goal of not having to explain and defend ("account" for)
a female perspective, of not functioning in terms of "the male bias
of psychoanalysis, the male bias of everything" (Dahlen 1985b,
p. 103). It conveys also a weariness with this interminable effort
and, more generally, with the effort of struggling with language at
the boundary of the real. Recognizing that this material appeared
in a portion of the text composed either a year earlier or, more
probably (judging from the seasonal material), seven years earlier,
helps one register the speaker's weariness.

Additionally, this reprocessing of earlier material encourages self-
consciousness about the dynamism of the reading process: that a
reader never steps in the same words twice, and that in the ateleo-
logical serial form no instance can be privileged. Dahlen is explicit
about this a couple sections further on in the same Reading, "A
Reading 8":

> when retyping it was found out there was no standard text but er-
> rors crept in which drifted changing the meaning ultimately and
> there was no way in which comparing notes the original could be
> discerned. there was no ideal text. there was nothing to check it
> against. there were not corrections to be made. no authority to
> whom regressing, reverting.
>
> (Dahlen 1992, p. 49)

Each moment of the writing is authoritative though none claims singular or lasting authority.

My third example of recurring material from "A Reading 2" is more characteristic for its brevity and for its demonstration of the way words and phrases cluster around particular intellectual issues that nag this speaker. The closing pages of "A Reading 6" (Dahlen 1985b, pp. 93–95)—in passages preoccupied with myths about women, beauty, and innocence—return to the earlier conjunction "the sign of the father. the sign of the lamb." (now as "our father, the lamb."). Here the myth of the unicorn is under particular scrutiny, as Dahlen ponders the fantasy of "white innocence" depicted (and criticized) in the following passage from Robert Duncan's "Three Pages from a Birthday Book":

> In the passion of the Unicorn, believing, he laid himself down to the White Lady's lap. The Butcher's men came then and slaughterd the heavy beast, Whose near-sighted eyes held to the Lady's dreamy eyes, fixd without flicker, most foreign. Because of the blood, the flayd flesh, the brutality, we picture (instead of the true monoceros, occult and impure) the white innocence of a fairy horse, of the crownd animal hero.
>
> (Duncan 1960, p. 21)

Where Duncan is concerned primarily with misrepresentations of the unicorn that deny both the occult and its brutal suppression, Dahlen focuses on the beautiful Lady and her double position. She is "working for the enemy, a spy, a trap, a snare. a man's lady" (Dahlen 1985b, p. 93). But she is herself "captive," though men label her condition "beauty." She is, then, "a maiden in both camps" yet exiled from both: "foreign, her foreign eyes." The speaker asserts her own similarity to this lady, though a male speaker denies her this complexity:

> that is not you, he said. but it was. it was some part of me disowned, disavowed. to reclaim it is to see that she was not first one and then another but the same. she is involved in it, implicated, silent, it is her silence we cannot bear, she is lovely.
>
> (Dahlen 1985b, p. 94)

Going further, at the poem's conclusion she calls into question all myths of innocence. She does so with help from Freud, under whose auspices the Lady becomes also the preoedipal mother from whom children must redirect their libido:

> we both loved her, swore allegiance to her. I a child and you a man. 'I a child and you a lamb.' we have been innocent after great difficulty, after wars among powers, fought out early and secretly. then we begin our lives. as innocent children. all it masks, little lamb who made thee. and Blake, who saw so many things upside-down and so shook the truth out, partly, still had the songs of innocence precede experience.
>
> our little little. our little thing. our little secret. our slash. our wound. our drawn up and wrinkled. our dirty mouth. child's play. it is all in the mind. we lost it at an early age. so long ago we don't remember. "let me remember, let me forget": Helen to Theseus [in *Helen in Egypt*], H.D. to Freud. let me be done with it. let me go. let me know so that I can be done with it. that is not you, he said. not now. little child, who made thee? our father, the lamb. o lamb of god, I come. in which the universe is redeemed of the perverse fantasies of children.
>
> (Dahlen 1985b, pp. 94–95)

Stein's notion that there is no repetition, only insistence, applies well to this reappearance of material from an earlier Reading. That insistence may, as Dahlen suggests in "Tautology and the Real," remind us of a limit we would perhaps rather not acknowledge—the limit of the real, and the "revelation of language at the boundary of the real" (Dahlen 1989b, p. 215). For if, as Lacan says in an aphorism Dahlen quotes several times in her essays, "The real is that which returns to the same place," language at the edge of the real may aspire to a return that is in fact impossible. In "A Reading 6," Dahlen puts it this way: "seeing it through in this 'non-repeating universe,' the repetition compulsion. each word falls where it may, non-repeatable" (Dahlen 1985b, p. 93). As a gesture of desire for return, verbal insistence may provide a form of at least provisional ordering. Yet inevitably it sets in motion a rereading.

The extended passage from "A Reading 6" just quoted reminds us that Dahlen "repeats" not only her own words, but the words of others as well. More telling than the explicit allusions to H.D. and Blake is the quoted feel of the language generally—a trait which pervades *A Reading* and contributes importantly to its polysemous texture. It hardly matters whether one knows the "source" texts;

reading Dahlen one constantly feels multiple layers of allusion, even as one wonders whether the echoes one hears are really there ("after great difficulty"—Dickinson? a formal feeling comes?). If nothing else, moments of gracefully leading cadence themselves recall the sound of canonical literary tradition—as in the following lines where repeated syntactic patterns and rhyming words create the effect of triple meter (dactyls and anapests) "let me be done with it. let me go. let me know so that I can be done with it." Alternatively, one often hears the inflection of common speech patterns and occasionally (though not in this passage) the sound bytes of mass consumer culture. In these ways Dahlen's writing announces itself as coming from within received culture and bearing the weight of historically accumulated association. Her writing/reading develops from the impulses of received phrases, even as it forms an argument in resistance to them.

Ultimately, resistance or refusal (the sort of thing Freudian psychoanalysis seeks to break down) seems to me a key concept for Dahlen's project; "at odds with what already exists," again and again she says, as Kristeva puts it, " 'that's not it' and 'that's still not it' " (1980b, p. 137). Yet another echoing of "A Reading 2," this time repetition of a quotation from Freud ("there is nothing in the unconscious that corresponds to *no*"), figures in thematizing this stance. Having been defined by others for so long, woman's efforts to define herself—like Dahlen's efforts to sing her own song of a maiden in "A Reading 2" or to affiliate herself with a complicating vision of the unicorn's lady in "A Reading 6"—require denying those constructions: "she is not who you think she is."

> the power of refusal all she has left. all she has left us, and that too we will be blamed for. that *no*. since there is nothing in the unconscious that corresponds to *no*, someone, she, has done it, 'that's torn it,' she is that wound in the side of the father, the son, who would otherwise live forever. the spear itself, of time, flung, in her name the movement begun, against the city, the walls, all that armor heaped, over and over, at the end of the play.
>
> because a woman said *no*. in the beginning a woman said *no*. no father, no son. I am not that she. bound she came. still she is coiled there, in that leap.
>
> never closer than now.
>
> (Dahlen 1992, p. 17)

Neither appearance of Freud's statement depends on the other, and neither one has greater importance. The recurrence itself lets us understand *A Reading*'s process of analysis as simultaneously destructive and constructive, as pushing beyond the bounds and bindings of received culture even if also constrained within them. Dahlen both weaves and unweaves, knots and unknots. She simultaneously breaks up what has been and generates forms of, or gesturing toward, what might be:

> what is language. a pattern, an archaic heritage. trees, listening,
> the next sound. a cat whispering. an energy in the break-up where
> we thought it might be out of order and dangerous. a serious
> flight, a leap which had not been anticipated. when in governance
> we, not guilt, but unknown, you have not seen that yet, it is out of
> bounds.
>
> (Dahlen 1992, p. 120)

In her 1992 essay, "On Drafts: A Memorandum of Understanding," Rachel Blau DuPlessis identifies her first reading of Dahlen's *A Reading* in the fall of 1985 as one of the experiences prompting *Drafts*, a "series of interdependent, related canto-length poems on which [she has] been working since 1986" (DuPlessis 1996, p. 145). Quoting her own essay on Dahlen (first published in *Ironwood 27*, 1986), DuPlessis notes as particularly significant for *Drafts* Dahlen's "heuristic establishment of form by the reading of those words she has 'happened' to write" (1996, pp. 146–47). Here DuPlessis suggests that both she and Dahlen conceive of the form of their serial works as speculatively instructive: form is provisionally established and subject to change according to immediate response, in the process of or as a means of investigation. DuPlessis's statement suggests, too, that the investigation such form serves is an attempted interpretation both of a female self—what she writes, what "happens" to emerge from her mind (and, in DuPlessis's case especially, from the happenstance of external events)—and, reflexively, of language—the accidents and events of her writing.

    That DuPlessis should focus on Dahlen's means of establishing form—here, through writing as (re)-reading—is particularly revealing in terms of her own project, for *Drafts* investigates a greater variety of formal possibilities for the feminist serial long poem than does *A Reading*. Dahlen attends less to formal issues than to her procedural model, Freudian associationalism. Free association requires a "non-judgmental attitude toward thought" that is anything but easy to achieve (Dahlen 1984a, pp. 3, 4); having labored toward this achievement, Dahlen mines its resources in much the same way from the first Reading through the seventeenth. The explorations of *A Reading* tend to focus inward, not only in terms of psychic process, but also in terms of language—toward the polysemous possibilities revealed by what happens in grammar or phrasing. The almost essayistic paragraphed appearance of most of *A Reading*, which is not characteristic of Dahlen's earlier poetry, suggests that a number of issues affecting poetic form, such as lineation, spacing, or rhythmic pattern, are deliberately deflected or downplayed here.[28] This work, which according to Dahlen "turns out to be something like a journal, at times like poetry, or prose narrative . . . [,] was not preconceived in terms of these or any other forms or genres originally" (Dahlen 1984a, p. 3; ellipsis added). While the generic hybridity she notes in this passage overlaps suggestively with modernist traditions of the long poem, Dahlen's *A Reading* engages in fairly muted fashion with issues involving the formal possibilities and problems of the long poem per se.

DuPlessis's serial work, less an exploration of psychological depths and Freudian methodologies, was from the start more self-consciously positioned within and against the modernist tradition of the encyclopedic long poem. The earliest experiences she lists in "On Drafts" as leading up to that work were first, her initial readings of *Paterson* and *Spring & All* in the mid-sixties, and second, "unfinished issues in [her] intractable dissertation, *The Endless Poem* (1970), on *Paterson* and *The Pisan Cantos*" (DuPlessis 1996, p. 146). Given that *Drafts* is haunted by such "monumental works of modernism," it is hardly surprising that DuPlessis should be grappling quite deliberately with the question, "still fresh after eighty years or more: What to do about the long poem?" (1996, p. 153).

DuPlessis's serial poem, then, takes the exploration of useful poetic form as one of its central aims. The epigraphs to *Drafts 3–14* identify this quest: the first, from Clark Coolidge, points to DuPlessis's determination (shared by Dahlen) to gather the details of ongoing daily experience into her boundlessly extending form: "The minutest details of / sunlight on a shoe . . . / had to be scribbled down, / and with *extensions*."[29] The second, from Louis Zukofsky, raises questions about the formal consequences: "Feeling this, what should be the form / Which the ungainliness already suggested / Should take?"

The disjunctions of *Drafts*, like much innovative modernist writing, extend the model not of psychoanalysis but, as DuPlessis notes, of collage, "with its ethos of accumulation, clarity of the excerpt, preservation of edges, and juxtaposition. (In my vision, Schwitters, perpetually. . . .)" (1992, p. 73). That Schwitters is a visual artist and collage initially a visual art form is significant, for the appearance of the page proves key to DuPlessis's collage forms, as it is for Howe's compositions as well. Unlike Dahlen's Readings, DuPlessis's Drafts tend to be what she calls (in an essay on Anne-Marie Albiach's poem, *Mezza Voce*) "page poems or visual texts," in which the white space of the page becomes "a deliberate ground for the text's typography and placement" (DuPlessis 1989, p. 168).

For instance, the page space of "Draft #1: It" is dominated by two large handwritten letters, N and Y ("the necessary // no and yes") that appear, each with a smaller version of the letter nestled within a larger one, near the beginning and end of the piece, as if to frame it. They call attention to the poem's equivocating announcement about the importance to the interpretive process of visual markings and slight visible shifts:

> A mark, a tuft, a makr   a/ a\
> makes meaning it's
> framed marks that make
> meaning is, isn't
> it?   Black
>
> coding inside   A
> white fold open   eye
> open   a little
> slip

(DuPlessis 1987, p. 87)

Conventionally, we rely on the white margin's framing of our marks to make meaning but, through both content and formal arrangement, DuPlessis here asserts a desire to unsettle our usual procedures. This first Draft also shifts frequently toward two-column format, so one must choose whether to read across or down, constantly reassessing and readjusting relationships among phrases as one proceeds. Some passages are arranged to achieve a density and line length suggesting prose, while elsewhere words and lines are widely spaced, awash with silence or lending grand space to the smallest words, "a" or "it." Deliberately, no single frame holds, and the poem's visual dynamics both contribute to and dramatize the way meanings "slip."

Examples of visual heuristics in DuPlessis's form abound: The fourth Draft, "In," for instance, experiments with interpolated boldface, while the eighth, "The," humorously accomplishes its exploration of small-scale precisions partly through glosslike passages in reduced fonts. "Draft 5: Gap," contains black rectangles of varying dimensions suggesting censorship and other forms of obliteration. "Schwa"'s thematic concern with the half-sayable that goes unsaid is reinforced mimetically by proliferating ellipses. Typically, however, DuPlessis does not deploy visual elements as simple mimetic cues, what she describes as "the poster-like advertising hit of much Concrete Poetry which does visually what the affable dinosaur 'onomatopoeia' does for sound" (1989, p. 168). Rather, her approach to typography (like Howe's) extends Olson's field poetics, by which "open-form" poets such as Duncan have charted the movements of voices and discourses, scoring the poem's intellectual and emotional structure. Nathaniel Mackey observes:

> The shapeliness of Olson's poems tends toward the idiosyncratic, each poem bringing into being a unique instance of the myriad possibilities to which the poet strives to remain open. The pursuit of shape is consistent with the poetry's open aspirations, Projectivism's exploratory bent manifesting itself in the often desultory, nomadic sprawl into which the words extend: [here appears a passage from the *Maximus Poems*] Passages like this graphically embody the instantaneity of thought, the multiple margins and highly variable line-lengths contributing to a ruminative, improvisatory effect.

> (Mackey 1993, pp. 137–38)

In visual character, DuPlessis's *Drafts* and Duncan's "Passages"—improvisatory nomadic explorations, both—are quite similar. Though Duncan's left-hand margins tend to be somewhat more fluid while DuPlessis employs more typographic variation, both poets vary their line lengths and their spacing between lines or groups of lines; both frequently use visible caesuras breaking up their lines.[30] These similarities point to DuPlessis's and Duncan's sharing desires, inherited from Williams, " 'to write down that which happens at that time . . .' and 'To practice skill in recording the force moving' " (Williams quoted by DuPlessis in her essay on Dahlen, *PG*, p. 110). Some of Duncan's Passages, like some of the Drafts, contain nonalphabetic symbols ("The Collage" ["Passages 6"]; "Benefice" ["Passages 23"]) or interpolate typographic gestures such as italics and boldface. The visual character of letters themselves, an interest in "Draft 1: It," is particularly important in "Spelling" ["Passages 15"], Duncan's charming demonstration of language changing over time.[31]

DuPlessis's approach to the formal field can be distinguished from Duncan's in terms of her particular political commitments; as I have argued is the case with her and Dahlen's exploitation of semiotic elements or with Dahlen's embrace of "alternative paths," DuPlessis's use of a visual poetics is often deliberately feminist. Gender is only one of many subjects she addresses in *Drafts*, but gender issues, DuPlessis acknowledges, "suffuse" her formal choices (1996, p. 151). She regards the "page poem" as having "a transgressive aim, especially in relation to the normal shape of reading" (DuPlessis 1989, p. 170); ultimately, reading cannot escape linearity, but the visual text can initiate a "silent struggle between seeing and reading" (1989, p. 171). (Dahlen's work, in contrast, accepts a linearity of reading—left to right, top to bottom—though it disrupts linearity through the semantic and syntactic disjunctions within and between her sentences.) Although such transgression need not serve feminism, it certainly may do so. The possibilities for page space have a *"double inheritance,"* so that DuPlessis finds a work like Albiach's *Mezza Voce* to be *"paradigmatic of general modernist possibilities for the page, and of specifically female apprehensions of it"* (DuPlessis 1989, p. 172). DuPlessis's interrogative and speculative reading of *Mezza Voce* in " 'A White Fiction': a woman and a page" suggests that the woman writer's page poem—in repositioning the writer, destablizing the reader's consumption of the text, remapping silence and consciousness, and/or compromising narrative—permits the poet to *"[rearrange] the cultural situation of women."* That essay demonstrates DuPlessis's intense (and, I sense, increasing) interest in the possibilities visual form offers for *"this work cut out for all of us, this writing as feminist practice"* (DuPlessis 1989, p. 174).

DuPlessis reinforces the subversive possibilities of modernist/projectivist field poetics by approaching page space as a register of

the social dynamics, including the gender dynamics, of marginaliza-
tion. Claiming "marginality and marginalization" as central inter-
ests—and in this DuPlessis is very close to Susan Howe—she sees
the visual text's "freeing" of the margin as allowing margin and
center to exchange force (DuPlessis 1992, p. 75; 1989, p. 170). Visi-
ble gaps—analogous to the archival gaps in which Howe finds (the
absence of) her historical female subjects—assume for DuPlessis
particular political and gender-inflected meanings, as do verbal
overlays and scatterings or the imposing structures of regular verse.

Even a punctuation mark may have or acquire gendered over-
tones and possibilities, as DuPlessis's thematic play with em dashes
in "Draft 7: Me" suggests. On the page, "Me" is irregular but—
except for a prominent drawing of a two-toned hieroglyphic eye—
not radically unusual: the lines are consistently left-justified; their
length varies from one to a dozen syllables; they cluster in stanzalike
units anywhere from one to six lines long that are separated by con-
sistent spaces. The poem opens with the image of a sealed lid on
which writing appears. Polysemously suggested are the sealed and
heavily graffitied subway stop at New York's 91st Street, the closed
eye of a dreamer, and a closed box in which letters or other writing
is stored. The term "sky-writing," which notes inform us comes
from one of Emily Dickinson's letters, is soon introduced. Allusion
to Dickinson reinforces the sense of the sealed lid as containing the
secreted production of the woman writer. There is a disorienting
sense, too, of shifting scale, as vast sky merges with or emerges from
casket, whether a chest containing precious letters, or a coffin, per-
haps an inscribed sarcophagus:

> Thru the sealed lid
> "91st St"
> wherein
> mazed letters rem
>
> was wrote, note, she
>
> tolled sky writing:
>
> (DuPlessis 1991, p. 23)

Sky writing becomes a spatialized metaphor for the possibilities
and difficulties of women's writing, with the sky a figure simulta-
neously for the woman's undefined or evacuated sense of herself

and for the vast threatening world in which her self-inscription is so difficult:

> and it was wide and it was
> black—er—blank
> a blue A
> byss, ab
> cess, am
> bush,
>
> em space.
>
> —Sky writing—
>
> (1991, p. 23)

Typed em dashes first enter the poem as a gesture of correction suggesting self-censorship ("black—er—blank"), as if the speaker feels compelled to treat her revelatory slip about the sky's blackness as merely an error. This denial of despair follows the decorum of typically "feminine" self-effacement. The sky's "blue A"—evoking Hester Prynne's letter of a complementary color—suggests the historical oppression of woman's sexuality. The mid-word line break between "A" and "byss" introduces, too, the disorienting fracturing of women's sky writing. Wrenched syllables on the edge of nonsense suggest the restriction on expression and subjectivity imposed by conventional identification of woman with inferiority (etymologically, byss means bottom), with unspeaking nature (am / bush), with silence (speech in cessation), even with filth (as in cesspool). What remains available for the woman writer is the space of a shift or disjunction, the "em space" opened by the em dash (not coincidentally Dickinson's most common and expressively used punctuation mark).

Subsequently, however, the difficulty of locating the voice or identity that belongs in this liminality is asserted and enacted in the increasing frequency of hesitant spacings:

> Lucid cool green twi-day (say) a struggle
> between different
> voices competing   don't use that, meaning
> that model   that word   to identify
> things that   this   isn't it   isn't my   voice
> it?
>
> (1991, p. 23)

"what // speaks? // 'me'— // her memoirs?" the poem goes on to ask (1991, p. 24). Here the lexigraphical reversal of "me" and "em," and the embedding of "me" and "moi" in "memoirs," point to the female writer's multiplicitous subjectivity. Her struggle is to sing not the I, the ego-subject which she rejects, but her "polyphonous voy- / sizz."

By the final pages of the poem (after exploring the possibilities for self-inscription in the "sounding" of largely domestic "luminous things"), the speaker reconsiders the em dash, now as a figure of enlarged possibility for herself:

> Am, em a variable space
> switched tracks, or dashing marks
> which lie in wait
> in every dark and light
> that gleaming round or rounds this very spot.
>
> (1991, p. 26)

This expansive sense of oneself as a variable space, a dispersed potential that may be located here and everywhere, enables acceptance even of occasional blockages of her speech ("So what, that's it it's just like that").

It also appears to lead to writing procedures reminiscent of "the reading of those words she has 'happened' to write":

> And so I started putting writing
> into my poems
> and writing over and writing my poems
> over—
>
> (1991, p. 27)

The things of her world, luminous or otherwise, become the "fodder foods" she offers her poems; the heart of the poem is not "the thing itself" or the self, but the writing itself, and the reading and rewriting of the writing. From this perspective, the perspective of the woman writer in process and in motion (on the subway, dashing from place to place, or following the multiple tracks of her writing), the marks of the em dash expand into "streaking lines":

> Of streams my eyes my hums their streaking lines
> they

were all others, live and dead
others they brought
with them dashed into me—
some "me,"
that is, or
no me.

                                        (1991, p. 27)

Here, at the poem's close, under pressure of feminist re-vision, the em dash is not a mark of hesitation, separation, or correction, but of conjunction and community (bringing others—additional people/ marginalized people—who dash into me, or one of my multiple selves); its extending lines help construct a self-in-language that may escape the sense of blank isolation or confinement conveyed by the poem's initial imagination of sky writing and sealed sarcophagi.

As in Dahlen's serial long poem, and Duncan's, biographical information enters *Drafts*—"Me," for instance, contains suggestions of a train-riding commuter who may well be DuPlessis and a child's dream narration about "big-mouth / bears" that may be her own or her daughter's. But however much these poems may derive from immediate lived experience, biography is not focal and does not serve to reveal personality ("no me"); the speaking subject is construed as constructed within—or within and beyond—language, not represented through it. Consequently, the structure of the serial long poem on Duncan's *grand collage* model cannot be episodic, as *is* the case in poetic sequences like Hacker's, Dove's, and Osbey's, and neither narrative progression nor repeating metaphors and images that suggest continuities of personal history unify the work. How, then, does the form of the whole emerge? To what extent and how is the collage long poem, in Pound's aching phrase, to "cohere" for the postmodern poet who distrusts totalizing gestures?

For Dahlen, the very regularity of her dominant paragraphlike form may be one way of giving the separate parts of the work a recognizable feel signaling they are components of *A Reading*, without having to suggest any progression toward resolution. In addition, as she herself notes in "Forbidden Knowledge," *A Reading* demonstrates a thematic preoccupation with limits that runs counter to its interminable form. She postulates that the rejection of formal limit may bespeak an unconscious wish for immortality. In that case, the work's "concern for limits, for boundary, a working out of ideas of time, and of space, of person, parentage, and of the limits of history, both in the larger sense, but especially as one lives it through one's individual life" may be an anxious response to "what is given in the form as a lack, or absence of limitation" (Dahlen 1984a, pp. 10–11). This dialectic between the endlessness of language and the boundedness of life may itself generate a sense of structure, a pattern that partially contains the centrifugal energy of *A Reading*.

We have also seen that Dahlen loosely links the numbered parts of *A Reading* through unsystematic recurrence of preoccupation (including her scrutinizing of the texts and master narratives of psychoanalysis and Christianity) and through apparently random repetition of phrase. These links, as I noted earlier, provide readers with some of the satisfactions of textual unity at the same time that they thwart a sense of closure; each recurrence invites a new reading and helps "[postpone] completion of the thought indefinitely" (Hejinian 1984, p. 135). DuPlessis's Drafts, similarly, are linked by seemingly haphazard repetition across the series of thematic concerns and of verbal material. Where words are repeated exactly or nearly exactly in either serial work, they may well be phrases of no particular centrality or mnemonic power (for example, "cup of creamy tea," "pinholes," or "4:32" in *Drafts*; "a country road," "before that and before that," and "hinged in the middle" from *A Reading*). Their repetition gives the reader a sense of continuity, even déjà vu, often without commanding the recognition of a specific recurrence that thematically significant motifs in more conventional poems require.

But DuPlessis remains particularly conscious of how the modernists—who wanted both openness and coherence, a rendering of impulse and a crystallization of order—wrestled with the problem of the long poem's form. Without sharing their dreams of stable order, she nonetheless desires a sense of structure, though it must not interfere with the processive flexibility, the centrifugal energy of *grand collage*. Duncan, who trusted in the coherence of the universe's order, minimized pattern and insisted on the dispersal of his "Passages." He left them literally "unbound"—never collected into one volume—and seems deliberately to have left loose ends whenever neat containment might threaten. For instance, nine Passages in *Ground Work II: In the Dark* are grouped under "Regulators," which is identified as a "Set of Passages." (One of these is identified as "Passages 22"; years earlier *Bending the Bow* contained a poem "In

The Place Of A Passage 22." By the time of *Ground Work*, Duncan
was no longer numbering the Passages.) Yet one of the "Regula-
tors" poems is in fact not one of the "Passages," while three addi-
tional Passages are included in the volume but not as "Regulators."
DuPlessis, however, perhaps because she does not share Duncan's
mystical faith in cosmic order and unity, is more drawn to organiz-
ing patterns for her own "endless poem." She initially planned, for
instance, to investigate some pronouns and pronominals, beginning
in the first and second Drafts with "it" and "she." Not wanting to
follow on mechanically, however, she allowed developments emerg-
ing from the series as it unfolded to override her plans (see Du-
Plessis 1996, pp. 147–48), so that patterns in subject matter or title
turned out to provide little organizing structure.

Recently, DuPlessis has proposed an approach to the work's
larger form that provides a more regular sustainable structure yet
leaves her long poem open to endless continuance and responsive
to "the force moving." The structure she calls a "fold" has a prede-
termined mathematical element, yet prescribes almost nothing
about how the mathematically determined recurrence will be en-
acted.[32] Describing her work since the collection of *Drafts 3-14*, Du-
Plessis explains "the fold" as follows:

> even as I completed five more works (in 1991–1993, through
> "Draft 19"), I began to be bothered that my organizational strate-
> gies were (to oversimplify) only horizontal. [She refers to her prac-
> tice of linking successive Drafts through randomized thematic or
> verbal repetitions.] In November 1993, in an incredibly exciting
> moment of realization, I came to a further structural principle
> which impacts on all the Drafts, but begins functioning after the
> nineteenth (called "Working Conditions"). I decided in a flash to
> create a "fold," so that this new set of works corresponds in some
> sensuous, formal, intellectual, or allusive way to a specific former
> Draft, and to create this fold in sequential order. Thus "Draft 1"
> is implicated in "Draft 20"; hence the title "Draft 20: Incipit"
> with the pun on "It" (the title of Draft 1) but also the word for *be-*
> *ginning*, or, better, "it begins" or "she begins" in Latin. "Draft 2:
> She" provoked "Draft 21: Cardinals" and is evoked by it, with the
> maternal materials, the color red, and so on, all the way along to a
> projected relationship between "Draft 19" and "Draft 38." This
> pattern can then be repeated in a third group of nineteen works

(and a 4th, and a 5th etc), which "fold over" all of the prior groups of nineteen. This tactic creates a regular, though widely spaced, recurrence among the poems, and a chained or meshed linkage whose periodicity is both predictable and suggestive. This strategy of "the fold," layering and reconsidering materials, does something very interesting to my conception of the work. It's my way of "solving" the insoluble problem of the long poem.

(Letter to author, 11 October 1994; *Drafts 15–XXX*, *The Fold* has since been published by Potes & Poets Press, 1997)

This principle, which seems an extension of DuPlessis's long-standing interest in palimpsestic texts, calls to mind the meaning of her polysemous title that would suggest rewriting a single poem again and again.

This procedure might become burdensome to the poet or reader by the fourth or fifth round; at the moment, however, DuPlessis's innovation of the fold is proving a fruitful response to the formal problems of that "baggy monster," the modernist long poem. To see how the fold works, and in the process to demonstrate one last time that belatedness has not entrapped contemporary women poets assaying the long poem into mere repetition or imitation of earlier models, I will close by examining the fold of one pair of Drafts, "Draft 3: Of" (February–July 1987; May 1991) and "Draft 22: Philadelphia Wireman" (March–August 1994).

A statement from Dahlen's blurb on the back of *Drafts 3–14* provides a helpful point of entry to "Of," the first poem in the book:

> Modernism's impulse to defer the "end of history" (both as *telos* and *terminus*) is central to these *Drafts*. Rachel Blau DuPlessis is writing a kind of history of the end in which all knowledge is temporary or tentative, unremembered, censored or distorted, lapsed, smashed, decayed. The figure of the writer picking through the detritus is associated metonymically with the fractured parts of the world, parts of speech, the departed, the dead.

Urban debris fills the opening passages of "Of," which are bracketed by a dark line along which is vertically inscribed, as if an instruction, "CUT" (see figure 5). (There is a reflexive joke here: we are reading a "trashed" passage about "trash.") The title perhaps positions us as "of" this world of degraded fragments, an unlovely realm omitted from most conventional lyric, and often from suburban middle class consciousness. The catalogue begins:

> Hinge-loss door, lack latch
> ice-ribbed, straws, wad
> T-top conglomerate, gritty glass
> smash, street-glacier moraine. Pressed
> particle board, its jujubes of shellack,
> sweet sweet plastic lobbed hither
> shredding rips, not too much shelter anyway,
> guttering.

(1991, p. 1)

The word "of" appears only once here, because the versatile preposition functions as a linguistic "hinge," a "latch," a word that bridges. The word "of" establishes relation—derivation, cause, composition, association, connection, possession, etc.—while the scene is one in which the things littering the urban landscape at winter's bleak close have no relation beyond that of chance accumulation. It is a scene suggesting cultural failure and skewed values as much as material degradation; descriptions suggest foulness ("Flop donut. Scat Pretzel."), unhealthy sweetness ("sweet sweet plastic"), pain ("[l]ittle howling water marbles ice"), and violence ("[u]neased acceleration and diesel heavy / smoke shot straight rays / at an unseasoned toddler") (1991, p. 1).

The poet considers the way writing figures in this environment and the possibilities for language use in poetry that might thereby be suggested:

> Everything
> but weed slack's
> loose with melted
> writing.
> Like one wrote IMPISM right on that rude wall.
>
> Words come just like that, vision.
> beak black bleak
> cut back through arced site protocol,
> member the day. Each micro-face splice gutted,
> that
> brekkkl they brekk the lyric ruck.

(1991, p. 1)

Of

Hinge-loss door, lack latch
ice-ribbed, straws, wad
T-top conglomerate, gritty glass
smash, street-glacier moraine. Pressed
particle board, its jujubes of shellack,
sweet sweet plastic lobbed hither
shredding rips, not too much shelter anyway,
guttering.

Little howling water marbles ice.
Peaked cans junk cubist shingles.
Trounce state cultivated motor auto.
Flop donut. Scat pretzel.
Uneased acceleration and diesel heavy
smoke shot straight rays
at an unseasoned toddler, some unformed
particles strain to come
"eye-shaped." The rest
could care less.
Everything
but weed slack's
loose with melted
writing.
Like one wrote IMPISM right on that rude wall.

Words come just like that, vision.
beak black bleak
cut back through arced site protocol,
member the day. Each micro-face splice gutted,
that
brekkkl they brekk the lyric ruck.

"don't call me a chef honey
I'm a crook"

CUT

Figure 5. Opening page of Rachel Blau DuPlessis's "Of," the first poem in *Drafts 3–14*. ©1991 by Rachel Blau DuPlessis. All rights reserved. Reproduced with the permission of the author.

The debris-filled scene is overlayered with graffiti. Just as the "gut-tering" of a candle entails the release of its wax, the environment's being "loose with melted / writing" might signal its potential for freeing and renewing linguistic forms. But "IMPISM"—with its jarring suggestions of mischief (imp), of codified system (-ism), and of fracture (as if this were the left-over piece of some longer term)—doesn't convey a constructive or uplifting "vision." (And the gutter-ing of a candle reduces rather than enhances vision.) Instead, the words that "come" to the poet follow a grim associative logic suited to the scene: "beak black bleak." At least such uses of language offer oral pleasures.[33] And, based as they are on an honest vision of gutted, guttered fragments, they may serve to brake/break "the lyric ruck." That line may recall Pound's bragging about breaking the pentame-ter; here what is braked or broken, stopped or shattered, is the ruckus of the ordinary lyric.

In the subsequent passages still bracketed as "CUT," such "brekkkl" writing (given play, the word brings to mind bric-a-brac, bricolage, brickle [meaning brittle], as well as breakage) is further juxtaposed against the "meditative / derivative" (DuPlessis 1991, p. 2). That phrase itself critiques continued production of medita-tive descriptive lyrics in the Romantic tradition, poems in which a present setting and a clearly separate remembered or imagined set-ting ("there's here, and there's there") are organized around the "pivot" of an "I." The writer of "Of" rejects "the pretty poem" in the meditative descriptive tradition "I might (therefore) of wrote," attacking in the process the protocols of grammar as well.

She chooses the obliquities of a writing practice not centered on an "I," not recollecting in tranquility some fixed landscape, but in-stead centered on words and their actions, in this case, "difficult OF":

> of words, enormous slant, difficult OF.
> Being. Junctures of saturation
> beyond catalogue, yet catalogue HAS TO DO
> do
> syntax; how, why, being beyond me.
> In the totality of its unstable relations
> unstatable: the what.
> This ice is treacherous.

Of is a voice and of is another, and there, here
of,
black and crest, the flair
"of things" in a langdscape.

(DuPlessis 1991, p. 2)

The landscape suggested by the catalogue of "junk / things junked"
in the poem's opening is the consequence of a consumer culture.
Language, of course, is implicated in this commodification. Hence
the "langdscape," in which one is deluged not just with consumer
products but with associated verbal formulas, as "[a]vocado green,
almond cream, blue heron, sunbeam / our choice / of colors our
choice of toppings 'rain' down."

Even unpretentious "of," treacherously unstable, is party to that
commodification because it marks possession. But as "a hinge from
word to word a thingk," "of" may remain also a flexible figure of
a "grammatical conjuncture" possible when the larger explanatory
structures of syntax (which establish "how, why") seem beyond
reach:

Hard to get home; but this is, this travelling
of
is
home.

(1991, p. 3)

Our unhealthy, unhomelike environment is depicted as if it were
Hansel and Gretel's wicked witch, fattening us with "empty food-
candy" in the guise of niceness. This realm of "little MACS and
diet YUMS and PUBS" lacks the pastoral space of Wordsworth's
meditation or the grand sweep of Whitman's catalogues. The poem
closes:

Quarrels, petitions, blanknesses, outrage,
collusions, buy-offs, conjunctions—
with something blown up
it is already here
the debris'

swift
exchange.

This gridlock of possessives
occupies the place
once held by distance.

(1991, p. 5)

Under the circumstances, perhaps the best one can do is "[t]o study
and inhabit . . . of." Working from the disheartening material and
social realities "of" our present surroundings ("The streets the
malls a homey homeless home / ahung with things"), the poet by
contemplating slippery "of" finds on the one hand evidence of the
processes of cultural/social degeneration—conjunctions and pos-
sessives gone awry—and on the other a model of humble, poten-
tially fruitful connective activity.

Sculptures made by binding together—conjoining—fragments
of urban detritus inspired the folded "Draft 22: Philadelphia Wire-
man" (first published in the Fall 1995 issue of *Hambone*). "Of," we
saw, explicitly calls attention to its difference from and criticism
of meditative descriptive lyric; "Philadelphia Wireman," however,
follows a procedure more usual in *Drafts*: DuPlessis's "commitment
to a critical rupture of the standpoints and ideologies of the lyric,"
which have had so many designs on the female figure, is manifest
in "an attempt simply to ignore the lyric and the issues of beauty,
unity, finish, and female positions within these ideas, and to instead
articulate the claims and questions of Otherness" (DuPlessis 1992,
p. 74). Otherness, of course, is not necessarily female; "the question
of being a woman writing these works comes and goes" (1991,
p. 74). The Philadelphia Wireman is a figure of racial and aesthetic
otherness. He is categorized as an "outsider artist," one who pro-
duced his art outside of the institutional structures of art training
and consumption. DuPlessis provides the following information in
her notes to the poem:

> "The Philadelphia Wireman sculptures were found abandoned on
> a side street in Philadelphia on a trash night in 1982. . . . The en-
> tire collection totals approximately six hundred pieces and appears
> to be the creation of one person." It is surmised that the person is
> dead, because the objects were thrown out en masse. It is sur-

mised that he was strong (i.e. male) because the thick wires seem
to have been twisted without the help of pliers or other tools. And
it is surmised that he was African-American because of the particu-
lar Philadelphia neighborhood in which they were found and be-
cause of the tradition of Kongo power objects on which these
works seem to draw.

(DuPlessis 1995, p. 113; ellipsis hers)[34]

Like DuPlessis in "Of" (herself a Philadelphia artist), this man
constructed his distinctive art from urban residue, wrapping wires
around materials probably found on the streets—ticket stubs, ex-
pired bus passes, bottle caps, campaign buttons, nails, bits of foil or
cellophane, matchbook covers, flattened cans, an earring, a plastic
straw, and the like (see figures 6, 7, and 8). The relevance of the
Wireman's art to DuPlessis's poetic practice is particularly evident
if one recognizes this poem's reconsideration of earlier materials in
its folding over "Draft 3." In this folding, "Of," with its suggestions
of icy littered streets and a solitary figure walking in a gloomy space
at once populous and silent, exposes the problems confronted by
the contemporary artist/citizen. "Philadelphia Wireman" points
with less detachment and more passion to the possibility of power-
ful, even change-inducing art achieved through irregular, random-
ized, tortuous forms that may bind the exploded pieces and frac-
tured spirits of our world.

In general terms, most of the links between the two poems can
be subsumed within their shared fascination with urban debris and
their didactic implication that this realm of "thicngs" (a coinage
combining "thick" and "things" and evoking "think" as well) is nec-
essarily the founding material for contemporary art. The catalogue
is a central device for both poems, which share also a number of
key phrases and terms—"travelling," "juncted," "hinge," etc. Yet
the Wireman's achievement, to which DuPlessis seems to respond
so powerfully, propels more searching examination of what such
art might achieve than she attempted in "Of." Both the wireman's
method—twisting—and his predominant material—wire—pro-
vide important images for "Draft 23," prompting DuPlessis to ex-
tend her thinking about conjunctions (punning on junk, of course)
and hinges to fuller consideration of artistic and sociopolitical
power.

of wattage,
wire wadding inside TV backs crushed and matched.

Raygun downtime wire
wound round talisman. *Can you tie*
Hard store spiky columnmojo
talismum   circulations
of wrapping.
Bottle-cap, bracelet, bundled scrap, conductor wire
tape ribbon condensed ballast erased ballads *travelling the rage of signs.*

Wrapped this, wrapped this, wrapped this, wrapped this in the upbuilded.
Allegro, largo, presto, dominato, and elegy.
Cifar, naam, vak, datum, klas,
plastic, glass, package, trademark, umbrella,
batteries, pen, leather, reflector shatter,
cellophane, spring spirals, filigree naturewire,
cap nut, square nut, wing nut, lug,
bolts and clamps, telephone listings, bulb sprok,
nails, foil, coins, toys, watch,
tools, trinkets, tickets
AND quivering filament.

Can you tie up Spirit Writing *the hinge from void to word to work*
on the wadded page randomize the flow of paths. *DO bottle-cap talism-*
um ur flicker inside the upbuilded. Be *in the OF*
and MAKE deep spurts from depths of cursive scrimmage.

Electrodynamic powered surge. *Can you tie*
up round bent, wicked wrinkled
wrung out, folded up
time to do it
in.
Stroked electricity. *Chromatic*
conjunctures hingeknob crushed
HERE. and HOW.
Cans glittery sharp. Spilling onto the street. *Flicker inside the upbuilded*
bits. *Foldit* matter
dreckbundle wireloaf static mingled whirlwind
wound whorl work.
Street light greeny-silver
glittery sharp. Play "8."

Figure 6. Page 112 of Rachel Blau DuPlessis's "Draft 22: Philadelphia Wireman,"
as printed in *Hambone* 12 (Fall 1995): 110–13. ©1995 by *Hambone*/Nathaniel
Mackey. Used by permission of the author and the publisher. This poem is also
in *Drafts 15–XXX, The Fold* (Elmwood, CT: Potes & Poets Press, 1997). © Rachel
Blau DuPlessis. All rights reserved.

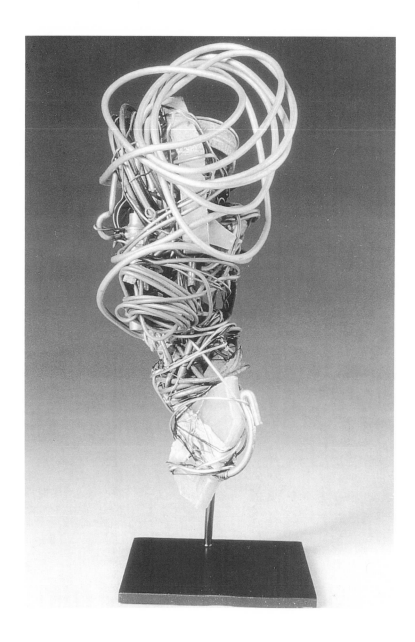

Figure 7. Sculpture by Philadelphia Wireman, c. 1970. Wire, large bottle cap, hanger handle; dimensions: 8 × 3¼ × 3½ inches. Photo courtesy of Janet Fleisher Gallery, Philadelphia, Pennsylvania. Photographer, Joe Painter.

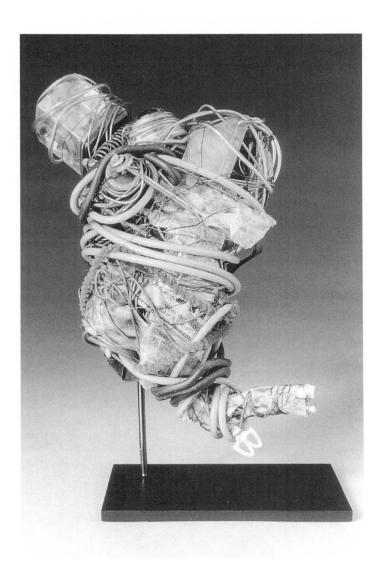

Figure 8. Sculpture by Philadelphia Wireman, c. 1970. Green wire, flash bulb, blue pipe cleaner; dimensions: 7½ × 5 × 3 inches. Photo courtesy of Janet Fleisher Gallery, Philadelphia, Pennsylvania. Photographer, Joe Painter.

"Philadelphia Wireman" follows the twists of language, particu-
larly the generative twining of alliterative words and of hybrid spell-
ings, more exuberantly than "Of." Visually, it follows a more freely
twisting course through space as well (see figure 6 for an illustration
of a sample page). The poem opens:

> Red "8" dreamscrip double
> > travelling red "8" inside the train; these twists *are twinned, are*
> tricky tracks following the trail of any conjuncture, fused in the yard where
> signals web, and spoked electricity
> > > spooks furrows, making kaolin
>
> the moon.
>
> > > > > > > (1995, p. 110)

The figure of a web in which spokes radiate from a central point
while strands wrap concentrically as well offers an alternative to the
binary oppositions of centrifugal and centripetal, open and closed
form. Such an alternative seems to be precisely the aspiration of
"the fold," and the Wireman's art confirms its feasibility. The
Wireman's small intricate sculptures (most of them about fist-size)
enact the possibility of an art that twists to follow any associative
or chance conjuncture presenting itself, yet nonetheless generates
a contained space or form. The opening "dreamscrip double" sug-
gests something analogous: the path of the numeral eight—turned
sideways, the sign of infinity—may be traveled endlessly, even as
one remains, at once still and moving, "inside" a train.

Early parts of the poem emphasize the question of "HOW" such
an art (specifically, the Wireman's) was or is "MADE." This is a
query not just about method and form but about emotional energy
as well:

> > > HOW hung the hinge from void to word
> from word to work   the rage *of signs*
> > from work to bode   *asymmetrically*
> > > > wherever *agendas* TRAVELLED.
>
> > > The detritus
> > lucking the traumscrapt: lucking
> > > transcript, trauma, script, and scrap. How scraped
> > > > down to
> > radiobones—*spurts and flecks* of awe, and joy-
> > > rigged jerrybuilt trash dense ovoids   zig-filled zeros

> *forsaken bridges:*
> So much for structure, triple,
> odelike, but *twisted together, fused*
> the same, the same, the same again.
>
> (1995, pp. 110–11)

Rage, awe, joy—somehow the Wireman has captured these intense emotions. "[T]he detritus / lucking the traumscrapt: lucking / transcript" suggests that his incorporation of debris in transcribing trauma—the culture-wide psychic damage resulting from capitalism, racism, etc. so evident in "Of"—(or in giving form to *traum*, German for dream) is precisely what enables such valuable communication.

The phrase "so much for structure" may be read in two very different ways, depending on how one hears its tone. If dismissive, the line and those immediately following embrace this outsider's defiance of conventional structural principles, represented for instance by the complexly organized lyric form of the ode. "The same, the same, the same again," may express a complaint that the "triple" structure of the classical ode's strophe, antistrophe, and epode—or turn, counterturn, and stand—doesn't offer a meaningful development. If instead the tone is one of wondering appreciation, then the phrase remarks on the exciting quantity of material and imaginative resources the inventive outsider may draw upon. The two readings are not mutually exclusive. Both lead to the admiring acknowledgment of what this artist has startlingly achieved through repetitive twisting together of his wires. The Wireman's example appears to reinforce DuPlessis's faith in what her fold might achieve: where he "Foldit the wire" she "Foaled OF. / Did OF again."

Thereafter, the poem's emphasis shifts from how made to "WHO MADE," (or in terms echoing the opening lines, "*Who / heard the mixing of the tracks*" [1995, p. 111]) so that social marginalization comes more in focus. The artist remains unknown. We have "Clusters of electricity and notation / from the dump ditch," but when it comes to answering the question "WHO DID the work?" "mum's the word." The punning term "mum" reminds us that many anonymous works—though not the Wireman's—have in all likelihood been produced by women, ordinary mothers, say. The immediate re-entry of detritus from a woman's poem, "Of," might reinforce the same point. The lines "Glisten of bright glass bits /

thru the work dirt" recall "Thick, this smashed bottle / green / on glaciated street ice" from the earlier Draft (as well as William Carlos Williams's "Between Walls" and Marianne Moore's "An Octopus"). But this woman poet, DuPlessis, is marginal not just because of her gender but also because she is an experimental writer. The play on mum, mummy, talismum, etc., throughout may underscore our culture's tendency to think of the Other *in terms of* the feminine. Yet through the example of the Wireman, DuPlessis cautions against simple identification of such femininization with the biologically female. The point is the erasure of the outsider's subject position. In the Wireman's case, his work was saved, but only by the most unlikely of accidents.[35]

With "*can you tie*," about two-thirds of the way through the poem, enter the first stutterings of the final question that will not be fully stated until the closing lines: "*can you tie up / the anger / of the dead?*" This image might suggest either a dangerous or an admirable achievement, depending on whether one understands tying up as restraining and repressing or as channeling and putting to use. This ambiguity highlights the risks of the project that DuPlessis and the Wireman share, but the notes' mention of Kongo objects indicates that the primary meaning here is a positive one.

DuPlessis's notes refer us to Robert Farris Thompson's *Flash of the Spirit*, where we learn that Kongo and Kongo-American tombs "are frequently covered *with the last objects touched or used by the deceased*," thought to be charged with the strength and spirit of the dead person:

> The Kongo believe that the deposit of such objects safely grounds the spirit, keeping it from harming the living remains. The arrest of the spirit in last-used objects (*kanga mfunya*, literally, "tying up the emanations or effluvia of a person," or in another translation, "tying up the anger of the dead") directs the spirit in the tomb to rest in peace and honors its powers on earth.
>
> (Thompson 1984, p. 134)

An artist such as the Wireman, if he or she arrests the spirit in used (if not last-used) objects, can perhaps act as a healer who brings peace to the spirits of the living (those who touched the objects but are not dead) as well as the dead. To the extent that DuPlessis's grieving for her mother, who died of cancer in May of 1990, is palpable in the Drafts from "Draft X: Letters" on, the desire to give peace and honor to a dead person has a particular personal cast. At the same time, in a culture where so many are marginalized, in this "overspill / exilic" nation where all sorts of outsiders—whether women, self-trained artists, experimental artists, members of under-classes or of ethnic and religious minorities—find themselves "*travelling the rage of signs*," peace-bringing art has far wider social implications.

The electrified energy of this poem whose words and catalogues twine, surge, and spiral down the page conveys to the reader how the Wireman's sculpture focuses for DuPlessis the challenge she must undertake in her own verbal medium. The poet demands of herself and her readers, can you "Be *in the OF* / and MAKE deep spurts from depths of cursive scrimmage"? Somehow all of this trash, irregularly wrapped and twisted, can constitute "the up-builded." Such a "dreckbundle" can be a talisman helping counter the considerable evils of contemporary American society.

That the talismanic power of the Wireman's sculpture draws on non-Western tradition adds material to the fold that was absent from "Of." DuPlessis's notes concerning "the instruction 'to randomize the flow of paths'" refer us to a page from *Flash of the Spirit* providing information about certain African traditions of design which employ the "suspension of expected patterning" as protection against evil, thought to travel in straight lines (Thompson 1984, pp. 221–22). That same page informs us that "discretionary irregularities" of design may also serve to empower the individual who dons them:

> hunters and warriors, heroic wearers of off-beat textiles . . . venture into disordered regions, mirroring them, deflecting them with their dress, and come back, as Mary Douglas has memorably phrased a parallel accomplishment, "with a power not available to those who have stayed in the control of . . . society."
>
> (first ellipsis added; Thompson 1984, p. 222)

Thompson presents such art as part of "a history of resistance to the closures of the Western technocratic way" (1984, p. 222). "Philadelphia Wireman" suggests, as "Of" did not, that looking to a broader range of "outsider" traditions may expand the resources available to contemporary American experimental poets who resist these same closures.

That DuPlessis or anyone can succeed in tying up the anger of the dead remains only a possibility. The poem ends with a question, and the task it presents sounds as daunting as those set for Psyche:

> *Can you*
> pin to place ELECTRIC
> websaw system, *tie*
> IT   from the square-law curve of light,
> mark another point OF, dots, *can you tie*
> flicker and hiss, neon spark rune *can you tie up*
> *the anger*
> *of the dead?*

(1995, p. 113)

Nonetheless, I think DuPlessis's poem—the draft, the fold, and the whole of the unfolding series—places considerable hope in its own voracious and eccentric methods. DuPlessis's *Drafts*, and Dahlen's *A Reading* as well, suggest that interminable "pattern-breaking" experiments like theirs may succeed in exploding inherited restrictions/inscriptions of gender. They do so by resisting the deliberately beautiful, by devouring dense sediment of intellectual and material detritus, by approaching all experiential and cultural materials as matter for incorporation and ever-extending feminist analysis. In the process, they may expose alternative forms of enlightenment and empowerment, and even alternative models of beauty, just as the Wireman's "whirlwind / wound whorl work" reveals the delicate flicker of the "quivering filament."

This Genre Which Is Not One: A Short Wrap-up on Long Poems by Women

In "This Sex Which Is Not One," Luce Irigaray, attempting to open a space in which to theorize female sexuality, insists on woman's rendering definition inadequate and on the plurality, diversity, and complexity of woman's sexual pleasure. Similarly, in attempting to expand critical understanding of the long poem, I propose that this is a genre which is not one, being "far more diversified, more multiple in its differences, more complex, more subtle than is commonly imagined—in an imaginary rather too narrowly focused on sameness" (Irigaray 1985, p. 28). One of my primary aims in bringing together into a single book readings of eight very different long poems by contemporary women has been to convey a sense of the amazing variety—and vitality—of women's work in extended forms. In addition, I have intended to call attention to the flowering of women's long poems in recent decades, to demonstrate the variety of traditions giving rise to contemporary long poems, and to suggest the centrality of the long poem to current developments in contemporary poetry more generally. Having immersed my reader in close readings of individual poems, it seems appropriate before closing to elaborate briefly upon these general points.

Collectively, the preceding chapters demonstrate that all kinds of experience and intellectual discourse find their way into women's long poems, as do resources from a range of generic and ethnic traditions. The poets may see themselves as engaged in retrieving historical truths, voicing what has been muted, correcting past misconceptions, or inventing utopian fictions; as reappropriating old myths or creating new ones; as interrogating or elaborating upon earlier intellectual constructs, or generating alternatives; as "de-poeticizing" (DuPlessis's term), repoeticizing, or poeticizing for the first time. Their political commitments vary widely; though often subversive of dominant ideology, women's long poems need not be so. The subject matter they treat may be highly theoretical, intimately personal, or public. If historical, it may be restricted to a carefully defined place, time, and community, as in Osbey's *Desperate Circumstance, Dangerous Woman* and Dove's *Thomas and Beulah*, or given cross-cultural and chronological sweep, as in Grahn's and Doubiago's epics. The forms may be compressed or expansive, contained or open-ended, disjunctive or fluid, narrative or ateleological, or some combination thereof. The language may be densely imagistic or abstract, tightly controlled or diffuse, the diction heterogeneous as Hacker's or restricted to a particular vernacular like Osbey's. The long poem's parts, closely or loosely bound, may stand in hypotactic or paratactic relation.

This study's six chapters have organized this wealth of material by treating representative poems organized according to three categories: epic-based poems, lyric sequences, and radically experimental works. These categories are neither exclusive, rigid, nor comprehensive; they function here only heuristically, enabling readers to perceive (among other things) how different approaches to the form may suit particular feminist projects. Epic, for example, a comprehensive genre bound up, even in its modern modifications, with myth, sweeping history, and individual heroism, lends itself to revisionary myth-making. It offers a logical venue for poets who wish to shift the female subject from margin to center and enlarge their readers' understanding of women's agency and powers. Alternatively, lyric sequences, because traditionally less comprehensive, may invite exploration of more contained material—the history of a particular individual or community, the dynamics of a single love affair. And for those poets whose feminist project is not so much to bring women from margin to center or to substitute presence and voice for women's past erasure and silence as it is to create new forms of intelligibility hospitable to the feminine, the long poem offers an extended format for more radically innovative, destabilizing experiments with language.

Considering the long poem in terms of several types, themselves subject to considerable variation, also encourages an understanding of the long poem as a flexible generic category that cannot be associated with a single generic tradition, such as epic or lyric. Its multiplicity of traditions and precedent models is precisely what renders the long poem an attractive field of possibilities for such a diversity of contemporary poets. And although women have entered this terrain late, well aware that they are not the first explorers, their writings suggest they have not been hampered by their sense of belatedness. Rather, their poems reveal energetic commitments to investigate and expand the potential of precedent modes, to challenge and modify their androcentrism, and, where deemed necessary, to invent new forms capable of rendering female difference.

The relations women establish between their poems and the male-dominated traditions of the long poem prove even more varied than the traditions themselves. We have seen, for instance, that Doubiago lovingly ventures toward a corrective complementarity with modern male epic precedent in *Hard Country*, while Grahn in "Queen of Swords" largely ignores male epic since Homer, finding both her story line and her primary models in texts authored (at least probably) by women. Through playful mimicry, Hacker succeeds in denaturalizing elements of the sonnet sequence that have expressed masculine and heterosexual desire, while Howe, in a somber work, turns to dramatic disruptions of inherited genres, syntax, and visual space in order to trace in poetry and history an absent female presence. Some women writing long poems engage with particular male predecessors (Doubiago's Olson; Hacker's or Howe's Shakespeare; Dahlen's Duncan), finding in the work of individual antecedents varying degrees of permission or constraint. They may also position themselves in relation to broader traditions, as in Dove's adoption of slave narrative patterns or DuPlessis's modifications of modernist collage epic. Alternatively (or supplementarily) they may draw upon multiple male—and, where available, female—traditions and predecessors, as Howe does in analyzing the masculine cultural imaginary in "The Liberties."

The marked increase since the late 1960s in women's interest in composing long poems follows from struggles in the "second wave" of feminist activism for expanded attention to women's experience, history, and artistic powers. Evidently, women now feel empowered to embrace a scale of artistic ambition, public material, and intellectual quest that once seemed legitimate only to masculine authority. Moreover, the long poem's inclusive range—its openness to sociological, anthropological, and historical material—proves particularly suited to exploration of women's roles in history and the formation of culture. The genre's history of iconoclasm, and particularly the disruptive strategies of the modernist collage long poem, heightens the genre's appeal for women at this time, while the form's generic hybridity makes it easily adaptable to some current understandings of female subjectivity as multiplicitous, polymorphous, fractured. The long poem seems a kind of expansive frontier whose ample space and varied formal options invite female poets to explore in uncharted directions, inscribing women's experiences, gynofocal mythologies, female sexualities, and their senses of the feminine imaginary.

Some of the reasons for women's increasing turn to long poems, however, have little to do with gender, and shed light on the contemporary literary scene more generally. Women's long poems constitute one manifestation of current efforts by both male and female poets to counter the limitations of the kind of personal lyric that had by the 1970s come to dominate poetry in the United States. This mode's brief first-person depictions of revelatory instants, inevitably limited in intellectual depth, historical sense, or political insight, in effect relegate poetry to the cultural margins. As a corrective response, a widespread shift toward longer, more inclusive poetic forms is under way—whether toward book-length long poems like the eight examined here, mid-length lyric sequences, or collections of lyrics so artfully arranged and unified that the individual lyric demands interpretation within the framework of the entire volume.

The poems I have examined exemplify a widespread desire to generate poetries consonant with the needs and challenges of our era, capable of engaging seriously with its central ethical, linguistic, and social dilemmas. Epic, recognized since Aristotle as a genre of central civic importance, provides some obvious strategies for returning to poetry the cultural centrality that has slipped away with the rise of prose fiction. Lyric sequences enable poets to build large structures more developed in their intellectual substance and emotional range than individual lyrics can be, without having to sacrifice in their component parts the intensity of focus that particularly recommends post-Romantic lyric. Avant-garde forms which more dramatically subvert received genre codes may, by pushing the limits of intelligibility and disrupting conventions of representation, demand thorough reconsideration of what poems may do; experimental long poems aspire to destabilize the master narratives and conventions of mastery that shape far more than our conventions of lyric.

The long poem is as important to the literature of our time as it was to the modernist era, but now it is a form—or rather a plurality of formal options—employed as frequently by women as by men. Women's long poems, in all of their restless diversity, deserve recognition for their rich contributions to current efforts to repossess history in literature, to discover fresh ways of conceptualizing and representing gendered subjectivity, and to expand the powers of poetry itself.

NOTES

Introduction

1. For an overview of the production of American long poems in this century, see my essay "The Twentieth Century Long Poem" in *The Columbia History of American Poetry* (Keller 1993).

2. Several dozen titles come quickly to mind, and they are just a beginning: A. R. Ammons's *Sphere*, John Ashbery's *Flow Chart*, Julia Budenz's *From the Gardens of Flora Baum*, Jill Breckenridge's *Civil Blood*, Hayden Carruth's *Sleeping Beauty*, Fred Chappell's *Midquest*, Leo Connellan's *The Clear Blue Lobster-Water Country*, Diane DiPrima's *Loba*, Robert Duncan's "Passages," Donald Finkel's *Endurance: An Antarctic Idyll*, Carolyn Forché's *Angel of History*, Suzanne Gardinier's *The New World*, Albert Goldbarth's *Different Fleshes*, Judy Grahn's *The Queen of Wands*, Carla Harryman's *Vice*, Lyn Hejinian's *My Life*, Susan Howe's *A Bibliography of The King's Book or Eikon Basilike*, Galway Kinnell's *The Book of Nightmares*, Bernadette Mayer's *Midwinter Day*, James Merrill's *The Changing Light At Sandover*, Simon Ortiz's *From Sand Creek*, Robert Pinsky's *An Explanation of America*, Minnie Bruce Pratt's *Crime Against Nature*, Joan Retallack's *Errata 5uite*, Vikram Seth's *Golden Gate*, Ron Silliman's *Tjanting*, Melvin Tolson's *Harlem Gallery*, Frederick Turner's *The New World*, Diane Wakowski's *Greed*, Ruth Whitman's *The Testing of Hanna Senesh*, Jay Wright's *The Double Invention of Komo*.

3. Several essays by Susan Stanford Friedman have called attention to women's production in the long poem and examined its dynamics: "Gender and Genre Anxiety: Elizabeth Barrett Browning and H.D. as Epic Poets," "When A 'Long' Poem is a 'Big' Poem: Self-Authorizing Strategies in Women's Twentieth-Century 'Long Poems,'" and "Craving Stories: Narrative and Lyric in Contemporary Theory and Women's Long Poems." My own essay, "The Twentieth-Century Long Poem," also discusses numerous works by women. Of the book-length studies, only Rosenthal's and Gall's (1983), Baker's (1991), and Kamboureli's (1991) treat poems by women at all and not one gives women's poems anything approaching proportional representation: Kamboureli devotes part of a chapter to work by

Daphne Marlatt and discusses more briefly poems by such women as Margaret Atwood, Betsy Warland, and Dorothy Livesay. Baker treats long poems by Gertrude Stein and Bernadette Mayer, and in his closing chapter, " 'Language' Theory and the Languages of Feminism," he considers the place of experimental writing in feminist theories of literary production. For discussion of women's texts in Rosenthal's and Gall's study, see note 11 below.

Friedman's "Craving Stories" (1994) and my "The Twentieth-Century Long Poem" are the only scholarship I know of that considers works by writers of color within the framework of the long poem. This book's single chapter on one type of African American sequence can only begin to suggest how specific ethnic traditions may inflect and enrich long poems.

4. Altieri notes that such lyrics resist the intellect "by focusing self-consciousness on the fineness of feelings anchored in resonant sensations" (1982, p. 458). By narrowing the powers of mind in this private and ahistorical poetry, "poets purchase an emotional theater incapable of staging any generalization with respect to the present or any encounter with the concerns about power, motive, social contradictions, and delusive rhetorics that appear to be the basic interests of our literate community" (1982, pp. 458–59). The ideas developed in this essay form the basis for Altieri's book *Self and Sensibility in Contemporary American Poetry* (1984).

5. Evidence of a tendency to identify the long poem with grand ambition is widespread. In the recent issue of *Parnassus* that is devoted to the long poem (17, no. 2, and 18, no. 1), the following statements by different authors appear: "the long poem remains a daunting but tempting challenge, like climbing the Himalayas" (pp. 9–10); "At a time when all the big themes—the gods, the hero, the artist-hero, truth, the imagination, the past redeemed, the utopian dream—are definitely lowercase, it would seem to require a certain hubris to write a very long poem" (p. 40); "[s]ome of the traditional grandeur of the long poem is its spectacular comprehensiveness. For it sets out upon a marathon of language that, once completed, will have run up a spacious, trustworthy point of view" (p. 270); "metaphysics not only engages the spirit of late twentieth-century people but also inspires poets to embark on such spiritual journeys in a statelier, heavier vessel than mere lyric" (p. 423). In opening her study of modernist long poems, Margaret Dickie asserts "the long poem is an attempt at the major poem" (1986, p. 1). Thomas Vogler in his study of Romantic epics by Blake, Wordsworth, Keats, and Crane identifies as one of his assumptions that "almost all great poets have had and still have a desire to write a long, serious poem, a total embodiment of their poetic vision" (1971, pp. 17–18).

6. Although the label "experimental," along with terms like "avant-garde" or "innovative," is widely used now to describe the poetic practices I have in mind, I would have preferred to substitute a term designating specific formal or structural traits for this one suggesting an attitude toward language and form. After all, today's experiment may be tomorrow's convention. But, formally and structurally, radically experimental practice in the long poem is markedly varied; descriptors like "anti-narrative," "anti-lyric," "palimpsestic," "non-voice-based" or "syntactically disrupted" either have limited applicability or reduce experimental practice to mere opposition/reaction. At the same time, characteristic traits that might provide the basis for a label—polysemous, disjunctive, heterogeneric, etc.—are not exclusive

to such experimental writing. Unable to discover or generate a more satisfactory designation, I rest with the currently accepted terminology.

7. There are other studies of long poems not treated in this survey of the criticism because the character of the long poem *per se* is not a central interest. For instance, Margaret Dickie's *On the Modernist Long Poem* (1986) is concerned primarily with narrating the composition of *The Waste Land, Paterson, The Bridge*, and *The Cantos*, seeing in the composition of these poems the history of modernism.

8. In *Conceptions of Reality in American Poetry*, L. S. Dembo seconds Pearce's insight that in "modern American neo-epics" the poet has become his own hero; as Dembo sees it, the quest is for poetic creativity itself, enacted usually in the "pursuit of a goddess, a muse, a personification of beauty, or an embodiment of natural or divine forces, with whom union means self-realization" (1966, p. 6).

9. Alan Golding's discussion of the inadequacy of the paradigms offered by Pearce, Miller, and Bernstein for reading serial poems like George Oppen's corroborates this observation (1988, pp. 222–23). Golding presents Rosenthal's and Gall's model, which I discuss below, as also inappropriate for Oppen's work.

10. For instance, David Kalstone, who is interested in poems that are "autobiographical mutants," positions long poems as outgrowths of lyric; they take the form of lyric sequences, or have lyrics embedded in them, or depend on the poet's earlier work in lyric forms (1983, pp. 126–27). Hayden Carruth identifies as one of the three principal traits of the modernist long poem that "it is lyrical in its mode" (1993, p. 210).

Joseph Riddel (1978) asserts that the theory of the lyric is the only theory of the long poem, but his understanding of lyric is a deconstructive one that emphasizes the way in which the lyric undoes its own frame, its own closure. (Riddel's essay is an introduction to an issue of *Genre* devoted to the twentieth-century long poem. The essays in that issue treat the following texts: Lautreamont's *Chants de Maldoror, The Cantos, Four Quartets, Paterson, The Bridge*, "Auroras of Autumn," and Ashbery's "Self-Portrait in a Convex Mirror" in concert with a few other poems by Ashbery.)

11. Interestingly, Rosenthal and Gall (1983) identify Dickinson's fascicles as a second nineteenth-century example of the sequence. In general, however, poems by women occupy a minor position in their book. After discussion of Fascicles 15 and 16 in chapter 3, the next discussion of a poem by a woman appears 350 pages later, in a section devoted to Plath's " 'final' poems" and Sexton's "The Divorce Papers." Then, in the last section of the concluding chapter, sequences by H.D., Laura Riding, Muriel Rukeyser, and Adrienne Rich are examined briefly.

12. This is not a necessary consequence of focusing on a single mode. Bernstein, for instance, uses the generic traits of verse epic as tools for understanding and analyzing the failures as well as the successes of the poems he examines.

13. Rosenthal and Gall admit only the possibility that "some genius will find a way of writing a long, continuous narrative poem or logically or thematically developed one that will satisfy the most knowledgeable and sensitized of contemporary readers." They claim that "a fatal ennui with such efforts does seem to have set in" (1983, p. 6).

14. Gardner provides insightful readings of John Berryman's *Dream Songs*, Galway Kinnell's *Book of Nightmares*, Theodore Roethke's "North American Se-

quence," Robert Duncan's "Passages," John Ashbery's "Self-Portrait in a Convex Mirror," and James Merrill's *The Changing Light at Sandover*.

15. My perspective on the criticism evolved independently of Kamboureli's. I first presented a critique of the lyric and epic models of the long poem at the 1987 MLA convention in a paper titled "Poems Containing History: Some Problems of Definition of the Long Poem." Vincent Sherry published an insightful article in 1985 pointing out the inadequacy of most critical models of the long poem for such British texts as David Jones's *The Anathamata*, Basil Bunting's *Briggflatts*, and Geoffrey Hill's *Mercian Hymns*. Only Altieri's approach does Sherry find useful. Sherry does not, however, question the appropriateness of existing (American) models for American poems.

16. The differences between my perspective and Kamboureli's can also be attributed to our different national emphases. It may well be that Canadian long poems—Kamboureli's subject—exhibit traits that do not correspond entirely with the American literature I know or that Canadian long poems fit more easily within a single model than American poems do. In addition, Kamboureli's Canadian focus determines her taking a postcolonial critical perspective in which discontinuity and difference from colonial traditions comes to the fore.

17. Friedman's "Craving Stories: Narrative and Lyric in Contemporary Theory and Women's Long Poems" is one example of scholarship that refuses to see narrative long poems as necessarily anachronistic or socially conservative. Friedman argues that despite the poststructuralist association of narrative with "the repressive masculine, paternal, and oedipal," women's practice in the contemporary long poem demonstrates the invalidity of "a totalizing association of narrative with the tyranny of the social order" (1994, pp. 15, 18). She sees narrative functioning in contemporary women's long poems as a claim to historical and mythic discourses.

18. In this essay, Friedman goes on to argue that two exceptional women poets who dared produce epic poems, Elizabeth Barrett Browning and H.D., did so by a hybridization of two genres regarded as more appropriate for women—the lyric and the novel—which they fused with the epic.

19. DuPlessis does not suggest that there is a single female aesthetic and explicitly rejects the idea of "one single constellation of strategies." Here I follow her practice of consequently referring to "female aesthetic" without either "a" or "the" preceding. She defines the term as follows:

> the production of formal, epistemological, and thematic strategies by members of the group Woman, strategies born in struggle with much of already existing culture, and overdetermined by two elements of sexual difference—by women's psychosocial experiences of gender asymmetry and by women's historical status in an (ambiguously) non-hegemonic group.
>
> (1990, p. 5)

Later in the essay, she acknowledges that female aesthetic turns out to be "a specialized name for any practices available to those groups—nations, genders, sexualities, races, classes—all social practices which wish to criticize, to differentiate from, to overturn the dominant forms of knowing and understanding with which they are saturated" (1990, p. 16).

20. In two essays in *The Pink Guitar*, "Family, Sexes, Psyche: An Essay on H.D. and the Muse of the Woman Writer" and "Pater-Daughter: Male Modernists and Female Readers," DuPlessis discusses the problematic example male modernist practice has posed for women poets, especially H.D., and for women readers. DuPlessis's ideas on this topic are crucial to her own poetry and will be discussed further in chapter 6.

21. Sonnet sequences such as Edna St. Vincent Millay's *Fatal Interview* or Elizabeth Barrett Browning's *Sonnets from the Portuguese* appear to have held less importance as long poem models for contemporary women, perhaps because composing them did not require dramatically transgressing accepted models of "poetess" as conventional lyricist. Similarly, long poems by some modernist women such as Edith Sitwell, Charlotte Mew, and Vita Sackville-West have not generated excitement among contemporary women poets, who seem not to find their example useful.

22. In identifying various strategies by which women have "feminized the genre" of long poem, Friedman notes that all involve "dismantl[ing] the boundaries so as to position themselves *as women* writing inside a tradition in which women have been outsiders" (Friedman 1990b, p. 12).

23. I am not denying the value also of gynocritical studies, which focus exclusively on women as a distinct literary group and explore the difference of women's writing; these may yield insights not available otherwise. My only partial embrace of gynocritical methodology in this study, where I focus on women writers but not, for the most part, in terms of female precursors and traditions, reflects my desire to insure that future genre-defined studies—unless they have an explicit gender focus—will include more than a token representation of works by women writers.

24. In addition, Victor Li's analysis of length in several modernist long poems can temper our tendency to think of length only as a matter of volume or even ambition and not as a "quality of discourse." At least in some cases, Li's argument suggests, length signals the poet's attempt—at once hopeful and despairing—to heed the expansive and inclusive nature of language, to escape the "imprisoning grip of personality" (Li 1986, p. 6), to embrace the multiple realities of the phenomenal world. Longer works, then, may point to perspectives on poetic authority, and on the subject and the subject's relation to the objective world, different from those readily conveyed in shorter works.

25. Consequently, it is not surprising that readers can disagree about whether some volumes should be considered long poems. Friedman identifies Diane Glancy's *Lone Dog's Winter Count* as "a volume of discrete poems that cohere as a long poem in reference to Lone Dog's spiral representation of Dakota history" and asserts that the five parts of Louise Erdrich's volume *Baptism of Desire* "can be read together as a long poem whose narrative of spiritual quest is reconstructed by the reader based on the ordering and sectioning of the discrete lyrics" (Friedman 1994, pp. 30, 32). I myself do not regard these collections as long poems, but I heartily endorse Friedman's suggestion that these books "can be read" (and productively so) with the relation of their parts in mind. Collections of short poems may well reveal their richest ore to those who mine across as well as within the seams of the individual poems.

Chapter One

1. Friedman argues that "epic and the lyric have continued to invoke the inscriptions of gender implicit in Homer and Sappho as the mother and father of contrasting discourses of deeds and feeling" (1986, p. 203). Epic portrays action in the public domain, and its norms coincide with western norms for the masculine, while lyric, whose norms accord with the feminine, conventionally presents private and personal material. For male poets, "writing within the epic tradition has been an extension of a culturally granted masculine authority to generate philosophical, universal, cosmic, and heroic discourse" (1986, p. 205). Because women have not had that cultural authority, "the epic has been the last bastion among poetic genres for women to approach" (1986, p. 205).

2. This is not to say that Grahn's or Doubiago's poems are free from literary allusions. Rather, the allusions remain generally inconspicuous, and one need not recognize their sources to understand the poetry. At the back of *Hard Country*, Doubiago provides several pages of notes identifying her sources, most of which have little to do with the high cultural canon the male modernists often invoked.

3. In this chapter, quotations from *Hard Country* (Doubiago 1982) will be cited as *HC*, followed by page numbers.

4. Since my concern in this chapter dictates a focus on the speaker's heterosexual quest, I do not explore her search for a maternal connection to the extent that it is developed in the poem. An essay parallel to this one might compare the narrator's relation to the mothers with Doubiago's relation to her most significant female literary predecessor, H.D. *Hard Country* recalls *Helen in Egypt* in presenting a woman who seeks transformation of her male companion via contact with his mother, whom she sees in his eyes. Friedman's discussion of H.D.'s use in *Helen of Egypt* of the concept of androgyny in both "the individual search for wholeness and the parallel transcendence of duality in the patterns of society itself" overlaps suggestively with this chapter's claims about Doubiago's version of complementarity (Friedman 1990a, pp. 396–97).

5. Marilyn Farwell's distinction between two concepts of androgyny—of balance (an interplay between separate and unique elements) and of fusion (one element incorporated into the other)—is useful here. In "Virginia Woolf and Androgyny" (1975; written when the term androgyny had considerable critical currency), Farwell points out that the fusion model, which has been the dominant western concept, has meant subsuming the female principle into the supposedly universal male one. When I refer to the phallocentric model of complementarity, it is such a union that I have in mind. The balance model, exemplified by the dualities of Yin and Yang, considers both principles valid; interdependent rather than antagonistic, each transforms itself into the other without dominating or incorporating the other. Each side contributes to a dynamic tension that defines the unity. The balance model is the primary one underlying Doubiago's quest. Where there are suggestions of fusion in her work, the feminine incorporates the masculine, rather than the reverse.

6. Doubiago concludes her discussion: "How many years I wasted having to refute this simple but dangerous lie. It prevented me from seeing, in my own life, the crucial issues of feminism" (*SE*, pp. 57–58).

7. The best known statement of this view is Adrienne Rich's "Compulsory Heterosexuality and Lesbian Existence" (1986b).

8. Like many feminist writers today who wish to validate lived female experience, Doubiago uses a first-person speaker who invites identification with the author; her fiction and poetry construct a consistent history for "Sharon Doubiago." I will refer to the speaker as Sharon and the author as Doubiago. That procedure should not obscure the extent to which Sharon in *Hard Country* is a synthetic mythic figure, an American Isis named

> variously, Ramona, Santana, Sacajawea, Sasquatch, Marilyn, Donna, Nga-My, Emanuelle, Lilith, Daughter of Albion, Rose of Sharon, The Linga Sharira, Amazon, Loretta, Cinderella, Sappho, Black Buffalo Woman, Eliza, Lady of the Lake, Mama, Evangeline, fata morgana, La Llorona, La Chingada, Sahaykwisa, Eve, Psyche, I Am, Old Woman Geographer, Angel, Charon, etc.
>
> (*HC*, p. 259)

9. A supposed slip revealing the size of his penis (*SE*, p. 331), this is a complex gesture since the narrator claims greater sexual satisfaction from a large penis, at the same time that this kind of crude joke deflates the achievement of Olson's massive epic and enlarged protagonist by reducing it to a sophomoric striving for genital size.

The unnamed husband in *Hard Country* seems closely related to the Max character of the stories in *The Book of Seeing with One's Own Eyes*. The earlier cross-country journey with her husband that the narrator frequently mentions appears to be the same journey Doubiago describes taking with Max in the story "Chappaquiddick." The husband and Olson/Maximus are associated near the epic's close in a section entitled "The Pornographer: The Mind in Which We All Participate" by brief reference to the husband "[a]s a boy in Dogtown" (*HC*, p. 250).

10. The closest male precedent among twentieth-century epic poets for Doubiago's interest in Native American experience of white colonization would be Williams in his prose study *In the American Grain*.

11. Olson's interest in myth and in Jungian archetypes is particularly pronounced in *Maximus IV, V, VI*.

12. It may be worth recalling that Pound formulated many of the important tenets of poetic modernism in a series of columns entitled "I Gather the Limbs of Osiris." Alluding to these would be another way in which Doubiago invokes the tradition she writes out of and whose imbalances she attempts to correct.

13. Catherine Stimpson also notes that Doubiago does not question gender difference itself. Rather, "Doubiago asserts a profound causal relation between sex and gender. The bodies and sexualities of men and women are different, naturally so. Therefore, the gender roles of men and women are different, naturally so. . . . *South America Mi Hija* poeticizes, as Lawrence and Olson do, a heterosexuality charged with archaism and nostalgia that is meant to redeem the sexualities of our grubby, steely, killing moment" (Stimpson 1993, pp. 264–65).

14. Charon, of course, provides a further link to epic tradition as a figure crucial to the hero's descent into the underworld. This descent is associated with a movement into the past that enables the hero's progress into the future and toward completion of his quest.

15. The line I refer to is syntactically ambiguous, so that the hardness may be the man's or the woman's:

He lies in me long, searching quietly, as with a free hand, a deep and great
place.
I stir on him slowly, rising upwards, as through a flood.
He becomes a part of what is there, a hard, gold depth.

(*HC*, p. 150)

I read this syntactic ambiguity as part of the passage's deliberate mixing of attri-
butes conventionally assigned to one gender or the other.
16. The earlier passage, which describes those who have moved to the ridge of
Albion where Sharon and her husband lived, reads:

We are learning to sing
though our tongues were cut out long ago.
. . . .
We have brought our hearts to the very end of the world,
to live on this edge as prophets of form, as artists and farmers,
knowing love is not to transcend the horrors we have known,
or the earth we have never loved
but to know and contain them
within our bodies
as when you come into me
it is the body of America you enter,
her dark unwritten stories.

(*HC*, p. 89)

Chapter Two
1. I capitalize Lesbian because Grahn does so throughout her work. Similarly,
I will sometimes follow Grahn's simplifying spellings—dike, fem—and I will use
without the distancing device of quotation marks words like dyke or faggot, which
appear frequently in Grahn's writing and for which she attempts, sometimes
through unorthodox etymology, to reclaim dignified meanings. Grahn is particu-
larly attached to the label dyke because it is "a lower-class word, not written into
literature or the dictionary" (1990, p. 135); in her writing dyke/dike sometimes
also carries connotations of public ceremonial function not necessarily present in
the term Lesbian.
2. The volume has two main sections (supplemented by an introduction, several
appendices concerning the ancient tale of Inanna's descent to the underworld,
notes, and a bibliography of additional readings): "The Queen of Swords: A Play
with Poetic Myth" (pp. 7–126) and "Two Poems" (pp. 129–48). The first of the
two poems, "Descent to the Roses of the Family," is particularly closely related
to the play in theme and imagery. It depicts, among other things, "What happens
when the women abdicate their powers, / and let the red rose go / in favor only
of the white" (p. 140). The play is preceded by a "List of Poems" which provides
titles for selected sections of each gate or scene. These poems are not titled in the
text, though small dagger symbols in the right margin signal their beginning and
end; frequently a single "poem" includes speeches by several characters. Following

Grahn's practice in the book's introduction, I use italics to distinguish the title of the volume from the title of the play, which appears in quotation marks.

3. In the list of "Players" that precedes the play proper, modern names and ancient Sumerian names, each with a brief gloss, appear opposite one another in parallel columns.

4. Listening to Malcolm X was what taught Grahn that "separatism and the centrality of a group of people to themselves were powerful social tools" (Grahn 1985, p. xvii).

5. Of course, the two works which I identify as of primary importance are not the only significant antecedents for "The Queen of Swords"; Grahn draws upon the example of other authors as well as different works by Stein (for example, "Patriarchal Poetry") and H.D. (*Trilogy*).

6. That Grahn identifies Stein as literally the butch figure in her relationship with the femme Toklas and H.D. as literally femme in relation to the butch Bryher (Grahn 1990, p. 145) may have pointed me toward this metaphor, but I intend the figure of the butch-femme couple to operate apart from the literal realm.

7. See also Judith Butler, *Gender Trouble:* "The idea that butch and femme are in some sense 'replicas' or 'copies' of heterosexual exchange underestimates the erotic significance of these identities as internally dissonant and complex in their resignification of the hegemonic categories by which they are enabled" (1990b, p. 123).

8. Grahn's theories about the cultural function of gay people correspond interestingly with Case's proposal. Grahn argues in *Another Mother Tongue* that gays mediate between worlds, transferring "power, information, and understandings from one 'world' or sphere of being to another" (1990, p. 269) and that, consequently, gay men and lesbian women play crucial roles in making cultural change possible.

9. Grahn's personal involvement in the lesbian bar scene of the 1950s may have contributed to this stance as well, since it was accepted practice for butches to defend their fems through fist-fights and comparable displays of physical toughness and strength (see Kennedy and Davis 1992).

10. For a quick summary of the autobiographical dimensions of *Helen in Egypt*, see Albert Gelpi, "H.D.: Hilda in Egypt" (1985), especially 75–78.

11. Friedman persuasively argues in "Creating a Women's Mythology: H.D.'s *Helen in Egypt*" that H.D. portrays war as central to the masculine world (associated also with such things as darkness, disorder, hate, rape, and death) that is "always shown in head-on conflict" with the women's world (valued for its association with life, love, joy, regeneration, etc.) (Friedman 1990a, p. 381). Helen ultimately discovers that both she and Achilles androgynously contain their opposites, so that the polarized worlds of love and death "relate to each other dialectically as well as confrontationally" (1990a, p. 399). But the new polarity this dialectical interaction makes possible—like the new complementarity to which Doubiago aspires in *Hard Country*—is one that places the women's world at the center; no positive value accrues to the "warrior cult."

12. Grahn elaborates her menstrual analysis of the Inanna descent story in *Blood, Bread, and Roses* (1993, pp. 211–14).

13. Similarly, Helen's wish to think of nature and beauty in terms of "Some-

thing pinker and more austere— / something traditional, stars or / sea anemones, or flowers . . . "(Grahn 1987, p. 44) may even allude to H.D.'s early poetry in *Sea Garden*.

14. Although set in Egypt, H.D.'s epic does not in fact provide a simple explanation of where Helen was during the war. When at last able to address Achilles's question about whether the Helen with whom he exchanged glances at Troy was real or a phantom, Helen asserts that they were one. She has by this time recovered memories of being in Troy with Paris. Nonetheless, H.D.'s Helen and the world she represents remain largely separate from the masculine world of war in which Achilles was so invested.

15. In her most recent work of feminist cultural theory, *Blood, Bread, and Roses*, Grahn identifies war as an "extension of old warrior games of ritual sacrifice—a parallel menstrual practice" (1993, p. 269). Having argued that in early civilizations menstruation and the female rituals surrounding it were key to social regulation and to a sense of human control over events, Grahn claims that men developed parallel rites, including warlike sacrificial games, in order to establish the same sense of comprehension and control.

16. Grahn's representation of hell as a lesbian bar draws on recollections of her first trip to a Gay bar: "I remember the fear I felt on the bus ride downtown. The bus passed through a dark tunnel and the driver had a black curtain wrapped around his seat. I felt I was on a journey to hell and had to laugh at my young self for undertaking such a perilous journey. There would be no turning back for me once I had entered such a place; I knew very distinctly that I had 'crossed over' " (Grahn 1990, p. 30). She identifies lesbian bar culture as "a strong underbase" for the movement known by 1970 as Lesbian feminism (1990, p. 276).

17. Friedman anticipates my argument here when she identifies Grahn's *Chronicle* as a "working class re-vision of H.D.'s work, which seems to presume a classical education" (Friedman 1990b, p. 18). Friedman regards Grahn as engaged in more direct revising of such modern epics as *The Waste Land* than I perceive, at least in "The Queen of Swords" (some passages of *Wands* do allude to Eliot).

18. Maria Damon is among the academic critics who have seen Stein in a similar light. In *The Dark End of the Street*, Damon claims that "the matter with which Stein carried out her 'abstract,' nonrepresentational experiment in art and her 'nonreproductive' experiment in domestic life is not esoteric in the least: What could be more complacently democratic than everyday language and human affections in domestic relationship? . . . she 'unmeans' English by turning the simplest and most conversationally domestic syllables into literary and philosophical discourse" (Damon 1993, p. 221). Damon's chapter considering Stein's writing as minority discourse often stresses, as Grahn does, the proximity of Stein's language to everyday conversation and vernacular. Like Grahn, Damon emphasizes the subversive elements in Stein: "In cutting the ground out from under the geopolitical, literary, semantic territory on which the drama of difference and exclusion/inclusion is played, Stein unmeans and unmaps—deterritorializes—the language of difference and exclusion/inclusion" (1993, p. 235). Damon's discussion of doggerel sheds light on the implications of Grahn's reliance on obvious rhyme (1993, pp. 208–14).

19. As is often the case when one artist admires another, Grahn's vision of Stein

selectively stresses what Grahn finds compatible. In emphasizing egalitarianism Grahn discounts, for instance, Stein's allegiance to genius, and in stressing an atypical work like "Dr. Faustus," she exaggerates Stein's engagement with myth, which is discussed below.

20. In discerning a degree of mysticism in Stein, through linking Stein's concern with numbers to kabbalism (Grahn 1989, p. 141), Grahn further emphasizes commonalities between Stein and H.D.

21. Grahn notes that "Stein apparently took some of Helen's multiple names [Marguerite and Helena] from Goethe's *Faust*" (1987, p. 1). Goethe is not Stein's only source for the Faust story. According to Richard Bridgman, Stein had in mind neither Marlowe's nor Goethe's versions of the legend; her "most direct experience" with the story is likely to have come through Gounod's opera (Bridgman 1970, p. 289). Neuman argues that "Stein's libretto descends from two operatic and literary Faustus traditions: one derived from Goethe and used by Gounod and Berlioz, the other derived from the German puppet plays and Marlowe and modified by Ferruccio Busoni" (1988, pp. 171–72). Neuman identifies specific links between Stein's play and both Berlioz's and Gounod's versions, W. G. Will's 1886 adaptation of Goethe, and the political allegory of Busoni's *Doktor Faust* (1988, pp. 172–75).

22. Neuman, responding partly to the autobiographical dimensions of the play, presents Marguerite Ida and Helena Annabel's position as more mixed; she is "both strengthened by her knowledge and undermined by her position as public idol" (1988, p. 186). As Neuman explains, the serpent here is not a Christian symbol but a pagan one representing the immortal wisdom of the goddess. That a term like "symbolic" is appropriate here, when it has so little place in discussion of most of Stein's work, signals the atypicality of this myth-based play.

23. Friedman rightly observes that "For H.D., the inner reality reflects the outer; the same pattern shapes the individual, the interpersonal, the societal, and the mythic" (1990a, p. 399). However, this patterning in the "outer" realms is not represented through mimetic realism.

24. The autobiographical dimensions of the play are discussed by Bridgman (1970, p. 290), Betsy Alayne Ryan (1990, p. 128), and Neuman (1988, pp. 173–74). There would seem to be some autobiographical dimensions to "The Queen of Swords" as well. The contents of the personal poem "Descent to the Roses of the Family" ("an open letter to my brother" that follows the play) overlap with the scene at Gate Six in which Helen recollects the "carefully buried splinter memories of childhood"—memories of suffering sexual and psychic abuse by various members of her family. Like both Stein and H.D., then, Grahn finds in myth a generalizing context that translates her private experience into communal pattern.

25. This is true of Stein's work generally. Grahn relays that Richard Wright credited Stein's *Melanctha* with opening up his ears so that he could hear black speech and thereafter "tap that vast reservoir of living speech that went on about me" (Grahn 1989, p. 144).

26. Damon's characterization of Stein's deterritorializing language—discussed in terms of her Yiddish—comes to mind: "Yiddish is a language of movement, which binds to each other, with infinite permission for change, the languages it travels through and connects. Even changes in spelling, affecting changes in con-

sciousness, are part of an unpredictable, unteleological progression" (Damon 1993, p. 215).

27. Though Grahn's word play derives more from Stein than from H.D., again the harmonies of their combined example are notable. *Helen in Egypt* is dramatically antilinear in structure and relies heavily on incantatory repetitions, as does "The Queen of Swords." *Trilogy* in particular is filled with punning associative word patterning. H.D. explicitly pursues "the meaning that words hide," explaining, "For example: / Osiris equates O-sir-is or O-Sire-is; // Osiris, / the star Sirius, // relates resurrection myth and resurrection reality" (1983, p. 540). Grahn in "Swords" plays differently on Sirius: "*Nin:* Are you serious? *Helen:* No, I'm only Venus. You can be Sirius" (1987, p. 123). A Crow's lines, "We're here to seriously, or is it cereally, or is it / surlily, or is it surely or is it sorely or is it / scornfully or is it scorefully" (Grahn 1987, p. 93) might recall the kind of progression H.D. creates, for instance, in "mer, mere, mère, mater, Maia, Mary" (H.D. 1983, p. 552).

28. To clarify Stein's ideas about naming (her "creating it without naming it"), Grahn quotes at length from Stein's "Poetry and Grammar" (1985, p. 68–69).

29. Some of Wood's theories about homosexual paradox (only a portion of which I outline here) apply to male homosexuality and the male body but do not fit lesbian practice or the female body. In this context, it is worth noting that I had originally planned to compare Grahn's play with a dramatic long poem by W. H. Auden, *The Age of Anxiety*, thinking to find there an example of a gay male writer mediating the dominant tradition for a lesbian poet. On the surface, the two dramatic poems have a good deal in common: In both the characters are emblematic of human powers; their interactions, at once contemporary and timelessly mythic, take place largely in a bar; the underlying quest, both psychological and spiritual, is for an integrated full selfhood; same-sex desire is directly addressed; both works' seriousness is relieved by humor and verbal play; the theatrical form suggests a shared authorial sense of the ceremonial function of poetry. The archaism of Grahn's epic patterns and incantatory verse find an analogue in Auden's use of alliterative verse. The journey Auden stages into the unconscious, leading to the Magna Mater, is even a kind of journey into the underworld. Bringing the two texts together, moreover, seemed in keeping with Grahn's belief in common functions shared by gay male and female cultures.

Yet I decided not to pursue this comparison, both because Grahn when she wrote "The Queen of Swords" was unaware either of Auden's poem or of his being gay (letter to the author, 8 July 1993) and because the differences between the two works seemed far more profound than their commonalities. Auden's outlook is that of a gay man in the pre-Stonewall era who disapproved of homosexuality. Although one of the four characters in *Age of Anxiety* is gay, the play is far from a celebration of homosexuality. Moreover, Auden writes as a Christian intensely conscious of human sin, limitation, and failure, believing in no redemption except that offered by a Divine intercession; human progress is illusory, and the individual is fundamentally alone and lonely. Grahn's celebration of Gay bonds and powers, and her insistence on the possibility of social and personal improvement possible purely within the context of human communities are fundamental to "Swords."

For valuable discussion of homosexuality in Auden's work, including how Auden himself disguised it and his critics have failed to see it, see Gregory Woods, *Articu-*

late Flesh: Male Homo-Eroticism and Modern Poetry (1987, pp. 168–94) and Clive James, "Auden's Achievement" (1973, pp. 53–58).

30. Significantly, Grahn throughout *Another Mother Tongue* presents Gay people as especially empowered because they are able to identify with both sexes and consequently able to see from more than one point of view at a time.

Chapter Three

1. Geneva Smitherman defines "testifyin" at greater length as "a ritualized form of black communication in which the speaker gives verbal witness to the efficacy, truth, and power of some experience in which all blacks have shared. In the church, testifyin is engaged in on numerous symbolic occasions; newly converted ex-'sinners' testify to the church congregation the experience of being saved, for instance. . . . A spontaneous expression to the church community, testifyin can be done whenever anybody feels the spirit" (Smitherman 1977, p. 58).

2. Other works in this category by women of color include *The Homeplace* by Marilyn Nelson Waniek (though the narrative is more dispersed since more figures and generations appear) and *Shallow Graves: Two Women and Vietnam* by Wendy Wilder Larsen and Tran Thi Nga, a sequence Larsen links to the Vietnamese tradition of the verse novel, or *truyen*. A number of mid-length lyric sequences pursue comparable aims: for example, "The Butcher's Wife" in Louise Erdrich's *Jacklight*, Mitsuye Yamada's "Camp Notes," or, in epistolary form, Sherley Anne Williams's "Letters from a New England Negro." While my label "testifying"— being steeped in African American tradition—deliberately emphasizes the non-Anglo-European elements of such poems, some white poets have employed the lyric sequence in similar fashion. For instance, in "The Journals of Susanna Moodie," Margaret Atwood conveys a strong sense of minority identity, both as a woman and as a Canadian in a continent dominated by the United States.

3. Exceptions include Friedman's "Craving Stories" (1994), "When a 'Long Poem' Is a 'Big' Poem" (1990b), and my own essay, "The Twentieth Century Long Poem" (Keller 1993).

4. In its early years, this debate, tied to issues of constructivism versus essentialism and of racial integration versus racial separatism, was carried on by such intellectuals as W. E. B. Du Bois (writing in *Crisis* magazine), E. Franklin Frazier, and Alain Locke. For an early overview, see Frazier's "Racial Self-Expression" (1927). Recently the debate has surfaced in arguments among black intellectuals about the relevance of poststructuralist thought and theory to black literature— arguments involving Joyce A. Joyce versus Henry Louis Gates, Jr., and Houston A. Baker in the Winter 1987 issue of *New Literary History*, as well as essays by bell hooks, Barbara Christian, and others.

5. She has not, however, been embraced by white feminists; Dove is not mentioned, for instance, in Alicia Ostriker's groundbreaking study of women's poetry, *Stealing the Language* (1986).

6. Dove calls attention to Tolson's uses of the "tradition of great black ballads," of signifying, of the toast, of spirituals, blues, and jazz, and of specific characteristics of black speech such as "mimicry, exaggerated language, spontaneity, and braggadocio." She places particular emphasis on "narrative sequencing," a term she takes from Smitherman's *Talkin and Testifyin*, referring to African American stories as

abstract observations about the larger questions of life rendered into concrete narratives which may appear digressive or tangential to white readers.

7. Gates's view has a long intellectual tradition behind it; Ralph Ellison, for instance, thought similarly. Lawrence Levine's historical scholarship similarly presents African American culture from slavery on as a hybrid creation, evolving from a vital West African base but also from interaction with Euro-American traditions. See for instance, Levine's discussion of the origins of slave song (1977, pp. 19–30).

8. Walcott's critical success renders him parallel with Pulitzer-prize-winning Dove, who registers in this essay a sensitivity to the "double-edged" fate of any member of a minority who "makes it":

> As a model, he or she must be perfect; no slip-ups or "you've let us down." As a special case, he or she is envied, even reviled. Move away from the home court and you're accused of being "dicty" [black slang for snobbish—Levine 1977, p. 150]; return and you're a prodigal. Write about home and you blaspheme; choose other topics and you're a traitor.
>
> (Dove 1987, p. 67)

Dove is married to a white German novelist, has spent extended periods in Europe, and has written a number of poems dealing entirely with European historical figures and cultural traditions.

9. The three works Dove mentions having had close by while she was writing *Thomas and Beulah* represent diverse formal models and cultural traditions. They are Robert Penn Warren's lyric sequence *Audubon: A Vision*, which portrays selected aspects of Audubon's biography from a highly internalized perspective emphasizing guilt, passion, imagination; Aimé Césaire's semisurrealist autobiographical statement of negritude, *Return to My Native Land;* and Charles Wright's *Bloodlines*, containing his abstractly autobiographical sequence "Tattoos" (Rubin and Ingersoll 1986, p. 363).

10. Marjorie Perloff, focusing on self-consciously postmodern work, has explored the "return of story" in recent poetry in quite different terms. Where modernist poets spurned story, she sees story reappearing in postmodern work but as "a point of reference, a way of alluding, a source . . . of parody. To tell a story is to find a way . . . of *knowing* one's world. But since, in the view of many of our poets . . . the world just doesn't—indeed shouldn't—make sense, the *gnosis* which is narration remains fragmentary" (Perloff 1985, p. 161). She predicts that as "our conceptions of the relation of self to world become more closely adjusted to the phenomenology of the present" we will see more use of narrative, "but it will be a narrative fragmented, dislocated, and often quite literally non-sensical" (1985, p. 169).

Dove's and Osbey's long poems demonstrate that less radically disrupted uses of narrative in contemporary poetry by African American writers may arise from premodernist, ethnically specific traditions that often relied on fragmentation and dislocation as strategies for coding perspectives alternative to the dominant ones.

11. Friedman argues that narrative "functions in two main ways in women's

contemporary long poems: first, as a claim to historical discourse and, second, as a claim to mythic discourse" (1994, p. 23). Here I emphasize the historical dimension, wishing to distinguish what poets like Dove and Osbey are doing from the larger-than-life portraits that emerge from the myth-based and mythically scaled epics of poets like Grahn or Doubiago.

12. Dove explains that her earlier collection *Museum* similarly aimed to "get the underside of the story, not to tell the big historical events, but in fact to talk about things which no one will remember but which are just as important in shaping our concept of ourselves and the world we live in as the biggies, so to speak. So, that's why the dedication to the book is 'for nobody who made us possible' " (Rubin and Ingersoll 1986, p. 232). Dove underscores her concurrence with mainstream lyric aesthetics when she stresses her desire "to present this underside in discrete moments, because for me as a poet the apprehended moment is of supreme importance" (Taleb-Khyar 1991, p. 356).

13. According to George B. Tindall, "In all, the Southeast lost some 323,000 native Negroes by migration during the 1910's, or some 4.9 per cent of the native Negro population in 1910, and 615,000 during the 1920's or 8.2 per cent of the native Negro population at the beginning of that decade. By 1930, 26.3 per cent of all Negroes born in the Southeast were living elsewhere, a total of some 1,840,000" (Tindall 1967, p. 148).

14. In her recent, more extended treatment of the sequence in *The Given and the Made*, Vendler does not pursue the importance of the great migration. In that problematic essay, she is eager to downplay race as a determinate of experience in the United States. While relying on a reductive vision of African American poetic traditions (according to which Gwendolyn Brooks, for instance, exemplifies only "populist linguistic practice" [Vendler 1995, p. 62]), Vendler presents the sequence as marking an important moment in Dove's development away from a preoccupation with blackness. Her discussion of *Thomas and Beulah* focuses on how "Dove solves the 'color question' by having everyone in the central story be black; daily life, then, is just daily life, even though it is in part controlled by a white context appearing occasionally at the edges of the story" (Vendler 1995, pp. 77–78).

15. These forces include the general economic subordination of blacks in the south, crop failures and floods in the early 1910s threatening the southern economy, and the north's need for labor generated by decreased European immigration and by war industries' depletion of the northern labor force.

16. "In the ten years 1918–1927 . . . American lynch mobs slaughtered 454 persons, of whom 416 were Negroes, including 11 women, 3 of them pregnant" (Tindall 1967, p. 172). Black migrants frequently identified lynching as their reason for heading north; mistreatment by police—suffered by far greater numbers—was a significant factor as well (Johnson and Campbell 1981, pp. 84–85).

17. Thomas's betrayal of the obligations of friendship is underscored by evocations of *Huck Finn*, another story of a black escapee traveling with a friend upriver. "The Event" recalls the scene in which Jim and Huck have to dive from their raft and stay deep underwater to escape a river-boat wheel. This follows immediately after Huck earns a scolding from Jim for behaving like "trash" in toying with Jim's emotions. When Huck surfaces, he sees no sign of Jim, but the two are reunited a few chapters later. In Thomas's case, however, the dive, which proves

fatal, is a solo affair prompted by a careless dare he (in a trashlike moment?) offers his "inseparable" friend.

18. John Shoptaw, stressing the severance between Thomas's and Beulah's stories, argues that Lem is the love of Thomas's life. He sees the half-shell image as ringing changes on "that Orphic half-shell, the surviving Aristophanic hemisphere of their round of love" (Shoptaw 1990, p. 376). Shoptaw sees Tennyson's *In Memoriam* as the "closest relative of Thomas's elegiac side of the story" (1990, p. 377). His interesting and useful essay seems to me to overstate significantly the gap between Thomas and Beulah in order to underscore the homosexual bond.

19. Thomas's embellishing of experience in his own version of testifying provides a useful caution against imagining that Dove's sense of telling the truth through story involves a naive understanding of "truth." As I will subsequently argue, Dove's insistence on different individual perspectives on lived history functions similarly.

20. Though some reviewers have interpreted Dove's two-sides narration as emphasizing isolation in marriage, she sees it otherwise. Dove recounts being "absolutely amazed" by the letter of a student who thought that the pair

> didn't like each other at all, that the marriage was very sad. . . . It must have something to do with our concept of love—that if we are young it is going to be romantic all the way through. In the poem "Company" Beulah said: "Listen: we were good, / though we never believed it." I remember that absolutely calm feeling that my grandparents had, a sense of belonging together. Today I see young lovers struggling to find earth-shattering ecstasy in every second. That's a part of love, but it's a small part.
>
> (Schneider 1989, p. 121)

Levine's comparison of black and white popular song from 1920 to 1950 may illuminate this interpretive disparity. He indicates "how important the elements of idealistic, dreamlike, magical love were in the hit tunes" made by and for whites (Levine 1977, p. 271). The blues, in contrast, recorded by blacks for a black audience, depicted love not as the etherial, ideal relationship of the white popular songs but as "a fragile, often ambivalent human relationship between imperfect beings" (1977, p. 276). Music in African American traditions does not indulge in romantic sentimentality; thus "[t]he blues were filled with descriptions of imperfect mates" (1977, p. 277). Those who regard Dove's sequence as a "sad" portrait of a marriage may be reading with a set of expectations shaped more by white cultural traditions than black ones.

21. Vendler understands Beulah to be employed as a domestic (1995, p. 78). Although one poem describes Beulah dusting, I see no evidence that she worked outside her own home before her postwar employment in a dress shop depicted in "The Great Palaces of Versailles."

22. I am drawing on Gates's discussion in *The Signifying Monkey* of Hurston's resolving the tension between standard English and black dialect through dialect-informed free indirect discourse. According to Gates, Hurston is responsible for introducing free indirect discourse into African American narration (1988, p. 191),

using it in *Their Eyes Were Watching God* to express Janie's divided self (1988, p. 207) and to represent the black community's speech and thoughts (1988, p. 214).

Dove reveals her appreciative awareness of Hurston's techniques in her forward to *Jonah's Gourd Vine:* "Hurston's language is superb, rich with wordplay and proverbs—not only compelling when it comes to rendering the dialect of the Southern rural black but also as an omniscient narrator who neither indulges nor condemns the actions of her characters but offers the complexity of life in a story that leaves judgment up to the reader" (Dove 1990, pp. xiv–xv).

23. Only some of the many critics identifying specific black traditions emphasize gender separation as Hernton does here. Gloria Hull in "Afro-American Women Poets: A Bio-Critical Survey" asserts that Afro-American women poets "have forged and developed their own unique tradition" (1979, p. 166). Critics who have examined specifically female African American traditions in the novel include, among others, Michael Awkward, Barbara Christian, Missy Dehn Kubitschek, Mary Helen Washington, Susan Willis.

24. These passages come from a review of six books of poetry, including Dove's *Museum* and Osbey's *Ceremony for Minneconjoux,* both of which were published in 1983. Hernton distinguishes Dove collection from the other volumes under review in its being for the most part removed from the narrative poetic tradition he describes. Identifying hers as "a 'European Sensibility,' " he declares that the bulk of the poems in *Museum* "decidedly lack anything suggesting they were written by a person of African, or African-American, artistic cultural heritage" (Hernton 1985, p. 544).

25. Downing does grant the poem "modest success." He acknowledges the poignancy of the protagonist's emotional crisis and her haunting "sense of erasure extending back through generations" (1993a, p. 225); recognizes that the "New Orleans ethnic expressions" in Osbey's poem form a "communal body of speech" that "allow and articulate the survival of the urban tribe"; and attributes to Osbey the ability to "be evocative when she wants to." The flaws he identifies in the work include a "thinness of texture," excessive reticence and over-reliance on atmospheric effects, too little "mercury" in the language, and a failure to individuate voices or "[quicken] the pulse" to build toward dramatic crisis (Downing 1993a, p. 228).

26. Never mentioning the maroons, Downing (mis)understands Marie instead to be belatedly recognizing the "nefarious" nature of her mother's extramarital liaison (1993a, p. 226).

27. Some scholars emphasize the Haitian origins of New Orleans voodoo, but from what I can discern, more recent scholarship stresses its earlier evolution by the slaves imported directly from Africa. For discussion of specific African religious practices incorporated into voodoo, see Jessie Gaston Mulira, "The Case of Voodoo in New Orleans" (1990) and Bryan Ott, "Voodoo in New Orleans 1990" (1991, pp. 30–38).

28. The use of voodoo charms is recorded in New Orleans courts as early as 1773, well before the massive immigration of Haitians in 1809.

29. Maroon communities within the continental United States have garnered strikingly little attention from either creative artists or historians. In contrast, a

good deal of imaginative and scholarly literature treats the maroons in the Caribbean islands and in Central and South America.

30. In 1746, there were nearly twice as many black people in New Orleans as white; people of color were in the majority from the 1780s to the 1830s (Logsdon and Bell 1992, p. 206). According to John Blassingame, the first free Negroes appeared in New Orleans in the 1720s (1973, p. 9).

31. "Free people of color represented nearly 29 percent of [the city's] population in 1810, 23 percent in 1820, 25 percent in 1830, and 18 percent as late as 1840" (Hirsch and Logsdon 1992, p. 192).

32. See, for instance, the opening section of Missy Dehn Kubitschek's *Claiming the Heritage: African-American Women Novelists and History*, entitled " 'My Mother Talking: Ancestral Voices and the Quest for Identity" (1991).

33. From the earliest days of New Orleans, blacks and Indians mixed a good deal. Indian and African slaves often escaped together (and often in Indian-African couples), seeking refuge among Indian tribes. Africans fought on the side of the Indians in the uprising of the Natchez against the French. Interbreeding was common. Indian survival skills and knowledge of the local environment were important for maroon survival (see Price 1973, pp. 11–12, 15–16). Gwendolyn Hall discusses the relation of Indians to blacks in early New Orleans (1992, pp. 64–65, 71–78) as does Berndt Ostendorf (1993, pp. 391–92). Jerah Johnson's essay in the Hirsh and Logsdon collection (1992) discusses in detail colonial policies toward the Indians. Eugene Genovese (1979, pp. 69–76) explores the relations of black slaves and maroons to the Indians in the South, claiming that "[e]ffective white manipulation of Indians and blacks against each other reduced possibilities for the organization of stable maroon colonies" (p. 71). He adds, however,

> The magnificent unity of the blacks and Seminoles [in Florida] had precedents, the most notable of which was the black support for the great rising of the Natchez in Louisiana in 1729. In the aftermath of that event, the whites moved to placate the blacks and drive a wedge between them and their Indian allies. They scored some success, but, as the conspiracy at Pointe Coupee demonstrated anew in 1795, the threat of black-Indian cooperation remained acute so long as the French and Spanish held Louisiana.
>
> (1979, p. 73)

34. Osbey depicts Marie's subsequent renewal as the rain comes in terms recalling *The Waste Land*. Gardner McFall notes other echoes of *The Waste Land* in her review, "What Hunger Is" (1992). These can be seen as a signifying critique. Their presence reinforces the argument, represented in this essay by Gates, that the intertextual network for even the black tradition of narrative poetry Osbey identifies is interracial.

Chapter Four

1. This revival is evident in the publication of individual volumes of formalist verse; of formalist anthologies like Philip Dacey's and David Jauss's *Strong Measures* (1985), Robert Richman's *The Direction of Poetry* (1988), and Annie Finch's *A Formal Feeling Comes* (1994); and of proformalist critical studies such as Timothy

Steele's *Missing Measures: Modern Poetry and the Revolt Against Meter* (1990) and Wyatt Prunty's *"Fallen From the Symboled World": Precedents for the New Formalism* (1990).

2. Though not of central concern in this chapter, the rise of Language writing has added further dimensions to current debates about the politics of poetic form. From the perspective of Language writers, the dominant "workshop" mode of contemporary free verse and new formalist verse do not represent alternative poetics (or politics) so much as they enact a shared conservative aesthetic dependent on the order of syntax, the coherence of the subject, and the representational character of language.

3. Ariel Dawson, for instance, claims that "the reemergence of formalism is perfectly harmonious with the yuppie knack for resurrecting elitist traditions" (1985, p. 5). In "The Closing of the American Line: Expansive Poetry and Ideology," Thomas B. Byers argues at length that although "history gives the lie to any intrinsic link between meter and ideology," "in aesthetics and cultural criticism, both implicitly and, surprisingly often, explicitly, the preponderance of [the current New Formalist movement's] utterances range from moderately conservative to virulently reactionary" (1992, pp. 401, 398).

4. Statements in an interview conducted by David Montenegro in May of 1987 suggest Rich may be moderating her position so as to place more emphasis on the resources of formal tradition. As part of her response to a question about whether traditional metric implies a frame of mind or limits content, Rich asserts that she never wanted to "get rid of" the iambic pentameter line and adds,

> I guess what I'm searching for always is a way of staying linked to the past, pulling out of it whatever you can use, and continuing to move on. And I'm not sure that a new textual form creates—it certainly *doesn't* create—a new consciousness. It can equally well be said that a new consciousness, a radically divergent one, doesn't necessarily create a new form either. I hate that form/content bifurcation, but sometimes it has to be used, for an attitude, a stance, a positioning of the poet.
>
> (Montenegro 1991, pp. 18–19)

She goes on to describe the effectiveness of Derek Walcott's use of iambic pentameter in an explosive "fusion of old form and old consciousness with new form and new consciousness" (Montenegro 1991, p. 19).

5. In " 'Openness,' 'Closure,' and Recent American Poetry," Alan Golding calls attention to the New Formalists' invocation of organicist rhetoric more typically employed by free verse practitioners, the formalists' putative opponents. The quoted material derives from Golding's paraphrase of Timothy Steele's organicist justification of metered verse.

6. This point is humorously demonstrated by Language poet Charles Bernstein's *The Nude Formalism* (1989).

7. For examples of homosexual critics pointing to the tendency of the (straight) critical tradition to deny the homosexuality in the sonnets, see W. H. Auden (1973, p. 99) and Joseph Peguiney (1985, p. 1), whose entire book refutes such denial.

8. Montefiore acknowledges that the Lacanian model on which her analysis of

sonnets as mirror poems rests is "vulnerable to the criticism that it is universalist and ahistorical and that its ready acceptance of such potentially antifeminist notions as the castration complex colludes with the patriarchal bias of their originators" (1987, p. 104); nonetheless, she finds the model too useful to relinquish in her analysis of women poets' flawed attempts to intervene in the masculine sonnet tradition.

9. In the context of this chapter's larger argument, it is worth noting that in the latter poem, Hack also considers issues of poetic form. While playing upon marriage rituals, she makes fun of organicist, mimetic understandings of poetic form: "will measured feet / advance processionally, where before / they scuff-heeled flights of stairs, kicked at a door, / or danced in wing-tips to a dirty beat?" (*LD*, p. 65). Her proclaimed uncertainty about poetic meter and pace points to the sonnet tradition's lack of precedent for treating satisfied, settled love, while nonetheless emphasizing the form's flexibility.

10. In these terms, we can distinguish this project from the more radical one exemplified in, for example, Monique Wittig's *The Lesbian Body*. As Elaine Marks has noted in "Lesbian Intertextuality" (1979), Wittig is creating a new mythology in which the female body as well as woman's relation to language are thoroughly undomesticated; Wittig wants only the wild, unfettered by the safe and familiar.

11. Sue-Ellen Case makes a similar argument in "Toward a Butch-Femme Aesthetic" (1989), claiming that the butch-femme couple plays on the phallic economy rather than to it. Case sees the discourse of camp, associated with the butch-femme masquerade, as a potential key to the liberation of the "feminist subject" who has the agency to change ideology.

12. See also Judith Butler's book, *Gender Trouble: Feminism and the Subversion of Identity*, especially the section titled "Bodily Inscriptions, Performative Subversions" (1990b, pp. 128–41).

13. Perhaps she refers also to Marilyn Hacker's having been a married heterosexual earlier in her life.

14. Her outrageous procedures find precedent in the work of Byron, and of others influenced by him, such as Auden and Merrill. That fixed form can determine word choice and shape content is precisely what free-verse advocates like Rich deplore, while they claim that free verse can render poetic form a more genuine extension of content. Hacker, presumably, would see "organic" or "open" forms as no closer to truth or naturalness, only to its pretense.

15. One could invoke here the notion of postmodernism's "complicitous critique" developed by Linda Hutcheon in *The Politics of Postmodernism* (1989). However, Hacker's work seems to me less concerned with commenting on and critiquing dominant conventions than in opening them up, and Hutcheon's terminology might obscure the playfulness of Hacker's stance.

16. Nor does either pretend to be moved by love toward virtue or the spiritual life. That idea is mocked in the semantic ambiguity generated by the mid-word line break in lines describing their first night together: "we did everything / two punchdrunk girls on second wind, whose strength / was tenfold, because, hey, our hearts were pure- / ly bent on it, could" (*LD*, p. 61). These lines also demonstrate the liberties Hacker takes with syntax.

17. I am drawing on Margaret Homans's insights in " 'Syllables of Velvet':

Dickinson, Rossetti, and the Rhetorics of Sexuality," although Homans, like Montefiore, sees the sonnet tradition as masculine in ways Hacker does not. Homans argues that the "I" of the romantic lyric that developed from the Petrarchan love poem is "constitutively masculine . . . because in Western poetic and philosophical traditions, self-expressive subjectivity is represented as a male prerogative" and that lyrics in the Petrarchan tradition "[depend] on an implicit plot . . . of masculine, heterosexual desire" which negates women's pleasure (1985, p. 570). This plot, conveyed in a rhetoric reliant on specular metaphor, depends on a distance between speaking subject and silent object. Homans sees Emily Dickinson as having in some poems escaped this plot, having imagined "a place from which female sexuality can speak for itself, a rhetoric of female pleasure to replace the silencing rhetoric of male desire" (1985, p. 576). Depending not on distance but on contiguity, and privileging touch rather than sight, this rhetoric relies on metonymy rather than metaphor, since metaphor "assumes a subject-object relation and an order of priority" (1985, p. 585).

Chapter Five

1. Pound remarked in a late interview,

> An epic is a poem containing history. The modern mind contains heteroclite [deviating from ordinary forms or rules] elements. The past epos has succeeded when all or a great many of the answers were assumed, at least between author and audience, or a great mass of audience. The attempt in an experimental age is therefore rash. Do you know the story: "What are you drawing, Johnny?"
> "God."
> "But nobody knows what He looks like."
> "They will when I get through!"
> That confidence is no longer obtainable.
>
> (Plimpton 1963, p. 57)

2. Howe's work is frequently included in anthologies of Language writing, such as Ron Silliman's *In the American Tree* (1986) and Douglas Messerli's *"Language" Poetries: An Anthology* (1986), and it is both published and discussed in journals associated with that movement; her poetry is considered in critical studies devoted to Language writing, such as Linda Reinfeld's *Language Poetry: Writing as Rescue* (1992); the poetics program in which she teaches at SUNY Buffalo is led by Language poet (also a key theorist for the movement) Charles Bernstein. In an interview with the author, however, she suggests a complex relation to Language writing; despite some important commonalities, she feels herself removed from the Language writers by difference in generation (she is older), in major influences (hers are modernist), and in the philosophical and political impulses behind her work (Keller 1995, pp. 19–20).

3. In her most recent book, *Hatshepsut, Speak To Me* (1992), Ruth Whitman modifies the single speaker frame of her earlier persona poems to engage in dialogue with the only woman pharaoh of ancient Egypt, a figure whose crossing of gender boundaries mirrors Whitman's sense of her own experience. As in her other historical poems, Whitman conveys a sense of the surrounding earlier culture, but

only her focal character has any depth. The explicitly comparative frame of this dialogic poem makes particularly clear how much of that depth derives from projection of Whitman's own personality and experience.

4. When asked why Pound does not appear on this list, which actually contains six rather than the announced seven poets, Howe replied that she should have put him there, adding "the first few Cantos and the *Pisan Cantos* are *very very* important to me" (letter to author, 23 August 1992).

5. An association between fragmentation and the feminine is widespread, both in the female/feminist avant-garde and elsewhere. We shall encounter it again in chapter 6 in the work of DuPlessis and Dahlen. Luce Irigaray, who may well have influenced Howe's thinking on this matter, posits that "the rejection, the exclusion of a female imaginary certainly puts woman in the position of experiencing herself only fragmentarily, in the little-structured margins of a dominant ideology, as waste, or excess" (1985, p. 30).

6. Irigaray's "Questions" in *This Sex Which Is Not One* contains the phrase "aporia of discourse" (1985, p. 149) in connection with the female sex and provides a helpful overview of why Irigaray considers the articulation of the reality of her sex impossible in discourse, which presumes an exclusively male model.

7. Howe wrote in a letter, "I don't understand why it is I get obsessed by particular people in history. But I do. And that seems to be often what fuels my work. I was completely caught up with Stella—then with Mary Rowlandson—then Hope Atherton, Anne Hutchinson, and most recently Clarence Mangan. . . . it's as if they enter my imagination as characters in a play but the play is not a play, it's real" (letter to author, 23 August 1992).

8. The authenticity of several existing portraits said to represent Stella is a subject of scholarly debate. See Henry Mangan's discussion in "Appendix VII" to Swift's *Journal to Stella* (Swift 1948, pp. 687–703).

9. In arriving at this statement, I was assisted by Henry Louis Gates, Jr.'s discussion of a "critical double bind" in "Critical Fanonism"; Gates addresses the problems of agency and responsibility raised by critical treatments of the native vis-à-vis the repressive operations of colonialism (Gates 1991, p. 462).

10. That the structure of the *Cantos* is best understood as a pattern of "rhymes" was first suggested, I believe, by Hugh Kenner who asserted in *The Pound Era* that "the *Cantos* affords a thesaurus of subject-rhymes" and that, in addition, "two sensibilities may rhyme, there are culture rhymes" (Kenner 1971, pp. 93, 92). This concept, which I find useful in discussing Howe, has been adopted by a number of Pound scholars.

11. Here my view differs somewhat from that of Marjorie Perloff, who writes, "How, then, to give life to a 'poem containing history'? There is Ezra Pound's way: the documentary collage with its 'repeats' and 'subject rhymes,' but, except in prose pieces like the Mary Rowlandson essay, this is not Howe's. Emily Dickinson's punning, wordplay, and syntactic ambiguity are closer" (Perloff 1990, p. 305). Certainly, Howe is not engaged in Pound's version of documentary collage, but "repeats" and "subject rhymes" seem to me essential to her work's analysis of historical processes. Rather than choosing between Pound's way and Dickinson's, she draws on both.

12. The actual passage (with parts Howe did not include italicized) reads: "*I*

must not write too much—so adieu deelest Md Md Md FW FW Me Me Me *Lele I can say lele yet oo see*—Fais I dont conceal a bitt. as hope savd." In the letter, Swift has been describing his recent serious illness; editor Harold Williams explains Swift's declaring he conceals nothing as meaning that he has confessed the full gravity of his illness (he has just declared that he's "in no danger of Life, but miserable Torture") so that Stella and Dingley will not worry about him unduly (Swift 1948, p. 529, note 35).

13. In "Four Part Harmony," Howe presents this dichotomy in slightly different terms: her mother's side of the library was "magic and expressive and wild" and her father's was "history and biography and authority." She adds, "It seems to me that my definition of poetry all these years later moves between those two poles" (Howe and Creeley 1994, p. 21).

14. In most of her historical works, Howe explores American history, tracing aspects of the American character and voice. "Defenestration of Prague" and "The Liberties" are unusual in their focus on Ireland. Recently, however, "Melville's Marginalia" has drawn her back toward Ireland through the poet Clarence Mangan.

15. The liberties of a city are the district extending beyond the city's bounds, subject to the control of the municipal authority. St. Patrick's, too, had its own liberty, or surrounding district under its control, referred to, for instance in Swift's *Drapier's Letters* as quoted in the *OED*, "I will begin the experiment in the liberty of St. Patrick's."

16. In his review, "Singing into the Draft," Hank Lazer accurately observes that Howe, in revisualizing notions of field-composition, renders the page, rather than the line or the sentence, the unit of composition (1991, p. 10). I will sometimes refer to these units as lyrics, for although they lack some of the traits associated especially with Romantic and post-Romantic lyric (such as the focus on the poet-speaker's sensibility), they are shaped as much by sound and musical expression as are the works of any conventional lyricist. Howe has remarked that despite her interest in the visual aspects of her pages, "the strongest element I feel when I am writing something is acoustic" (Keller 1995, p. 13).

17. What I suggest here is similar to Peter Quartermain's observation that "while her reassessment and indeed her poetics, rejecting the possibility of definitive statement, invite elliptical commentary (if they invite commentary at all), there are indeed identifiable and even definable concerns and themes recurring throughout Howe's work. I think that the great energy of Howe's writing arises from a series of tensions, between the more-or-less explicit themes and subject matter of the work, and the unstated verbal and schematic activity of the poem . . . ; between Howe's enchanted fascination with and desperate possession by history and with language, and her intense desire to be free of them; between her desire for the secure, the stable, and the defined, and her apprehension of them as essentially false." Like Quartermain, I would add that "What I offer is only *one* way of reading Howe" (Quartermain 1992, p. 183).

18. Howe's prose essays on historical subjects are more obviously didactic than her poetry. In 1988, when Charles Bernstein asked her, "Do you see it as a political role of a poet doing historical and textual inquiries in the way that you do?" she replied,

> I wouldn't want to decree what the political role of any poet should be. . . . For a long time I thought it was my political purpose to find some truth that had been edited out of our history. For example, I thought it was urgent that I bring Mary Rowlandson's narrative back into our consciousness. I love words. I hope they are allowed to suggest all meanings possible. I hope that language will always be an undiscovered country. All poetry that sets words free is political. The irony is that "political poetry," poetry with a specific political agenda for improvement, tends to imprison knowledge. But words will always escape into their own mystery.
>
> (Howe 1990, p. 195)

"The Liberties" is a product of that time when Howe wanted to call attention to truths edited out of our history, but her desire to convey her "truths" has always been countered by a desire to leave words free.

19. Some take Medb as a figure of sovereignty to whom a king must be symbolically married in order to reign legitimately (Ellis 1991, p. 166).

20. This notion of the ninth wave being the largest appears in Tennyson's *The Holy Grail*, where "the two . . . watch'd the great sea fall, / Wave after wave, each mightier than the last, / Till last, a ninth one, gathering half the deep / And full of voices, slowly rose and plunged / Roaring, and all the wave was in a flame." The drawing included in the text (though omitted from the version in *The Europe of Trusts*) is by Howe's husband, David von Schlegell.

21. Hero may also evoke the story of Hero and Leander, lovers separated by a body of water, as sometimes were Stella and Swift, as well as Hero in Shakespeare's *Much Ado About Nothing*, whose word carries no power when she is unjustly accused.

22. Howe links the danger of madness with women's attempt to transgress patriarchal limitations on their literary production in an interview where she describes her passionate love of the writing of both Dickinson and Woolf, two women who were "accepted into the male pantheon but they had to pay the price of otherness. Virginia Woolf . . . ended by drowning herself. Emily Dickinson did not go mad but she had to make severe choices. She had to become very 'odd' in order to be left alone to write." Howe goes on to recall her early feeling that Woolf's madness was punishment for hubris. "I remember being afraid that if I worked too hard with words *I* might start hearing voices. I had this lesson of these two writers whose language was exemplary but whose mastery told the other story that a woman could go too far" (Falon 1989, pp. 33–34).

23. Ibsen's *The Wild Duck* is a significant intertext at multiple points in "The Liberties." Here, for instance, the shooting death of Hedvig is relevant; although she kills herself, responsibility for her death lies with several male characters, especially Hjalmar, whom she has loved as her father.

24. There is an Irish tradition associated with the Feast of St. Stephen of men and boys hunting the wren and then going from door to door carrying the dead bird on a holly bush. In this passage Howe echoes the "Hunt the Wren" song, one version of which goes:

We'll hunt the wren, says Robbin the Bobbin
We'll hunt the wren, says Richie the Robin
We'll hunt the wren, says Jack o' the Lan'
We'll hunt the wren, says everyone.

(Killip 1975, p. 185)

In this ancient tradition, some of the hunters "were dressed as fools, others wore straw, and some were disguised as women" (Foster 1951, p. 34).

25. I suspect that the presence of a play script here also identifies the work as in part a tribute to the author's mother, from whom she acquired her love of theater.

26. It is worth recalling here that Howe's father was named Mark.

27. Howe explores this aspect of women's conversion narratives in "Encloser" and in the longer version of that essay published in *The Birth-mark*, "Incloser" (Howe 1993).

28. Here and later in "God's Spies" are further echoes of Hedwig's death— her self-destructive, love-seeking collusion with the fathers—in Ibsen's *The Wild Duck*. "Depths of the sea" on page 109 and the image of submerged bodies "on the bottom— / tangle and seaweed" on page 110 are among these allusions.

29. Just as the Lir story appears in Pound's Canto II, Acteon and his leaping hounds appear in Canto IV. Clearly, Pound is another writer central to the male imaginary through which Howe "goes back."

30. In *My Emily Dickinson*, Howe comments on this profound doubleness in *King Lear*. After quoting Lear's diatribe against women, she adds that if Shakespeare "at the height of his power demonstrated his volcanic loathing for women, constantly colliding with his aversion, he revealed and reviled it in a play tender beyond comparison. In *King Lear* Shakespeare has gone down to the deeps of sexual terror, into the violence of primal exile from our mother" (Howe 1985, p. 107).

31. Howe complains in the discussion transcribed at the end of "Encloser": "In history individuals get lost. Particularly women, as we well know by now, but not only women—individuals. The individual voice tends to get erased. Singularities are surrounded and erased by factions" (1990, p. 191). Her interest in specific historic individuals, shared by such mainstream poets as Dove and Whitman, contrasts with the more generalizing project of poets like Grahn or Doubiago who bring to light the history of marginalized factions or groups.

32. In this elliptical work, Howe only once uses the punctuation that conventionally encodes blanks and silences, and when she does do so, she ponders the implications of those marks: "do those dots mean that the speaker lapsed / into silence?" (*DP*, p. 72).

Chapter Six

1. Elsewhere in *The Pink Guitar* DuPlessis notes that racial narratives too remain unchallenged. She is examining this issue in a critical study currently in progress.

2. See Linda A. Taylor's discussion of Kathleen Fraser's development in "'A Seizure of Voice': Language Innovation and a Feminist Poetics in the Works of Kathleen Fraser" (1992), along with Fraser's essay, "The Tradition of Marginality"

(1989). A number of critics and theorists have considered the relation between experimental writing and the feminine; for a fascinating recent discussion, see Joan Retallack, ":RE:THINKING:LITERARY:FEMINISM:" (1994).

3. In "The Tradition of Marginality," Kathleen Fraser traces the origin of *HOW(ever)*, a San Francisco-based journal which she founded in 1983. Fraser, Frances Jaffer, and Beverly Dahlen were the initial editors, with Carolyn Burke and Rachel Blau DuPlessis serving as contributing editors. Dahlen withdrew after two years. "The name represented for us an addendum, a point of view from the margins, meant to flesh out what had thus far been proposed in poetry and poetics." The journal asserted "a point of view that defines itself as female and often feminist" and was devoted solely to the publication of women writers, exploring "a female tradition of language inventiveness" (Fraser 1989, p. 26).

In the May 1984 issue of *HOW(ever)*, Dahlen commented on the complexities of tracing a female tradition. One possible response she outlines to the woman writer's discovery that "the tradition *is* male" is "the necessity that some of us feel to work out the specifically female line of descent in our tradition, that line which has been, by all accounts, so obscured. . . . It is my belief that [a woman] cannot simply enter the tradition, identifying with it as if she were male; she is, I think, in grave risk to do so. But what other identity is there? Surely, to ask that is to bring us to the heart of the matter: woman as absence and the consequent risks involved in the invention of our own traditions" (Dahlen 1984b, p. 14).

4. The quoted phrase is the subtitle of DuPlessis's 1986 book-length study of H.D., which focuses on her struggles for authority. H.D.'s relationship to Pound and his work figures centrally in DuPlessis's essay "Family, Sexes, Psyche" in *The Pink Guitar*.

5. The poet Lynn Lonidier, a friend of both Duncan's and Dahlen's, invited Duncan to a reading Dahlen gave and introduced them there in the mid-1970s. He subsequently wrote the "Afterword" to Dahlen's "The Egyptian Poems," published by Hipparchia Press in 1983 (reprinted in *Ironwood* 27).

6. In the same letter Dahlen identifies Stein as another example of a writer whose influence is not proportional to the amount of material read.

7. In *Unending Design*, Joseph Conte presents serial form, which he carefully distinguishes from sequential form, as a distinctly postmodern poetic innovation "virtually unanticipated by existing formal types" (1991, p. 5). See the section of his "Introduction" titled "Seriality and Proceduralism: A Typology of Postmodern Poetry" for extended consideration of the series and its relation to other types of the long poem. Alan Golding also discusses the serial poem in relation to common critical paradigms of the long poem or poetic sequence in "George Oppen's Serial Poems" (1988, pp. 222–24).

8. Dahlen continues, "At any rate, I took George to be my mentor for a while and my poem to him ("A Letter at Easter") is, I think, in the mode of the serial poems he was writing at the time" (letter to author, 10 January 1995).

9. Duncan knew both Oppen and Spicer. Duncan (along with Robin Blaser) was one of Spicer's closest associates in the San Francisco scene beginning in the late 1940s; the two influenced each other a good deal, although a rift between them was evident by the early 1960s. Oppen and Duncan were corresponding by 1969, when Oppen expressed admiration and a sense of kinship with *Bending the Bow*

(Oppen 1990, p. 183). Oppen's book-length serial poem *Discrete Series* was published in 1934; he then stopped writing poetry for many years. He resumed publishing in 1962, and some of his later volumes contained serial poems.

10. Other important discussions of Duncan's sense of tradition include Michael Davidson's chapter in *San Francisco Renaissance*, " 'Cave of Resemblances, Cave of Rime': Tradition and Repetition in Robert Duncan" (1989) and Christopher Beach's chapter in *ABC of Influence*, "Objectivist Romantic" (1992).

11. In DuPlessis's case, Duncan's influence was most powerful and direct on her practice, not of poetry, but of the essay. Examining the literary character of her essays is, however, beyond the scope of this book.

12. Duncan himself draws the distinction in the interview conducted by Bernstein and Burton Hatlen, where Duncan also claims that Pound is really a noncollagist (Bernstein and Hatlen 1985, p. 117).

13. Duncan's gracious acknowledgment of debt to women extends in his later years to Dahlen and DuPlessis as well. DuPlessis in "For Duncan" quotes from a letter Duncan wrote to her in 1979 in which he credits her writing with giving him the impetus to return to the *H.D. Book* (DuPlessis 1988, p. 9). And in his "Afterword" to Dahlen's "The Egyptian Poems," Duncan not only speaks of months of returning to Dahlen's poetry but asserts "[s]he has deepened my apprehension of the oracular voice in Poetry" (Duncan 1986, p. 145).

14. Michael Davidson and Maria Damon, among others, link Duncan's literary innovations to his homosexuality. Davidson sees "Duncan's thematics of dispersion and sexual plurality as being defined not only by means of a Neoplatonic Orphism but in terms of the homosexual writer attempting to enter modernism on his own terms" (Davidson 1989, p. 149). Damon's reading in *The Dark End of the Street* (1993) positions Duncan's invocation of and dissolution of opposites within patterns characteristic of gay writing.

15. For instance, Duncan's interview comment: "I'm a development in a language, but I certainly didn't develop the language, so I refer to myself as derivative entirely" (Cohn and O'Donnell 1980, p. 537).

16. A Stein-like passage from "A Reading 16" addresses this issue at length:

> somehow the writer was a different person writing. the writer did not look like her writing. she may have been fair or dark but that did not perhaps enter her writing. . . . then there was another person. the person of the writing.

> but of course there was the reading also. first one would have been a reader. then one was helpless. then one knew nothing but the writing. as the reader one knew nothing but the writing. then the person disappears. then, and then the writing is all. all there is. then there is nothing but reader, reader of the writing.

>   (Dahlen 1989a p. 86, ellipses mine)

17. Conte, among other critics, has linked such ideas to Barthes's conception of the writerly text (Conte 1991, pp. 57–58; see also Reid 1979, pp. 178–79); such understandings of the reader's role typify Language writing.

18. Duncan's phrase, taken from one of the epigraphs preceding "Passages 1"

quoting Emperor Julian, *Hymn to the Mother of the Gods*, echoes also with Thoreau's plea for extra-vagance in the "Conclusion" of *Walden:*

> I desire to speak somewhere *without* bounds; like a man in a waking moment, to men in their waking moments; for I am convinced that I cannot exaggerate enough even to lay the foundation of a true expression. . . . The volatile truth of our words should continually betray the inadequacy of the residual statement.
>
> (Thoreau 1991 [1854], pp. 260–61)

Thanks to Tom Schaub for pointing this out.

19. Alan Shima similarly links Dahlen's practice and Kristeva's notions both of the subject-in-process and of the dissolution of symbolic modes (see, for instance, Shima 1993, pp. 118, 121–22, 127, 128, 141, 146). However, his claim that Dahlen's "process-oriented writing experimentally relinquishes the privileges of referentiality, personality, and control," with its language of sacrifice, does not adequately convey the positive, politically motivated choice that Dahlen deliberately makes (Shima 1993, p. 118).

In this connection, it is worth noting DuPlessis's assertion of her own deliberate entry into "a complex, ongoing, everlasting and unstable negotiation with the patriarchal, some border-crossing mix of 'symbolic' and second term 'semiotic.' . . . The practice is trying to articulate critical leverage in form or language, to cite and transpose, to encircle and enter wedge-wide, to parody, to exaggerate, to slow up, to offer gesture inappropriate to genre, and genre riddled with its own gestures" (*PG*, p. 66). All this because, she says, "I want writing. / Writing, as feminist practice" (*PG*, p. 67). Dahlen in "A Reading: Emily Dickinson: Powers of Horror" mulls over a statement DuPlessis made in correspondence about the risk women writers—as opposed to men writers—take when they try to get the semiotic into their writing (Dahlen 1986a, pp. 20–21).

20. This lack of definition is probably reinforced by the historically modern condition Dahlen outlines in her essay on Dickinson. Noting a "progress of subjectivity" in the two hundred years separating Vaughan and Dickinson, she observes, "[w]hat's lost to us in the progress of subjectivity is a sense of the reality of the other, that third person for whom or which the abstract noun 'the world' might be a sign" (Dahlen 1986a, p. 10). In our own time "[t]he world is displaced by a mourning for its loss" (1986a, p. 11).

21. In "A Reading: a Reading" Dahlen herself undertakes a far more thorough analysis than I attempt here. Devoted to the first section of "A Reading 14," Dahlen's essay is instructive not only in its interpretive statements and the information it provides about what "the writer" has been reading, but even more in its modeling of interpretive procedures. Speaking impersonally of "the writer," Dahlen moves through the section phrase by phrase, reporting multiple possible suggestions and unpacking nuances of tone. (She mentions irony with marked frequency.) She also offers paraphrasing overviews, as a clause like the following suggests, "The first two sentences might possibly be rendered: . . . " (Dahlen 1985a, p. 115, ellipses mine). And she sometimes circles back to a passage analyzed earlier so as to "read much more into" it (1985a, p. 117). Despite the multiple possibilities of meaning she notes, she builds a single reading as she goes, pointing to the unfolding of

"basic themes" or of patterns (such as a pattern in which "[f]antasy gives way, over and over, to humor, to irony, to observation of details from the concrete objective world" [1985a, pp. 129–30]). She also insists, "Other readings are possible and I do not mean, by offering this, to privilege it as *the* intended reading" (1985a, p. 113).

22. I will refer to the visual groupings in *A Reading* as paragraphs because that is what they resemble and because they do, by and large, function as units. (In "A Reading: a Reading" Dahlen herself uses the word "section" for what I call a paragraph; I am reserving "section" to refer to the collections of paragraphs separated by some sort of graphic marker—*A Reading 1–7* uses what looks like a bold centered dash.) Similarly, I will refer to any phrase or group of phrases followed by a period as a sentence (terminology that corresponds with Dahlen's), since these units seem to function analogously to grammatical sentences. Although most of *A Reading* does not employ the lineated form conventional to poetry, I regard "poem" as an appropriate generic label both because of the work's affiliations with the traditions of twentieth-century long poem and because the language is "poetic" in the Kristevan sense important to its author.

23. Dahlen frequently thematizes a resistance to narrative and narrative literary conventions in her work. One sample, in which she first imitates novelistic techniques and then criticizes them, will suffice: "his hat, knocked off in the wind, went rolling down the hill. he bent and ran after it, doggedly. one novel like another though 200 years separate them." (Dahlen 1992, p. 151). Such passages explicitly position Dahlen's aesthetic against that evident in sequences by Dove, Osbey, and Hacker, which rely heavily on novelistic narrative structures.

24. Shima also discusses this passage (1993, p. 131). I treat "red" as less thoroughly arbitrary than he does.

25. Dahlen suggests her own perspective on the double in (among other places) a short piece entitled "In Re 'Person.'" Linking our impoverished notions of the person to spatialized conceptions of the world as drama, and the person as persona (mask), Dahlen ties this to a larger set of shabby relations in capitalism:

> [T]he *value* of perspective to nascent capitalism was that it eventually aided in the creation of a new reality, a rationalized objectified space which could then be opened to exploitation. The value of providing a "double" for nature was the same as the value of providing a soul for the human individual: it split the world into sacred and profane, private and public usage. . . . Just as perspective created the uncanny mirror of nature, so the mirror itself was instrumental in the creation of the human soul, the ghost of oneself which is seen to walk abroad in dreams, which is said to be immortal, the "true" or "real" self as distinct from this "person" who, after all, is merely a mask of flesh and bones.
>
> (Dahlen 1991, pp. 74–75)

In her essay on Dickinson, she identifies the middle of the nineteenth century as the time when the ghost that is the I's double "begins to haunt literature" (Dahlen 1986a, p. 11). This—Dickinson's time—is when "the world is already beginning to disappear. There is no assurance that the existence of a first person implies the other two" (1986a, p. 10). A fuller analysis of this section of "A Reading 2," which mentions also a "schizophrenic episode," would elaborate on the role of the double.

26. For discussion of the opening lines and their recursiveness, see Shima (1993, pp. 120–23).

27. In "While These Letters Were A-Reading," DuPlessis also presents Duncan's ideas about "plans" and how to do without them to make a related point about Dahlen's writing as a "reading of those words she has 'happened' to write" (*PG*, p. 118).

28. Not all the Readings follow this paragraphlike form, however, or follow it consistently. The fourth, which is only six pages long, looks like free verse and uses the paragraph form only briefly. "A Reading 4" also contains the most notable visual experiment in the serial to date: on p. 53 some words and phrases recording environmental sounds appear in columns; these sections are set off by horizontal lines and heavy brackets and each is followed by a line in which "*tik tik tik*" repeats across the page. "A Reading 17" contains a grid of words similar to what Howe uses in "The Liberties" and Duncan in "Passages 13" (though Dahlen's words derive from a test used to determine reading levels, called the Wide Range Achievement Text [Davis 1986, p. 149]). Although the overall effect is unquestionably of proselike blocks of texts, a number of the Readings contain a passage or passages that look like verse.

29. Due to a printer's error, the final s on *extensions* was omitted from *Drafts*. The plural form more accurately conveys DuPlessis's method.

30. In Duncan's work, this last technique is especially noticeable in the Passages of *Ground Work: Before the War* and *Ground Work II: In the Dark*, where he experiments with caesuras in a wide-page format that accommodates long lines.

31. I say charming because of the character of Duncan's examples of earlier English, as well as the poem's often-quoted ending in which the pleasures of language merge so delightfully with erotic pleasure:

And Jesperson recites:

> She was a maid • the maiden kween.
> It is made of silk • a silken dress.
> The man is old • in olden days.
> The gold is hid • the hidden gold.
> The room is nice • all nicen warm.

and quotes from Conan Doyle's *The Great Shadow:*

> "I wish your eyes would always flash like that, for
>   it looks so nice and manly."
>
> It looks so nicen manly.

(Duncan 1968a, p. 50)

32. One might think of DuPlessis's formal model of "the fold" as a cross between what Conte calls "serial" and "procedural" postmodern poetic forms. The

former are protean and provisional, open to chance; the latter follow predetermined and arbitrary constraints.

33. Sound progressions into which semiotic play may enter are characteristic of DuPlessis's writing; like Duncan, she not only loves words' music but allows their babble to lead her lines.

34. DuPlessis's notes provide citations for phrases quoted from others, such as the one opening this passage; I choose not to repeat the citations here.

35. The sculptures were discovered by a Philadelphia designer who "was driving home from a party one night when his headlights flashed across a heap of shiny metal objects." That this person happened to be an artist and one "fascinat[ed] with urban residue and lost trinkets" is probably crucial to the survival of the Wireman's artworks, which within hours would have been compacted in one of the city's garbage trucks (Jarmusch 1986, p. 166).

WORKS CITED

Altieri, Charles. 1978. "Motives in Metaphor: John Ashbery and the Modernist Long Poem." *Genre* 11: 653–87.

———. 1982. "Sensibility, Rhetoric, and Will: Some Tensions in Contemporary Poetry." *Contemporary Literature* 23: 451–79.

———. 1984. *Self and Sensibility in Contemporary American Poetry.* New York: Cambridge University Press.

Auden, W. H. 1973. "Shakespeare's Sonnets." In *Forewords and Afterwords,* pp. 88–108. New York: Random House.

Baker, Houston. 1990. Review of *Grace Notes,* by Rita Dove. *Black American Literature Forum* (Fall): 574–77.

Baker, Peter. 1991. *Obdurate Brilliance: Exteriority and the Modern Long Poem.* Gainesville: University of Florida Press.

Beach, Christopher. 1992. *ABC of Influence: Ezra Pound and the Remaking of American Poetic Tradition.* Berkeley: University of California Press.

Becket, Tom. 1989. "The Difficulties Interview." *The Difficulties* 3, no. 2 (Susan Howe Issue): 17–27.

Bernstein, Charles. 1989. *The Nude Formalism.* Illustrated by Susan Bee. Los Angeles: Sun & Moon.

Bernstein, Michael André. 1980. *The Tale of the Tribe: Ezra Pound and the Modern Verse Epic.* Princeton: Princeton University Press.

———. 1982. "Bringing It All Back Home: Derivations and Quotations in Robert Duncan and the Poundian Tradition." *Sagetrieb* 1: 176–89.

———. 1985. "Robert Duncan: Talent and the Individual Tradition." *Sagetrieb* 4: 177–90.

Bernstein, Michael André, and Burton Hatlen. 1985. "Interview with Robert Duncan." *Sagetrieb* 4: 87–135.

Blassingame, John W. 1973. *Black New Orleans 1860–1880.* Chicago: University of Chicago Press.

Bridgman, Richard. 1970. *Gertrude Stein in Pieces.* New York: Oxford University Press.

Bryan, Violet Harrington. 1987. "An Interview with Brenda Marie Osbey." *The Mississippi Quarterly* 40: 33–45.

Butler, Judith. 1990a. "Gender Trouble, Feminist Theory, and Psychoanalytic Discourse." In *Feminism/Postmodernism*, edited by Linda J. Nicholson, pp. 324–40. New York: Routledge.

———. 1990b. *Gender Trouble: Feminism and the Subversion of Identity.* New York: Routledge.

Byers, Thomas B. 1992. "The Closing of the American Line: Expansive Poetry and Ideology." *Contemporary Literature* 33: 396–415.

Carruth, Hayden. 1993. "Narrative Anyone?" *Parnassus* 17, no. 2, and 18, no. 1: 210–18.

Case, Sue-Ellen. 1988. "Judy Grahn's Gynopoetics: *The Queen of Swords.*" *Studies in the Literary Imagination* 21, no. 2: 47–67.

———. 1989. "Toward a Butch-Femme Aesthetic." In *Making a Spectacle: Feminist Essays on Contemporary Women's Theatre*, edited by Lynda Hart, pp. 282–99. Ann Arbor: University of Michigan Press.

Clayton, Jay. 1993. *The Pleasures of Babel: Contemporary American Literature and Theory.* New York: Oxford University Press.

Cohn, Jack R., and Thomas J. O'Donnell. 1980. "An Interview with Robert Duncan." *Contemporary Literature* 21: 513–48.

Conte, Joseph M. 1991. *Unending Design: The Forms of Postmodern Poetry.* Ithaca: Cornell University Press.

Dacey, Philip, and David Jauss. 1985. *Strong Measures: Contemporary American Poetry in Traditional Forms.* New York: Harper & Row.

Dahlen, Beverly. 1984a. "Forbidden Knowledge." *Poetics Journal* 4: 3–19.

———. 1984b. Letter to Jed Rasula, under "Postcards." *HOW(ever)* 1 (May 1984): 14.

———. 1985a. "A Reading: a Reading." In *Writing/Talks*, edited by Bob Perelman, pp. 113–34. Carbondale, IL: Southern Illinois University Press.

———. 1985b. *A Reading 1–7.* San Francisco: MOMO's Press.

———. 1986a. "A Reading: Emily Dickinson: Powers of Horror." *Ironwood* 28: 9–37.

———. 1986b. "Something/Nothing." *Ironwood* 27: 170–75.

———. 1989a. *A Reading (11–17).* Elmwood, CT: Potes & Poets Press.

———. 1989b. "Tautology and the Real." *Temblor* 10: 215–18.

———. 1991. "In Re 'Person.'" *Poetics Journal* 9: 74–75.

———. 1992. *A Reading 8–10.* Tucson: Chax Press.

Damon, Maria. 1993. *The Dark End of the Street: Margins in American Vanguard Poetry.* Minneapolis: University of Minnesota Press.

Davidson, Michael. 1983. "Robert Duncan." In *Dictionary of Literary Biography*, vol. 16, *The Beats: Literary Bohemians in Postwar America*, edited by Ann Chambers, pp. 169–80. Detroit: Gale Research Co.

———. 1989. *The San Francisco Renaissance: Poetics and Community at Mid-century.* Cambridge: Cambridge University Press.

Davis, Gayle. 1986. "The Question of Authority in *A Reading.*" *Ironwood* 27: 149–53.

Dawson, Ariel. 1985. "The Yuppie Poet." *Associated Writing Programs Newsletter* (May): 5–6.

DeKoven, Marianne. 1989. "Male Signature, Female Aesthetic: The Gender Politics of Experimental Writing." In *Breaking the Sequence: Women's Experimental Fiction*, edited by Ellen Friedman and Miriam Fuchs, pp. 72–81. Princeton: Princeton University Press.

Dembo, L. S. 1966. *Conceptions of Reality in Modern American Poetry.* Berkeley: University of California Press.

———. 1972. "George Oppen." In *The Contemporary Writer: Interviews with Sixteen Novelists and Poets*, edited by L. S. Dembo and Cyrena N. Pondrom, pp. 172–90. Madison: University of Wisconsin Press.

Dickie, Margaret. 1986. *On the Modernist Long Poem.* Iowa City: University of Iowa Press.

Doubiago, Sharon. 1982. *Hard Country.* Minneapolis: West End Press.

———. 1988. *The Book of Seeing With One's Own Eyes.* Saint Paul, MN: Graywolf.

Dove, Rita. 1985. "Telling it Like it I-S *IS:* Narrative Techniques in Melvin Tolson's *Harlem Gallery.*" *New England Review and Bread Loaf Quarterly* 8 (Autumn): 109–17.

———. 1987. " 'Either I'm Nobody, or I'm a Nation.' " Review of *Collected Poems*, by Derek Walcott. *Parnassus: Poetry in Review* 14, no. 1: 49–76.

———. 1990. "Forward" to Zora Neale Hurston, *Jonah's Gourd Vine*, pp. vii–xv. San Bernadino, CA: Borgo Press.

———. 1993. *Selected Poems.* New York: Vintage. (*Thomas and Beulah* originally published by Carnegie-Mellon University Press, 1986.)

Downing, Ben. 1993a. "Big City, Long Poem." *Parnassus: Poetry in Review* 17, no. 2, and 18, no. 1: 219–34.

———. 1993b. "A Response." *Parnassus: Poetry in Review* 18, no. 2, and 19, no. 1: 482–83.

Duncan, Robert. 1960. *The Opening of the Field.* New York: Grove Press.

———. 1968a. *Bending the Bow.* New York: New Directions.

———. 1974. "Preface to a Reading of Passages 1–22." *Maps* 6: 53–55.

———. 1985. *Fictive Certainties.* New York: New Directions.

———. 1986. "Afterword." *Ironwood* 27: 142–46.

———. 1987. *Ground Work II: In the Dark.* New York: New Directions.

———. *The H.D. Book.*

    1963. "From the Day Book." *Origin* 10 (July): 1–47.

    1967a. Part I, Chapter 2. *Coyote's Journal* 8: 27–35.

    1967b. Part I, Chapter 6, "Rites of Participation, Part I." *Caterpillar* 1 (October): 6–29.

    1968b. Part I, Chapter 6, "Rites of Participation, Part II." *Caterpillar* 2 (January): 125–54.

    1969. Part II, Chapter 2. *Caterpillar* 6 (January): 16–38.

    1979. Part II, Chapter 9. *Chicago Review* 30 (Winter): 37–88.

DuPlessis, Rachel Blau. 1986. *H.D.: The Career of that Struggle.* Bloomington: Indiana University Press.

———. 1987. *Tabula Rosa.* Elmwood, CT: Potes & Poets Press.

———. 1988. "For Duncan." *H.D. Newsletter* 2: 8–10.

———. 1989. " 'A White Fiction': a woman and a page." *Temblor* 10: 168–74.

———. 1990. *The Pink Guitar: Writing as Feminist Practice.* New York and London: Routledge.

———. 1991. *Drafts 3–14.* Elmwood, CT: Potes & Poets Press.

———. 1992. "On Drafts: A Memorandum of Understanding." *To: A Journal of Poetry, Prose, + the Visual Arts* (Summer): 72–77.

———. 1994. " 'Corpses of Poesy': Some Modern Poets and Some Gender Ideologies of Lyric." In *Feminist Measures: Soundings in Poetry and Theory,* edited by Lynn Keller and Cristanne Miller, pp. 69–95. Ann Arbor: University of Michigan Press.

———. 1995. "Draft 22: Philadelphia Wireman." *Hambone* 12: 110–13.

———. 1996. "On Drafts: A Memorandum of Understanding." In *Onward: Contemporary Poetry and Poetics,* edited by Peter Baker, pp. 143–55. New York: Peter Lang.

———. 1997. *Drafts 15–XXX, The Fold.* Elmwood, CT: Potes & Poets Press.

Ellis, Peter Berresford. 1991. "Medb." In *A Dictionary of Irish Mythology,* pp. 165–66. Oxford: Oxford University Press.

Falon, Ruth. 1989. "Speaking with Susan Howe." *The Difficulties* 3, no. 2 (Susan Howe Issue): 28–42.

Farwell, Marilyn R. 1975. "Virginia Woolf and Androgyny." *Contemporary Literature* 16: 433–51.

———. 1988. "Toward a Definition of the Lesbian Literary Imagination." *Signs* 14: 100–118.

Felski, Rita. 1989. *Beyond Feminist Aesthetics: Feminist Literature and Social Change.* Cambridge, MA: Harvard University Press.

Finch, Annie, ed. 1994. *A Formal Feeling Comes: Poems in Form by Contemporary Women.* Brownsville, OR: Story Line Press.

Foster, Edward. 1990. "An Interview with Susan Howe." *Talisman: A Journal of Contemporary Poetry and Poetics* 4 (Spring): 14–38.

Foster, Jeanne Cooper. 1951. *Ulster Folklore.* Belfast: H. R. Carter.

Frank, Robert, and Henry Sayre, eds. 1988. *The Line in Postmodern Poetry.* Urbana: University of Illinois Press.

Fraser, Kathleen. 1989. "The Tradition of Marginality." *Frontiers* 10: 22–27.

Frazier, E. Franklin. 1927. "Racial Self-Expression." In *Ebony and Topaz,* edited by Charles S. Johnson, pp. 119–21. New York: National Urban League. (Reprinted in *Black Protest Thought in the Twentieth Century,* second ed., edited by August Meier, Elliott Rudwick, and Francis L. Broderick, pp. 116–21. Indianapolis: Bobbs-Merrill.)

Freud, Sigmund. 1950. "The 'Uncanny.' " In *Collected Papers, Volume IV,* edited by Ernest Jones, pp. 368–407. London: Hogarth Press.

———. 1963. "Analysis Terminable and Interminable." In *Therapy and Technique,* edited by Philip Rieff, pp. 233–72. New York: Macmillan.

Friedman, Susan Stanford. 1986. "Gender and Genre Anxiety: Elizabeth Barrett Browning and H.D. as Epic Poets." *Tulsa Studies in Women's Literature* 5: 203–28.

———. 1990a. "Creating a Women's Mythology: H.D.'s *Helen in Egypt.*" In *Signets: Reading H.D.,* edited by Susan Stanford Friedman and Rachel Blau DuPlessis, pp. 373–405. Madison: University of Wisconsin Press.

———. 1990b. "When a 'Long' Poem Is a 'Big' Poem: Self-Authorizing Strategies in Women's Twentieth-Century 'Long Poems.' " *LIT* 2: 9–25.

———. 1994. "Craving Stories: Narrative and Lyric in Contemporary Theory and

Women's Long Poems." In *Feminist Measures: Soundings in Poetry and Theory*, edited by Lynn Keller and Cristanne Miller, pp. 15–42. Ann Arbor: University of Michigan Press.

Fussell, Paul. 1979. *Poetic Meter & Poetic Form*, rev. ed. New York: Random House.

Gardner, Thomas. 1989. *Discovering Ourselves in Whitman: The Contemporary American Long Poem*. Urbana: University of Illinois Press.

Gates, Henry Louis, Jr. 1988. *The Signifying Monkey: A Theory of Afro-American Literary Criticism*. New York: Oxford University Press.

———. 1991a. "Critical Fanonism." *Critical Inquiry* 17: 457–70.

———. 1991b. "Introduction: On Bearing Witness." In *Bearing Witness: Selections from African-American Autobiography in the Twentieth Century*, pp. 3–9. New York: Pantheon.

Gelpi, Albert. 1985. "H.D.: Hilda in Egypt." In *Coming to Light: American Women Poets in the Twentieth Century*, edited by Diane Wood Middlebrook and Marilyn Yalom, pp. 74–91. Ann Arbor: University of Michigan Press.

Genovese, Eugene D. 1979. *From Rebellion to Revolution: Afro-American Slave Revolts in the Making of the New World*. Baton Rouge: Louisiana State University Press; rpt.: New York: Random House, 1981.

Goethe, Johann Wolfgang von. 1950. *Faust, Parts One and Two*. Translated by George Madison Priest. New York: Knopf.

Golding, Alan. 1988. "George Oppen's Serial Poems." *Contemporary Literature* 29: 221–40.

———. 1991. " 'Openness,' 'Closure,' and Recent American Poetry." *Arizona Quarterly* 47: 77–91.

Grahn, Judy. 1978. *The Work of a Common Woman: The Collected Poetry of Judy Grahn, 1964–1977*. Trumansburg, NY: The Crossing Press.

———. 1981. "Red and Black with Fish in the Middle." In Linda Koolish, "A Whole New Poetry Beginning Here," pp. 538–60. Stanford University Ph.D. Thesis.

———. 1982. *The Queen of Wands*. Trumansburg, NY: The Crossing Press.

———. 1985. *The Highest Apple: Sappho and The Lesbian Poetic Tradition*. San Francisco: Spinsters, Ink.

———. 1987. *The Queen of Swords*. Boston: Beacon Press.

———. 1989. *Really Reading Gertrude Stein: A Selected Anthology with Essays by Judy Grahn*. Freedom, CA: The Crossing Press.

———. 1990. *Another Mother Tongue: Gay Words, Gay Worlds*, updated and expanded edition. Boston: Beacon.

———. 1993. *Blood, Bread, and Roses: How Menstruation Created the World*. Boston: Beacon.

Grover, Jan Zita. 1990. "Words to Lust By." *The Women's Review of Books* 8 (November): 21–23.

Gubar, Susan. 1984. "Sapphistries." *Signs* 10: 43–62.

H.D. 1974. *Helen in Egypt*. New York: New Directions (first published in 1961).

———. 1983. *Collected Poems, 1912–1944*, edited by Louis L. Martz. New York: New Directions.

Hacker, Marilyn. 1986. *Love, Death, and the Changing of the Seasons*. New York: Arbor House; rpt., New York: Norton, 1995.

———. 1989a. "An Invitation to My Demented Uncle." *Ploughshares* 15: 1–5.

———. 1989b. " 'Begin to Teach.' " Review of *Time's Power*, by Adrienne Rich. *The Nation* 249: 464–67.

Hall, Gwendolyn Midlo. 1992. "The Formation of Afro-Creole Culture." In *Creole New Orleans: Race and Americanization*, edited by Arnold R. Hirsch and Joseph Logsdon, pp. 58–87. Baton Rouge: Louisiana State University Press.

Hammond, Karla. 1980. "An Interview with Marilyn Hacker." *Frontiers* 5: 22–27.

Hejinian, Lyn. 1984. "The Rejection of Closure." *Poetics Journal* 4: 134–43. Reprinted in *Onward: Contemporary Poetry and Poetics*, edited by Peter Baker, pp. 27–40. New York: Peter Lang, 1996.

Hernton, Calvin. 1985. "The Tradition." *Parnassus: Poetry in Review* 12, no. 2, and 13, no. 1: 518–50.

Hirsch, Arnold R., and Joseph Logsdon. 1992. "Introduction to Part III." In *Creole New Orleans: Race and Americanization*, edited by Arnold R. Hirsch and Joseph Logsdon, pp. 189–200. Baton Rouge: Louisiana State University Press.

Hirsh, Elizabeth A. 1990. "Imaginary Images: 'H.D.,' Modernism, and the Psychoanalysis of Seeing." In *Signets: Reading H.D.*, edited by Susan Stanford Friedman and Rachel Blau DuPlessis, pp. 430–51. Madison: University of Wisconsin Press.

Homans, Margaret. 1985. " 'Syllables of Velvet': Dickinson, Rossetti, and the Rhetorics of Sexuality." *Feminist Studies* 11: 569–93.

Homer. 1995. *The Odyssey*. Translated by A. T. Murray, revised by George E. Dimock, 2d ed. Cambridge, MA: Harvard University Press.

Howe, Susan. 1983. "The Liberties." In *Defenestration of Prague*, pp. 64–112. New York: Kulchur Foundation.

———. 1985. *My Emily Dickinson*. Berkeley: North Atlantic Books.

———. 1990. "Encloser." In *The Politics of Poetic Form: Poetry and Public Policy*, edited by Charles Bernstein, pp. 175–96. New York: ROOF Books.

———. 1993. *The Birth-mark: unsettling the wilderness in American literary history*. Hanover: Wesleyan University Press; published by University Press of New England.

Howe, Susan, and Robert Creeley. 1994. "Four-Part Harmony: Robert Creeley and Susan Howe Talk It Out." *Voice Literary Supplement* 124 (April): 21–22.

Hull, Gloria T. 1979. "Afro-American Women Poets: A Bio-Critical Survey." In *Shakespeare's Sisters: Feminist Essays on Women Poets*, edited by Sandra M. Gilbert and Susan Gubar, pp. 165–82. Bloomington: Indiana University Press.

Hutcheon, Linda. 1989. *The Politics of Postmodernism*. London: Routledge.

Irigaray, Luce. 1985. *This Sex Which Is Not One*. Translated by Catherine Porter with Carolyn Burke. Ithaca, NY: Cornell University Press.

James, Clive. 1973. "Auden's Achievement." *Commentary* 56 (December): 53–58.

Jarmusch, Ann. 1986. "Mysterious Stranger." *ART News* 85 (Summer): 166.

Johnson, Daniel M., and Rex R. Campbell. 1981. *Black Migration in America: A Social Demographic History*. Durham, NC: Duke University Press.

Kalstone, David. 1983. "Persisting Figures: The Poet's Story and How We Read It." In *James Merrill: Essays in Criticism*, edited by David Lehman and Charles Berger, pp. 125–44. Ithaca: Cornell University Press.

Kamboureli, Smaro. 1991. *On the Edge of Genre: The Contemporary Canadian Long Poem*. Toronto: University of Toronto Press.

Keller, Lynn. 1987. "Poems Containing History: Some Problems of Definition of the Long Poem." Paper delivered at 1987 MLA Convention.

———. 1993. "The Twentieth-Century Long Poem." In *The Columbia History of American Poetry*, edited by Jay Parini and Brett C. Millier, pp. 534–63. New York: Columbia University Press.

———. 1995. "An Interview with Susan Howe." *Contemporary Literature* 36: 1–34.

Keller, Madeleine. 1987. Interview: "Carol Ascher and Rachel Blau DuPlessis." *Bench Press Series on Art*, edited by Madeleine Keller. New York: Bench Press.

Kennedy, Elizabeth Lapovsky, and Madeline Davis. 1992. " 'They was no one to mess with': The Construction of the Butch Role in the Lesbian Community of the 1940s and 1950s." In *The Persistent Desire: A Femme-Butch Reader*, edited by Joan Nestle, pp. 62–79. Boston: Alyson Publications.

Kenner, Hugh. 1971. *The Pound Era*. Berkeley: University of California Press.

Killip, Margaret. 1975. *Folklore of the Isle of Man*. London: B. T. Batsford.

Kolodny, Annette. 1975. *The Lay of the Land: Metaphor as Experience and History in American Life and Letters*. Chapel Hill: University of North Carolina Press.

Kristeva, Julia. 1977. *About Chinese Women*. Translated by Anita Barrows. New York: Urizen Books (first published in France in 1974 as *Des Chinoises*).

———. 1980a. *Desire in Language: A Semiotic Approach to Literature and Art*, edited by Leon S. Roudiez. New York: Columbia University Press.

———. 1980b. "Woman Can Never Be Defined." In *New French Feminisms*, edited by Elaine Marks and Isabelle de Courtivron, pp. 137–41. Amherst, MA: University of Massachusetts Press.

Kuberski, Philip. 1985. "Charles Olson and the American Thing: The Ideology of Literary Revolution." *Criticism* 27: 175–93.

Kubitschek, Missy Dehn. 1991. *Claiming the Heritage: African-American Women Novelists and History*. Jackson: University of Mississippi Press.

Lazer, Hank. 1991. "Singing into the Draft." *American Book Review* 13, no. 4 (October/November): 9–11.

Levine, Lawrence W. 1977. *Black Culture and Black Consciousness: Afro-American Folk Thought from Slavery to Freedom*. New York: Oxford University Press.

Li, Victor P. H. 1986. "The Vanity of Length: The Long Poem as Problem in Pound's *Cantos* and Williams' *Paterson*." *Genre* 19: 3–20.

Logsdon, Joseph, and Caryn Cossé Bell. 1992. "The Americanization of Black New Orleans, 1850–1900." In *Creole New Orleans: Race and Americanization*, edited by Arnold R. Hirsch and Joseph Logsdon, pp. 201–61. Baton Rouge: Louisiana State University Press.

Ma, Ming-Qian. 1994. "Poetry as History Revised: Susan Howe's 'Scattering As Behavior Toward Risk.' " *American Literary History* 4: 716–37.

Mackey, Nathaniel. 1993. *Discrepant Engagement: Dissonance, Cross-Culturality and Experimental Writing*. New York: Cambridge University Press.

Marks, Elaine. 1979. "Lesbian Intertextuality." In *Homosexualities and French Literature: Cultural Contexts/Critical Texts*, edited by George Stambolian and Elaine Marks, pp. 353–77. Ithaca: Cornell University Press.

McFall, Gardner. 1992. "What Hunger Is." *American Book Review* (April/May): 28.

Messerli, Douglas, ed. 1986. *"Language" Poetries: An Anthology.* New York: New Directions.

Miller, James E., Jr. 1979. *The American Quest for a Supreme Fiction: Whitman's Legacy in the Personal Epic.* Chicago: University of Chicago Press.

Moi, Toril. 1988. *Sexual/Textual Politics: Feminist Literary Theory.* Methuen, 1985; London: Routledge, 1988.

Montefiore, Jan. 1987. *Feminism and Poetry: Language, Experience, Identity in Women's Writing.* London: Pandora Press (Routledge & Kegan Paul).

———. 1987–88. " 'What Words Say': Three Women Poets Reading H.D." *Agenda* 25, nos. 3–4: 172–90.

Montenegro, David. 1991. "Adrienne Rich." In *Points of Departure: International Writers on Writing and Politics,* interviews by David Montenegro, pp. 5–25. Ann Arbor: University of Michigan Press.

Mulira, Jessie Gaston. 1990. "The Case of Voodoo in New Orleans." In *Africanisms in American Culture,* edited by Joseph E. Holloway, pp. 34–68. Bloomington: Indiana University Press.

Neuman, Shirley. 1988. " 'Would a viper have stung her if she had only had one name?': *Doctor Faustus Lights the Lights.*" In *Gertrude Stein and the Making of Literature,* edited by Shirley Neuman and Ira B. Nadel, pp. 168–93. Boston: Northeastern University Press.

Olson, Charles. 1966. *Selected Writings,* edited by Robert Creeley. New York: New Directions.

———. 1983. *The Maximus Poems,* edited by George Butterick. Berkeley: University of California Press.

Oppen, George. 1990. *The Selected Letters of George Oppen,* edited by Rachel Blau DuPlessis. Durham: Duke University Press.

Osbey, Brenda Marie. 1991. *Desperate Circumstance, Dangerous Woman.* Brownsville, OR: Story Line.

———. 1993. "Letter to *Parnassus.*" *Parnassus: Poetry in Review* 18, no. 2, and 19, no. 1: 480–81.

Ostendorf, Berndt. 1993. "Urban Creole Slavery and Its Cultural Legacy: The Case of New Orleans." In *Slavery in the Americas,* edited by Wolfgang Binder, pp. 389–401. Würzburg: Königshausen & Neumann.

Ostriker, Alicia Suskin. 1986. *Stealing the Language: The Emergence of Women's Poetry in America.* Boston: Beacon.

Ott, Bryan M. 1991. "Voodoo in New Orleans 1990: Contemporary Beliefs and Ritual Practices." M.A. Thesis. University of Wisconsin-Madison.

Peabody, Richard. 1985. "A Cage of Sound: An Interview with Rita Dove." *Gargoyle* (no. 27): 2–13.

Pearce, Roy Harvey. 1961. *The Continuity of American Poetry.* Princeton: Princeton University Press.

Peguiney, Joseph. 1985. *Such Is My Love: A Study of Shakespeare's Sonnets.* Chicago: University of Chicago Press.

Perloff, Marjorie. 1982. "From Image to Action: The Return of Story in Postmodern Poetry." *Contemporary Literature* 23: 411–27.

———. 1985. *The Dance of the Intellect: Studies in the Poetry of the Pound Tradition.* New York: Cambridge University Press.

———. 1990. *Poetic License: Essays on Modernist and Postmodernist Lyric.* Evanston, IL: Northwestern University Press.

Plimpton, George, ed. 1963. Interview with Ezra Pound. In *Writers at Work: The Paris Review Interviews*, Second Series. New York: Viking.

Price, Richard, ed. 1973. *Maroon Societies: Rebel Slave Communities in the Americas.* Garden City, NY: Anchor Press.

Prunty, Wyatt. 1990. *'Fallen From the Symboled World': Precedents for the New Formalism.* New York: Oxford University Press.

Quartermain, Peter. 1992. *Disjunctive Poetics: From Gertrude Stein and Louis Zukofsky to Susan Howe.* New York: Cambridge University Press.

Rampersad, Arnold. 1986. "The Poems of Rita Dove." *Callaloo* 9: 52–70.

Reid, Alec. 1975. "From Beginning to Date: Some Thoughts on the Plays of Samuel Beckett." In *Samuel Beckett*, edited by Ruby Cohn, pp. 63–72. New York: McGraw-Hill.

Reid, Ian W. 1979. "The Plural Text: 'Passages.' " In *Robert Duncan: Scales of the Marvelous*, edited by Robert J. Bertholf and Ian W. Reid, pp. 161–80. New York: New Directions.

Reinfeld, Linda. 1992. *Language Poetry: Writing as Rescue.* Baton Rouge: Louisiana State University Press.

Retallack, Joan. 1990. "Non-Euclidean Narrative Combustion (or, What the Subtitles Can't Say)." In *Conversant Essays: Contemporary Poets on Poetry*, edited by James McCorkle, pp. 491–509. Detroit: Wayne State University Press.

———. 1994. ":RE:THINKING:LITERARY:FEMINISM: (three essays onto shaky grounds)." In *Feminist Measures: Soundings in Poetry and Theory*, edited by Lynn Keller and Cristanne Miller, pp. 344–77. Ann Arbor: University of Michigan Press.

Rich, Adrienne. 1978. *The Dream of a Common Language: Poems 1974–1977.* New York: Norton.

———. 1979. "When We Dead Awaken: Writing as Re-vision." In *On Lies, Secrets, and Silence: Selected Prose 1966–1978*, pp. 33–49. New York: W. W. Norton & Co.

———. 1986a. "Blood, Bread, and Poetry: The Location of the Poet." In *Blood, Bread, and Poetry: Selected Prose 1979–1985*, pp. 167–87. New York: W. W. Norton & Co.

———. 1986b. "Compulsory Heterosexuality and Lesbian Existence." In *Blood, Bread, and Poetry: Selected Prose 1979–1985*, pp. 23–75. New York: W. W. Norton & Co.

———. 1989. *Time's Power: Poems 1985–1988.* New York: W. W. Norton & Co.

———. 1990. " 'Sliding Stone from the Cave's Mouth.' " *American Poetry Review* 19 (September/October): 11–17.

Richman, Robert. 1988. *The Direction of Poetry: An Anthology of Rhymed and Metered Verse Written in the English Language Since 1975.* Boston: Houghton Mifflin.

Riddel, Joseph N. 1978. "A Somewhat Polemical Introduction: The Elliptical Poem." *Genre* 11: 459–77.

Roche, Thomas P., Jr. 1989. *Petrarch and the English Sonnet Sequence.* New York: AMS Press.

Rosenthal, M. L., and Sally M. Gall. 1983. *The Modern Poetic Sequence: The Genius of Modern Poetry*. New York: Oxford University Press.

Rubin, Stan Sanvel, and Earl G. Ingersoll. 1986. "A Conversation with Rita Dove." *Black American Literature Forum* 20: 227–40. Reprinted as " 'The Underside of the Story': A Conversation with Rita Dove." In *The Post-Confessionals: Conversations with American Poets of the Eighties*, edited by Earl Ingersoll, Judith Kitchen, Stan Sanvel Rubin, pp. 151–65. Cranbury, NJ: Fairleigh Dickinson University Press.

Ryan, Betsy Alayne. 1990. *Gertrude Stein's Theatre of the Absolute*. Ann Arbor: UMI Research Press.

Sadoff, Ira. 1990. "Neo-Formalism: A Dangerous Nostalgia." *American Poetry Review* 19 (January/February): 7–13.

Schneider, Steven. 1989. "Coming Home: An Interview with Rita Dove." *Iowa Review* 19: 112–23.

Sedgwick, Eve Kosofsky. 1985. *Between Men: English Literature and Male Homosocial Desire*. New York: Columbia University Press.

Shakespeare, William. 1972. *King Lear*, edited by Kenneth Muir. Rev. ed. London: Methuen & Co.

———. 1961. *Sonnets*, edited by Douglas Bush and Alfred Harbage. Baltimore: Penguin.

Sherry, Vincent B. Jr. 1985. "Current Critical Models of the Long Poem and David Jones's *The Anathemata*." *ELH* 52: 239–55.

Shima, Alan. 1993. *Skirting the Subject: Pursuing Language in the Works of Adrienne Rich, Susan Griffin, and Beverly Dahlen*. Uppsala: Studia Anglistica Upsaliensia 82.

Shoptaw, John. 1990. "Segregated Lives: Rita Dove's *Thomas and Beulah*." In *Reading Black, Reading Feminist: A Critical Anthology*, edited by Henry Louis Gates, Jr., pp. 374–81. New York: Penguin.

Silliman, Ron, ed. 1986. *In the American Tree*. Orono, ME: National Poetry Foundation/U of Maine Press.

Smitherman, Geneva. 1977. *Talkin and Testifyin: The Language of Black America*. Detroit: Wayne State University Press (also Houghton Mifflin 1977).

Spicer, Jack. 1973. "Excerpts from the Vancouver Lectures." In *Poetics of the New American Poetry*, edited by Donald Allen and Warren Tallman, pp. 227–34. New York: Grove Press.

Steele, Timothy. 1990. *Missing Measures: Modern Poetry and the Revolt Against Meter*. Fayetteville: University of Arkansas Press.

Stimpson, Catharine R. 1993. "Demeter in South America." *Parnassus: Poetry in Review* 17, no. 2, and 18, no. 1: 258–71.

Swift, Jonathan. 1948. *Journal to Stella*, Volumes I and II, edited by Harold Williams. Oxford: Oxford University Press.

———. 1958. *The Poems of Jonathan Swift*, edited by Harold Williams, 2d ed., Vol. 2 of 3 vols. Oxford: Oxford University Press.

———. 1962. *Miscellaneous and Autobiographical Pieces*, edited by Herbert Davis. Oxford: Basil Blackwell.

Taleb-Khyar, Mohamed B. 1991. "An Interview with Maryse Condé and Rita Dove." *Callaloo* 14: 347–66.

Taylor, Linda A. 1992. " 'A Seizure of Voice': Language Innovation and a Feminist Poetics in the Works of Kathleen Fraser." *Contemporary Literature* 33: 337–72.

Teish, Luisah. 1983. "Women's Spirituality: A Household Act." In *Home Girls: A Black Feminist Anthology*, edited by Barbara Smith, pp. 331–51. New York: Kitchen Table.

Terrell, Carroll F. 1980. *A Companion to the Cantos of Ezra Pound*. Berkeley: University of California Press.

Thompson, Robert Farris. 1984. *Flash of the Spirit: African and Afro-American Art and Philosophy*. New York: Random House.

Thoreau, Henry David. 1991. *Walden or, Life in the Woods. 1854*, edited by Edward Hoagland. New York: Random House (Vintage Books).

Tindall, George Brown. 1967. *The Emergence of the New South 1913–1945*. Volume 10 of *A History of the South*, edited by Wendell Holmes Stephenson and E. Merton Coulter. Baton Rouge: Louisiana State University Press.

Vance, Jane Gentry. 1982. "An Interview with Ruth Whitman." *The Kentucky Review* 3: 59–76.

Vendler, Helen. 1986. "In the Zoo of the New." *New York Review of Books*, Oct. 23, 1986: 47–52.

———. 1995. *The Given and the Made: Recent American Poets*. London: Faber and Faber.

Vickers, Nancy J. 1981. "Diana Described: Scattered Woman and Scattered Rhyme." *Critical Inquiry* 8: 265–79.

Vogler, Thomas A. 1971. *Preludes to Vision: The Epic Venture in Blake, Wordsworth, Keats, and Hart Crane*. Berkeley: University of California Press.

Walker, Alice. 1983. "In Search of Our Mothers' Gardens." In *In Search of Our Mothers' Gardens: Womanist Prose*, pp. 231–43. San Diego, New York, London: Harcourt Brace Jovanovich.

Walsh, William. 1994. "Isn't Reality Magic? An Interview with Rita Dove." *The Kenyon Review* 16, no. 3: 142–54.

Waniek, Marilyn Nelson, and Rita Dove. 1991. "A Black Rainbow: Modern Afro-American Poetry." In *Poetry After Modernism*, edited by Robert McDowell, pp. 217–75. Brownsville, OR: Story Line.

Whitman, Ruth. 1977. *Tamsen Donner: A Woman's Journey*. Cambridge, MA: Alice James Books.

———. 1986. *The Testing of Hanna Senesh*. Detroit: Wayne State University Press.

———. 1987. "History, Myth, and Poetry: Writing the Historical Persona Poem." *Iowa English Bulletin* 35: 65–73.

———. 1992. *Hatshepsut, Speak to Me*. Detroit: Wayne State University Press.

Williams, William Carlos. 1963. *The Collected Later Poems*. Rev. ed. New York: New Directions.

Wittig, Monique. 1986 [1975]. *The Lesbian Body*. Translated from the French by David Le Vay. London: Peter Owen, 1975; Boston: Beacon Press, 1986.

———. 1992. *The Straight Mind and Other Essays*. Boston: Beacon Press.

Woods, Gregory. 1987. *Articulate Flesh: Male Homo-Eroticism and Modern Poetry*. New Haven: Yale University Press.

———. 1990. "'Absurd! Ridiculous! Disgusting!': Paradox in Poetry by Gay Men." In *Lesbian and Gay Writing: An Anthology of Critical Essays*, edited by Mark Lilly, pp. 175–98. London: Macmillan.

INDEX

abortion, 43
Achilles, 70, 71, 72, 75, 173–74
Aeneid, 77
African American music, 123–27, 324n.20
African American writers: and Anglo-European tradition, 104, 111, 142–43, 321n.4; Black Arts Movement, 105, 107, 109; black subjects prescribed for, 105–6; double voicedness of black texts, 109, 322n.7; episodic structure in, 114; female poetic tradition of, 139, 325n.23; first-person form used by, 137–38; maternal history in African American women's fiction, 148; musical references by, 123; narrative in, 111–14, 130, 141; slave narratives, 111, 114, 117, 118, 139, 144
Age of Anxiety, The (Auden), 320n.29
Albiach, Anne-Marie, 278, 280
Alexander, Pamela, 190
Allen, Paula Gunn, 63
Altieri, Charles, 3, 10–11, 310n.4, 312n.15
Amazons, 62, 71, 75, 76
American Indians. *See* Native Americans
"Analysis Terminable and Interminable" (Freud), 267, 269

androgyny: as androcentric concept, 28; in Doubiago, 27, 41, 314n.5; Doubiago on the land as androgynous, 54–56; Hacker on, 172–73; in H.D., 314n.4; two concepts of, 314n.5
Anglo-Mongrels and the Rose (Loy), 16
"Anniad" (Brooks), 20–21
Another Mother Tongue: Gay Words, Gay Worlds (Grahn), 60, 317n.8
"Architecture, The" (Duncan), 253
"Art of Seeing With One's Own Eyes, The" (Doubiago), 35, 36
Ashbery, John, 11, 17, 21
assimilation, 110
associationalism, 277
Atherton, Hope, 193, 330n.7
Atwood, Margaret, 153, 321n.2
Auden, W. H., 10, 18, 320n.29, 328n.14

Baker, Houston A., 106, 107–8, 321n.4
Baker, Peter, 11, 309n.3
Baptism of Desire (Erdrich), 313n.25
Barthes, Roland, 335n.17
Beckett, Samuel: *Happy Days,* 236; *Waiting for Godot,* 227–28, 231
Bending the Bow (Duncan), 249, 285, 334n.9

matriarchy: in "Doctor Faustus Lights the Lights," 81–82; Trojan War marking end of, 69–70; voodooism as, 149

Matthiessen, F. O., 201

Maximus Poems, The (Olson): Algonquin legends in, 39, 46; M. A. Bernstein on, 8; and Doubiago's *Hard Country*, 6, 17–18, 23–24, 30, 51–52, 315n.9; erratic numbering in, 207; Rosenthal and Gall on, 10; women in, 45–46

Mayer, Bernadette, 11

Medb, Queen, 217, 332n.19

"Melville's Marginalia" (Howe), 331n.14

men: epic as territory of, 4, 69, 314n.1; male ideology in modernist collage epic, 15–16; male modernist practice and women poets, 313n.20; male writers treating the land as female, 54; separate spheres ideology, 129. *See also* masculinity; patriarchy

Merrill, James, 160, 328n.14

Messerli, Douglas, 329n.2

Mezza Voce (Albiach), 278, 280

Millay, Edna St. Vincent, 155, 313n.21

Miller, James E., Jr., 7

Miller, Perry, 201, 216

misogyny: in heterosexual social structures, 29; love stories as tales of, 230; of Olson, 30, 46; of Shakespeare, 178, 202; of Swift, 202

"Miss Furr and Miss Skeene" (Stein), 95

Mitchell, Juliet, 249

modernism: allusive texture of modernist epic, 23; collage long poem in, 1; *Drafts* positioned within and against, 277; Duncan on, 244, 249; DuPlessis on, 240–41, 252–53, 285; female aesthetic and, 15, 312n.19; Imagism, 79; lyric voice ruptured by, 240; male modernist practice and women poets, 15–16, 313n.20; male modernists on women, 240;

mythical method of modernist epic, 47; and "The Queen of Swords," 80

Moi, Toril, 252

Monroe, Marilyn, 38, 50–51, 59

Montefiore, Jan: on the beloved in sonnets, 155, 162, 180, 327n.8; on Grahn's reading of H.D., 80; on the sonnet as masculine, 160, 329n.17

Montenegro, David, 327n.4

Moore, Marianne, 21

motherhood: in Dahlen's *A Reading*, 256–57; in Doubiago's *Hard Country*, 31–32; in Hacker's *Love, Death, and the Changing of the Seasons*, 175, 183–84; maternal histories in African American women's fiction, 148

Mulira, Jessie Gaston, 147, 149, 325n.27

Museum (Dove), 323n.12, 325n.24

My Emily Dickinson (Howe), 188, 330n.30

"My Life Had Stood a Loaded Gun" (Dickinson), 202

mythic realism, 81, 85

"Mythology" (Hacker), 173

narrative: in African American writing, 111–14, 130, 141; in Dahlen, 337n.23; in long poems, 3, 112, 312n.17, 322n.11; Osbey on, 143, 158; in postmodern poems, 3, 322n.10; Rosenthal and Gall on, 311n.13; slave narratives, 111, 114, 117, 118, 139, 144

Natchez, 326n.33

Native Americans: and African Americans, 150, 326n.33; in *Hard Country*, 39, 40–42; in *The Maximus Poems*, 39, 46; sexism in, 41; Williams's interest in, 315n.10; women compared with, 41, 43

Neuman, Shirley, 81–82, 84, 319nn.21, 22, 24

New Formalism, 156, 184, 327n.5

Niedecker, Lorine, 21

53; glamorization of woman, 33; heterosexuality as concept of, 28; the hunt in, 229; the lesbian as removed from, 163–64, 183; madness resulting from opposing, 332n.22; religious transformation in, 59; self-destructive desire of women in, 44; sexism of, 29; Stein's "Doctor Faustus Lights the Lights" on, 84; subversion of not limited to single mode, 19; violence of, 226, 228, 230; and war, 44; women losing control of their reproductive functions in, 43; worst aspects of both genders in, 47–48

Pearce, Roy Harvey, 7

Pen, 61, 75

Penthesilea, 71, 75

performative formalism, 156, 185

Perloff, Marjorie, 3, 4, 322n.10, 330n.11

Perse, Saint-John, 11

Petrarchan sonnet: the beloved in, 176, 177–78; female practitioners of, 155; gender in, 162–63; and Hacker's *Love, Death, and the Changing of the Seasons*, 160, 161, 164–65, 170, 173, 178, 182; the romantic lyric developing from, 329n.17

Philadelphia Wireman, 292–301, 339n.35

Pisan Cantos (Pound), 240, 277, 330n.4

poetic sequence, 9–10; of Auden, 10; defined, 9; of Dickinson, 311n.11; and Dove, 114; serial poems distinguished from, 334n.7; sonnet-sequence distinguished from, 9; of Stevens, 10

poetry: Howe on transcendence in, 188; iambic pentameter, 157, 159, 327n.4; midlength poems by women, 20; New American concept of, 34; poet as critic of dominant cultural values, 8; poets increasingly drawn to expansive forms, 22, 306; regular poetic forms, 156, 185; repe-

tition in, 270, 285. *See also* formalism; genre; long poems; modernism; narrative; poetic sequence; postmodernism; writers of color; *and poets and poems by name*

"Pomade" (Dove), 133–34, 137

postmodernism: complicitous critique, 328n.15; serial and procedural poetic forms, 338n.32; story in poetry of, 3, 322n.10; totalizing gestures distrusted in, 284

Pound, Ezra: and coherence, 21, 284; Duncan contrasted with, 245, 269, 335n.12; eccentric view of history, 39; on epic, 187, 329n.1; *Helen in Egypt* influenced by, 79–80; and Howe, 330n.4, 333n.29; Howe's language compared with, 198–99, 330n.11; "I Gather the Limbs of Osiris," 315n.12; as model for epic-based poems, 2; openness to the world, 11; traditional ideologies in, 16; on verse epic, 8, 24. See also *Cantos, The*

"Projective Verse" (Olson), 33–34, 37

Quartermain, Peter, 331n.17

Queen of Swords, The (Grahn), 60, 316n.2

"Queen of Swords, The: A Play with Poetic Myth" (Grahn), 59–101; autobiographical dimensions of, 319n.24; Boudica in, 74–75; butch/fem interaction represented in, 60; characters' Sumerian counterparts, 61–62; colloquial speech in, 86–89; the Crow Bar, 61–62, 77–78; the Crows, 73–74, 87–89, 90, 91; and deconstruction, 65; as descent into the underworld, 76–78; Dumuzi, 61, 77; Enki, 61, 62, 78, 93, 100; Ereshkigal, 60–62, 67, 72, 78–79, 91, 93–94, 96; *Hard Country* contrasted with, 98; and H.D., 18, 69, 317n.5; and H.D.'s *Helen in Egypt*, 69; Helen of Troy, 60–61, 66, 68,

"Satisfaction Coal Company, The"
(Dove), 122
Scalapino, Leslie, 17
scenic lyric, 3, 22, 310n.4
Schlegell, David von, 332n.20
Schwitters, Kurt, 278
Sea Garden (H.D.), 318n.13
Sedgwick, Eve, 163
semiotic, the, 252, 260, 266, 269,
336n.19
separate spheres ideology, 129
sequential form. *See* poetic sequence
serial poems: and Dahlen, 243, 253,
334n.8, 336n.19; defined, 6, 242;
and Duncan, 18, 242; DuPlessis on,
242, 243; epic contrasted with, 242;
Oppen on, 242, 243, 311n.9; se-
quential form distinguished from,
334n.7; Spicer on, 243. *See also*
Drafts; Reading, A
sexism: complementarity and, 29; of
Native Americans, 41; of Olson, 45.
See also misogyny; patriarchy
sexuality. *See* female sexuality; hetero-
sexuality; homosexuality
sexual violence: Achilles' rape of
Penthesilea, 71; war compared with,
43
Shakespeare, William: and Hacker's
*Love, Death and the Changing of the
Seasons*, 160, 162, 164, 177; homo-
erotic elements in the sonnets, 162,
163, 327n.7; *King Lear*, 218, 226,
234, 237, 333n.30; misogyny of,
178, 202; procreation sonnets,
174
Sherry, Vincent, 312n.15
Shima, Alan, 336n.19, 337n.24
Shoptaw, John, 324n.18
Silliman, Ron, 17, 253, 329n.2
singularities, 195–96
slave narratives, 111, 114, 117, 118,
139, 144
slave revolts, 145, 147
Smitherman, Geneva, 321nn.1, 6
Song of Myself (Whitman), 7, 9

sonnet sequences: and contemporary
long poems by women, 313n.21;
the feminine expressed by, 155,
160, 162–63, 171; gender in, 155–
56, 162–63, 171, 327n.8; and Hack-
er's *Love, Death, and the Changing of
the Seasons*, 6, 17, 154; homoerotic
elements in Shakespearean, 162,
163, 327n.7; lesbian love repre-
sented by, 160, 163; poetic se-
quence distinguished from, 9; Rich
dismissing, 158. *See also Love,
Death, and the Changing of the Sea-
sons;* Petrarchan sonnet
South America Mi Hija (Doubiago),
27, 315n.13
"Spelling" (Duncan), 280, 338n.31
Spencer, Anne, 130, 139
Spicer, Jack, 243, 334n.9
Stanley, George, 243, 334n.8
"Stanzas in Meditation" (Stein), 16
Stein, Gertrude: as butch, 68, 82,
95, 317n.6; and Dahlen, 334n. 6;
as democratic, 80–81, 318n.18;
gerund forms in, 94; and Grahn,
63, 80–81, 95, 318n.19; and
Grahn's "The Queen of Swords,"
18, 81, 84–85, 87, 91–92, 317n.5;
Grahn's *Really Reading Gertrude
Stein*, 63; idiomatic speech in, 85–
86, 319n.25; on lesbian experi-
ence, 95; "Lifting Belly," 16; "Miss
Furr and Miss Skeene," 95; mysti-
cism in, 319n.20; mythic realism
of, 81, 85; openness to the world,
11; paradox in, 92; "Patriarchal
Poetry," 16, 317n.5; play of lan-
guage in, 89–90; principle of polar-
ity in, 95; on repetition and insis-
tence, 274; "Stanzas in Meditation,"
16; as subversive, 81, 318n.18;
Tender Buttons, 16; unnaming by,
90, 320n.28; and Yiddish, 319n.26.
See also "Doctor Faustus Lights the
Lights"
Steiner, George, 248

Stella (Hester Johnson): diary of, 204–5; as erased from history, 196–97; Howe's obsession with, 330n.7; language shared with Swift, 200; poems of, 197; portraits of, 197, 330n.8; as representative of western woman, 198; and Swift, 197, 200–201, 216; Swift's *Journal to Stella*, 199, 212; Swift's "On the Death of Mrs. Johnson," 216, 221; Swift's "To Stella, Visiting Me in my Sickness," 216; Swift's "To Stella, Who Collected and Transcribed his Poems," 229; "To Dr. Swift on his birth-day, November 30, 1721," 228

Stesichorus, 69, 83

Stevens, Wallace: Howe on, 191; "Notes Toward a Supreme Fiction," 7; Rosenthal and Gall on sequences of, 10

Stevenson, Anne, 153

Stimpson, Catharine R., 27, 315n.13

"Straw Hat" (Dove), 120, 124

Strickland, Stephanie, 153

"Sunday Greens" (Dove), 133, 134

"Sunday Night" (Hacker), 177

Swift, Jonathan: feminine position of, 199; and Ireland, 200, 203; *Journal to Stella*, 199, 212; language shared with Stella, 200; "On the Death of Mrs. Johnson," 216, 221; and Stella, 197, 200–201, 216; Stella's "To Dr. Swift on his birth-day, November 30, 1721," 228; "To Stella, Visiting Me in my Sickness," 216; "To Stella, Who Collected and Transcribed his Poems," 229; and Vanessa, 199

Tabula Rosa (DuPlessis), 239

Tamsen Donner: A Woman's Journey (Whitman), 153, 190

"Tautology and the Real" (Dahlen), 260, 261, 264–65, 274

Teish, Luisah, 149

Tender Buttons (Stein), 16

Tennyson, Alfred, Lord: *The Holy Grail*, 332n.20; *In Memoriam*, 9, 324n.18

testifying, 103–4, 321nn.1, 2, 324n.19

Testing of Hanna Senesh, The (Whitman), 153, 190

Thom, Rene, 196

Thomas and Beulah (Dove), 103–36; African American music in, 123–27; Beulah's poems ("Canary in Bloom"), 116, 128–36; black migration north as central to, 116–17, 120, 323nn.13, 15; "The Charm," 119; "Chronology," 116, 135, 153; "Company," 324n.20; "Compendium," 122; "Courtship," 120; "Courtship, Diligence," 130; "Daystar," 131; "Definition in the Face of Unnamed Fury," 122; discontinuous storytelling in, 152–53; Dove's grandparents as models for, 116; "Dusting," 130–31, 135; "The Event," 113–14, 119–20, 124, 125, 135, 323n.17; frustration and complaint as undertones of, 115; "Gospel," 126, 127, 131, 135; "The Great Palaces of Versailles," 132; "Headdress," 134–35; "A Hill of Beans," 129; "Lightnin' Blues," 122; "Magic," 130; as mainstream work, 18; "Nothing Down," 117–18, 121; "Obedience," 131–32; "The Oriental Ballerina," 135; originating in oral narrative, 113; poems to be read in sequence, 116; "Pomade," 133–34, 137; publication date, 20; "Refrain," 124–25, 126; "Roast Possum," 127–28; "The Satisfaction Coal Company," 122; sources of, 6; in speakerly text tradition, 136–37; specificities of place in, 153; "Straw Hat," 120, 124; "Sunday Greens," 133, 134; third person in, 137; "Thomas at the Wheel," 122; Thomas's poems ("Mandolin"), 116, 118–28; two